NOLO Products &

Books & Software

Get in-depth information. Nolo publishes hundreds of great books and software programs for consumers and business owners. Order a copy—or download an ebook version instantly—at Nolo.com.

Legal Encyclopedia

Free at Nolo.com. Here are more than 1,400 free articles and answers to common questions about everyday legal issues including wills, bankruptcy, small business formation, divorce, patents, employment and much more.

Plain-English Legal Dictionary

Free at Nolo.com. Stumped by jargon? Look it up in America's most up-to-date source for definitions of legal terms.

Online Legal Documents

Create documents at your computer. Go to Nolo.com to make a will or living trust, form an LLC or corporation or obtain a trademark or provisional patent. For simpler matters, download one of our hundreds of high-quality legal forms, including bills of sale, promissory notes, nondisclosure agreements and many more.

Lawyer Directory

Find an attorney at Nolo.com. Nolo's consumer-friendly lawyer directory provides in-depth profiles of lawyers all over America. From fees and experience to legal philosophy, education and special expertise, you'll find all the information you need to pick the right lawyer. Every lawyer listed has pledged to work diligently and respectfully with clients.

Free Legal Updates

Keep up to date. Check for free updates at Nolo.com. Under "Products," find this book and click "Legal Updates." You can also sign up for our free e-newsletters at Nolo.com/newsletters.

1st edition

Contracts

The Essential Business Desk Reference

by Attorney Richard Stim

FIRST EDITION   JANUARY 2011

Cover Design   JALEH DOANE

Book Design   TERRI HEARSH

Proofreading   SUSAN CARLSON GREENE

Printing   DELTA PRINTING SOLUTIONS, INC.

Stim, Richard.
  Contracts : the essential business desk reference / by Richard Stim. -- 1st ed.
     p. cm.
  Summary: "An A to Z, plain-English encyclopedia of contract terminology that
dissects important contract concepts for business owners, law students, managers, and
consumers. It also includes sample agreements with explanations on how to complete
them"--Provided by publisher.
  ISBN-13: 978-1-4133-1281-2 (pbk.)
  ISBN-10: 1-4133-1281-0 (pbk.)
  ISBN-13: 978-1-4133-1289-8 (e-book edition)
  ISBN-10: 1-4133-1289-6 (e-book edition)
  1. Contracts--United States--Popular works. I. Title.
  KF801.Z9S75 2010
  346.7302--dc22
                         2010021161

Please note

We believe accurate, plain-English legal information should help you solve
many of your own legal problems. But this text is not a substitute for
personalized advice from a knowledgeable lawyer. If you want the help of a
trained professional—and we'll always point out situations in which we think
that's a good idea—consult an attorney licensed to practice in your state.

Acknowledgments

Thanks to Lisa Guerin, editor extraordinaire, and to Terri Hearsh, for design and layout.

Your Legal Companion

Contracts may sound like a topic of interest only to lawyers and perhaps some high-level business executives. But the rest of us need to know about contracts, too, whether we're running or managing a business, buying a house, signing up for a credit card, or insuring a car. The truth is, contracts pervade every aspect of our lives. Many everyday transactions and activities, from shopping to working to marriage and more, are contractually based. Consider a typical day:

Welcome to your day. You get up at 7 a.m. because you have an employment contract that requires you to appear at work. In exchange for the eight hours you spend reviewing spreadsheets, going to meetings, and hanging around the water cooler, you receive certain benefits and a paycheck twice a month (Hey, today's payday!). On the way to work, you stop at the gas station where you accept a contractual offer to buy 16 gallons of gas at $3.15 a gallon. You take the freeway to the bridge tollbooth, where you exchange money for the opportunity to cross the bridge (actually you signal your electronic acceptance of this contractual arrangement via your FastTrak card—VALID!).

You arrive at the parking garage where you accept the parking garage's offer to store your car for the day for $15. At the local coffee shop, the waitress offers you coffee and a vegan donut; you accept the offer by handing over $3. At work (when you should be preparing spreadsheets), you click the "I accept" button to enter into a contract to buy a download of an Elmore Leonard novel for $12. Later—also, in violation of your employment contract—you hook your iPod to the work computer and accept Apple's offer to sell you an application that makes gastrointestinal sound effects (a bargain at only 99¢).

On the way home from work, you stop at the gym and renew your membership, agreeing to the gym's new terms of service and arranging to have the gym charge your credit card every month. Then, you accept the supermarket's offer to sell you a salmon dinner and apple juice for $12. By using your new credit card for these transactions, you accept the credit card company's offer to extend credit on the terms provided in its consumer contract. Because it's the first day of the month, you make sure to drop off the rent check; by doing so, you renew your month-to-month rental contract with your landlord. Finally, you click to accept Amazon.com's offer to sell you a download of *Toy Story 3*, and you sit at home happily watching Buzz Lightyear.

See what we mean? Our days are built on a series of transactions. Almost every waking hour, we are constantly entering into, enjoying the benefits of, and possibly even violating, contracts. And that's just in our personal lives: Those who run or manage businesses deal with contracts all the time, in their relationships with employees, contractors, vendors, commercial landlords, banks, utilities, insurance companies, and, of course, customers and clients. Every contract we accept, whether for business or pleasure, is connected to other supply and service contracts, employment agreements, leases, real estate sales, debt agreements, insurance contracts, and the like. We all live and operate within a massive web of contractual relationships.

Who needs to know about contracts? There may have been a time when small businesses could avoid learning much about contracts, because commerce was based on a handshake, lawyers were more affordable, or transactions were just simpler. But, alas, those days are long gone. In today's world, every business (and many consumers) could use some help understanding the language and rules of contracts—and few want (or can afford) to pay a lawyer $250 an hour for this information. This book is intended for the thousands of nonlawyers who must prepare, review, explain, or abide by contracts every day—from the parking attendants who have to explain the contract painted on the wall at the parking garage to the landlord who has to decide what to include in a lease agreement to the small business owner who needs to understand the fine print in a new rider to the company's liability insurance policy.

How this book can help. If you regularly deal with contracts, especially at your business, you probably want to know:

- **How to write a contract or contract provision.** For example, you may want to draft a simple confidentiality provision to insert in an agreement to give a contractor.
- **What particular contract terms mean.** For example, perhaps you're wondering what "indemnity" is, how to figure out whether you "breached" an agreement, or what it means when "time is of the essence."
- **How to make sure you can enforce important business agreements down the road.** For example, you may be wondering whether it's okay to do a handshake deal for a $5,000 loan, which provisions should be in your contractor agreements, or which types of contracts should be put in writing.

This book will help you with all of these concerns—and many more. Although this is not a contract form book—that is, it doesn't include a disk full of generic forms—it does provide more than a hundred examples of clauses, contracts, and sample language you can use right away. Most importantly, this book makes it easy to look up the essential terms that appear in most common contracts (along with some of the more obscure ones—mutatis mutandi, anyone?). And, it explains the rules that determine how contracts are interpreted and enforced by courts, so you can make sure you get the benefit of your business deals.

If you've already begun exploring the world of contracts by entering into a contract to buy this book, congratulations! If you haven't yet purchased this book, we hope you'll consider entering into a contract to do so. Hopefully, as that great contractor Don Corleone once put it, we've made you an offer you can't refuse.

acceleration clause

It's true of cars, and it's true of contracts: An accelerator speeds things up. Acceleration clauses (also known as "demand clauses"), commonly found in loans, leases, mortgages, or other payment agreements, require the party who borrowed money to speed up the payments. If you're required to make monthly payments on a loan and you miss a payment, an acceleration clause makes the entire amount you borrowed due. In other words, you must immediately pay back the entire loan.

Unenforceable clauses. Courts won't enforce an acceleration clause that is so grossly unfair as to be unscrupulous (or "unconscionable"). This issue is more likely to arise in a lease, because the acceleration clause forces tenant to pay for something not yet received (time spent in the rented space or using the rented equipment), while in other loan agreements, the debtor has already gotten the money, home, car, or other purpose of the loan.

Minimizing the damages. In general, courts don't like it when acceleration clauses are used as penalties. A court is more likely to enforce a clause that approximates, at least to some degree, the damages cause by the missed payment(s), as estimated when the contract was signed.

> EXAMPLE: A company leased ATM machines. When one of its customers missed a payment, the company tried to enforce an acceleration clause that made all future payments immediately due. An Ohio Court of Appeal ruled that the acceleration clause was unenforceable because it did not impose any obligation on the leasing company to minimize (or "mitigate") its damages.

For example, if the leasing company repossessed the ATM machine and then immediately leased it to someone else, the amount it earned from the new rental should have been offset from the amount owed by the first customer. Otherwise, the ATM company is getting paid twice for use of the same machine.

A court will also decline to enforce an acceleration clause if the parties have an honest dispute about the amount owed.

Mortgages. Most mortgages provide a grace period before the acceleration clause kicks in. During the grace (or "cure") period, the borrower has the chance to make up missed payments. If the borrower is unable to bring the payments current, then the lender can demand full payment and start foreclosure proceedings or work with the borrower to avoid foreclosure. An acceleration clause in a mortgage may be triggered by other events besides a failure to make timely payment—for example, the sale of the property (sometimes referred to as a due-on-sale clause) or refinancing.

Related term: promissory note.

acceptance

See offer and acceptance.

accord and satisfaction

It may sound like an archaic maneuver from *The Three Musketeers*, but accord and satisfaction is actually a relatively simple contract principle: The parties can always agree to modify the terms of their contract. When one party agrees to accept something other than what's promised in the contract—for example, the seller of a car agrees to accept less money because the brakes need to be replaced— then the parties have reached an "accord." When the buyer pays the lesser amount and the seller accepts it, that's "satisfaction." So, an accord and satisfaction is when the parties agree to an alternative way to perform the deal. An accord and satisfaction often involves the payment of a debt. For example, a creditor who loaned money to a failing business and wants to cuts his losses might agree to accept less than the full amount due.

How is it done? In an accord and satisfaction, one agreement (the new arrangement) is substituted for another (the original contract). The new agreement (sometimes referred to as a "discharge of debt," or a "mutual settlement and release of debt") spells out the accord and satisfaction and terminates the old agreement.

What about accepting checks that say "payment in full"? Let's say you borrow money from a friend and then have a dispute as to how much is owed—you say $500; she says $1,000. What happens if you send a check for $750 that states "payment in full"? Your friend says she is going to cash it but she thinks you still owe her $250, so she crosses out "payment in full" on the check. Can she go after you for the rest of the money if she cashes the check? Not according to most court rulings. As one judge put it, "What is said is overridden by what is done." This rule applies only if there is a dispute over how much is owed, however. If you and the other party agree on what you owe, you can't try to scratch out a better deal by writing "paid in full" on your check for half the amount. Finally, if there is a dispute but the check is cashed inadvertently, the rule may not apply (courts are split on that issue).

Related terms: amendment, integration.

accretion

When something gradually increases in size—for example, your spouse's waistline or your boss's ego—the process is known as accretion. The term appears in the following types of contracts:

- **Financial contracts.** Accretion refers to the process by which payments or value increases over time. For example, accretion occurs when a bond purchased at a discounted price ($175) matures to its face (or "par") value ($250).

- **Real estate contracts.** Accretion refers to the increase in land size due to the forces of nature. For example, accretion occurs if a river changes course and sediment deposits increase the size of the property.
- **Labor union contracts.** An accretion clause dictates what happens to employees in one company if they are transferred to another company whose employees are already represented by a union.

An accretion clause spells out how the extra money, property, or people will be treated (for example, who will own the land created by sedimentation).

acquisition agreement (federal government)

The federal government needs to buy a lot of stuff, from jet engines and highway signs to paper clips and those nifty baseball caps with the presidential seal. It purchases these things via contracts known as acquisition agreements. All federal acquisition agreements must meet two criteria:

- Their purchasing power must come from a specific legislative source of funding. In other words, Congress—which holds the "power of the purse"—must have approved the expense or department budget.
- The agreement must follow the federal acquisition rules, most of which are derived in some way from the Federal Acquisition Reform Act (FARA) or the Federal Acquisition Regulations (FAR, found in Title 48 of the United States Code of Federal Regulations). These laws set guidelines, safeguards, fees, whistleblower protections, administrative rules for contracts and many other regulations.

In addition, federal contracts must be executed or authorized by a contracting officer (usually the head of the appropriate agency) who has the authority to bind the federal government. Both goods and services can be the subject of federal acquisition contracts, although special performance-based rules apply to service agreements.

The acquisition regulations and process are provided in detail at Acquisition Central (www.acquisition.gov).

acquisition agreement (sale of business)

Acquisition agreements are used when one company buys another. It's a rule of the corporate food chain that the bigger companies devour the smaller—for example, Google purchased YouTube, Coca-Cola bought Odwalla, and General Motors acquired Hummer (R.I.P.). All such deals, whether big or small, are made possible by acquisition agreements. These agreements occur in two ways:

- **Entity purchase agreements (also known as "stock purchase agreements").** In this arrangement, a buyer purchases a business entity by buying a majority (or more) of its stock. The new owner generally steps into the shoes of the previous owners, assuming all debts and obligations.
- **Asset purchase agreements.** In this arrangement, a buyer purchases all of a business's assets, both its tangible property (inventory, real estate, office equipment, and so on) and intangible property (copyrights, patents, trademarks, and trade secrets). The company's shell—its corporate or LLC ownership—remains in place with the same owners, even though there is no business to run anymore, as a practical matter. This is the deal of choice for the purchase of a sole proprietorship or a partnership because the business has no "shell" to speak of: Once the assets are gone, there's no structure left to worry about.

Which is better? There are two issues to consider when choosing an acquisition model: taxes and liabilities for debts and obligations. Taxwise, an asset sale is usually better for a buyer because the buyer can begin depreciating the assets sooner. A seller usually prefers an entity purchase because the seller pays taxes only at the low, long-term capital gain rate. Sellers are especially wary about using an asset sale for a C corporation, because that will leave them at risk for double taxation, once for the corporate entity and then again for the shareholders.

As for debts and liabilities, an asset sale is usually preferable for a buyer, because the buyer won't be responsible for existing debts of the business unless the buyer agrees to take them on. That's not the case with an entity sale, in which it's assumed that all liabilities are included in the sale. (To make the deal happen, however, the selling shareholders or LLC members may have to accept responsibility for some specified liabilities, such as a recent bank loan.) The choice of acquisition arrangement also affects how ownership is transferred and whether a lease for the business can be transferred or assigned to the new owners.

Related terms: assignment (of contract); due diligence; merger; reformation; remedies; rescission (court ordered); restitution; successors and assigns; void (voidable).

act of God

Even atheists can avoid liability for breaching an agreement by claiming that performance was delayed by an act of God—an unforeseen natural event, such as a flood, tornado, an earthquake, or lightning. However, whether a court accepts this argument often depends on the contract language in a "force majeure" clause. Humanists please note: Although the reference to "God" implies a supernatural cause for such events, it is accepted that some of these events are (at least partially) human induced—for example, flooding caused by the use of reclaimed land or earthquakes caused by human activity, such as drilling or excavation.

Related terms: force majeure; impossibility (of performance).

addendum

An addendum is simply any document attached to—and made part of—a contract. If you're a busy manager who uses the same contract repeatedly with multiple clients, then addendums are your

BFFs. Using an addendum makes it easy to change schedules, prices, standards, product lists, or any other information that may vary regularly over time or from customer to customer. In some cases, the addendum is also known as a rider, an exhibit, or a schedule (although technically, the latter two terms are specific types of addendum).

How can you be sure the addendum is binding? Because an addendum is attached *after* the signature page, parties often initial each page of the addendum to guarantee that it will be considered part of the agreement. Another (or complementary) approach is to include the words "incorporated by reference" the first time an addendum is mentioned in a contract (for example, "The parties shall abide by the delivery specifications in the attached Addendum, incorporated by reference"). You can also use a special clause within the main body of the contract to make this point, as shown below.

Addendum: Sample language

> **Addendum.** Any attached Addendums and any other attachments or exhibits to this Agreement are incorporated in this Agreement by reference.

Related terms: boilerplate; incorporation by reference.

additional insured

Being named as an additional insured allows someone to be protected from liability under another person's or company's insurance policy. When an entertainer like Britney Spears appears at the Hard Rock Café, she (probably through her lawyer) requests, as a condition of her contract, that she be named as an additional insured (or as a "named insured") under the Hard Rock's liability insurance policy. That way, if anyone is injured during her show, the insurance policy will protect her—along with the club—from liability. Similarly, a toy designer will want to be named as an additional insured under a toy company's product liability insurance.

Additional insured versus named insured. Do not confuse the term "named insured" with "additional insured." If you are added to a policy as a "named insured," the protections of the policy extend beyond you to your partners, officers, employees, agents, and affiliates. Because the coverage is so broad, it may cost as much as 50% of the original premium to add a named insured to a policy. That's why being added as an additional insured is relatively inexpensive; it covers only the individual whose name appears on the certificate.

How is it done? A contract clause—commonly entitled "Insurance"—establishes the type and amount of insurance coverage required, how proof will be provided that the party has been named, and other details. These clauses can be quite lengthy. Below is an example of an abbreviated version.

Insurance: Sample language

> **Insurance.** Company shall obtain and maintain during the term of the agreement, at Company's sole cost and expense, standard product liability insurance coverage naming Customer as an additional insured.

Related terms: beneficiary; insurance contract (insurance policy); product liability; third-party beneficiary; underwriter.

ADR

See alternative dispute resolution (ADR).

agent

An agent is authorized to act on behalf of someone else (the "principal"). Remember Tom Cruise as a sports agent in *Jerry Maguire,* or Jeremy Pivens as the Hollywood agent Ari Gold, in

Entourage. In return for their deal making, agents like these usually receive a cut of the money the principal makes on a deal. Because an agent commonly has authority to negotiate contracts that are binding on a principal, the agent has a legal duty to be scrupulously loyal and honest to the principal, fully disclosing all of the information the principal needs to make a fully informed decision. (This higher standard is known as a "fiduciary relationship.") For example, it would be a breach of your agent's duty if she failed to disclose that she also represented your competitor.

An agent is not the principal's employee because the principal does not control how the agent performs (a standard requirement for employees). Also, most agents typically represent a number of clients. To ensure that a court does not misinterpret the relationship, agency contracts often contain a clause like the one below. Note, this clause references other relationships besides agent-principal, including joint ventures (any joint economic activity between two or more people) and partnerships.

No joint venturer: Sample language

Nothing contained in this Agreement is deemed to constitute either agent or company as a partner, joint venturer, or an employee of the other party for any purpose.

When an agent can bind the principal ("actual authority"). The agent's power to enter into contracts and make promises that the principal must keep usually happens in one of two ways:

- **By contract.** The agent and principal sign an agency contract, establishing the agency's power to bind the principal.
- **By law.** Either a statute or case law establishes the relationship. For example, in a general partnership, any partner can bind the other partners.

When an agent's power to commit the principal is explicitly spelled out by law or contract, the agent is said to have "actual authority." This means that the agent and principal both know, and agree to, the agent's role in acting for the principal.

Apparent authority. In some cases, someone can be lead to reasonably believe that an agent who lacks actual authority has the power to enter into contracts. This is called "apparent authority." In order to protect a party that was misled, a court will uphold the agreement if that party reasonably believed that the principal endorsed the deal, because of statements, actions, or even inaction.

> **EXAMPLE:** A former insurance agent, recently fired by SLYCO, arrives at Max's home. The ex-agent was supposed to turn in his company car (emblazoned with the SLYCO logo) but kept it for an extra week. The ex-agent convinces Max to pay several thousand dollars for a newer policy. The agent pockets Max's money and disappears, never informing SLYCO. Later, after a car accident, Max asks for repayment under his policy. Max reasonably relied on the fact that the ex-agent had a company car in assuming that he still worked for SLYCO. Because Max's assumption was reasonable, SLYCO would probably be obliged to provide the coverage purchased by Max. Courts refer to situations like this, in which someone who once had actual authority but no longer does, as "lingering apparent authority."

How to avoid apparent authority problems. To avoid being bound to contracts by someone with apparent authority, the principal should:

- **Provide notice.** Alert third parties that an agent no longer has authority. For example, if you've switched agents, notify your customers.
- **List actual agents.** Periodically distribute a statement to customers and clients on company letterhead indicating the agents who have actual authority, and update the list quickly when necessary.
- **Keep the agent informed.** Let the agent know, in writing, whether or not you have conferred actual authority, and as to which issues.

Related terms: authority to bind; escrow; fiduciary (duty, relationship); power of attorney.

agreement in principle

An agreement in principle (like a "letter of intent") is an "agreement to agree"—the parties *want* to make a deal but they haven't agreed on all of the details. Because it doesn't contain all of the essential elements for a contract, an agreement in principle cannot bind the parties to particular terms. However, most courts agree that once an agreement in principle is made, the parties have a duty to act in good faith as they proceed to finalize the agreement. If one party fails to negotiate in good faith, the other may sue for damages. On the other hand, if the parties reach an agreement in principle, and then take action on it—that is, they act as if a contract is in place—courts will presume that a contract exists and will do their best to determine and enforce its terms.

Related term: letter of intent.

aleatory

An aleatory contract is one in which the consideration paid by each party is usually unequal because the outcome is dependent upon chance or a future event—for example, a wager or an insurance contract.

Related term: insurance contract (insurance policy).

alternative dispute resolution (ADR)

Alternative dispute resolution (ADR) is an umbrella term for various ways to settle a legal dispute short of full-blown litigation. For example, in 1992, Herb Kelleher, president of Southwest Airlines, offered to arm-wrestle a rival airline company's president for the right to use the slogan, "Plane Smart." Kelleher lost, but he demonstrated the outer boundaries of ADR. Few executives have followed Kelleher's lead; most prefer more common ADR procedures, such as:

- **Mediation.** A neutral third person helps the parties talk through their dispute and come up with a mutually acceptable solution. Some mediators suggest possible outcomes, but a mediator generally can't impose a resolution on the parties.
- **Arbitration.** Much like a judge, an arbitrator hears from both parties, sometimes in a trial-like proceeding. The arbitrator then decides how the dispute should be resolved.
- **Negotiation.** The parties resolve the dispute themselves, with or without the aid of a third party.
- **Collaborative law.** Lawyers, trained in special, less adversarial procedures, represent each party and work together to reach a mutually acceptable resolution. Collaborative law is used most commonly in divorce proceedings.

Although ADR is considered an "anything but court" approach, many courts have incorporated ADR-type programs. For example, the federal courts use Early Neutral Evaluation (ENE), a variation on mediation—in order to alleviate their increasing caseloads. With the exception of court-ordered ADR procedures, all ADR is voluntary.

Contracting parties who want to resolve potential disputes by ADR rather than litigation should include a clause in their contract to that effect. Although the parties could decide to use ADR after a dispute arises, it's better to put an ADR clause in the contract ahead of time. Once the parties are engaged in a contract dispute, it will be much harder for them to reach an agreement on dispute resolution procedures.

Related terms: arbitration; boilerplate; mediation; negotiation.

ambiguity

Ambiguity occurs when contract language can be reasonably interpreted in more than one way. For example, if an artist-model agreement states, "The artist shall paint the model nude," is it the artist or the model who should appear sans clothing? Although some ambiguities are semantic—a word has multiple meanings—most are the result of misuse or improper placement of words, making the language confusing or inconsistent, or in some cases, producing an absurd result. For example, one employment contract we've seen states that the employee "must wear the uniform in the employee locker." (Claustrophobic applicants need not apply.)

Consider a contract between a lawyer and a client that provided for payment of the attorney's out-of-pocket expenses. The clause stated:

> These [out-of-pocket] expenses include court reporting services, expert witness fees, reasonable travel expenses, if any, fees paid to trial witnesses, and the cost to create demonstrative trial exhibits.

In this case, the client argued that the word "include" was a term of limitation that should be interpreted as "include only." Therefore, he shouldn't have to pay for anything that wasn't on the list, such as photocopies and online research. The lawyer argued that "include" was a term of expansion, used to preface a few common examples. In other words, the client had to pay for *all* reasonable out-of-pocket expenses, whether or not they were on the list.

The court agreed that both interpretations were reasonable but concluded that as a matter of public policy—and perhaps, poetic justice—ambiguities in attorney fee agreements should be construed against the attorney, who after all wrote the agreement. The client didn't have to pay the extra fees.

How do courts interpret ambiguity? Some ambiguities may not be obvious to the ordinary observer but may arise because the contract language has an unusual meaning under the circumstances. For example, in one historic case, a contract for horsemeat provided a discount if the meat was less than 50% protein. This seems clear enough on its face, but the supplier successfully claimed that trade custom in the horsemeat business was that 49.5% protein meets a

50% standard. In other words, the term "50%" was ambiguous in this context, in that it could actually mean "49.5%."

What evidence is considered? Courts differ as to what types of evidence they will consider when resolving ambiguities in a contract. For many years, courts looked only to the "four corners" of the document and to the "plain meaning" of its words. In a 1968 case, however, the California Supreme Court broke with the past and considered evidence outside of the contract in interpreting its meaning.

> **EXAMPLE:** A contractor agreed to indemnify a public utility for any harm caused during the replacement of a turbine cover. ("Indemnify" means that the contractor would compensate the utility for damages.) When the contractor caused $25,000 in damage, the public utility sued to get the money back under the indemnity clause. The contractor argued that the indemnity clause was meant to insure only against harm to third parties, not to the utility itself. The words "third party" didn't appear in the contract, but other evidence of trade practices by the parties proved that the contractor's interpretation was correct. The California Supreme Court ruled in favor of the contractor stating that evidence outside a contract (extrinsic evidence) should be admitted as long as it is offered to prove a meaning to which the language of the writing is "reasonably susceptible."

In summary, although courts sometimes differ, external evidence—for example, previous contracts between the parties or previous courses of action between the parties—can generally be used to clarify or explain an ambiguity, as long as that evidence does not vary or contradict the terms of the contract. A different result may occur, however, if similar evidence is used to contradict the meaning of the agreement. In that situation, the parol evidence rule—a principle governing in the admission of prior negotiations—is applied.

Two other things to consider about ambiguity.

- **Vague language is not necessarily ambiguous.** Common contract terms—for example, "reasonable," "satisfactory," and "immediately"—are vague but not necessarily ambiguous within the context of an agreement.
- **Plain language can avoid many ambiguities.** Lawyers have a fondness for unusual word order ("as in this deed provided") as well as obscure language ("therein referenced"). In addition, a paranoia among lawyers leads to over drafting—for example, saying "shall not now, or in the future" instead of just saying, "shall not." The solution is unambiguous: Use plain language whenever possible.

Ambiguities clause. Sometimes—as in the fee agreement mentioned above—ambiguities are interpreted against the drafter of the contract. In other words, if terms could be reasonably interpreted in different ways, a court will likely rule in the way most beneficial to the person who didn't write the contract. After all, the drafter was responsible for writing the ambiguous language in the first place, and shouldn't get to benefit from a lack of clarity. Parties who don't want this default rule to apply can include the following clause (sometimes referred to as an "ambiguities clause") in their contract.

Ambiguities: Sample language

> **Ambiguities.** Both parties and their attorneys have participated in the drafting of this Agreement and neither party will be considered the "drafter" for the purpose of any statute, case, or rule of construction that might cause any provision to be construed against the drafter of the Agreement.

Related terms: any/each; interpretive provisions; mistake; parol evidence rule; plain meaning rule; rules of interpretation (rules of construction.

amendment

Didn't get your contract *exactly* right? Amend it.

Amendments are ideal if you and the other party want to modify some of the elements of a contract—for example, one party wants to make an addition, deletion, correction, or similar change. An amendment doesn't replace the whole original contract, just the part that's changed by the amendment (for example, the delivery date or price for goods). If a contract requires extensive changes, it's generally wiser to create an entirely new agreement or, alternatively, to create an "amendment and restatement," an agreement in which the prior contract is reproduced with the changes included.

Can you prohibit oral amendments? Some contracts contain clauses (such as the one below), which require that any amendments be made in writing and signed by both parties.

Prohibition against oral amendments: Sample language

Entire Agreement. This is the entire agreement between the parties. It replaces and supersedes any and all oral agreements between the parties, as well as any prior writings. Modifications and amendments to this agreement, including any exhibit or appendix, are enforceable only if they are in writing and are signed by authorized representatives of both parties.

Surprisingly, the prohibition against oral modification provided in this clause is not always enforced. The reasoning, as expressed by one court, is this: Parties to a contract cannot, even by a written provision in the contract, deprive themselves of the power to alter or terminate that contract by a later agreement; so a written contract may be modified by the parties in any manner they choose. In other words, a contract clause requiring written amendments will not always be enforced. The chances of it being enforced go down if one or both parties relied on the oral modification.

EXAMPLE: An insurance company had an employment contract with an agent that required any modifications to be in writing. The agreement also stated that the agent's employment had to be terminated in writing. The agent was offered $500 to resign. When he refused to resign, his boss said, "You are fired." The agent left the job, accepted his severance pay and accrued vacation pay, and stopped coming to work. However, he argued that he was still entitled to collect commissions because his employment was never terminated in writing, as required by the contract. A federal court of appeal did not agree. Despite the contract language requiring modifications in writing, the court determined that the agent and the insurance company had accepted, through their statements and actions, an oral amendment to the contract regarding notice of termination. Most importantly, the insurance company had reason to rely on the agent's behavior *after* he was told he'd been fired.

This is not to say that you should disregard clauses prohibiting oral amendments or avoid using such clauses in agreements. Written amendments—like written agreements in general—have many advantages over oral agreements, and a party seeking to enforce an oral modification despite a clause prohibiting them will face an uphill battle in court. In addition, the law requires that some amendments be in writing—for example, amendments for transfers of real or intangible property and certain financial contracts must be in writing.

Amendments, consents, and waivers. There are times when parties want to deviate from an agreement but don't need to modify it. For example, one party to a nondisclosure contract might give the other party permission to disclose certain facts to certain people, even though that might technically violate the language of the contract. These deviations—in which a party waives a provision or permits something that is otherwise prohibited—are sometimes considered amendments, although they are more properly defined as "waivers" or "consents." Unlike an amendment, a consent or waiver doesn't modify the agreement itself; instead, it excuses or permits activities that are otherwise prohibited by the contract. Consents and waivers should be in writing.

Creating amendments. The goal when creating a contract amendment is to be as specific and concise as possible. As James Brown might have stated, "You should hit it and quit it." The document can appear informal—for example, like a letter agreement—or it can resemble the original contract in font and layout. Generally, amendments come in a few different styles, as shown below.

Redlines and strikeouts. Additions and deletions are shown visually, with additions underlined and deleted text crossed out. (Most word processing programs allow you to choose "strikeout" as a font.) A statement describing the process commonly precedes it.

The parties agree to amend the Agreement by the following additions (indicated by underlining) and deletions (indicated by strikethroughs):

Section 7 is amended to read as follows:

7. Term. The Term of this Agreement is from July 31, 2009 to July 31, ~~2010~~ 2011. The Agreement may be renewed ~~on an annual basis~~ for additional two-year terms following the initial term, upon written agreement of the parties. The parties must mutually inform each other of their intention to renew the Agreement no later than ~~January 31~~ June 1 of each year in which the Agreement is set to terminate.

"Replaced in its entirety." In this manner, you simply state that a whole clause has been replaced and provide the new clause.

> Section 7 is replaced in its entirety by the following:
>
> **7. Term.** The Term of this Agreement is from July 31, 2009 to July 31, 2011. The Agreement may be renewed for additional two-year terms following the initial term, upon written agreement of the parties. The parties must mutually inform each other of their intention to renew the Agreement no later than June 1 of each year in which the Agreement is set to terminate.

Describing without restating the amendment. Using this approach, the changes are described. This is often shorter but requires the parties to check against the existing text of the contract.

> "The first sentence of Section 7 is amended by modifying "2010" to "2011." The second sentence is amended by striking "on an annual basis," and replacing it with "for additional two-year terms." The date in the last sentence is modified from "January 31" to "June 1."

You can choose whichever method suits you or combine them if you wish. The important thing, as with all contract drafting, is that your intentions are clear to all parties as well as to third parties reading the amendment. In addition, be sure to change any cross-references, if necessary.

TIP

Modifications before the contract is signed. If a contract is modified before it is signed, such changes are not "amendments." If you wish to handwrite a change into an agreement that been printed out for signature—for example, because you noticed a typo at the last minute—you can use a pen to do so and have both parties initial it. Although not technically an amendment, these modifications are sometimes labeled as such.

CAUTION

Amending certain assigned UCC agreements. If your contract is a secured transaction—a loan or a credit transaction in which the lender acquires a security interest in collateral you owned—then there may be complications involving amendments to assigned agreements under Section 9-405 of the Uniform Commercial Code (UCC). You should consult with an attorney before amending an assigned contract for a secured transaction.

Completing the amendment. Here's how to complete the sample amendment shown below:

- **Introductory paragraph.** Type your name or the name of your company and the other side's name (an individual or a company).
- **Describe the amendment(s).** Type in the amendments to the existing contract using any one of the three methods described above.
- **The concluding paragraph.** This paragraph should be included to guarantee that other than the amendment, the contract remains as it is written.
- **Proofread and sign your amendment.** Under the printed party names, each of you should sign and write in the date. Below, each should print his or her name and title, such as "Chief Operating Officer," or "General Partner." You'll want to make sure the person signing the agreement has the authority to do so, and equally important, that you have fulfilled any signing or notice requirements included in the original agreement. Generally, agreements require the contracting parties to sign all amendments. However, in some cases—for example, corporate amendments or amendments to financial agreements—other signatures or notices may be required.
- **Manage amendments.** Contracts may undergo multiple amendments, so it's usually a good idea to number each amendment—for example "Amendment No. 1" or "First Amendment." In addition, amendments should be filed and

Amendment

Amendment

1. This amendment (the "Amendment") is made by _____ and _____ ,
parties to the agreement _____ dated (the "Agreement").

2. The Agreement is amended as follows: _____
_____ .

3. Except as set forth in this Amendment, the Agreement is unaffected and will continue in full force and effect in accordance with its terms. If there is conflict between this Amendment and the Agreement or any earlier amendment, the terms of this Amendment will prevail.

_____

By: _____

Printed Name: _____

Title: _____

Dated: _____

_____

By: _____

Printed Name: _____

Title: _____

Dated: _____

maintained with the original agreement so that anyone viewing the file will know that the agreement has been amended.

Related terms: accord and satisfaction; addendum; integration.

amortization

Using an amortized payment plan, the borrower—for example, in a mortgage or car loan—gradually pays less interest (and more principal) as the payment plan progresses.

A little history. During the 1930s, homeowners purchased homes with much shorter mortgages (three to five years) than today's 20- to 30-year loans. Down payments for these short mortgages ranged from 50% to 80% of the purchase price and ended with a large balloon payment. That may explain why more than half of the population rented and most of the rest were in danger of losing their homes during the Great Depression. In 1934, the Federal Housing Authority stepped in with a new system of government-backed mortgages, which required a much lower down payment, and spread repayment of the loan amount (the principle) and the cost of the loan (the interest) over a longer period, using a system that was called amortization.

> **EXAMPLE:** Jake borrows $100,000 to purchase a condo at 8% interest and plans to pay it back over ten years. Although each of his 120 monthly payments will be for the same amount ($1,213), less than half of his first payment will go toward paying off the principal; the rest will pay the interest on the loan. As the principal is paid off, the interest owed decreases and the amount of each payment that goes toward the principal increases over the life of the loan, until only $8 of his final payment goes toward interest.

Related terms: APR; compounding (compound) interest; debt; equity; interest rates (usury); mortgage; promissory note.

antecedent, rule of the last (also last antecedent rule, last antecedent doctrine)

In 1891, attorney Jabez Sutherland wrote a book on interpreting contracts and statutes. He created a simple rule for deriving the meaning of contract clauses that contained multiple obligations or conditions. Sutherland said that when a qualifying word or phrase is used with a group of obligations or conditions, the qualifying terms are presumed to modify only the condition or obligation that immediately precedes it (the "last antecedent").

Rule of the last antecedent: Sample contract language

> Subject to the termination provisions of this Agreement, this Agreement is effective from the date it is made and will continue in force for a period of five (5) years, and thereafter for successive five (5)-year terms, unless and until either party terminates it by providing one-year prior notice in writing to the other party.

The **qualifying phrase** in this sample is "unless and until either party terminates it by providing one year prior notice in writing." The **last antecedent** is "successive five year terms." Applying the rule to this clause, either party could terminate the agreement under the notice provision *only* during "successive five (5)-year periods," not during the initial five (5)-year period.

Rule of the last antecedent: U.S. Constitution

> No person except a natural born Citizen, or a Citizen of the United States, at the time of the Adoption of this Constitution, shall be eligible to the Office of President...

The **qualifying phrase** in this sample is "at the time of the Adoption of this Constitution." The **last antecedent** is "a Citizen of the United States." If the rule were not applied and the phrase was intended for both of the conditions, then the United States would have run out of presidential possibilities—any "natural born Citizen at the time of Adoption of this Constitution"—sometime in the 19th century.

Unfortunately for those seeking contractual clarity, Jabez Sutherland muddied the waters by added a qualifier to his rule: "Evidence that a qualifying phrase is supposed to apply to all antecedents instead of only to the immediately preceding one may be found in the fact that it is separated from the antecedents by a comma." Although still used by some American courts, this exception could lead to unintended results, because it conflicts with common grammatical usage of commas. Like all rules of construction, courts generally apply this one with a dose of common sense in order to avoid potentially absurd results.

Related terms: mistake; plain meaning rule; rules of interpretation (rules of construction).

anticipatory breach (anticipatory repudiation)

Anticipatory breach occurs once one party to a contract indicates—either through words or actions—that it's not going to perform its contract obligations. For example, in April 1852, Mr. De La Tour hired Mr. Hochester as a courier. Hochester was supposed to start work on June 1, but on May 11, De La Tour told him he wouldn't need his services. On May 22, Hochester sued for breach and De La Tour responded that no breach could occur until the services were due to begin, on June 1 (which had been the rule until that time). The English court, in a landmark case, ruled that a contract is breached once one party unconditionally refuses to perform as promised, regardless of when performance is supposed to take place. This unconditional refusal is known as "repudiation." When that occurs, the other party can immediately claim a breach and seek remedies such as payment.

When does repudiation occur? Courts usually recognize three types of repudiation:

- **A positive and unconditional refusal is made to the other party ("express repudiation").** The other party must tell you, in essence, "I'm not going through with the deal." It's not enough to make a qualified or ambiguous refusal ("Unless this drought breaks, I won't be able to deliver the apples"). The repudiation must be clear, straightforward, and directed at the other party ("I will not be delivering the apples as promised").

- **A voluntary act makes it impossible for the other party to perform.** When it comes to repudiation, actions speak as loudly as words. For example, a couple was supposed to repay two loans from the profits of their business. Instead, the couple voluntarily ran the business into the ground, incurring lots of other debts and making it impossible to pay back their original loans. Their reckless actions counted as a repudiation of the original loan agreements.

- **The property that is the subject of the deal is transferred to someone else.** If the contract is for the sale of property, repudiation occurs when one party transfers (or makes a deal to transfer) the property to a third party. For example, if you've contracted to buy a house and you learn that the other party has subsequently sold it to his brother, your sales contract has been repudiated (even if you never heard a word about it from the other party).

UCC rules for sale of goods. The Uniform Commercial Code (UCC)—legal rules governing the sale of goods—prescribes a procedure for dealing with anticipatory breach. If you have reason to believe that the other party is not going to fulfill its obligations, you have a right to demand "adequate assurance of performance," and you can suspend your own performance until the assurance is provided. If, after 30 days, the other party fails to comply with your request for assurances, the contract is officially over ("repudiated").

EXAMPLE: In April, Steve orders 100 computers from Compco. He is supposed to pay $50,000 on May 1 and receive the computers on July 1. On April 29, Compco's CEO tells a television reporter, "Unless chip production increases, Compco may have trouble filling its summer orders." Steve demands an assurance from Compco and withholds payment of the $50,000 due on May 1. When Compco hasn't responded to Steve's request for assurance by the end of the month, Steve terminates the contract.

As you can see, under UCC rules, a qualified repudiation ("Compco may have trouble filling its summer orders") is enough to stop the clock on the contract, at least until the other side provides the requested assurances. Many commentators have argued that all contracts—not just those governed by the UCC—should follow these rules for requesting and providing assurance.

Retracting repudiation. It's possible for a party to repudiate the contract and then later retract the repudiation, as long as the other party hasn't made a "material change" in position because of the repudiation.

> **EXAMPLE:** Tom is supposed to deliver 100 cases of cauliflowers to Bob. Tom's tractor breaks down, and he tells Bob he can't fill the order. Bob immediately makes a new cauliflower deal with Sam. Two days later, Tom buys a new tractor and tells Tom he can fulfill the order. But it's too late to retract the repudiation because Bob relied on it in making his new deal with Sam (a "material change").

When only a payment remains. In what may seem like an odd quirk, the rules described in this section don't apply if the *only* contract obligation remaining is for one party to pay money to the other. In these cases, the party seeking the payment must wait until the due date for the payment has passed. (No claim of anticipatory breach can be made.)

> **EXAMPLE 1:** Greta agrees to steam clean Sam's houseboat on May 1; Sam will pay Greta $2,000 on June 1. Greta completes

the steam cleaning on time and on May 15, Sam tells Greta he can't pay her. Because the only contract obligation remaining is payment, Greta must wait until June 1 to sue for breach.

EXAMPLE 2: Same facts as above: Greta agrees to steam clean Sam's houseboat on May 1; Sam will pay Greta $2,000 on June 1. This time, Greta starts the work but within the hour Sam announces he can't pay her. In this case, Greta does not have to wait until June 1 to sue for breach because Greta hadn't completed her steam cleaning (her obligation). She can claim an anticipatory breach.

Duty to mitigate. There's one last twist to anticipatory breach: If one party repudiates the contract, most courts require the other party to act swiftly to avoid incurring unnecessary costs or expenses. This is referred to as "mitigating damages" and generally means that you can't sit around and let the situation get worse. This also explains why some parties repudiate a contract: It gives the other party more time to cut its losses, which reduces the damages available for the breach. For instance, in our houseboat example, if Sam repudiates two weeks before Greta starts work, she may be able to find another client to fill that slot—and limit or even wipe out any damages she could have collected from Sam as a result of the breach. If she can make up the money with another job, it's essentially a situation of "no harm, no foul."

Related terms: breach, material; mitigation of damages; Uniform Commercial Code.

antidilution clause

This provision prevents the value of a stock from decreasing as a result of additional shares being issued (a process known as "dilution"). For example, in 1995, a U.S. company, Alantec, was sold for $770 million. The founders, who thought they owned 90% of the stock, received a measly $600,000. Why? Venture capitalists who owned a small share of the company had been issuing the company's common stock to many investors, which diluted the founder's ownership to .007 percent. To prevent this type of dilution, stock sale and stock transfer contracts typically contain antidilution clauses.

Related terms: acquisition agreement (sale of business); blue-sky laws; fraud (misrepresentation); merger; private placement.

antitrust

Federal and state antitrust laws prohibit businesses from engaging in monopolistic activities—that is, these laws make illegal any practices purposely designed to unfairly give a business dominant control over a particular market segment. In addition to preventing monopolistic activities, antitrust laws prohibit business practices that restrain the free flow of commerce (called restraint of trade). The purpose and goal of these laws—most notably the Sherman Antitrust Act, the Clayton Antitrust Act, and the Robinson-Patman Act of 1936—is to preserve competition and protect consumers.

Antitrust violations are often associated with contracts because it is through business agreements that companies enforce their monopolistic behavior. Among the more common types of business activity that may potentially cause restraint of trade antitrust violations are:

- **Price fixing.** This occurs if two or more businesses enter into an agreement (formal or informal) to maintain their prices at a certain level—for example, several drug companies secretly conspire to set prices for a certain class of generic drugs. The flip side of price fixing is "bid rigging" when several competitors conspire to determine which one them will win a bidding competition.
- **Exclusive dealing agreements.** It's not illegal to make an exclusive contract with someone, but exclusive dealings that unreasonably restrain trade are prohibited under federal law.

For example, in 2005, several chain stores grouped together to pressure a glassware supplier to deal exclusively with them and not to deal with another chain, Bed Bath & Beyond. The effect of the deal was to unfairly suppress trade.

- **Tying agreements.** These are contracts that require a customer who wishes to purchase one product to also purchase another. For example, a clothing manufacturing company patents a new machine for sewing buttons. The clothing company that licenses the machine also insists that manufacturers buy its buttons as a condition of the license.

- **Requirements contracts.** These are agreements prohibiting a purchaser of goods from purchasing comparable items from another source. Sometimes this is accomplished expressly—for example, by a mandatory contract condition—and sometimes it is done secretly—for example, as Standard Oil did at the turn of the 20th century by secretly providing rebates to customers.

- **Territorial restriction agreements.** These are agreements where competitors agree not to compete within each other's territories, much like when a criminal gang agrees to not engage in activities on the other gang's turf.

Practically speaking, antitrust laws should not be a concern for most small business owners, as few agreements have a large enough impact on the related market or industry to raise the antitrust warning flag. If, however, a larger company insists on certain contractual requirements—for example, pricing requirements or exclusionary conditions—and the flow of commerce might be affected by it, then the arrangement might violate antitrust laws. In general, antitrust enforcement is subject to the political climate at the time. Deciding whether a particular activity violates the antitrust laws involves such variables as the intent of the actors, the degree of harm done to other companies, and the level of commerce that is affected (local, state, national, or international).

Related terms: franchise agreement; license agreement.

any/each

"Any" and "each" are often (and incorrectly) used interchangeably in contracts. Here's the scoop. "Any" refers to one member of a group without specifying which member—for example, "any general partner" refers to one (unspecified) general partner from a partnership. If "any" is used with a plural noun—for example, "any general partners"—then it refers to two or more partners from the partnership without specifying which partners. "Each" refers to every member of a group considered individually—for example "each officer" refers to every officer in the company from vice-president to CEO. Because "any" and "each" are adjectives that sometimes cause contract ambiguity, contracts expert Tina L. Stark recommends using "any" when creating discretionary authority—for example, when someone *may* do something ("Any officer may sign checks without the consent of the board"), and to use "each" when creating affirmative obligations—for example, when somebody *must* do something. ("Each officer shall furnish proof of citizenship prior to commencing employment.")

Related terms: mistake; plain meaning rule; rules of interpretation (rules of construction).

appurtenance

Real estate contracts often reference things that "run with the land." These are called "appurtenances," and they come in two forms:

- **a right associated with land**—for example, the right to access land using a horse trail, or
- **property that's attached to land**—for example, a barn or a shed.

Related terms: easement; real estate contract.

APR

Americans owe a staggering $900 billion to credit card companies. That's why most card-carrying members of the credit-card class aren't surprised when the credit card company adds some sticker shock each month (for failing to pay their credit card off in full). These additional monthly interest payments are calculated using an annual percentage rate (APR) established by the federal government The APR is divided by twelve to arrive at a periodic interest rate, then multiplied against your monthly balance to come up with your monthly interest payment. References to APRs are often found in loan agreements and mortgages, or may be used in a contract as the standard for determining interest on late payments.

Related terms: amortization; compounding (compound) interest; debt; equity; interest rates (usury); mortgage; promissory note.

arbitration

Though often considered a 20th-century phenomenon, arbitration— an out-of-court proceeding in which one or more neutral third parties hear evidence and then make a binding decision—has a long and checkered past, starting with King Solomon's famous approach to child custody. It was used in England back in the 13th century (and before the existence of the so-called common law—rules based upon court rulings), and George Washington even included an arbitration provision in his will. Today, arbitration is the most commonly used method of alternative dispute resolution (ADR).

Binding or nonbinding. Arbitration can be binding (which means the participants must follow the arbitrator's decision and courts will enforce it) or nonbinding (in which either party is free to reject the arbitrator's decision and take the dispute to court, as if the arbitration had never taken place). Binding arbitration is more common.

Who can arbitrate disputes? Arbitration can be voluntary (the parties agree to do it) or mandatory (required by law). Most contract arbitrations occur because the parties included a clause requiring them to arbitrate any disputes "arising under or related to" the contract. If a provision like this isn't included, the parties can still arbitrate if they both agree to it (although it's tough to reach an agreement like this once a dispute has arisen).

Advantages and disadvantages. For simple contract disputes in which the matter can be heard in one day, arbitration is usually a good choice. However, if in doubt, consider the advantages and disadvantages, below:

- **Advantages.** Arbitration is usually faster, simpler, more efficient, and more flexible for scheduling, than litigation. Also, it avoids some of the hostility of courtroom disputes, perhaps because it's a private proceeding versus the public drama of the courtroom. If the subject of the dispute is technical—for example, about a patent—the parties can select an arbitrator who has technical knowledge in that field.
- **Disadvantages.** Unlike a court ruling, a binding arbitration ruling can't be appealed. It can be set aside only if a party can prove that the arbitrator was biased or that the ruling violated public policy. Unlike a court battle, there is no automatic right to discovery (the process by which the parties must disclose information about their cases). However, you can include a requirement for discovery in your arbitration provision or agree to it under arbitration rules. The costs of arbitration can be significant; in some cases, they may even exceed the costs of litigation (see below).

What does it cost? According to a survey by Public Citizen, a consumer watchdog group, the cost of initiating arbitration is significantly higher than the cost of filing a lawsuit. On average, it costs about $9,000 to initiate a claim to arbitrate a contract claim worth $80,000 (versus about $250 to file that action in state court). Keep in mind that the people in the dispute pay the arbitrators, and arbitration fees can run to $10,000 or more. Add in administrative costs and your own attorney fees (if you hire one) and the process might even cost more than litigation.

Arbitration checklist. A simple arbitration provision, such as the one shown below (see "Arbitration: Sample of simple language"), may be suitable for basic contract disputes. But more complex contracts or those involving large sums of money may require the parties to consider some of the questions below. (Note: When you agree to arbitrate with an organization such as the American Arbitration Association, their rules permit the parties to work out some of these details later. Still, it's generally easier to agree on these things *before* there's a dispute.)

☐ **Do you want an arbitrator knowledgeable in a specific field of law or business?** If so, include that in your arbitration provision— for example, "Arbitration will be conducted by an arbitrator experienced in the toy and licensing industry."

☐ **Do you want to understand why the arbitrator ruled a certain way?** In this case, you should include a request for a written record of the decision.

☐ **Do you want to prevent some issues from being arbitrated?** If so, then you need to make exceptions—for example, "All claims and disputes arising under or relating to this Agreement are to be settled by binding arbitration, except for disputes relating to the validity of patents ...."

☐ **Are you worried that the potential award may be astronomical?** If so, the parties may agree to limit the amount of the award— for example, by stating that the arbitrator cannot award more than $10,000 to any party.

☐ **Do you want the arbitrator to follow specific arbitration rules?** If so, include the name of the organization, for example, the California Lawyers for the Arts or the American Arbitration Association.

☐ **Should the winning party have its attorney's fees paid by the loser?** If so, include language regarding attorney's fees— for example, "the prevailing party shall be entitled to its reasonable attorney fees and costs." What are costs? The filing fees, charges for serving papers, court reporter charges for depositions (which can be very expensive), transcripts, costs of copying, and exhibits.

☐ **Does it matter where you arbitrate or what state's law applies to arbitration?** If so, indicate those preferences in the arbitration provision. Keep in mind that the location of the arbitration may seem unimportant now, but will prove a major issue if a dispute occurs and you have to book a flight to Anchorage for the arbitration hearing.

Sample arbitration clauses. The first sample shows a simple, no-frills arbitration clause; the second sample offers more conditions and obligations.

Arbitration: Sample of simple language

Arbitration. All claims and disputes arising under or relating to this Agreement are to be settled by binding arbitration in the state of [*insert state in which parties agree to arbitrate*] or another location mutually agreeable to the parties. An award of arbitration may be confirmed in a court of competent jurisdiction.

Arbitration: Sample of more complex language

Arbitration. All claims and disputes arising under or relating to this Agreement are to be settled by binding arbitration in the state of [*insert state in which parties agree to arbitrate*] or another location mutually agreeable to the parties. The arbitration will be conducted on a confidential basis pursuant to the Commercial Arbitration Rules of the American Arbitration Association. Any decision or award as a result of any such arbitration proceeding must be in writing and provide an explanation for all conclusions of law and fact and include the assessment of costs, expenses, and reasonable attorneys' fees. Any such arbitration will be conducted by an arbitrator experienced in [*insert industry or legal experience required for arbitrator*] and will include a written record of the arbitration hearing. The parties reserve the right to object to any individual who shall be employed by or affiliated with a competing organization or entity. An award of arbitration may be confirmed in a court of competent jurisdiction.

Do you need to hire a lawyer for arbitration? If you have a significant amount of money or property in dispute, you should consider hiring a lawyer. The arbitrator's decision will be binding, which means this is your only chance to win.

Arbitration variations. Arbitration is typically a straightforward matter. The parties submit evidence and arguments, and the arbitrator makes a binding decision. Over the years, however, a few variations have developed, including:

- **Mediation/arbitration** (sometimes known as "med/arb"). In this arrangement, the parties first attempt to mediate their dispute and, if they can't resolve it with a mediator, they submit the matter to arbitration.

- **Bracketed (high-low) arbitration.** The parties agree in advance to high and low limits on the arbitrator's authority. This method is best used when the only dispute is over how much money is owed.

- **Pendulum arbitration (also known as "baseball arbitration").** Both parties give the arbitrator figures for which they would be willing to settle the case. The arbitrator must then choose one party's figure or the other—no other award can be made.

- **Night baseball arbitration.** As in baseball arbitration, above, each side chooses a value for the case and exchanges it—with the other side, but not with the arbitrator ("night baseball" refers to the fact that the arbitrator is "kept in the dark"). The arbitrator makes a decision about the value of the case, and then the parties must accept whichever of their own figures is closer to the arbitrator's award.

When arbitration provisions are unconscionable. In order to avoid litigation, many companies routinely insert arbitration provisions into their nonnegotiable form contracts—for example, in agreements for medical insurance, cell phone services, employment contracts, and the like. Courts will not enforce such provisions if they are unconscionable—that is, they are considered to be so grossly unfair as to be illegal. Some states, most notably California, have been more active than others and have chipped away at these provisions, particularly when used in so-called contracts of adhesion (consumer agreements which one party must accept without question). In 2005, the California Supreme Court reviewed a form contract and ruled against the use of an arbitration provision that prohibited bringing class action lawsuits. And in a series of cases, courts have held that such a clause may be unconscionable if the provision is in a "take it or leave it"-type agreement and if the arbitration provision is one-way—that is, the party with less bargaining power must use arbitration but the other party with more bargaining strength can bring litigation. In 2010, the U.S. Supreme Court made it slightly more difficult to challenge arbitration provisions by requiring an attack on the provision and not the whole agreement.

Related terms: alternative dispute resolution (ADR); boilerplate; contract of adhesion (adhesion contracts); mediation.

arm's-length

In contract law, an agreement is considered to be arm's-length if the parties acted independently and the resulting agreement reflects what would be negotiated on the open market. (Wouldn't the world would be a better place, at least hygienically, if we could keep everyone at a distance equal to the length of an arm—the literal meaning of this term?) Whether an agreement is arm's-length is sometimes an issue of great interest to the government.

> **EXAMPLE:** A grandfather wants to give his granddaughter $100,000, but he is concerned about gift taxes. Instead, he prepares a "loan" agreement, lending her $100,000 interest free and with no schedule for repayment. The IRS would not consider that to be an arm's-length agreement and would instead insist that the amount be treated as a gift for tax purposes.

Contracts made with the U.S. government should be arm's-length and federal law determines what is and isn't arm's-length by using a "standard of comparability," in which the arrangement is measured against similar transactions on the open market. When courts measure an arm's-length decision, they commonly use three factors: market price, relationship of the parties, and comparable agreements.

Related terms: acquisition agreement (federal government); void (voidable).

arrears

Arrears refers to being "behind," in payments (and, no, it isn't Scottish slang for derriere). The term often appears in contracts referencing a failure to pay on a sales, loan, or mortgage agreement.

Related terms: compounding (compound) interest; debt; interest rates (usury); mortgage; promissory note.

as is

As long as the buyer had a reasonable opportunity to inspect the property beforehand, the as is buyer takes the goods in their current condition and cannot complain about problems later.

A little history. A century ago, all purchases were as is and the buyer had an obligation to seriously inspect every purchase before making it. The age-old legal rule was caveat emptor: Let the buyer beware. But during the 20th century, laws were enacted to protect consumers, including laws requiring that goods and services be merchantable and useful for their intended purposes. This implied warranty of merchantability does not apply when property is sold as is.

Related terms: breach, material; real estate contract; warranties.

as of

The magic words "as of" refer to the date that an agreement is effective. That's why a contract may state, "This Agreement is dated *as of* November 27, 2010," instead of "This Agreement is dated November 27, 2010." The "effective date" (or the as of date) can be different than the date of signature, so it's common practice to use "as of" in the preamble to indicate when an agreement was reached and to include a separate date for signatures. Another simple workaround is to state, "This Agreement is effective as of November 27, 2010 (the "Effective Date").

Related terms: effective date; recitals.

asset base loan

This is a type of loan agreement where the borrower pledges certain business assets—for example, equipment or inventory—as collateral for a loan.

Related terms: amortization; compounding (compound) interest; debt; equity; interest rates (usury); mortgage; promissory note; secured transaction.

assignment (of contract)

Did you ever start a magazine subscription with one company (say, *The National Scholar*) and midways into the subscription begin receiving another magazine (*The National Enquirer*)? That's usually because the first company has gone out of business and assigned all its subscription contracts to another company. An assignment of contract occurs when one party to an existing contract (the "assignor") hands off the contract's obligations and benefits to another party (the "assignee"). Ideally, the assignee steps into the shoes and assumes all of the contractual obligations and rights of the assignor. In order to do that, the other party to the contract must be properly notified.

> **EXAMPLE:** Tom contracts with a dairy to deliver a bottle of half-and-half every day. The dairy assigns Tom's contract to another dairy, and—provided Tom is notified of the change

and continues to get his daily half and half—his contract is now with the new dairy.

An assignment doesn't always relieve the assignor of liability; that depends on many factors, especially the language of the contract. Some contracts may contain a clause prohibiting assignment, others may require the other party to consent to the assignment, and others may include a guaranty that regardless of an assignment, the original parties (or one of them) guarantee performance.

EXAMPLE: Jonas and Murphy owned property in San Francisco that they leased to Schiller. Schiller assigned his lease to a battery manufacturing company, which became the new tenant under the lease. Jonas assigned his rights as a property owner to Kahn. When the battery manufacturer failed to pay rent, Kahn (the new owner) sued Schiller (the original tenant). The lease agreement included a guaranty clause, stating that if Schiller or "his assigns" failed to pay rent, than Schiller would be on the hook for it. Schiller's lawyers, looking for a creative way out of the payment, argued that the lease required Schiller to pay Jonas and Murphy, *not* Kahn (because Kahn was not mentioned in the original lease). The court disagreed, finding that Jonas was free to assign his rights to Kahn. The court said that if the lease was supposed to prevent Jonas from assigning rights, there should have been a prohibition written into it. In other words, if the parties want to prevent assignment of the contract, they must include an antiassignment clause. (By the way, the issue wouldn't have arisen if the lease had said that Schiller had to pay Jonas "and his assigns and successors.")

When assignments will not be enforced. An assignment of a contract will not be enforced if:

- **The contract prohibits assignment.** Contract language, typically referred to as an antiassignment clause, can prohibit (and "void") any assignments. We provide a sample, below. (See "No assignment or delegation permitted: Sample language.")

- **The assignment materially alters what's expected under the contract.** If the assignment affects the performance due under the contract, decreases the value or return anticipated, or increases the risks for the other party to the contract (the party who is not assigning contractual rights), courts are unlikely to enforce the arrangement.
- **The assignment violates the law or public policy**—Some laws limit or prohibit assignments. For example, many states prohibit the assignment of future wages by an employee, and the federal government prohibits the assignment of certain claims against the government. Other assignments, though not prohibited by a statute, may violate public policy. For example, personal injury claims cannot be assigned because doing so may encourage litigation.

Delegation or assignment? In some cases, a party may not wish to assign the whole contract but only to get somebody else to fulfill its duties.

> **EXAMPLE:** Phyllis enters into a written agreement with Robert's Bakery to provide cupcakes for her child's birthday party. Phyllis pays $200 in advance. Robert's Bakery has an emergency and can't deliver the cupcakes, so Robert pays $150 to Sylvia's Cupcakes to take over the delivery. Robert hasn't assigned the contract; he's delegated his duties to Sylvia. If Sylvia doesn't deliver, Phyllis' dispute would be with Robert. If Robert had properly assigned the contract, Phyllis' dispute would be with Sylvia. (Of course, to be effective as a delegation, the person to whom the task is delegated—in this case, Sylvia—has to accept or assume the duty or responsibility.)

Obviously, not all duties can be delegated—for example, some personal services are usually not delegated because they are so specific in nature. If you hired Ted Nugent to perform at your event, for example, he could not arbitrarily delegate his performing duties to Lady Gaga.

To prohibit delegation, the parties should include specific language to that effect in the agreement. For example, an antiassignment clause might state "Neither party shall assign or delegate its rights ...."

How is a contract assigned? There are three steps to follow if you want to assign a contract:

1. **Examine the contract for any limitations or prohibitions.** Check for antiassignment clauses. Sometimes the prohibition is not a separate clause but is included in another provision. Look for language that states, "This agreement may not be assigned ...." If you find such language, you may not be able to assign the agreement unless the other party consents.

2. **Execute an assignment.** If you are not prohibited from assigning, prepare and enter into an assignment of contract, an agreement transferring rights and obligations.

3. **Provide notice to the obligor.** After you have assigned your contract rights to the assignee, you should provide notice to the other original contracting party (referred to as the obligor). Unless otherwise prohibited by the contract or by law, this notice will effectively relieve you of any liability under the contract.

Assignment checklist. As you draft a contract clause about assignment or a later assignment agreement, consider these questions:

☐ **Do you want the freedom to delegate tasks in the agreement?** If so, be sure that the contract does not prohibit delegation. Usually that prohibition is included in an antiassignment clause. You can also include affirmative language if you wish, such as "Either party may delegate its obligations under this agreement."

☐ **Do you want the ability to assign the revenue you receive from a contract?** If you want to be able to assign revenue from a contract but not the performance obligations—for example, you want your nephew to receive the royalties from a licensing deal, but otherwise you are to be on the hook for all other obligations—then make sure you have made this freedom explicit if the contract has an antiassignment clause.

For example, you could include language such as, "Neither party may assign its rights or obligations except that Licensor may assign its right to receive revenue under this agreement."

- [ ] **Do you want the ability to assign all rights under the agreement to a company that acquires your business?** If so, review the antiassignment exceptions, below.
- [ ] **Do you want to make sure that the other party to the agreement will always be responsible to you, even if the agreement is assigned?** If so, you should include a guaranty similar to that mentioned in the example above, in which the assigning party guarantees performance after assignment.
- [ ] **Do you want to prevent the other side from assigning the contract or delegating its obligations?** Include a general antiassignment/ antidelegation clause and be sure that it includes language such as "Any assignment or delegation made in violation of this clause is void."

Antiassignment clauses. Below are three variations of antiassignment clauses that can be used in a contract. The first sample is a standard antiassignment clause barring any assignment or delegation. The second sample is used when the parties want to prohibit assignments except if they transfer the agreement to new owners or affiliate companies (and don't want to ask for permission). The last sample is similar to the second except it requires permission for such an assignment. The good news is that permission can't be withheld on a whim. Consent to the assignment to a new owner can only be made for a valid business reason. What's a valid reason? If the assignee is in terrible financial shape or is a direct competitor, that would qualify.

No assignment or delegation permitted: Sample language

Assignment. Neither party may assign or delegate its rights or obligations pursuant to this Agreement without the prior written consent of the other. Any assignment or delegation in violation of this section is void.

Consent not needed for affiliates or new owners: Sample language

Assignment. Neither party may assign or delegate its rights or obligations pursuant to this Agreement without the prior written consent of the other. However, no consent is required for an assignment that occurs (a) to an entity in which the transferring party owns more than 50% of the assets, or (b) as part of a transfer of all or substantially all of the assets of the transferring party to any party. Any assignment or delegation in violation of this section is void.

Consent not unreasonably withheld: Sample language

Assignment. Neither party may assign or delegate its rights or obligations pursuant to this Agreement without the prior written consent of the other. Such consent will not be unreasonable withheld. Any assignment or delegation in violation of this section is void.

Antiassignment clauses can be modified to prohibit only one of the parties from assigning rights. Also, when preparing an antiassignment clause, keep in mind that you can only prevent "voluntary" assignments; you cannot prevent assignments that are ordered by a court or that are mandatory under law—for example in a bankruptcy proceeding.

Related terms: acquisition agreement (sale of business); novation; successors and assigns.

assignor/assignee

The party assigning the contract (or legal rights) is the assignor; the party receiving them is the assignee.

Related terms: assignment (of contract); successors and assigns.

attachment

See addendum.

attest

An archaic term sometimes used to indicate that a party affirms or certifies something to be true or correct.

attorney-in-fact

An attorney-in-fact does not have to be an attorney; it can be any person named in a power of attorney document to act on behalf of someone else (the "principal"). The attorney-in-fact doesn't have unlimited powers, however. All of the powers and responsibilities are set forth in the power of attorney document. They often include the authority to sign contracts on behalf of the principal.

Related terms: agent; power of attorney.

attorneys' fees

Attorneys' fees are payments for a lawyer's services. You may have heard the joke about the new client who asked the lawyer, "How much do you charge?" "I charge $200 to answer three questions," replied the lawyer. The client asked, "Isn't that a bit steep?" "Yes," said the lawyer, "What's your third question?" As the joke indicates, it's important to get a clear understanding about how fees will be paid when you hire a lawyer.

Under the "American Rule," (applied in U.S. Courts), each party to a lawsuit must pay its own attorneys' fees, unless a statute provides otherwise. (For example, laws that the prohibit discrimination allow employees who win in court to collect their attorneys' fees from the other party.) However, parties can change this default rule by signing a contract that requires the losing side in a legal dispute to pay the winning (or "prevailing") side's attorneys' fees and costs. Below is a typical attorneys' fees provision.

A

Attorneys' fees: Sample language

Attorney fees. The prevailing party shall have the right to collect from the other party its reasonable costs and necessary disbursements and attorneys' fees incurred in enforcing this Agreement.

What are reasonable costs? Costs refer to filing fees, fees for serving the summons, complaint, and other court papers, fees to pay a court reporter to transcribe depositions (pretrial interviews of witnesses) and in-court testimony, and, if a jury is involved, to pay the daily stipend of jurors. Often, costs to photocopy court papers and exhibits are also included. Typically, court costs are paid by the parties to the dispute. But with the inclusion of an attorneys' fees clause, the losing party is held responsible for both parties' costs.

Watch out for one-way attorneys' fees provisions. Under a mutual provision, such as the example above, the party that wins the lawsuit is awarded attorneys' fees. This is fair and encourages the quick resolution of lawsuits. A "one-way provision" allows only one of the parties to receive attorneys' fees, usually the party with the better bargaining position. One-way provisions, no matter which side they favor, create an uneven playing field for resolving disputes. Some states, such as California, have recognized this unfairness and automatically convert a one-way attorneys' fees contract provision into a mutual provision.

Judicial enforcement. This type of clause is not always enforced. Courts are allowed to judge contracts for fairness and to change their terms if they decide that doing so is the more fair solution. If a judge decides that it would be unfair to enforce a requirement that one side pay the other's attorneys' fees or finds that one of the parties was forced into signing the agreement, the judge could cancel the requirement or change the amount of fees to be paid. But if a judge decides that an attorney fee provision is reasonable and that it was negotiated by two parties with equal bargaining power, then the judge will likely enforce it.

Related terms: alternative dispute resolution (ADR); arbitration; boilerplate; mediation.

authority to bind

This refers to someone with the power to sign agreements on behalf of another person or entity. (No, it is not borrowed from an S and M encyclopedia.) Under state laws, an officer of a corporation, a managing member of a limited liability company, or a general partner in a partnership all have the authority to bind their respective entities. The individual owner of a sole proprietorship can always bind that business, although in community property states, the signature of a spouse is sometimes also advised, just to make sure all parties are on board.

Status of authority. The status of the signing parties should be reflected in the signature block of the document, which should indicate whether that person is an officer, a general partner, and so on. In addition, many legal documents contain a statement such as "Each party has signed this Agreement through its authorized representative" or similar language.

Avoiding fraud. As a preventative measure—to avoid being improperly bound to contracts—businesses often take the following actions:

- **Furnish notice.** Companies often provide written notice to customers, vendors, and others as to who in the company has authority.
- **Provide contract notice.** Companies often include a notice on all contracts indicating the names of those persons who can bind the business.
- **Establish limitations.** Companies establish limitations on authority to bind in their agency and contractor agreements.

Related terms: agent; signatures.

avoidance (and frustration)

When a contract includes a mutual mistake, one party unfairly pressured the other ("duress"), or one party lied ("fraud"), then the goal of the contract has been "frustrated." In this situation, the injured party can void the contract ("avoidance"). In that case, all parties are released from their obligations. In cases of intentional fraud—for example, when someone deliberately lied to induce a deal, the injured party can elect avoidance or can instead seek additional damages for the fraud, under tort law.

Related terms: duress; fraud (misrepresentation); impossibility (of performance; mistake; restitution; void (voidable).

banker's acceptance

A banker's acceptance is an unconditional agreement to pay money on a certain date (the "date of maturity") and is often specified as a method of payment for deliveries or for international agreements. In some ways, it is also like a postdated check except that the bank has guaranteed (or "accepted") the arrangement, thereby assuring the contracting parties that the money is available. Banker's acceptances are considered to be negotiable instruments—agreements to pay money that can be transferred—that are bought and sold.

basket

This term occasionally appears in contracts to describe a group of (often diverse) securities purchased in a single stock sale (a "basket of stocks"). It can also refer to a group of currencies used to calculate foreign exchange rates.

beneficial ownership

Beneficial ownership occurs when you list someone as the official owner of property or a business while concealing the real owner (called the "beneficial" owner because that's the person who actually gets the benefits of ownership). This approach is often used in tax avoidance schemes although not all uses of beneficial ownership are illegitimate. For example, it's perfectly legal for the person who controls the voting power for stock shares (the beneficial owner) to be different than the person named as the registered owner of the stock.

Related terms: fraud (misrepresentation); Uniform Commercial Code.

beneficiary

Beneficiaries—the designated recipients of money or other property—
are commonly named in wills, trusts, life insurance policies,
retirement accounts, annuities, or trusts. Beneficiaries are always
at the mercy of the still-living person controlling the money or
property ("principal"), who can always change estate planning
documents.

> EXAMPLE: Cosima von Bulow was named as the beneficiary of
> her maternal grandmother's will—that is, the person entitled to
> receive her grandmother's property upon her death. But when
> Cosima came to the defense of her father Claus when he was
> accused of killing her mother, the socialite Sunny von Bulow,
> her grandmother removed Cosima's name from the will. It
> wasn't until Claus renounced any claims to Sunny's fortune that
> Cosima was reinstated as beneficiary of her grandmother's will.

Related terms: agent; fiduciary (duty, relationship); third-party
beneficiary.

best efforts

Best efforts is a contractual qualifier by which one party agrees
to use diligent efforts to fulfill an obligation. For example, what
if a third party has to assist in the performance of a contractual
obligation and you can't guarantee that will happen by the deadline
set in the contract? One solution is to insert the qualifier that you
will use "best efforts" to complete the work. That way, you're not
guaranteeing that the third party will come through in a timely
manner, only that you'll try your best to make it happen.

> EXAMPLE: Gerbik Engineering is supposed to complete
> reconstruction of a boat, but that requires a naval inspection
> and certification by the Coast Guard. Because the inspections

are done at the convenience of the Coast Guard, Gerbik can't guarantee that the boat will be ready to go by the contractual deadline, September 1. If the Coast Guard doesn't inspect until September 2, Gerbik would be in breach of the agreement. To avoid this problem but still assure the other party that Gerbik will do its part to meet the deadline, Gerbik's lawyer inserts a statement that "Gerbik Engineering will use reasonable efforts to have the boat reconstructed and inspected by September 1."

By using a best-efforts statement, a party can argue that missing the deadline doesn't constitute breach of the contract, as long as that party exercised reasonable efforts to complete the work on time.

Range of efforts. Lawyers have developed some different ways to describe the various types of "efforts" that a party can promise to use in a contract. These are listed below, with their usual definitions (as you'll see, despite the number of terms used, they all boil down to either "reasonable" or "best" efforts). However, keep in mind that courts might interpret these terms differently. To the surprise of some practitioners, courts often don't distinguish amongst the types of "efforts" a party might employ, and instead consider all "efforts" requirements to require only reasonable diligence from the person who promises to make them.

> **EXAMPLE:** A film distributor had agreed "to use its best efforts diligently and in good faith to exploit" two motion pictures. In analyzing this "best efforts" standard, the court held that the distributor need act only like the "average, prudent comparable distributor," a standard that sounds closer to the basic definition of "reasonable efforts" as described below.

So why bother to elaborate the differences between best efforts and reasonable efforts? Because some courts do recognize distinctions among these definitions. And, using more precise terms listed below allows each party to understand what the other is promising to do:

- **Reasonable efforts.** Someone who promises to make reasonable efforts must act like any other reasonable businessperson in a similar position; that is, the person must act diligently and responsibly, but doesn't have to do things that are commercially unfeasible.
- **Commercially reasonable efforts.** This is considered to be the same as reasonable efforts.
- **Good-faith efforts.** Again, this is interpreted to require reasonable efforts.
- **Best efforts.** A person who promises to make best efforts must do everything possible to make it happen, even to the point of suffering a commercial loss. As noted, courts often disagree with this interpretation. Many have held that a best-efforts promise does not require the party to act in a commercially unreasonable manner (for example, to risk bankruptcy). In Illinois, for instance, courts will not enforce a best efforts promise; they consider the terminology too vague.
- **Reasonable best efforts.** Considered to be the same as best efforts.

What are reasonable efforts? Regardless of whether courts differentiate between best efforts and reasonable efforts, they do require parties who make such promises to make *some* effort that involves diligence, reasonableness, and good faith. Because there are so many vagaries, it's often best for the drafter of such provisions to either specify exactly what the efforts will consist of or to specify what will not be required.

Related terms: ambiguity; rules of interpretation (rules of construction); warranties.

bilateral contract (versus unilateral contract)

A bilateral contract—a term that's tortured many law students—is made when both parties promise to do something. For example, you promise to pay Amazon.com for a George Foreman grill;

Amazon.com promises to ship your George Foreman grill. Almost all contracts are bilateral—from home sales to criminal plea bargains—because they are created by mutual promises. A bilateral contract is what people think of when they refer to a contract: I'll do this if you'll do that.

Unilateral contracts. The term "bilateral" is used to distinguish these agreements from unilateral contracts. A unilateral contract is an agreement in which one party promises to do something and the other party accepts by doing something. The classic law school example is a reward—for example, "Find my cat and I'll pay $200." You cannot accept the offer about the cat by *promising* to find the cat; you can accept it only by *finding* the cat.

> **EXAMPLE 1: Bilateral.** Tom accidentally drives his car into a shallow lake. Tom calls Sam's towing service and says, "Remove my car from the lake and I'll pay you $300." Sam accepts the offer. Sam and Tom formed a bilateral contract. Each party has made a promise to the other.

> **EXAMPLE 2: Unilateral.** Instead of hiring someone to tow his car, Tom posts a sign at the lake saying "I'll pay $300 to whoever removes my car from the lake." The only way to accept Tom's offer is to tow Tom's car (not to promise to tow it).

A unilateral contract is formed only if the other person acts in response to the offer. For example, what happens if Bob removes Tom's car from the lake just because it's an eyesore, without even seeing Tom's offer? Most courts would say that Tom doesn't owe Bob $300. And a unilateral contract cannot be accepted if the party attempting to claim the reward already had a legal obligation to perform the required act.

> **EXAMPLE:** Ms. Rheinhauer found a bracelet with 436 diamonds lost by Ms. DeKrieges. New York law makes it a crime to keep found property unless the finder makes a diligent effort to locate

B

the owner and notifies the police of the find within 10 days. Ms. Rheinhauer didn't do either. Later, she saw Ms. DeKreiges' notice of reward and tried to claim it by returning the bracelet. No reward for Ms. Rheinhauer because she was already required by law to return the bracelet.

bill of sale

The bill of sale is a hybrid legal document that confirms transfer of title to property and, in doing so, serves as evidence of a contract. For centuries, people have bought certain types of goods, such as horses, dogs, boats, or cars, using a bill of sale. Because it is commonly used for official purposes—to register a car or a boat, for example—a bill of sale may have to conform to state regulations. For example, many states require that a vehicle bill of sale include an odometer reading; some states require it to be notarized. Both parties can sign a bill of sale, but in many instances, only the seller needs to sign it.

When a bill of sale reflects a purchase on credit. Things can get complicated when a bill of sale is provided as security for a loan. For example, if someone pledges a car as collateral for a loan, he might provide the lender with a bill of sale for the car, to become effective only if he defaults on the loan. A bill of sale can also be used as an element of a loan. For example, if you're buying a car on payments, the complete agreement can be framed as a bill of sale, although, technically, the transfer of title might not happen until all payments required under the loan are made. State laws often regulate loan/bill of sale combinations because some sellers or lenders may abuse the practices described above.

Sample bills of sale. Below are of two types of bills of sale: one for a car; and one for a dog. Note that both contain extensive warranties (promises and assurances as to the condition or history of the item).

Motor Vehicle Bill of Sale

B

Motor Vehicle Bill of Sale

1. Seller hereby sells the vehicle (Vehicle) described here to Buyer: [*specify vehicle year, make, and model*].

   Its body type is: _____ .

   It carries the following vehicle identification number (VIN): _____

   Vehicle includes the following personal property items: _____ .

2. The full purchase price for Vehicle is $_____ . In exchange for Vehicle, Buyer has paid Seller [*choose one*]:

   ☐ single payment of the full purchase price.

   ☐ $_____ as a down payment, balance of the purchase price due by ____[*date*]____ .

   ☐ $_____ as a down payment and has executed a promissory note for the balance of the purchase price.

3. Seller warrants that Seller is the legal owner of Vehicle and that Vehicle is free of all legal claims (liens or encumbrances) by others except: _____
   _____ .

   Seller agrees to remove any lien or encumbrance specified in this clause with the proceeds of this sale and other funds if necessary, within _____ days of the date of this bill of sale.

4. Vehicle ☐ has ☐ has not been inspected by an independent mechanic at Buyer's request. If an inspection has been made, the inspection report ☐ is attached to and made part of this bill of sale ☐ is not attached.

5. Seller believes Vehicle to be in good condition except for the following defects: _____
   _____ .

Motor Vehicle Bill of Sale (continued)

B

6. To the best of Seller's knowledge, Vehicle:

   ☐ is   ☐ is not   a salvage vehicle.

   ☐ has   ☐ has   not been declared a total loss by an insurance company.

   ☐ has   ☐ has not   been repaired under the terms of a Lemon Law.

7. The odometer reading for Vehicle is: _____ .

8. Additional terms of sale for Vehicle are as follows: _____

   _____ .

Seller   Buyer

Signature: _____   Signature: _____

Name: _____   Name: _____

Date: _____   Date: _____

Bill of Sale for Dog

B

Bill of Sale for Dog

1. Seller sells to Buyer the dog (Dog) described as follows:

   Name: _____

   Breed: _____

   Sex: _____

   Birth date [*estimate if specific date not known*]: _____

2. The full purchase price for Dog is $_____ .

3. Buyer has paid Seller [*choose one*]:

   ☐ single payment of the full purchase price

   ☐ a down payment of $_____ with the balance of $_____ due _____[*date*]_____ , or

   ☐ other: ___[*explain*]_____ .

4. Seller warrants that:

   a. Seller is the legal owner of Dog.

   b. Dog has had the following vaccinations [*list all the vaccinations Dog has received, including the date the vaccination was given and the name of the vet who gave it*]: _____

   _____ .

   c. Dog was [*choose one*]:

   ☐ bred by Seller

   ☐ bought from a breeder. Name of breeder: _____ on _____[*date*]_____ .

   ☐ acquired from a previous private party owner. Owner's name: ____

   _____ .

Bill of Sale for Dog (continued)

B

d. Dog has had the following special training: _____

_____ .

e. Dog ☐ is ☐ is not purebred.

f. Dog is [*check one*]:

☐ registered with the American Kennel Club or another entity.
Provide details as appropriate: _____

_____ .

☐ not registered with the American Kennel Club or another entity
and is not eligible to be registered.

☐ not registered with the American Kennel Club or another entity
but is eligible to be registered. Explain: _____

_____ .

Seller will provide Buyer with the necessary papers to process
registration.

5. Seller believes that Dog is healthy and in good condition, except for the
following known problems: _____

_____ .

6. If a licensed veterinarian certifies, in writing, that Dog has a serious
disease or congenital defect that was present when Buyer took
possession of Dog, Buyer may, within 14 days of taking possession of Dog
[*choose one*]:

☐ return Dog to Seller. In this case, Seller will refund the purchase price
plus any sales tax and reimburse Buyer for the cost of reasonable
veterinary services directly related to the examination that showed
Dog was ill and emergency treatment to relieve suffering plus any
sales tax.

Bill of Sale for Dog (continued)

☐ keep Dog. In this case, Seller will reimburse Buyer for the cost of reasonable veterinary services directly related to the examination that showed Dog was ill and emergency treatment to relieve suffering, up to the amount of the purchase price plus any sales tax.

7. Dog will be delivered to Buyer in the following manner [*choose one*]:

☐ Buyer will take immediate possession of Dog.

☐ Buyer assumes responsibility for picking up Dog from _____ by __[*date*]_____ .

☐ In exchange for an additional delivery charge of $_____ , Seller will deliver Dog by _____[*date*]_____ to the following location:

_____ .

Seller   Buyer

Signature: _____   Signature: _____

Name: _____   Name: _____

Date: _____   Date: _____

blue-sky laws

Blue-sky laws were created to protect buyers against fly-by-night speculative stock schemes (in which what the purchaser actually gets is "so many feet of blue sky"). For example, are you interested in investing in a surefire beachfront real estate development in Florida? Oh, and did we mention that it's built on swampland, smells like a gas station, and the parking lot is home to a sizeable family of gators? That's exactly the kind of scam blue-sky laws seek to prevent.

The requirements of blue-sky laws vary from state to state, but generally they set rules for securities sales, intended to make sure that the buyers know—or could find out—what they're getting for their money. These laws require that certain securities offerings (and brokers) be registered, among other things. Seller can bypass many blue-sky requirements if they qualify for an exemption under SEC Regulation D (for example, if they are selling to a relatively small number of savvy investors).

Sometimes, a contract triggers blue-sky laws even though it doesn't refer to the sale of stocks and bonds. Blue-sky laws apply to all securities, and that term is broadly defined to include transactions in which one person invests money with the expectation of earning a return from someone else's efforts. Examples of securities include convertible promissory notes secured by stock, warrants (options to purchase shares), profit-sharing (or profit participation) agreements, stock option grants to company employees, and even "variable" annuities, which have a cash value or benefit tied to the performance of an investment account.

Related terms: fraud (misrepresentation); fraud in the inducement.

boilerplate

Boilerplate refers to standardized language used in contracts.

A little history. Back when newspapers were printed from typeset-pressed metal plates, some portions of the daily plates—such as the masthead and advertisements—rarely changed. These fixed plates were nicknamed "boilerplate" and that became common jargon for any unchanging text that is reused from document to document. Eventually, the term referred exclusively to "form" language in contracts.

Little in common. Although often grouped together, boilerplate provisions don't have much in common with one another except that they don't fit anywhere else in an agreement. For that reason, they are usually dumped at the end of the agreement under a title such as "Miscellaneous," "General," or "Standard."

Even though boilerplate is buried in the back of the agreement, these provisions are important. They affect how disputes are resolved and how a court enforces the contract. The effect of boilerplate is most often noticed when it is omitted from a contract—for example, if a contract doesn't include a provision awarding attorneys' fees to the winner of a dispute, it may prove tough for either party to find a lawyer willing to take the case, if there's a breach of contract.

Common contract boilerplate provisions. Here are some common boilerplate provisions:

- **Costs and Attorneys' Fees.** In the event of a legal dispute, the party that loses must pay the winning party's legal fees.
- **Arbitration.** Any disputes about the contract must be resolved through arbitration proceedings, not in a lawsuit.
- **Choice of Law.** In the event of a dispute, a choice of law provision determines which state's legal rules will be applied in the lawsuit.
- **Jurisdiction.** In the event of a dispute, a jurisdiction clause determines where (in which state and county) the lawsuit must be filed.
- **Waiver.** This permits the parties to forego or give up the right to sue for breach of a particular provision of the agreement without giving up any future claims regarding the same provision.
- **Severability.** This permits a court to sever (or take out) an invalid provision and still keep the rest of the agreement intact.

B

- **Integration.** An integration clause says that the written contract represents the final agreement of the parties. Often, it explicitly states the any prior statements or discussions of the agreement are replaced by the written contract, and that any further modification to the contract must be in writing.
- **Attachments.** This guarantees that attachments and exhibits will be included as part of the agreement.
- **Notice.** This describes how each party must provide notices to the other (for example, to terminate the agreement).
- **Relationships.** This prevents either party from claiming a business relationship with the other (for example, by stating that the parties are partners or that one is the other's employee).
- **Assignment.** This affects the ability of the parties to sell or transfer their rights under the agreement to another party.
- **Force Majeure** (pronounced fors- mazhoor') (also referred to as "Acts of God"). This establishes that the agreement will be suspended in the event of unforeseen disasters (such as earthquakes, hurricanes, floods, and so on).
- **Headings.** This provides that the headings used throughout the agreement have no special significance.
- **Escrow.** This allows you to place trade secrets, payments, or other information into a special account that will be opened only under certain conditions.
- **Jury Trial Waivers.** This establishes that when there is a court battle over the contract, the parties agree to have the dispute heard by the judge and to give up their right to a jury trial.
- **Limitations On Damages.** This sets a cap or otherwise limits the types of damages that may be awarded in a contract dispute.
- **Warranties.** These are promises or assurances made by each party regarding various contract obligations.
- **Indemnity.** In an indemnity provision, one party guarantees that it will cover the costs of certain disputes brought by third parties (that is, people who are not parties to the agreement).

- **Confidentiality.** This guarantees that the parties will not disclose certain information.
- **Announcements.** This establishes the manner in the parties can make public disclosures about the subject of the contract, such as statements about a forthcoming merger or joint business venture.
- **Counterparts.** This sets forth the right of the parties to execute copies of the agreement without everyone being present in one place at one time to sign them all.

Related terms: addendum; arbitration; assignment (of contract); attorney's fees; choice of law (governing law); confidentiality agreement; counterparts; escrow; force majeure; indemnity (hold harmless provision); integration; jurisdiction (subject matter; personal); jury trial, waiver of; notice; recitals; severability (savings clause); waiver; warranties.

breach, anticipatory

See anticipatory breach (anticipatory repudiation).

breach, material

In legal terms, a breach is material if it is so substantial that it defeats the purpose of making the contract in the first place. Or put another way, the breach must go to the very root of the agreement between the parties.

> **EXAMPLE:** In 2009, the company that produced the Miss California Pageant, K2 Productions, declared that the reigning crown holder, Carrie Prejean, had breached her contract. K2 stripped Prejean of her title and tiara, claiming that Prejean's contract violations allowed it to terminate the contract. From a legal standpoint, K2's actions were justified only if Prejean had committed a "material" breach: a breach that strikes so deeply at the heart of the contract as to render it "irreparably broken."

B

Had Prejean committed only a "partial" or "immaterial" breach, K2 would not be justified in terminating the deal, but would instead be obligated to try to patch up the problems.

What happens if there is a material breach? If there is a material breach (sometimes referred to as a "total" breach), the other party can simply end the agreement.

EXAMPLE: The wireless company Qualcomm entered into a patent agreement with Texas Instruments. The purpose of the agreement was to permit the two companies to share patents in order to avoid patent disputes. The contract contained a clause prohibiting the parties from discussing their royalty arrangements. After Texas Instruments revealed the royalties at a press conference, Qualcomm sued, claiming a material breach of the agreement. A Delaware court determined that it wasn't a material breach because the disclosure didn't defeat the purpose of the agreement—to achieve "patent peace." In other words, the disclosures didn't go the root of the agreement.

Material breach factors. In deciding whether a breach is material, courts often look to guidance from a legal guide known as the Restatement (Second) of Contracts, as well as to other court decisions. Generally, the following factors are relevant:

- **Is the other party deprived of the heart of what it bargained for?** For example, if the BMW dealer promised you a radio and fancy hubcaps, but the car that was delivered lacked both, that would probably not deprive you of the true purpose of your deal—the car—and would be less likely to be a material breach. On the other hand, if a used-car dealer promised you the very Ford Mustang driven by Steve McQueen in *Bullitt*, then presented you with a different Mustang, that would be a material breach. In this instance, your bargain wasn't about the make and model of the car; it was about one particular vehicle.

- **Can the other party be compensated for the loss?** Will money solve the problem, and if so, how much? If it's something that can be fixed with reasonable effort or expense, it's less likely to be material. Consider the hubcap-free, radio-less BMW, mentioned above. Because the dealer could easily fix the problem by installing the promised features, this probably isn't a material breach.

- **What will the breaching party lose (or forfeit)?** How much has the breaching party already done to fulfill its end of the deal? This factor often hinges on timing: how far along the parties are in carrying out their contractual obligations when the breach occurs. Consider a homeowner who hires a contractor to create a custom kitchen. If the homeowner declares a breach when the kitchen is near completion, the contractor will lose much more in time and money than if the breach was declared before construction began.

- **What are the chances that the breaching party will fix things?** The more likely it is that the breaching party can and will fix the problem, the less likely the breach is material. Obviously this is a tough call. If the other party provides security for its promised payment, or some other reasonable assurance that it will honor the deal, or if the economy or market shifts in favor of performance, then the breach is less likely to be material. On the other hand, signs of financial weakness or defaults on payments show that the problems are less likely to be corrected (and make a finding of material breach more likely).

- **Did the breaching party act in bad faith?** If the breach was willful or resulted from bad faith or unfair dealing, then a court is more likely to presume a material breach. For example, one court found that an executive who was insubordinate and refused to follow directions had materially breached his employment agreement. On the other hand, a breach that results from simple carelessness ("negligence") or circumstances beyond the party's control is less likely to be considered material.

B

Ready, willing, and able. It's not enough to simply claim that the other party committed a material breach. The nonbreaching party must also be "ready, willing, and able" to perform its obligations under the contract, if it hasn't performed them already. In one case, for example, a New York man contracted to buy a vacation house "as is" for $610,000. When the sellers refused to go through with the deal, the buyer claimed breach of contract. The court of appeals ruled for the sellers. The buyer could not show he was "ready, willing and able" to perform because he wanted substantial improvements to the heating and plumbing systems. In other words, he was not willing to take the house "as is."

What does the contract say? Some contracts provide guidance as to what constitutes a material breach. Rather than rely on a judge's discretion or interpretation of the law, the parties can include a provision in the contract stating that a breach of certain provisions will be considered material. For example, a clause may state that certain activities—a failure to make payments, a failure to maintain insurance, or a failure to achieve certain sales goals—will be considered material breaches. Because delays in performance and payment are not always considered material breaches, some contracts add a statement that "time is of the essence," which means that these types of delays will be considered a material breach.

Back to Carrie Prejean. According to K2's lawyers, Prejean failed to show up for events as promised, failed to disclose information about her background, failed to disclose the existence of racy photos and videos of herself, and signed an unauthorized post-pageant book deal—a no-no according to K2 lawyers. (K2 also sought the return of $5,200 loaned to Prejean for breast implants to "make her more competitive.") Based on the factors above, does this add up to a material breach?

Was K2 Productions deprived of the heart of the promised benefit? The core of the contract is that Prejean would serve as Miss California and render personal performances throughout the year. Her failure or refusal to make certain appearances strikes at the heart of the agreement and leans towards a finding of material breach.

Can K2 Productions be adequately compensated for the loss? Money cannot fix Prejean's failure to make personal appearances, nor can it undo Prejean's concealment of important facts—such as the existence of racy photos—that might have changed K2's decision to enter into the contract in the first place.

What will Prejean lose? Prejean had invested considerable time and effort into the competitions. However, her principal obligations didn't begin until she was chosen as Miss California. Because K2 Productions declared breach within weeks of the national pageant, a finding of material breach is more likely. In addition, in our world of instant celebrity and reality TV, Prejean might actually benefit from the termination. (After all, she had already landed a book deal.)

What are the chances that Prejean would fix things? Prejean had been offered a chance to fix things. "I told Carrie she needed to get back to work and honor her contract with the Miss California USA Organization and I gave her the opportunity to do so," Donald Trump told the press. (Trump is the owner of the Miss USA Pageant.) Based on the acrimony between the parties as played out in the press, however, it seems unlikely that Prejean could or would fix the problem.

Did Prejean act in bad faith? The failure to make appearances seems willful, unless Prejean had some justification for failing to perform her duties. Perhaps they were not as initially disclosed to her, for example.

Our conclusion. Based on publicly available information about the case, we think that a court would likely find that Carrie Prejean committed a material breach of her K2 Productions agreement and that K2 was justified in canceling the agreement.

Related terms: breach, anticipatory; damages, compensatory; damages, consequential; remedies.

breach, notice of

Notice of breach is the process of informing someone of a broken contract—the first formal step in resolving a contract problem

B

Unfortunately, Hallmark does not make a card that says, "To a very special former business associate: You're in breach of contract!" So you're going to have to come up with your own way to provide a notice of breach. The notice, generally in the form of a letter, (sometimes referred to as a "demand letter") explains why you believe there has been a breach (that is, what the other party did or didn't do) and lays out the actions that must be taken next, either to fix ("cure") the problems or to end the contract and compensate for the damage. Some notices are quite specific, laying out a detailed course of action and timetable for making things right. Other notices are less specific, serving primarily as invitations to talk things over.

Preserving the date. One important function of the notice is to create a record of the date when the breaching party is officially told of the breach. That date may be important if the dispute ends up in court. Before sending the notice, the nonbreaching party should confirm that the notice is going to the right person, via the proper method.

Check the notice clause. Contracts often have a clause—commonly referred to as a notice provision—setting forth contact information for each party. For example, notices may have to be communicated by email, fax, or overnight mail. Failing to follow these procedures may affect each party's rights. For example, a notice sent to the wrong address or by the wrong method may not "count" as notice of the breach, which gives the breaching party more time to cure the problem.

Describing the breach. The notice must indicate what part of the contract was breached. A breach—a failure to perform under the contract—usually comes in one of three flavors: (1) The other party failed to perform (for example, you haven't been paid or haven't received the goods you were promised); (2) the other party said that it *will not* perform its obligations in the future; or (3) the other party has made it impossible for you to perform your obligations under the agreement (for example, you were hired to modify a software program, but the company that hired you won't give you the code you need to do the work).

B

No matter why the breach occurred, you will need to identify which clauses of the contract are affected and list them in your letter. If more than one section has been breached, list all of them, leading with your strongest claims

Material breach. You may provide notice for any type of breach, but keep in mind that courts are most concerned with "material breaches"—actions by the other party that destroy the value of the contract. Although you can give notice of a "nonmaterial" breach (also known as a "partial breach" or an "immaterial breach"), a nonmaterial breach usually will not end the agreement.

The cure. In some cases, it may be too late to fix the problem. If so, the notice serves to terminate (cancel) the agreement and to seek damages. Much of the time, though, a breach of contract notice seeks to resolve contractual problems while keeping the agreement in effect. For that reason, the letter often provides a period of time during which the breaching party can fix ("cure") the breach. Most contracts include a clause establishing the cure period—often 30 days. Even if it seems like there's no point in offering a cure period, it may be in your best interest. The other party may be unaware of the problem or may have run into temporary setbacks that make compliance difficult.

Avoid passion. The breach of contract notice should have a dispassionate, business-like tone. Remember, this letter—like all correspondence preceding a lawsuit—could well become an exhibit to papers filed with the court. A judge or jury won't look kindly on a letter that is bullying, exaggerated, or melodramatic. Just stick to the facts.

Try to work it out. Before you send the notice—or perhaps at the same time—you should try to fix the problems informally. This can help you save time, money, and perhaps even your business relationship. Don't use the notice solely to intimidate the other party as some sort of business strategy—for example, to threaten a lawsuit in order to get out of a deal that's not as lucrative as you expected. That approach often backfires, especially if you're bluffing (and are then drawn into a long legal battle). Finally, if you and the other

B

party both want to formally end ("discharge") the agreement, it is best to do that by entering into a separate agreement terminating the contract. This is often done using a mutual rescission agreement. If one or both parties have already performed some of the contractual obligations—for example, a home has been partially constructed— you will need a more detailed settlement and release.

The response. After you send your notice of breach, be prepared for one of these responses:

- **No response.** If you don't hear anything within two weeks, send a second letter referring to your earlier letter. If you don't receive a response to the second letter, it's time to consult with an attorney. Perhaps a letter on a lawyer's stationery will have better results. If not, determine (with your attorney's advice) what your next steps should be.

- **Get lost.** You may receive a response telling you basically to "take a hike" or something equivalent—for example, "we have reviewed your letter and have determined that our company is not in breach of the agreement." You should consult with an attorney before you fire off an angry response; it's always possible that the responding party is correct.

- **Let's talk.** If the responding letter invites you to discuss the matter, then you may be on your way to resolving the problem. You may wish to consult an attorney for advice on how to proceed, particularly if you expect to reach a written settlement with the other party.

- **You're right; we give up.** Congratulations. You won. What happens next depends on how you want to end things. Depending on the scale or type of breach, you may want to use a formal settlement agreement. Again, an attorney can help you to wrap things up properly.

Below are two examples of breach of contract notices, one with a request for a cure, the other seeking termination of the contract.

Related terms: breach, anticipatory; breach, material; contract.

Breach of Contract Notice With Cure

Breach of Contract Notice With Cure

Dear _____ [*name of breaching party*] _____ ,

This letter concerns the [*name of contract or contract/agreement*] entered into between [*your name/your company's name*] and [*breaching party's or company's name*] on [*date of signatures*] (the "Agreement").

The purpose of this letter is to place you on notice that you have breached the above-referenced Agreement as follows: ___ [*describe each breach*] _____

_____

_____ .

You have _____ days from receipt of this letter to cure the breach.

[*Choose one the following ending*]

[**Conciliatory approach**]

Naturally, it is in the best interest of both parties to avoid litigation. My company is prepared and willing to work with yours to resolve this matter. We look forward to achieving a speedy resolution. By asserting our rights in this letter, we do not waive any other rights that we might be entitled to under the Agreement.

[**Aggressive approach**]

If you fail to cure this breach in a timely manner, we will take whatever legal action is required to enforce our rights under the Agreement. By asserting our rights in this letter, we do not waive any other rights that we might be entitled to under the Agreement.

Signature: _____

Printed name: _____

Breach of Contract Notice With Termination

B

Breach of Contract Notice With Termination

Dear _____ [name of breaching party] _____ ,

This letter concerns the [name of contract or contract/agreement] entered into between [your name/your company's name] and [breaching party's or company's name] on [date of signatures] (the "Agreement").

The purpose of this letter is to place you on notice that you have materially breached the above-referenced Agreement as follows: _____ [describe each material breach] _____

_____ .

Your company's actions have resulted in a material noncurable breach of the agreement and on that basis, the agreement is now terminated. According to the provisions of the agreement, your company must: _[describe the post-termination steps that the breaching party must take]_

_____

If you fail to take the steps outlined above in a timely manner, we will take whatever legal action is required to enforce our rights under the Agreement. By asserting our rights in this letter, we do not waive any other rights that we might be entitled to under the Agreement.

Signature: _____

Printed name: _____

bulletproof

A bulletproof contract is usually a reference to an agreement that has survived any attempt to be undone or circumvented. For example, a TV commentator might refer to Sandra Bullock's prenuptial agreement as being bulletproof. Many lawyers pride themselves on creating such Kevlar agreements; few contracts, however, fulfill this potential.

business interruption insurance

When your business is forced to close due to some unforeseen event, business interruption policies typically replace lost profits (determined using your business's earnings history as shown by its financial records) and pay any operating expenses you still have to pay even though you can't do business. In other words, if you must close your business due to a covered event, such as a fire or storm, this type of insurance policy replaces the income you won't be able to earn.

If you're the kind of business owner who worries about whether (and for how long) a tsunami will close down your surf shop, then consider a business interruption policy. These policies are not typically sold as stand-alone products; instead, they're added to property insurance policies or sold as part of a business insurance package.

When you're shopping for this type of insurance (or any other, for that matter), always check the exclusions and coverage. For example, some business interruption policies may provide an "extended period of indemnity," which kicks in after you reopen, to cover your continuing losses until you are fully back on your feet. If your customers don't immediately return after a temporary shutdown, this type of policy will pay for the business you're still missing during this transition period.

Related terms: additional insured; face amount; insurance contract (insurance policy).

business purchase agreement

See acquisition agreement (sale of business).

buy-sell agreement (buyout agreement)

Think of a buy-sell agreement as a business owner's prenup. A buy-sell agreement (also called a "buyout agreement") sets the price and terms for the sale of an owner's interest should that owner wish to depart in the future. Most buy-sell agreements are made when the business is formed. This is why they're like prenups: It's easier for the parties to agree on how they'll part terms when they're getting along (and planning to stay together forever) than after they're hopelessly locked in conflict.

Forced buyouts. One of the most appealing aspects of a buy-sell agreement is that it can include a requirement for co-owners to buy out the interests of a departing or deceased co-owner. This forced buyout provision creates a market for your ownership interest where one might not naturally exist. Not only does the provision guarantee that a departing owner can unload the interest, but it can also set the price in advance, so everyone knows exactly what they're agreeing to.

It's in the details. The buy-sell agreement can also limit ownership to a specific group of people, which prevents an owner from selling out to someone you don't want to do business with. And, it can be used to fund a company-owned insurance policy that can provide the funds to purchase a deceased owner's insurance. For more information, see: *Business Buyout Agreements: A Step-by-Step Guide for Co-Owners,* by Anthony Mancusco and Bethany K. Laurence (Nolo).

buyer in due course

This is a person who buys or otherwise legally receives a promissory note from a lender. The borrower's obligation to repay the note doesn't change just because the lender sells the note to someone else.

Related terms: compounding (compound) interest; cosigner; debt; interest rates (usury); mortgage; promissory note.

cap

A cap is a limitation, usually on the total amount to be paid for something. For example, if you intend to pay royalties to an artist but don't want to pay more than a total of $20,000, then you would cap the royalties by stating, "After total royalties of $20,000 have been paid to Artist, all royalty obligations will end."

Not everything can be capped, and some caps may be illegal. For example, an employer could not cap an employee's pay if that violated state employment laws relating to overtime or the minimum wage.

Related terms: ceiling; illegal contract.

capacity (to contract)

Certain people are always considered to lack the capacity to contract; as a legal matter, they are presumed not to know what they're doing. Those people—legal minors and the mentally ill, for example—are placed into a special category. If they enter into a contract, they can void it. That person can either end the contract or permit it to go ahead as agreed on. This protects the party who lacks capacity from being forced to go through with a disadvantageous deal. What if the producers of the *Girls Gone Wild* videos were to ply a young woman with Long Island iced teas and then pressure her into signing a release and lifting her T-shirt for the video camera; is that release enforceable? That depends on the woman's age and her mental capacity at the time she signed the release.

When minors contract. Because they lack capacity, minors (those under the age of 18, in most states) who make contracts can either honor the deal or void the contract. There are a few exceptions, however. For example, in most states, a minor cannot void a contract for necessities like food, clothing, and lodging. Also, a minor can void a contract for lack of capacity only while still under the age of majority. In most states, if a minor turns 18 and doesn't do anything to void a contract, then the contract can no longer be voided.

> **EXAMPLE:** Sean, 15, a snowboarder, signs an endorsement agreement for sportswear. He endorses the product and deposits his compensation for the endorsements for several years. At age 19, he decides he wants to void the agreement to take a better endorsement deal. He claims he lacked capacity when he signed the deal at 15. A court probably will not permit Sean to now void the agreement.

Mental incapacity. A person who lacks mental capacity can void, or have a guardian void, most contracts (again, except contracts for necessities). In most states, the standard for mental capacity is whether the party understood the meaning and effect of the words comprising the transaction. This is called the "cognitive" test. Some states use what's called the "affective" test: a contract can be voided if one party is unable to act in a reasonable manner and the other party has reason to know of the condition. And some states use a third measure, called the "motivational" test. Courts in these states measure capacity by the ability of the party to judge whether or not to enter into the agreement. These tests may produce varying results when applied to mental conditions such as bipolar disorder.

> **EXAMPLE:** Mr. Smalley contracted to sell an invention and then later claimed that the contract was void because he lacked capacity. Smalley had been diagnosed as manic-depressive and had been in and out of mental hospitals. His doctor stated that Mr. Smalley was not capable of evaluating business deals when he was in a manic state. A California Court of Appeals refused

C

to terminate the contract and stated that Smalley, in his manic state, was capable of contracting. "The manic phase of the illness under discussion is not, however, a weakness of mind rendering a person incompetent to contract ...." In other words, the Court viewed manic-depression as cognitive—that the condition may have impaired Smalley's judgment but not his understanding.

Alcohol and drugs. People who are intoxicated by drugs or alcohol are usually not considered to lack capacity to contract. Courts generally rule that those who are voluntarily intoxicated shouldn't be allowed to avoid their contractual obligations, but should instead have to take responsibility for the results of their self-induced altered state of mind. However, if a party is so far gone as to be unable to understand even the nature and consequences of the agreement, and the other (sober) party takes advantage of the person's condition, that contract may be voidable by the inebriated party.

EXAMPLE: In the late 19th century, Mr. Thackrah, a Utah resident and owner of $80,00 worth of mining stock, went on a three-month bender. Mr. T's fondness for alcohol was well known, and a local bank hired Mr. Haas to contract with the inebriated Thackrah. Haas did the deal, getting Thackrah to agree to accept $1,200 for his mining stock. When he sobered up (a month later), Thackrah learned that Haas had turned over the mining shares to a local bank (apparently the real culprits in the scheme). Thackrah sued Haas. The case went all the way to the U.S. Supreme Court, which ruled that the agreement was void because the bank and Haas knew that Thackrah had no idea what he was doing when he entered the contract. The bank had to return the shares to Thackrah, less the $1,200 he had already been paid.

Related terms: contract; void (voidable).

C

carve out

This term has many applications, all of them with a slightly surgical edge. Used as both a noun and a verb, carve out (sometimes spelled as one word) usually refers to an exception to a rule that would otherwise apply, or the process of creating that exception. For example, a condo agreement may restrict pet ownership, but carve out an exception for dogs under ten pounds.

Here are some other examples:

- **Securities.** A carve out is often used to describe the sale of a minor stake in a company or to the sale of a division of a company.
- **Licenses.** A carve out is used to retain certain rights while granting rights to others—for example, carving out the audio rights in a license agreement.
- **Real estate sales.** A carve out often refers to the separation of value between land and income generated from the land—for example, a landowner may carve out the oil rights to his land.

casualty loss

When bad stuff happens unexpectedly that causes physical damage to your business—for example, the power goes out and your frozen ice sculpture melts—it's usually categorized as a casualty loss. The term is commonly found in insurance contracts and refers to any financial loss from property that is damaged as the result of a sudden, unexpected event. The term also has a meaning in tax parlance. If you meet IRS conditions and can prove your loss, you can claim a "casualty loss deduction." The term "casualty" refers to your lack of fault. Like an innocent bystander, you were injured by circumstances beyond your control; in other words, you were a casualty.

Related terms: insurance contract (insurance policy); underwriter.

cause

This term has several legal meanings, including:

- **Cause of action.** This refers to a specific legal claim that can be made against another person or entity. For example, if someone breached your contract, then you have a cause of action for breach of contract. If someone published untrue statements about your business on a website, you would have a cause of action for libel.

- **Proximate cause.** Under the law of negligence, proximate cause refers to the direct or primary reason why an injury occurred. For example, if the seller of a home concealed a hole in the floor by laying carpet over it, and you later fell through, then the act of concealment would be the proximate cause of your injury.

- **Intervening cause.** An intervening cause is an event that interrupts the chain of causation. For example, let's go back to that hole in the floor. You twisted your ankle when you fell, but the doctor who examined you accidentally broke it while trying to force it into position to take X-rays. The doctor's actions would be an intervening cause of your injury.

- **Good cause.** Good cause (sometimes called just cause) is a standard applied to the dismissal of an employee. If an employee has an employment contract, good cause may be required to fire the employee. What constitutes good cause is often spelled out in written employment agreements. In the case of implied employment contracts or written contracts that don't define the term, it generally means that the employer must have a legitimate reason to fire, usually based on business needs and goals. Examples of good cause could include poor job performance, low productivity, refusal to follow instructions, habitual tardiness, absences from work, possession of a weapon at work, threats of violence, violating company rules, stealing or other criminal activity,

C

dishonesty, endangering health and safety, revealing company trade secrets, harassing coworkers, disrupting the work environment, preventing coworkers from doing their jobs, and insubordination.

Related terms: employment agreements; gross negligence; tort.

ceiling

Like a cap, a ceiling is slang for the upper limit for something. For example, the term is commonly used in real estate transactions to refer to the upper limit over which the interest rate on a variable rate mortgage may not rise over the life of the loan.

Related term: cap.

changed conditions clause

See impossibility (of performance).

choice of law (governing law)

A choice of law or governing law provision allows the parties to agree that a particular state's laws will be used to interpret the agreement, even if they live or the agreement is signed in a different state. For example, many big corporations choose Delaware law in their contracts, because that state's laws often favor corporations and, more importantly, the laws offer some predictability when it comes to disputes. Can this concept be utilized by every business? For example, let's imagine that you're a potato farmer in Michigan, and you're entering into a contract with a chain of food stores. Can you request that any disputes under your contract be decided under Idaho law (which you suspect really favors potato farmers) even though neither party has anything to do with Idaho? That depends.

Not every choice will be honored. Our example about Idaho potato farmers may not fly because courts usually look for some connection between the chosen state and either the transaction or the parties. A choice of law provision may also run into problems if it appears in an insurance contract, because some states want to make sure their consumer protection laws relating to insurance apply to those within their borders. (Massachusetts, for example, prohibits choice of law provisions in insurance contracts.) Some contracts involving secured transactions and the Uniform Commercial Code (UCC) may also conflict with choice of law rules. Also, contracts governing corporate behavior usually must be decided by the law of the state of incorporation. Generally, however, the differences in state law are not great enough to make this a major negotiating issue for most parties.

Don't confuse jurisdiction with governing law. Jurisdiction refers to where disputes will be settled; governing law indicates which state's laws will be used to resolve disputes. It's possible, for example, for a contract to require lawsuits over the contract to be filed in California but decided under New York law. The selection of which state is used for governing law is not often a crucial negotiating issue. But the selection of the state for jurisdiction can be more important: If there's a dispute, that's where everyone will have to go to resolve it Sometimes these two provisions are grouped in one paragraph.

Governing Law: Sample language

Governing Law. The laws of the Commonwealth of Massachusetts govern this agreement.

Related terms: boilerplate; conflict of laws; jurisdiction provision (forum selection provision).

clause

See proviso/provision.

clickwrap agreement

Clickwrap agreements are the digital spawn of shrinkwrap agreements—license agreements that were created once a consumer broke the shrinkwrap on boxed software. As boxed software slowly faded, consumers began making more agreements by clicking Okay to purchases, either to download software or other digital products or to enter into website agreements. Thus was the clickwrap agreement born.

Initial challenges. Clickwrap agreements were initially challenged over the issue of acceptance. Could clicking Okay on a screen really constitute acceptance of an agreement—and create a contract? And could all of this be done in the digital domain? In 2000, federal legislation—the Electronic Signatures in Global and International Commerce Act—was enacted, which helped remove much of the uncertainty that previously plagued clickwraps. This law confirms that contracts can be created electronically, among other things.

End-user licenses. Clickwrap agreements, like shrinkwraps, usually impose contractual restrictions on downloaders and are commonly known as end-user license agreements (EULAs). These clickwrap EULAs are considered enforceable agreements and "an appropriate way to form contracts."

> EXAMPLE: Mr. Hughes got into a dispute with America Online (AOL) and filed a lawsuit in Massachusetts. AOL insisted—based on AOL's standard clickwrap agreement—that Mr. Hughes bring the case in Virginia. A federal court agreed with AOL and enforced the clickwrap agreement.

Overreaching clickwraps. Like all contracts, a clickwrap cannot violate public policy or law. However, clickwraps tend to push the boundaries. For example, one company, as a condition of its clickwrap EULA, prohibited reverse engineering of its software—a legally acceptable method of inspecting and trying to reproduce a product after purchasing it. To the dismay of software programmers, a federal court upheld this provision.

Related terms: contract of adhesion (adhesion contracts); electronic agreements.

closing

In contracts, closing refers to the point when the parties exchange their performances—for example, in the case of a loan agreement, it's the meeting where the lender gives the money and the borrower agrees to pay it back. Anyone who's seen David Mamet's *Glengarry Glen Ross* knows that closing is what salespeople live for. The mantra "always closing" refers to the perpetual desire to get to that final point when the parties seal the deal by signing on the dotted line.

Closing is most often associated with real estate deals. In most of the country, the closing is the meeting in a real estate agent's or lawyer's office, in which the parties exchange the final documents and make the final signatures. (Some eastern states use the term "settlement" rather than "closing.") The seller walks out with the check and the buyer walks out with a deed to the property (and keys).

Related term: real estate contract.

cloud (on title)

A cloud is a question or defect in the title to property. It can be small (a misspelled address, for example) or it can be substantial (a lien on the property or a dispute about who really owns it). A real estate sale will be delayed while the cloud is removed, or it may be terminated if the cloud prevents transfer of title to the new owner.

Related terms: real estate contract; title insurance.

collateral

See secured transaction.

collateral assignment

Let's say you're borrowing money and the lender insists that you assign him ownership of your car until the loan is paid off. You transfer title of the car to the lender. Once you pay off the loan, the assignment is terminated and the car is yours again. This arrangement is called a "collateral assignment" (as distinguished from an absolute assignment, in which the lender maintains ownership no matter what).

Related terms: promissory note; secured transaction.

comfort letter

Like comfort food, a comfort letter is intended to make you feel better. It's usually prepared by an accounting firm and provides assurances about a company's stability, value, or all-round soundness. The letter is usually prepared for the benefit of companies seeking acquisitions, vendors preparing to contract, or investors preparing to seek an equity interest. The term may also be applied to letters providing assurances during an initial public offering or to letters providing assurances about a potential borrower. If time passes, and the recipient of the letter wants an assurance that the original letter is still accurate, the subsequent letter providing verification is known as a "bring-down" letter.

Related term: legal opinion.

commercially reasonable

See best efforts.

commitment

As a general rule, the term commitment refers to a pledge or a promise. It's not always clear, however, whether making a commitment triggers a binding obligation. That depends on the circumstances surrounding its use, the intentions of the parties, the context of the use, and trade practices. The term is more likely to trigger a binding obligation when used to signify a financial promise. For example, a lender who makes a commitment to lend money at a specific interest rate will be legally bound to follow through.

Related term: commitment letter.

commitment letter

A commitment letter is a lender's written statement that you have been approved for a mortgage, or more specifically, that the lender is making an offer to provide the purchase money under certain conditions. Unlike "letters of intent" and "agreements in principle," a commitment letter is actually an offer to enter a contract. Once the party receiving the letter accepts the offer, it becomes a binding contract.

Commitment letters come in two basic flavors: firm or conditional. In a firm commitment letter, the lender makes an unqualified promise to lend money to you. In a conditional letter, the lender spells out the conditions you must meet—most of which are taken care of as the buyer proceeds through escrow—before the contract is formed.

Related terms: agreement in principle; letter of intent; mortgage; real estate contract.

compliance (with laws)

A compliance with laws provision requires the parties to … well, comply with laws. Because all of us are legally required to follow laws and regulations anyway, what's the point of adding this type of provision? Because it allows one party to terminate the contract if the other fails to follow the law, which might not be possible absent the clause.

C

EXAMPLE: A software maker signs a contract to have its educational software sold in bundles prepared by a chain of box stores. The contract includes a compliance with laws provision. The box store bundles the educational software with gambling software, which violates several state laws. The software maker can terminate the agreement because the chain of box stores did not comply with state laws (in violation of the compliance provision). If the provision were not in the agreement, the software maker would have a more difficult time claiming a breach.

A typical compliance with laws provision includes language such as this:

Compliance with laws: Sample language

> **Compliance With Laws.** The rights and obligations expressed in this Agreement are conditioned on each party's compliance with all laws, regulations, rules, and ordinances applicable to the operation of its business and to this Agreement.

Related term: boilerplate.

compounding (compound) interest

Imagine the unbridled excitement when credit card company executives came up with compounding—a method for charging interest on interest. Compounding happens when all or some portion of the interest due on a loan becomes part the total loan debt (principal), which is then used to calculate subsequent interest payments. The result is that the person taking out the loan is considered to have "borrowed" both principal *and* interest—and must pay interest on the entire amount.

Compounding can also work in favor of consumers, such as when it's used to calculate the interest to be paid on a savings or investment account. Often, the interest earned by the savings account, for example, is paid directly into the account, where it can earn more interest.

Related terms: amortization; APR; interest rates (usury).

condition

Contracts often come with conditions—events or circumstances that trigger contractual obligations. For example, if you don't replace the gas in your rental car (the condition), you will have to pay for gas when you return it (the obligation). If you are late making a payment on a loan (the condition), you will need to pay a higher interest rate (the obligation). A condition is usually preceded by the use of qualifying words, such as "provided," "if," and "when."

Express and constructive conditions. Conditions are either express (explicitly agreed to by the parties) or constructive (imposed by law, although not stated in the contract).

> **EXAMPLE:** A Japanese manufacturer contracts to license Bob's software on the condition that Bob obtains export approval from the United States government. Bob gets a better offer from another company and loses interest in the original deal; he never bothers to seek export approval. Bob figures he doesn't have to go through with the contract because he never satisfied the condition—getting export approval—underlying the agreement. Wrong! The Japanese company wins its lawsuit against Bob for breach of contract because Bob can't take advantage of his own bad behavior—his deliberate failure to pursue the approval—to get out of the contract. In other words, obtaining export approval (express condition) requires cooperation by Bob (constructive condition).

Timing of conditions. Almost all conditions are **conditions precedent**, which means they must be satisfied *before* a party is obligated to do something. For example, the seller of a home must make certain repairs before the buyer is obligated to go through

C

with the purchase. **Concurrent conditions** refer to simultaneous events—for example, you hand over money at the same time as the seller hands you merchandise. Concurrent conditions are really just two simultaneous condition precedents. A **condition subsequent** terminates an obligation—for example, if you fail to timely report an auto accident, the insurance company's obligation to pay for damages is terminated. As scholars have noted, most conditions subsequent are also conditions precedent. For example, another way of looking at the insurance contract is that reporting accidents in a timely manner is a condition precedent to receiving coverage.

confidentiality agreement

Developers who tested the prototype iPads had to sort through a hefty 10-page confidentiality agreement, which required them (among other things) to keep the device isolated in a room with blacked-out windows, tethered to a fixed object, under lock and key—and, of course, no Tweeting about it or leaving it in a bar. Apple's secrecy standards might sound a bit Draconian, but they complement the company's covert marketing strategy (and allow for more suspense at the public unveiling of each Next Big Thing).

Every business has some valuable confidential information that it wants to keep under wraps. It could be a sales plan, a list of customers, a manufacturing process, or a formula for a soft drink. What all confidential information has in common is that its value would drop to zero if competitors knew it. In legal terms, these types of information are your business's trade secrets. Trade secrets are the only kind of information that can be protected by confidentiality agreements (also known as nondisclosure agreements or NDAs).

A confidentiality agreement is a legally binding contract in which a person or business promises to treat specific information as a trade secret and not to disclose it to others without proper authorization. If a trade secret is disclosed in violation of the confidentiality agreement, the trade secret owner can file a lawsuit, obtain a court order to stop further use of the trade secret, and recover money for the damage caused by the disclosure.

Use by employees. Although state laws require employees to maintain trade secrets, it's a good idea for employers to use confidentiality agreements as well, particular with employees who are exposed to valuable confidential business information. Competitors who learn of trade secrets through an employee's violation of a confidentiality agreement with a former employer may also be prevented from using the information commercially, even if they didn't know the employee had breached the agreement.

Implied confidentiality. Confidentiality agreements may be implied if the context of a business relationship suggests that secrecy was intended by the parties. For instance, a business that conducts patent searches for inventors is expected to keep information about the invention secret, even if no written confidentiality agreement requires it.

Using a confidentiality provision instead of a separate agreement. Instead of creating a confidentiality agreement from scratch, you may wish to include secrecy requirements in another contract—for example, an independent contractor agreement used regularly by your business. For example, you can insert the provision below into a license, an option, or a service contract.

Confidentiality Provision: Sample language

(a) Confidential Information. The parties acknowledge that each may receive or have access to confidential information (the "Confidential Information"). For purposes of this Agreement, Confidential Information includes all information or material that has or could have commercial value or other utility in the business in which the party disclosing the information ("Disclosing Party") is engaged. In the event that Confidential Information is in written form, Disclosing Party shall label or stamp the materials with the word "Confidential" or some similar warning. In the event that Confidential Information

Confidentiality Provision: Sample language (continued)

is transmitted orally, the Disclosing Party shall promptly provide a writing indicating that such oral communication constituted Confidential Information.

(b) Exclusions From Confidential Information. The party receiving the Confidential Information ("Receiving Party") shall not be obligated to preserve the confidentiality of any information that is: (a) publicly known at the time of disclosure under this Agreement or subsequently becomes publicly known through no fault of Receiving Party; (b) discovered or created by Receiving Party prior to the time of disclosure by Disclosing Party; or (c) otherwise learned by Receiving Party through legitimate means other than from Disclosing Party or anyone connected with Disclosing Party.

(c) Obligations of Receiving Party. Receiving Party shall hold and maintain the Confidential Information of the other party in strictest confidence for the sole and exclusive benefit of Disclosing Party. Receiving Party shall carefully restrict access to any such Confidential Information to persons bound by this Agreement, only on a need to know basis. Receiving Party shall not, without prior written approval of Disclosing Party, use for Receiving Party's own benefit, publish, copy, or otherwise disclose to others, or permit the use by others for their benefit or to the detriment of Disclosing Party, any of the Confidential Information. The Receiving Party shall return to Disclosing Party any and all records, notes, and other written, printed, or tangible materials in its possession pertaining to the Confidential Information immediately on the written request of Disclosing Party.

(d) Time Period. This Agreement and Receiving Party's duty to hold Disclosing Party's Confidential Information in confidence remains in effect until [*include year*].

(e) Survival. The nondisclosure provisions of this Agreement will survive the termination of any relationship between Disclosing Party and Receiving Party.

You can modify this provision to define trade secrets specifically or to make the time period unlimited.

Common provisions in an NDA. Below are explanations for the common elements of an NDA:

- **Defining the trade secrets.** Every nondisclosure agreement defines its trade secrets, often referred to as "confidential information." There are three common approaches to defining confidential information: (1) using a system to mark all confidential information (such as a stamp); (2) listing trade secret categories; or (3) specifically identifying the confidential information. Another approach to identifying trade secrets is to state that the disclosing party will certify what is and what is not confidential. For example, physical disclosures, such as written materials or software, may be clearly marked "Confidential." In the case of oral disclosures, the disclosing party provides written confirmation that a trade secret was disclosed.

- **Excluding information that is not confidential.** You cannot prohibit the receiving party from disclosing information that is publicly known, legitimately acquired from another source, or developed by the receiving party before meeting you. Similarly, it is not unlawful for the receiving party to disclose your secret with your permission. These legal exceptions exist with or without an agreement, but they are commonly included in a contract to make clear to everyone that such information is not considered a trade secret.

- **Duty to keep information secret.** The heart of a nondisclosure agreement is a statement establishing a confidential relationship between the parties. The statement sets out the duty of the receiving party to maintain the information in confidence and to limit its use. In some cases, you may want to impose additional requirements. For example, you may want to prohibit reverse engineering, decompiling, or disassembling software. This prohibits the receiving party (the user of licensed software) from learning more about the trade secrets.

You may also insist on the return of all trade secret materials that you furnished under the agreement.

- **Time periods—the duration of the agreement.** How long does the duty of confidentiality last? Duration is often a hot topic during negotiations. The disclosing party will usually want a longer or even an open-ended period; receiving parties typically want a short period. For employee and contractor agreements, the term is often unlimited or ends only when the trade secret becomes public knowledge. Five years is a common length in nondisclosure agreements that involve business negotiations and product submissions, although many companies insist on two or three years. If you are the disclosing party, you should probably seek the longest duration possible, preferably unlimited. But you should know that some businesses want a fixed period of time—and some courts, when interpreting NDAs, require the time period to be reasonable. Of course, the exact length of a "reasonable" period of time is subjective and depends on the confidential material and the nature of the industry. For example, some trade secrets within the software or Internet industries may be short-lived. Once the time period is over, the other party is free to reveal your secrets.
- **Boilerplate provisions and signatures.** The sample NDA includes four boilerplate provisions. Other provisions—injunctive relief, attorneys' fees, indemnity, arbitration and mediation, governing law, jurisdiction, and successors and assigns—could also be included here.

A sample confidentiality agreement. An example of a typical confidentiality agreement is provided below.

Basic Nondisclosure Agreement

Nondisclosure Agreement

This Nondisclosure Agreement (the "Agreement") is entered into by and between _____ ("Disclosing Party") with its principal offices at _____ , and _____ ("Receiving Party"), located at _____

for the purpose of preventing the unauthorized disclosure of Confidential Information as defined below. The parties agree to enter into a confidential relationship with respect to the disclosure of certain proprietary and confidential information ("Confidential Information").

1. Definition of Confidential Information. For purposes of this Agreement, Confidential Information includes all information or material that has or could have commercial value or other utility in the business in which Disclosing Party is engaged. If Confidential Information is in written form, the Disclosing Party will label or stamp the materials with the word "Confidential" or some similar warning. If Confidential Information is transmitted orally, the Disclosing Party shall promptly provide a writing indicating that such oral communication constituted Confidential Information.

2. Exclusions From Confidential Information. Receiving Party's obligations under this Agreement do not extend to information that is: (a) publicly known at the time of disclosure or subsequently becomes publicly known through no fault of the Receiving Party; (b) discovered or created by the Receiving Party before disclosure by Disclosing Party; (c) learned by the Receiving Party through legitimate means other than from the Disclosing Party or Disclosing Party's representatives; or (d) is disclosed by Receiving Party with Disclosing Party's prior written approval.

Basic Nondisclosure Agreement (continued)

3. Obligations of Receiving Party. Receiving Party shall hold and maintain the Confidential Information in strictest confidence for the sole and exclusive benefit of the Disclosing Party. Receiving Party shall carefully restrict access to Confidential Information to employees, contractors, and third parties as is reasonably required and will require those persons to sign nondisclosure restrictions at least as protective as those in this Agreement. Receiving Party shall not, without prior written approval of Disclosing Party, use for Receiving Party's own benefit, publish, copy, or otherwise disclose to others, or permit the use by others for their benefit or to the detriment of Disclosing Party, any Confidential Information. Receiving Party shall return to Disclosing Party any and all records, notes, and other written, printed, or tangible materials in its possession pertaining to Confidential Information immediately if Disclosing Party requests it in writing.

4. Time Periods. The nondisclosure provisions of this Agreement will survive the termination of this Agreement and Receiving Party's duty to hold Confidential Information in confidence will remain in effect until the Confidential Information no longer qualifies as a trade secret or until Disclosing Party sends Receiving Party written notice releasing Receiving Party from this Agreement, whichever occurs first.

5. Relationships. Nothing contained in this Agreement is deemed to constitute either party a partner, joint venturer, or an employee of the other party for any purpose.

6. Severability. If a court finds any provision of this Agreement invalid or unenforceable, the remainder of this Agreement will be interpreted so as best to effect the intent of the parties.

7. Integration. This Agreement expresses the complete understanding of the parties with respect to the subject matter and supersedes all

Basic Nondisclosure Agreement

prior proposals, agreements, representations, and understandings. This Agreement may not be amended except in a writing signed by both parties.

8. Waiver. The failure to exercise any right provided in this Agreement will not be a waiver of prior or subsequent rights.

This Agreement and each party's obligations are binding on the representatives, assigns, and successors of such party. Each party has signed this Agreement through its authorized representative.

Disclosing Party   Receiving Party

By: _____   By: _____

Printed Name: _____   Printed Name: _____

Title: _____   Title: _____

Date: _____   Date: _____

C

Completing the Confidentiality Agreement. In the sample agreement, the "Disclosing Party" is the person disclosing secrets, and the "Receiving Party" is the person who receives the "Confidential Information" and is obligated to keep it secret. The terms are capitalized to indicate that they should be interpreted as defined within the agreement. The sample agreement is a "one-way" (or in legalese, "unilateral") agreement—that is, only one party is disclosing secrets. If each side is disclosing secrets to the other, you should modify the agreement to make it a mutual (or "bilateral") nondisclosure agreement. To do that, substitute the following paragraph for the first paragraph in the agreement.

> This Nondisclosure Agreement (the "Agreement") is entered into by and between [*insert your name, business form and address*] and [*insert name, business form and address of other person or company with whom you are exchanging information*] collectively referred to as the "parties" for the purpose of preventing the unauthorized disclosure of Confidential Information as defined below. The parties agree to enter into a confidential relationship with respect to the disclosure by one or each (the "Disclosing Party") to the other (the "Receiving Party") of certain proprietary and confidential information (the "Confidential Information").

Related terms: covenant not to compete; nonsolicitation agreement; trade secret.

conflict of laws

This refers to the rules by which courts decide which state's law applies to a dispute.

A little history. As citizens from different nations began to interact, issues arose as to which nation's law governed a particular situation—for example, which country's laws should be used in disputes over shipwrecked sailors, an accident on a national border, or a contract gone bad between various European traders. Eventually, principles developed that enabled the parties to sort out these disputes over conflicting laws.

Applying these rules to states. These international concepts became the basis of U.S. laws describing how to choose which state's law should govern contract disputes. For example, Texas requires contract disputes to have some relationship to Texas if a party wants that state's law to apply to a case. So what happens if the parties are from California but choose Texas law to govern their dispute? Will the California court look to Texas law, decide that Texas doesn't want its laws to apply, and instead use California law (a procedure known as a *renvoi*)? Lawyers try to avoid that result by explicitly stating that the chosen state's conflicts of law rules don't apply to the contract.

The exclusion is usually written into the "governing law" provision.

Governing law: Sample language

Governing Law. Without giving effect to its conflicts of law principles, the laws of the Commonwealth of Massachusetts govern this agreement.

Do you need to include this magic language excluding conflicts of law principles? It can't hurt. However, in practical terms, it may not help. Many attorneys believe that courts routinely disregard this language and apply their own conflicts of law rules, even if that contract says they can't.

Related term: choice of laws (governing law).

conformed copy

Conformed copies refer to the making of two or more duplicates (conformed copies) of a contract.

C

A little history. In the old days (prior to 1960), in order to deal with the inability to make exact duplicates of signed documents, two or more duplicates were prepared. Later, in the early days of photocopying, Xerox machines were unable to pick up the blue ink often used for signatures, and so the need continued for conformed copies (often including written statements referencing any missing material—for example the mark "/S/" or "Signed By Party"). The conformed copies concept has found new meaning in the age of digital contracts. Companies often print out paper versions (conformed copies) of the original digital agreements.

consent

Consent refers to the process by which the parties agree to something that the contract prohibits. In other words, anything that is outlawed by a contract can be undone if the parties later consent to it. A typical example is when the parties consent to a particular assignment of rights, even though their agreement prohibits all assignments. Consent, like a waiver, does not modify the contract; it just prevents some condition or requirement of the contract from later being enforced.

A contract may require that consent be given in writing or at a specific time—for example, before a contractor incurs an expense. In some cases, the consent must meet a specific approval standard, often that consent shall not be "unreasonably withheld." In that case, you must have a good or reasonable basis (usually a sound business reason) for *not* consenting. Such provisions have occasionally led to litigation as the parties attempt to determine the standards for what is a reasonable basis for refusing to consent.

Related terms: assignment (of contract); waiver.

consequential damages

See damages, consequential.

consideration

Consideration is the answer to the question, "Why are you entering this contract?" It's the benefit that each party gets or expects to get from the deal—for example, Victoria's Secret gets your money; you get the studded halter top. For consideration to provide a valid basis for a contract, each party must make a change in its position (or what's referred to as "bargained-for detriment"). In other words, consideration is usually either the result of a (1) a promise to do something you're not legally obligated to do, or (2) a promise *not* to do something you have the right to do (often, filing a lawsuit).

> **EXAMPLE:** You backed into your neighbor's golf cart and damaged it. Your neighbor is legally permitted to sue you for the damage but instead agrees *not* to sue you if you pay him $1,000. This agreement provides adequate consideration for the contract, because each party is giving up something (your money for the neighbor's right to sue) in the exchange.

When a contract lacks consideration. In a few situations, courts will step in and declare that a contract is unenforceable because it lacks consideration. These include:

- **One of the parties was already legally obligated to perform.** For example, a police officer cannot claim the reward for capturing a crook because he is already legally obligated to capture and arrest crooks.

- **The promise amounts to a gift, not a contract.** If your rich uncle promises to give you money to buy a house, without any strings attached, that is a promise to make a gift. If he changes his mind, you can't force him to come up with the cash because his promise was one-sided; you have not done or promised to do anything in exchange. On the other hand, if you make a down payment on a house in reliance on his promise, and your uncle knows about it, a court may enforce his original promise. Although it still isn't a true contract, the law recognizes that it's necessary to hold people to their promises once others take action on the assumption that the promise will be kept. This legal theory—called "promissory estoppel"—treats promises that are reasonably relied upon as if they were contracts.

- **The exchange is for "past consideration."** When someone promises to give you something in return for something you've already done—"I'm going to pay you $500 because you quit smoking last year"—a court will not enforce the payment because the performance (quitting smoking) wasn't bargained for. You did it without knowing that someone would come along later and offer to pay for it.

- **The bargained-for promise is illusory.** For example, the laws in Maria's state prohibit firing an employee for refusing to sign a noncompete agreement. Maria signs one anyway, under threat of losing her job. The agreement is unenforceable because Maria's employer cannot do what it promised (or threatened) to do. A better approach would have been to provide Maria with some benefit or compensation if she signed, rather than threatening to fire her if she didn't.

What if the consideration seems disproportionate? In hindsight, many deals seem unfair ("You paid *how much* for that dress?"). However, courts rarely judge the value of the consideration exchanged unless the two promises are so disproportionate in value as to demonstrate bad faith (or "unconscionability") in the bargaining process. In such cases, however, the contract doesn't fall apart because of a lack of consideration in and of itself, but because the consideration is so disproportionate as to demonstrate that one party acted unfairly or concealed information necessary to make a fair deal.

Unless this type of bad faith exists, however, courts generally don't want to get into judging the relative value of particular promises or items. After all, what's worth a lot of money to one person may be worth very little to another; that's what bargaining is all about.

Do you need to use the word "consideration" in your contract? Many contracts provide a recital (a statement at the beginning of the contract) that the contract is being entered into "for good and valuable consideration, the sufficiency of which is acknowledged," or something to that effect. The writers of these contracts mistakenly believe that simply stating that consideration exists actually fulfills the requirement of contractual consideration. In a majority of states, however, this is not the case; such recitals don't prove anything. In other words, saying there is consideration doesn't necessarily mean there *is* consideration. Legal scholars agree that, generally, a contract doesn't need to include anything other than a statement that "the parties agree." The exception is for contracts that only one party signs, such as assignments, option agreements, or promissory notes. In these contracts, a recital that the consideration is sufficient should be included, because it's not self-evident that a bargained-for exchange has taken place.

Related terms: promissory estoppels; recitals.

construction agreement

A construction agreement is made when one party hires another to create, repair, or renovate a building or other structure. Popular films such as *Mr. Blandings Builds His Dream House* and *The Money Pit* conjure up the disasters commonly associated with constructing or renovating a home. In these films, good people (Cary Grant and Tom Hanks, respectively), watch their personal lives disintegrate in the face of endless construction, crooked contractors, and repeated technical setbacks. Perhaps these situations could have been avoided if only our heroes had used well-drafted construction contracts!

Although no contract can prevent every conceivable problem, a well-drafted construction agreement can establish rules and procedures, set standards and timetables, and preserve rights. The

C

challenge in drafting construction contracts is that there are so many parties involved, each with different interests. Among the cast of characters who may have a say in the construction process are owners, architects, decorators, vendors, contractors, subcontractors, insurers, and lenders. Each of these players has different duties, risks (and methods of allocating those risks), and plans for their business.

How the principals allocate risks. Private construction contracts are usually negotiated between the owner or other hiring party (such as a development company) and a general contractor (one person or entity that controls, oversees, and otherwise manages the details of the job). (In contrast, public construction projects are the result of competitive bidding between the government and a general contractor.) The negotiations typically depend on whether the owner has detailed plans and specifications for the project. If there are plans, the parties commonly go with a **fixed-value contract** (also known as a "stipulated value" or "lump sum"). Under this type of arrangement, the burden (and most of the risk) is on the general contractor to perform the tasks for the agreed-upon price.

A **cost-plus contract** creates more risk for the owner. Under this system, the owner pays all costs plus some of the overhead, as well as some fees. In this type of arrangement, the contractor has less motivation to cut costs and act efficiently (although price and efficiency incentives can be added to the agreement). An owner who doesn't already have a plan in place can avoid some risk with a hybrid agreement that uses a cost-plus framework with a cap (known as a guaranteed maximum price or GMP), which is subject to change as the plans develop. This gives the owner some control over the total cost of the project.

Prime contracts and side contracts/subcontracts. When people refer to a "construction contract," they usually mean the "prime contract": the main contract between the general contractor and the owner. However, both parties usually enter into numerous additional side agreements relating to the construction. Subcontractors that enter into agreements with the general contractor are especially vulnerable to additional risks and obligations. In many cases, they may be held to the terms of the prime agreement—for example, dispute resolution procedures that apply between the prime parties may also be enforced against subcontractors. For that reason, subcontractors should, when possible, review the prime agreement before signing a subcontractor agreement.

Ten provisions that should be in your construction contract. Every construction contract is different, but the following issues should always be addressed:

- **Services to be performed.** Defining the scope of the work to be done is the most important element in construction contracts. That's why preparing and including accurate plans is crucial (see below).

- **Payment.** Will the owner pay for materials directly (and pay the contractor only for services) or pay the contractor for labor *and* materials? One reason to pay for supplies directly has to do with liens. An unpaid supplier or subcontractor can place a lien on the owner's property (called a mechanic's lien or materials lien). A lien is a claim for payment made against your property that is recorded with the county recorder's office. If you want to sell your property, you can't pass good title to the buyer without clearing all liens. So, paying for things directly ensures there will be no liens. However, this bill-paying system can be unwieldy because the owner must be available during every step of a complex project. Other things to consider when it comes to payment is whether the contractor will be paid on a regular basis, on a schedule, in progress payments, or after invoicing.

- **Completion.** Everybody wants the construction to be over quickly (especially your neighbors). But when will that happy day arrive, and what constitutes "completion"? The contract must set a completion date (or dates, if the project is progressive) and establish standards of owner approval. The contract should also cover what will happen if the parties disagree as to whether completion has occurred.

- **Permits and approvals.** The contract should establish who gets and pays for building permits and approvals. Some owners like to be involved in this process in order to ensure compliance.

- **Warranty.** The owner wants an assurance as to construction standards for quality, quantity, and performance, and to guarantee (in some cases) that the owner will have adequate legal title if the property is sold. For example, the warranty may say that "construction will be completed in a workman-like manner in compliance with all building codes."

- **Liens and lien waivers.** As noted above, liens can get in the way of property sales. The owner typically wants an assurance that there won't be any problems with liens.

- **Site maintenance.** Some owners want to be sure that construction work takes place only at specific times, that equipment is stored in a particular location, or that cleanup takes place regularly.

- **Subcontractors.** It's common practice in the construction industry for contractors to subcontract out some of the work to other contractors, called subcontractors. For example, the contractor may hire an electrician to install electrical wiring. Most construction agreements include provisions that permit the contractor to hire subcontractors to help perform the services, but the contractor remains ultimately responsible for making sure that all of the work is completed properly.

- **Insurance.** The parties will want to guarantee that there is adequate liability insurance, in case anyone gets hurt on the job.

- **Attachments.** It's always wise to include plans, specs, building codes (if applicable), and designs as part of the construction contract, by attaching them to the document and incorporating them by reference.

Related terms: liens; mechanic's liens.

contract

According to Homer Simpson's lawyer, a contract is an agreement that "cannot be unbroken." Double negatives aside, the cartoon doesn't lie. What makes a contract special—and essential for business dealings—is that it is binding on the parties. (Or as the Latin maxim goes: *pacta sunt servanda*—agreements must be kept.) If one party doesn't hold up its end of the bargain, the other party has legal remedies. But to be enforceable by a court, every contract, whether written or oral, must meet several requirements:

- **Consideration.** As Cole Porter wrote in the song, "True Love," "You give to me and I give to you." That sums up consideration. Each party has to promise or provide something of value to the other. Without this exchange, there is no contract.
- **Offer and acceptance.** There must be a clear or definite offer to contract ("Do you want to buy this?") and an unqualified acceptance ("Yes!").
- **Legal purpose.** The purpose of the agreement must not violate the law. For example, you won't be able to enforce a loan agreement that charges interest in excess of what is allowed by usury laws or a service agreement to hire someone to rob a bank or kill your mother-in-law.
- **Capable parties.** To be "capable" of making a contract, the parties must understand what they're doing. For example, there is a presumption that minors and insane people usually don't know what they're doing and, for that reason, contracts they enter into won't be enforced under certain circumstances.
- **Mutual assent.** This is also sometimes referred to as a "meeting of the minds." The contracting parties must intend to be bound by their agreement and must agree on the essential terms.

In addition to these general rules, federal and state laws may impose more requirements on particular types of contracts. For example, certain consumer contracts must meet additional requirements, and some contracts must be in writing (as required by each state's "statute of frauds").

C

The contract as a document. The term contract often refers to a written agreement, typically including some or all of the following elements: introductory material (sometimes known as "recitals" or "whereas provisions"); definitions of key terms; a statement of the purpose or purposes of the agreement; the obligations of each party (and conditions that may trigger obligations); assurances as to various aspects of agreement (sometimes phrased as warranties, representations, or covenants); boilerplate provisions (about, for example, termination, indemnity, choice of law, or confidentiality), a signature block; and exhibits or attachments. (Most of these elements are discussed in more detail in separate entries.)

The contract as a process. "Contract" is a noun, but can be used as a verb, as well. When you contract with somebody, you participate in a process that typically involves three phases.

- **Phase 1: Contemplating the deal.** The parties each assess the prospective arrangement and its risks ("Can I trust her?") and attempt to predict the future ("Will I regret paying this price for the computer next month? Will it be outdated?").
- **Phase 2: Reaching an agreement.** During this phase the parties negotiate and agree on the terms, usually formalized in a written contract or some other documented evidence of the arrangement (such as a receipt or purchase order, for example).
- **Phase 3: Performance and enforcement.** Once the contract is in place, the parties are legally required to perform their mutual obligations. If one party fails to perform, the other can sue to enforce the deal.

When the term contract is used as a verb, you can best understand the essential human element of contracting: trust. Unless each party trusts the other to come through as promised, the deal will probably fall apart, no matter how many "whereases" and "heretofores" the contract includes.

Related terms: capacity (to contract); consideration; mutual assent; offer and acceptance.

contract interpretation

See rules of interpretation (rules of construction).

contract of adhesion (adhesion contracts)

If you hate to negotiate, then you'll love adhesion contracts. They are the ultimate "take or leave it" agreements, in which one party essentially says, "agree to all of my terms or there's no deal." As one court put, they are "imposed and drafted by the party of superior bargaining strength" and they relegate to the other party "only the opportunity to adhere to the contract or reject it."

To fit within the definition, the contract must be a standard, non-negotiable form agreement. Typical examples are insurance contracts, car rental agreements, parking agreements, preemployment arbitration provisions, and virtually any form contract spewed from a vending machine or computer. In fact, it was in a case about a machine-generated contract for airline insurance (*Steven v. Fidelity & Casualty Co.,* 58 Cal.2d 862 (1962)), that the California Supreme Court first decided that the standards for interpreting this type of contract should be different than the rules for contracts negotiated between parties with more equal bargaining power.

> **EXAMPLE:** Mr. Steven purchased round-trip flight insurance from a vending machine. When Mr. Steven's return flight was delayed, an airline agent arranged for him and three other passengers to take another carrier to Chicago. That flight crashed, killing all aboard. The insurer refused to pay Mr. Steven's widow, claiming that the charter plane that crashed wasn't covered under the policy. The clause in the agreement that pertained to Mr. Steven's circumstances was ambiguous, so the California Supreme Court had to decide how to interpret it. The Court decided that, when dealing with a contract of adhesion, the "burden of noncoverage" was upon the insurer, who had to prove the basis for the denial. Because the insurer in this case couldn't meet this burden, it lost the case.

Contracts of adhesion are not necessarily illegal or unethical. However, different standards apply when interpreting them. These standards are intended to provide some minimal protections to the party with less bargaining power. The two common standards include:

- **If it wasn't reasonably expected, it won't be enforced.** If a provision in a contract of adhesion goes beyond what a reasonable person would expect—or alternatively, if the person drafting an adhesion contract knew that a provision would be unacceptable but included it anyway—a court may not enforce the provision.
- **Unconscionability voids the contract.** If the adhesion contract goes beyond unequal bargaining power and starts to look oppressive and unreasonable ("unconscionable," in legal terms)—one that the party would not have entered into at all, had the provisions been negotiated—a court may refuse to enforce it.

Related term: void (voidable).

copyright

A copyright gives the owner of a creative work the right to keep others from unauthorized use of the work. Copyright law protects a variety of original expressions, including art, sculpture, literature, music, songs, choreography, crafts, poetry, software, photography, movies, video games, videos, websites, architecture, and graphics. Protection occurs automatically—that is, you acquire copyright once you fix the work in a medium—but this automatic protection can be enhanced by registering the work with the U.S. Copyright Office.

Copyright lasts for the life of the work's creator (its author) plus 70 years. In cases where the creator is a business, the copyright lasts between 95 and 120 years.

Under copyright law, a creative work (often referred to as a "work of authorship") must meet all of these three criteria to be protected:

- **It must be original.** The author must have created rather than copied it.
- **It must be fixed in a tangible (concrete) medium of expression.** That is, the work should be recorded or expressed on paper, audio or videotape, computer disk, clay, or canvas.
- **It must have at least some creativity.** The work must be produced by an exercise of human intellect. There is no hard-and-fast rule as to how much creativity is enough.

Copyright protects expression. Copyright does not protect ideas or facts; it protects only the unique way in which ideas or facts are expressed. For instance, copyright may protect an author's science fiction novel about a romance between an earthling and a space alien, but the author cannot stop others from using the underlying idea of an intergalactic love affair.

Copyrights and contracts. Copyrights are often the subject of three types of contracts:

- **Assignment.** An assignment is a contract (or a provision within a contract) in which a copyright is permanently transferred.
- **License.** A license is a contract by which the owner of a copyright gives someone permission to use or exploit intellectual property rights for a limited time or in a limited way.
- **Work made for hire agreement.** The term refers to a contractual relationship between a hiring party and someone who will create a copyrightable work.

Can a contract be protected under copyright law? Maybe, but the contract would probably have limited protection. One court held that insurance bond forms and indemnity agreements were entitled to copyright protection. However, the court said that because the forms contained standard language that would have to be included in any form designed to accomplish the same purpose, only verbatim copying of the exact wording would constitute copyright infringement. The principle at work here is that where there are only a few ways to express the facts and ideas contained in such contracts, there would be limited copyright protection (a legal rule

C

called the merger doctrine). So, for example, an attorney could not stop someone from copying a boilerplate provision regarding choice of law or jurisdiction since there are only a few ways to express those concepts.

The use of licenses to extend copyright. Copyright owners, particularly software and website publishers, often want to limit how purchasers use their products and services. For example, a software maker may insist that customers use its program only for personal, not commercial, purposes. To impose these restrictions, most publishers employ contract law in the form of a license agreement (or end-user license agreement or EULA). Technically, under a license agreement, the user is not purchasing a copy; the user is licensing the right to use the software under certain conditions. These license agreements may even prohibit acts that are otherwise legal under copyright law. For example, one company, as a condition of its EULA, prohibited users from examining its software code and determining how it functioned (reverse engineering). To the dismay of software programmers, a federal court upheld this provision.

corporation

A corporation is a business entity in which the owners hold shares (becoming shareholders) and elect a board of directors that directs management. Because a corporation is considered to be a legal entity separate from its shareholders, the company, not the owners (or directors and employees) is liable for debts and contractual obligations. That is, the owners (shareholders) of a corporation, as well as the directors and employees, are not personally liable for the business liabilities. (As satirist Ambrose Bierce put it, "It's an ingenious device for obtaining profit without individual responsibility.")

However, as with limited liability companies (LLCs), owners are liable for debts that are personally guaranteed, tax debts, and claims resulting from owners' negligence. The corporate entity is bound to the owners (and vice versa) by a set of federal and state corporation laws and through a series of corporate documents associated with the sale of stock and other paperwork associated with corporate formation and management.

Taxation: C corporations and S corporations. When we use the term "corporation" in this book, we always refer to a C corporation. Corporations are distinguished for tax purposes, as C corporations or S corporations. A C corporation is a regular for-profit corporation taxed under normal corporate income tax rules. In contrast, S corporations are taxed like partnerships—their income is passed on to the owners.

The C corporation files its own tax return (IRS Form 1120) and pays its own income taxes on the profits kept in the company. A C corporation is not a pass-through entity; it's taxed as a separate entity, at a corporate tax rate. When the corporate profits are passed to the owners, they are taxed again on individual returns.

Creation and management. To form a corporation, you pay corporate filing fees and prepare and file formal organizational papers, usually called Articles of Incorporation, with a state agency (in most states, the Secretary or Department of State). Directors must hold annual meetings and keep minutes, prepare formal documentation (in the form of resolutions or written consents to corporate actions) of important decisions made during the life of the corporation, and keep a paper trail of all legal and financial dealings between the corporation and its shareholders. The board of directors must appoint officers to supervise daily corporate business.

Corporations and contracts. A corporation can enter into a contract provided that the party signing the agreement has the actual authority or apparent authority (when the person leads someone to reasonably believe that he or she has the power to enter into contracts) to bind the corporation.

Related terms: limited liability company (LLC); partnership (general); personal liability; sole proprietor.

C

cosigner

A cosigner is a credit-worthy person who agrees to be fully liable for repayment of a loan if the borrower defaults. Federal law requires that commercial lenders give cosigners a notice of their potential liability when they agree to cosign a debt. This is not required for personal loans between friends and relatives.

Related terms: buyer in due course; promissory note.

counteroffer

See offer and acceptance.

counterparts

Counterparts are duplicates. The term arises when parties sign different copies of an agreement and exchange them, rather than everyone signing the same piece of paper. The procedure is used to speed up the execution of agreements and to facilitate the process of contracting between parties at a distance. To make sure all of the signed papers add up to one enforceable contract, many agreements contain a provision such as:

Counterparts: Sample language

Counterparts. This Agreement may be signed in any number of counterparts, all of which taken together constitute a single instrument.

Related terms: conformed copy; signatures.

covenant

A covenant is a promise to do something (or in the case of a negative covenant, *not* to do something). Many contracts are composed of big promises, such as "I promise to sell a house; you promise to buy the house." Covenants are smaller promises that augment or make possible the big promises, sometimes requiring activity before or after the major action that's the true subject of the agreement.

In real estate contracts, for example, covenants typically refer to actions that must be taken after the contract is signed and before the closing—for example, the seller covenants to preserve the outside deck with sealant and to not remove any of the lawn furniture. Covenants may require certain actions after a contract is performed, as well. For example, after an employment relationship ends, the ex-employee may still be obligated by a covenant not to compete for one year following termination.

Covenants are also used to provide assurances, as in a covenant to act in good faith and deal fairly or a covenant to use best efforts.

Related terms: representations and warranties.

covenant not to compete

A covenant not to compete is a contract in which someone agrees not to compete with a company (usually the person's current employer) for a certain period of time. For example, Don Draper, the advertising executive in the TV series "Mad Men," had a dilemma in Season Three. Should he sign a noncompete agreement—in which he would agree not to work for competing advertising companies after he left his employer—or should he retain his independence? If he didn't sign, his employer threatened to disclose some secret about his past. Although our hero hated losing the freedom to compete, he eventually caved in to his employer's demands.

Noncompetes and nondisclosure agreements. Noncompete and nondisclosure agreements (confidentiality agreements) both have the same goal: to prevent a competitor from using valuable business information. The difference is that a nondisclosure prohibits someone only from revealing information to a competitor; a noncompete prohibits someone from working for a competitor at all or starting a competing business, whether or not the person uses confidential

C

information in doing so. In other words, a noncompete is broader and more heavy-handed in its approach—so heavy-handed, in fact, that some states restrict or prohibit them.

In some cases, noncompetes and nondisclosure agreements complement each other. For example, an Internet business might use a noncompete agreement to prohibit former employees from working for competitors for a period of six months. Once the noncompete expires, former employees may work for a competitor but will still be prohibited, under the terms of a nondisclosure agreement, from disclosing trade secrets. The six-month noncompete period guarantees that short-term business strategies won't be compromised, while the nondisclosure agreement guarantees that fundamental long-term business information and methods won't be lost in subsequent years.

When to use a noncompete. As a general rule, a noncompete should be used only if it is necessary to protect competitive interests, and the restrictions are not unreasonably burdensome to the employee. Courts generally look on noncompete clauses with disfavor. In most states, these provisions will be enforced only if they serve a legitimate interest and are reasonably limited in scope and time. (Some states, such as California, won't enforce employee noncompete agreements at all.)

Also, an employer may not use a noncompete to bully an employee into staying. If a dispute arises over a noncompete agreement and a judge must review it, the judge will probably start with a presumption that restricting an ex-employee's right to work is unfair. The employer will have the burden of proving a valid business reason for using the agreement. If the employer's motive is anything other than a good-faith effort to protect the business, a court will probably refuse to enforce the agreement (not to mention that there will be an unhappy ex-employee who knows the company's trade secrets).

Noncompete Provision (to be added to an employee nondisclosure agreement that specifies which information the company considers confidential)

> Employee agrees that in order to protect the Confidential Information while Employee is employed by Company, and for a period of [*insert time period*] thereafter, Employee shall not:
>
> (a) plan for, acquire any financial interest in, or perform services for (as an employee, consultant, officer, director, independent contractor, principal, agent, or otherwise) any business that would require Employee to use or disclose any confidential information; or
>
> (b) perform services (as an employee, consultant, officer, director, independent contractor, principal, agent, or otherwise) that are similar to Employee's current duties or responsibilities for any person or entity that, during the term, engages in any business activity in which Company is then engaged or proposes to be engaged and that conducts its business in the following territory: [*insert territory—that is, region in which the employee cannot compete*].

Related terms: confidentiality agreement; nonsolicitation agreement; trade secret.

creditor

A creditor is the person or company that is owed money (by a debtor).

Related terms: debt; interest rates (usury); promissory note.

criminal plea bargain

Criminal plea bargains are a hybrid form of contract—an arrangement that must meet the standards of both contract law *and* criminal law. Galileo allegedly cut a plea bargain with the Catholic Church in 1633, abjuring some of the "errors" in his work

C

in exchange for detention on house arrest at his Italian villa (a significantly more comfortable result than remaining in prison at the pleasure of the Inquisition). Although plea bargains have been around for a while, American case law surrounding these deals (and making them enforceable) has evolved only during the last 75 years.

Making the deal. A plea bargain is essentially a contract between the defense and the prosecution, in which the defendant agrees to plead guilty or no contest in exchange for an agreement by the prosecution to drop some charges, reduce a charge to one that is less serious, or recommend that the judge impose a particular sentence acceptable to the defense. Because the plea bargain is recognized by United States courts as either a contractual or quasi-contractual arrangement, remedies such as specific performance—ordering one side to do what it promised—are commonly permitted when either the defendant or the prosecutor tries to back out of the deal.

> **EXAMPLE:** Mr. Santobello had a long criminal record. When he was busted for promoting gambling and possession of gambling devices he was concerned that he would get the maximum sentence. After negotiations with the prosecutor, Santobello agreed to plead guilty to a lesser offense in return for the prosecutor's promise to make no recommendation as to his sentence. At Santobello's appearance for sentencing many months later, a new prosecutor recommended the maximum sentence, which the judge imposed. Santobello attempted unsuccessfully to withdraw his guilty plea but the court would not permit it. He appealed to the U.S. Supreme Court, which held that original prosecutor's promise not to recommend sentencing should either be enforced (specific performance), or Santobello should be able to withdraw his guilty plea. It wasn't fair to require only Santobello—and not the prosecutor—to keep his end of the deal.

What are the benefits? As is true of most contracts, a plea bargain offers benefits to both sides. A defendant may benefit from a reduced sentence, a lesser criminal conviction, a speedier resolution, and less hassle or publicity. A prosecutor gets an assured conviction, less congestion on the court docket, and more flexibility in dealing with codefendants or others involved in a crime. Plea bargains have been extremely popular in recent decades and have been negotiated by politicians (Spiro Agnew), assassins (James Earl Ray), traitors (John Walker Lindh), and crooks (Michael Milken and Enron's Michael Kopper).

Can the parties make a deal without the judge's approval? No, a judge's approval is always required. In many courts, prosecutors recommend the bargained-for sentence without obtaining any explicit agreement beforehand from the judge. But many prosecutors know from past experience and the judge's reputation whether the judge can be counted on (as many can) to rubber-stamp the prosecutor's recommendation. If the judge rebels or simply doesn't follow the track record and imposes a harsher sentence than the one the defendant was led to expect, the defendant is usually allowed to withdraw the plea and reassert his or her right to go to trial.

Get it in writing. Sometimes, prosecutors agree to certain deals outside of court, only to change their minds once in front of the judge. In most places, the defendant caught in such a situation would have the right to simply withdraw a guilty plea. To deter prosecutors from going back on a deal, defendants should have the terms put in writing before going before the judge. If the prosecutor agrees only to make a recommendation or to not oppose the defense lawyer's request for a certain sentence, however, the court, in some cases, may refuse to allow the defendant to withdraw the plea.

Not all plea bargains are equal. As with all contracts, plea bargains differ from case to case. However, unlike traditional contract factors, such as supply and demand, plea bargains depend on:

- whether the defendant has any prior convictions ("priors")
- how serious the offense was (especially whether it was a violent crime), and
- how strong the prosecution's case (evidence) is.

C

For many common offenses, prosecutors in a given courthouse will have worked out a "price list," setting out the typical sentences for different offenses. For example, in one area, it may be the prosecutors' practice to uniformly reduce all first-time DUI (driving under the influence) offenses in which blood alcohol tests reveal a marginal or borderline level to a lesser offense, such as reckless driving.

Plea bargains are usually binding. Defendants cannot get out of deals just because they changed their minds. In certain (though rare) circumstances, however, where it would be unfair to allow a deal to stand, defendants may be allowed to withdraw guilty pleas. Examples of such circumstances may include that a defendant:

- did not have the "effective assistance of counsel" in making the deal—for instance, the defendant was forced to plead before a public defender could be appointed
- was not informed of the underlying charges before agreeing to the deal or does not voluntarily agree to the deal, or
- was given a sentence that differs from the agreed-upon deal.

cross-collateralization

If you're familiar with the expression "robbing Peter to pay Paul," then you understand how cross-collateralization works. It's a process by which a company uses income from one source to pay off a debt to another. It is standard for companies that contract for creative rights to cross-collateralize debts and income from subsequent projects. For example, a manufacturer may cross-collateralize income from several of an inventor's creations; a publisher may cross-collateralize income from several books by an author, or a record company may cross-collateralize various sources of a musician's income.

> EXAMPLE: Sheila's first album is in the red for $5,000. (The album cost $10,000 to make and earned only $5,000 in royalties.) Sheila assigned some merchandising rights to her

record company; under that arrangement, she has earned $15,000 in merchandise royalties. The record company will cross-collateralize the debt for the first album with the income from the merchandise. As a result, Sheila will receive only $10,000 of the merchandising income; the rest will go to pay the outstanding cost of making her album.

Related terms: license agreement; royalty.

cross-reference

Drafters of contracts often refer to related information elsewhere in the agreements. For example, a statement that "payment will be made as provided in Exhibit A" sends the reader to the end of the agreement for a schedule of payment due dates. Using cross-references avoids unnecessary repetition while ensuring that the reader gets all the information necessary to understand the contract.

cure (cure period)

Cure refers to the right of one party to fix a contract problem. Consider, for example, why some companies breach agreements. Sometimes it's bad behavior, but sometimes it's unintended—the result of cash flow problems, bookkeeping errors, or scheduling snafus, for example. Because a breach may be unintended, it is considered unfair to terminate an agreement until the breaching party has an opportunity to fix (or cure) the problem. Typically, each party is given 30 or 60 days (the cure period) from the time of notification to cure the defect. For example, if you don't receive your royalty payment from a manufacturer, you would provide notice of the breach to manufacturer. The manufacturer's receipt of your notice triggers the cure period. If you don't get paid within the cure period, then you can terminate the agreement. A typical cure provision is part of a termination provision as shown below.

Termination: Sample language

> **Termination.** This Agreement may be terminated by either party on written notice of termination, upon material breach of any obligation by the other party, if such other party fails to cure such breach within sixty (60) days after written notice.

Not every breach is curable. One party's failure to obtain insurance, for example, may not be curable, because the other party will be exposed to liability even during the cure period. In addition, even if a cure period or right to cure is not written into the agreement, most courts (including small claims court) require that the parties try to cure a breach within a reasonable time (usually 30 days).

Related term: remedies.

damages, compensatory

Damages are the financial measure of the harm caused by a legally recognized injury. (The term refers both to the harm caused and to the amount the other party must pay to make it right.) When lawyers refer to contract damages, they are usually talking about compensatory damages, which (as the name indicates) are intended to compensate for a breach.

Expectations count. The general rule for compensatory damages (also known as direct damages) is that they are based on expectations. For example, if you agree to sell your camera for $200 and the other party fails to pay after receiving the camera, your compensatory damages are what you expected to get: $200. Compensatory damages are intended to put you where you would have been if the contract had been performed. So, for example, if you are providing services or goods, your damages are typically measured by your anticipated profit on the deal (that is, your price minus out-of-pocket costs).

> **EXAMPLE:** Charlie contracts with BJ, a crafts artist, to make him a custom wall hanging for $1,000. BJ calculates that she will pay $350 for fabric, parts, and delivery. BJ starts the design but before she buys any materials, Charlie tells her he's changed his mind and hired someone else to make the piece. BJ sues for the $1,000 promised under the contract, but the court awards her only $650 because she has not yet incurred the out-of-pocket expenses for materials (the court subtracts the $350 from the $1,000 Charlie was going to pay her).

There must be actual damage. You cannot just guess at how much you could have made from a deal and claim that as your damages. You must prove that you had a realistic and foreseeable expectation of receiving a particular amount; in other words, you must show proof of your loss. This is where a well-drafted contract can help, because it sets out each party's expectations clearly.

> EXAMPLE: **A tale of three ostriches.** In 1990, Mr. and Mrs. Doner started an ostrich breeding business. They purchased a trio of ostrich chicks from Mr. and Mrs. Snapp for $9,000. In ostrich parlance, a "trio" refers to two hens and a male. But the Doners later learned they had received two males and a female. (Apparently, it can be difficult to determine the sex of an ostrich for the first two years of its life.) The Doners found other ostrich breeders and traded the two males: one for another male, and the other for two female chicks. Then, three years later, the Doners sued the Snapps for $15,000, claiming they would have earned that much if the Snapps had provided them with the original trio as promised. The problem for the Doners was that they could not prove they had a realistic expectation they would earn $15,000 when they signed their contract—or alternatively, that the mismatched trio was what prevented them from earning the $15,000. Their estimate was speculative—a best guess at what they might earn—and had nothing to do with what they paid for the chicks (or any other amounts mentioned in the contract).

Over the years, general guidelines have evolved for determining compensatory damages in various contracts, as follows.

Services contract: breach by seller (service provider). When the service provider breaches, the buyer is usually entitled to whatever it costs to complete the work (typically, the cost of hiring someone else to finish the job).

EXAMPLE: Tom's in-laws will be staying with him for a month, so he hires Sanford to retile his guest bathroom for $700. Sanford starts the job and then quits. Tom must pay $800 to Bob to complete the work on time. For breaching the contract, Sanford owes Tom $100 (the difference between what Tom expected to pay and what he actually paid) as well as the return of any sums already paid to him by Tom.

D

Services contract: breach by buyer of services. When the buyer breaches, the seller of services is entitled to the contract price minus any reasonable out-of-pocket expenses. (If the out-of-pocket expenses have already been paid, then they are included in the damages.)

EXAMPLE: Tom hires Sanford to retile his bathroom for $700 (including $200 for the tiles). Sanford buys the tiles and shows up to do the work, but Tom has changed his mind. Tom owes Sanford $700 (unless Sanford can use the tiles at another job in which case their value would be deducted from the damages—a principle known as mitigation).

Sales contract for goods: breach by seller. If the goods are unique—for example, a rare coin or a vintage automobile—the buyer may not be satisfied by a financial payment. Under these circumstances, the buyer may demand that the item be delivered—that is, that the contract be carried out exactly as agreed. (This remedy is called "specific performance.") In the case of goods that are fungible (not unique), the buyer has two choices: (1) The buyer may sue for the market value of the goods minus the contract price (that is, the anticipated profit); or (2) the buyer can purchase the goods elsewhere and sue for the difference between that price and what should have been paid under the contract.

EXAMPLE: Sam, the owner of a restaurant, orders 200 chairs from Billie's Furniture. Sam will pay $20 a chair, for a total of $4,000. Billie later announces he is unable to fill the order.

It costs Sam $5,000 to buy replacement chairs after Billie breaches the contract. Sam is entitled to $1,000 in damages (the difference between what he expected to pay and what he actually paid).

D

Sales contract for goods: breach by buyer. If the buyer of goods breaches, the seller is entitled to lost profits, measured by the difference between the contract price and either the market value of the goods at the time of breach or what the seller was able to charge someone else for them.

EXAMPLE: Sam, the owner of a restaurant, orders 200 chairs from Billie's Furniture. Sam will pay $20 a chair for a total of $4,000. Sam decides not to open the restaurant and tells Billie not to deliver the chairs. Billie is entitled to his expected profit on the deal (the contract price minus the wholesale price of the chairs). However, Billie doesn't want to be stuck with 200 chairs in his inventory so he sells them to Alice for $3,000. Sam owes Billie $1,000 ($4,000 minus the $3,000 Billie earned by selling the chairs).

If the goods can't be sold to anyone else, the seller may be able to collect the full price. In some cases, the seller may be entitled to the difference between the out-of-pocket cost of the goods and the contract price.

Sales contract for real property: breach by seller. The jilted buyer of real property is (in some cases) entitled to actually receive the property (this remedy is known as "specific performance"). Alternatively, the buyer is entitled to the difference between the market price and the contract price.

EXAMPLE: Smith contracts to buy a vacation cottage from Catano for $200,000. At the last minute, Catano changes his mind. At the time of Catano's change of heart, the cottage is valued at $225,000. A court may order Catano to hand over the cottage (specific performance) or to refund any money already paid and to pay Smith compensatory damages of $25,000 (the difference between the market price and the contract price).

Sales contract for real property: breach by buyer. Real estate contracts often set out specific remedies when a buyer breaches. For example, the buyer may have to forfeit the down payment, deposit, or fees. At the same time, the seller is entitled to the amount by which the contract price exceeds the property's value at the time of the breach (if the value has declined), together with out-of-pocket losses and interest. If the property can be sold for more than the contract price, the seller has no damages and can recover only the amounts set forth in the contract.

> **EXAMPLE:** Smith contracts to buy a vacation cottage from Catano for $200,000. At the last minute, Smith changes his mind. At the time of the breach, the cottage is valued at $225,000 and Smith had paid $25,000 as a down payment. The contract states that if Smith backs out, Catano can keep the down payment, which he does. He later sells the cottage for $225,000. Catano cannot recover any additional money from Smith because the property sold for more than the original contract price.

Construction contract: breach by owner. If the owner breaches a construction contract, the damages depend on the stage of construction. If the breach occurs before construction has begun, the contractor can recover lost profits (the contract price less the cost of materials and labor). If the breach happens during construction, the contractor is entitled to lost profits, plus the cost of the construction that has already taken place. If the breach occurs after construction, the contractor is entitled to the contract price, plus interest.

> **EXAMPLE:** Melvin hires Emily's Construction to build a guest cottage on his property for $130,000 (including materials of $30,000). If Melvin terminates before Emily starts work,

D

he owes her $100,000 (her expected profit). If he terminates midway, she is entitled to $100,000 plus the cost of any materials she already bought (unless the materials can be used at another job in which case their value would be deducted—a principle known as mitigation).

Construction contract: breach by contractor. If the contractor breaches in the middle of the project, the owner is entitled to be paid what it will cost to finish the job. If the breach causes delays, the owner is also entitled to damages for loss of use of the property. In some cases, the owner may be entitled to the difference between what the property would have been worth if the work had been completed and the market value of the property at the time of breach.

EXAMPLE: Melvin hires Emily's Construction to build a guest cottage on his property for $130,000 (including materials of $30,000). Melvin pays Emily $50,000 upon commencement of the project. He also pays for the materials. Emily walks out midway into the project, and Melvin has to pay $70,000 to Weldon to complete the work. Melvin has spent a total of $150,000 for work and materials that he expected to get for $130,000. Emily owes Melvin the difference: $20,000.

Compensatory damages are not the only remedy. When a contract breaks down, the parties sometimes may be entitled to a range of remedies (legal resolutions) in addition to compensatory damages (each is described in more detail in other entries in this book):

- **Consequential damages.** These include all "reasonably foreseeable" losses that would flow from a breach. For example, if a groundskeeper failed to prepare a baseball park, it is reasonably foreseeable that the home team would have to postpone the game that day.
- **Incidental damages.** These are minor costs of dealing with the breach, such as relisting fees for an auction to sell property after the original highest bidder backed out of the deal.

- **Specific performance.** This is where the court orders the breaching party to actually do what was promised in the contract, such as finish construction or hand over an item, rather than just paying money.
- **Liquidated damages.** This is a specifically agreed upon amount, stated in the contract, that will be paid in the event of a breach. Often, liquidated damages are used when both parties recognize that it will be difficult to put a dollar amount on the damages a breach would cause. These clauses are also the subject of scrutiny by a court.
- **Mitigated damages.** This is a reduction in compensatory damages to reflect the hurt party's obligation to minimize its losses. For example, if a tenant breaches a lease, the landlord cannot sit by idly and allow the apartment to remain vacant. If the landlord can lease the apartment for some portion of the preexisting lease period, then that amount should be deducted from the landlord's damages against the former tenant.
- **Punitive/exemplary damages.** These extra damages are awarded to punish someone for extremely bad behavior, such as fraud. They are not awarded for claims of breach of contract but may be awarded if a tort claim—a form of personal injury, such as negligence or fraud—is made along with the contract case.

Related terms: consequential damages; exemplary damages; incidental damages; liquidated damages; mitigation of damages; remedies; specific performance; tort.

damages, consequential

Consequential damages (also known as "special damages") are claims for contract injuries that are foreseeable, though not necessarily a direct result of the contract breach. Typically, they arise when one party's losses from a broken contract exceed the costs (or value) associated with the deal. For example, the cost to complete a boat ($10,000) may not adequately compensate for the revenue lost by a fisherman if the boat is not ready by fishing season ($100,000).

When should the party who breaks the agreement be liable for these potential losses? That depends on whether the losses are foreseeable when the contract is made. Consider Mr. Siegel's dilemma.

D

> **EXAMPLE:** Mr. Siegel delivered $200 to Western Union with instructions to transmit it to a friend. The money was to be bet (legally) on a horse, but this was not disclosed in the instructions. Western Union misdirected the money order, and it did not reach Siegel's friend until several hours after the race had taken place. The horse that Siegel intended to bet on won and would have paid $1,650 on Siegel's $200 bet. Siegel sued Western Union for his $1,450 lost profit, but the court held that Western Union was not liable. The company "had no notice or knowledge of the purpose for which the money was being transmitted."

This rule that damages must be foreseeable is derived from a 19th-century English case (with which every first-year law student is familiar): *Hadley v. Baxendale.*

> **EXAMPLE:** Hadley hired Baxendale to transport the broken shaft from his corn mill to the manufacturer, who was to make a new one using the broken shaft as a model. Baxendale failed to deliver the shaft within the time promised. With the engine shaft out of service, the mill was shut down. Hadley sued for profits the mill lost during the additional period that it was shut down because of Baxendale's breach. The English court refused to grant the award because the damages were not foreseeable— that is, they had never been communicated at the time of the contract.

Using contract language to limit consequential damages. The key to an award of consequential damages is whether the breaching party was aware of the string of consequences that resulted from a breach. Sometimes, this knowledge can be inferred from language in a contract pointing to the consequence ("Contractor acknowledges that the failure to complete the construction by July 4 will delay the opening of the amusement park"). At the same time, in an attempt to prevent an award of consequential damages, many contracts contain a provision (usually entitled "Limitation of Liability" or "Limitation of Damages") in which the parties agree that one or both parties will not be liable for these types of losses. Because these provisions limit legal rights that would otherwise exist under the law, courts scrutinize them carefully to make sure they are fair and voluntary. For that reason, lawyers often format these provisions in capital letters or bold print either to satisfy state laws (some require special typefaces for these provisions) or just to make sure that the other party can't later claim it was unaware of the limitation.

Limitation on damages: Sample language

LIMITATION OF LIABILITY: EXCEPT AS OTHERWISE PROVIDED IN THIS AGREEMENT, UNDER NO CIRCUMSTANCES SHALL EITHER PARTY BE LIABLE TO THE OTHER PARTY FOR INDIRECT, INCIDENTAL, CONSEQUENTIAL, SPECIAL, OR EXEMPLARY DAMAGES ARISING FROM THIS AGREEMENT, EVEN IF THAT PARTY HAS BEEN ADVISED OF THE POSSIBILITY OF SUCH DAMAGES.

Courts will generally enforce a provision that limits or prohibits these damages, unless the provision is grossly unfair or violates public policy (that is, it's unconscionable). As a general rule, this happens only when the provision seeks to override consumer protection laws or relates to personal injury damages.

Related terms: exculpatory clause; exemplary damages; liquidated damages; mitigated damages; remedies; specific performance.

damages, incidental

Incidental damages are reasonable (and usually minor) expenses incurred when dealing with a breach of contract—for example, the seller's delivery and storage charges if a buyer rejects goods or a property owner's fees to relist a property after the buyer breaches. The term is a catch-all for unidentifiable damages that are neither compensatory (expected losses) nor consequential damages (foreseeable losses).

Related terms: exculpatory clause; exemplary damages; liquidated damages; mitigation of damages; remedies; specific performance.

DBA (doing business as)

See fictitious business name.

debenture

A debenture is an unsecured bond. Bonds are pieces of paper that certify a debt. They're usually issued by the government (such as a U.S. Treasury bond) or a corporation to raise money. Typically, the purchaser of a bond makes money because the bond earns interest or is discounted (in other words, the buyer purchases it for less than its face value). Some bonds are secured by property. This means that if the corporate or government debtor defaults, the owner of the bond can take the property securing the debt. (For example, if the government defaults on a Treasury Bond, you would *not* be entitled to a few acres of a national park or a night in the Lincoln bedroom.) Because no money or assets are set aside to back the value of a debenture, the buyer must rely solely on the general creditworthiness of the issuer.

debt

A debt is anything that's owed to someone. Because debt is an essential tool for running businesses and transferring property, debts (and their repayment) have evolved into a specialized area of contract law that includes promissory notes, mortgages, and loan agreements. At the same time, the unequal bargaining power of a lender and borrower has led to government regulation of debt agreements. This regulation dictates what you must, can, and cannot do in certain key areas of debt contracts, such as how much interest may be charged, how the creditor may obtain the collateral or security on a loan, the warnings required in consumer contracts, or the ability of third parties to collect on debts.

Related terms: debt security; debtor: interest rates (usury); mortgage; promissory note.

debt security

Debt securities (also known as "fixed-income securities") include any government or corporate interest-paying debt (usually in the form of a bond, note, bill, or money market instrument) that can be bought and sold. If you buy a debt security, you're betting on someone else's ability to repay a loan. Many banks did this when they purchased mortgage-backed bonds and ultimately contributed to a minor collapse of the United States economy in 2008.

debtor

A debtor is anyone who owes money. The term is also used in bankruptcy court to describe the person or entity declaring bankruptcy.

Related terms: creditor; debt security; interest rates (usury); mortgage; promissory note.

deduction

A deduction is just a cost, expense, or another amount that's subtracted from something else. Deductions are your friends when you're the one paying (for example, at tax time), because they reduce your total bill. When you're the one collecting money, however, deductions lower your ultimate payoff.

Contractual payment provisions often include many deductions that diminish what one party is supposed to receive. For example, a recording agreement may permit the record company to deduct returns, advertising, commissions, and recording costs from payments otherwise due to a musician. In general, if you're receiving a payment, it's in your best interest to keep contractual deductions to a minimum.

Related term: royalty.

deed

A deed is the document that transfers ownership of real property. Deeds come in many forms:

- **Quitclaim deed.** A quitclaim transfers ownership but doesn't guarantee it.
- **Grant deed.** A grant deed implies certain promises—for example, that the title hasn't already been transferred.
- **Warranty deed.** A warranty deed—commonly used in home sales—transfers ownership and explicitly promises the buyer that the transferor has good title to the property, meaning it is free of liens or claims of ownership.
- **Deed of trust.** This transfers property to a trust that holds it as security for a loan.
- **Transfer-on-death deed.** This transfers property only after the title holder is deceased.

Related terms: mortgage; real estate contract.

default

A default is a failure to do something, whether it's a football team that fails to show up for the game or a debtor who fails to make a payment. In contract law, the term is most often associated with the failure to make timely payments on mortgages and loan agreements.

defenses (breach of contract)

When accused of wrongdoing, your defenses comprise any plausible legal argument that justifies your position. As in sports, the best defense in a contract dispute is a good offense. It's usually not enough to simply deny legal wrongdoing; you must respond with every possible defense. And if you don't raise defenses in the early stages of lawsuit, you may be prevented from raising them later.

Most of the contract defenses listed below are referred to as affirmative defenses. As a legal matter, this means that the party raising the defense has the burden of proving it, if the dispute goes to trial. An affirmative defense does not contest the primary claims or facts (for example, that there was a breach of contract), but instead asserts mitigating facts or circumstances that render the breach claim moot. In other words, it is like saying, "Even if I breached the contract, the other party should not win the suit."

> EXAMPLE: Dodd, a teenage singer, failed to show up for a concert and is accused of breaching his contract to provide entertainment services. Regardless of whether he breached the agreement, he may assert the affirmative defense that he lacked the capacity to enter into the contract in the first place because he's a minor.

Arguing in the alternative. The law permits you to claim as many alternative defenses as you want, even if they contradict each other. For example, you may argue that the contract is invalid or unenforceable, that you performed as required by the contract, and alternatively, that your failure to perform was justified by the other party's actions—even though they can't all be true. (It's a little bit like the criminal defense attorney who argues his client was 100 miles from the scene of the murder and, alternatively, that the murder was in self-defense.)

In some cases, you may admit to the breach and assert defenses only to the damages claimed by the other side.

Common affirmative defenses. How you frame your legal defenses in a lawsuit is limited only by your lawyer's imagination (and your ability to bankroll legal fees). The most common defenses are listed below (see the separate entries for more details on each defense):

D

- **The contract was supposed to be in writing.** If the other side argues that an oral agreement should be enforced against you, you may be able to defend yourself by claiming that the a state law (known as the "statute of frauds") requires this type of contract—for example, for the sale of real property—to be in writing.

- **The contract is indefinite.** If the essential terms were never agreed upon, you may be able to defend by arguing that the contract is indefinite. This means either the parties did not consider the deal to be final or that a court could not discern the essentials, even by implication (for example, if it's not clear how long an agreement should last or what the specifications are for a construction project). Agreements to agree (such as letters of intent or agreements in principle) are usually considered indefinite and therefore unenforceable, although courts will require the parties to act in good faith to reach an agreement.

- **There is a mistake.** You can defend yourself by proving that a mutual mistake was made as to an essential fact in the contract—for example, both parties were mistaken as to the authenticity of a painting. You cannot use this defense when referring to a mistake in judgment by one party ("*Oops, I could have gotten so much more for my painting!*").

- **You lacked capacity to contract.** If you lacked capacity (that is, you couldn't understand what you were doing when you entered into the deal), the contract may be voidable. This defense is most likely to succeed in the case of minors and those with impaired mental capacities.

- **You were fraudulently induced to enter into a contract.** A contract will be invalid if it was induced by lies, under duress ("Sign this or we'll take your cat"), or by a trusted person's undue influence (your real estate agent advises you to buy because she secretly gets a kickback from the seller).

- **The contract is unconscionable.** A contract won't be enforced if it is grossly unfair. This almost always occurs in situations where the bargaining power is severely imbalanced (as in a contract of adhesion) and the party with more power takes advantage by forcing unfair conditions, clauses, or waivers on the other party.

- **Estoppel.** When one party makes a statement excusing performance and the other party relies on that statement, the first party may be prevented from later denying that statement and claiming a breach. For example, if a bank president calls a homeowner and tells her that the bank won't foreclose for six months in order to give the homeowner a chance to sell the home, the bank will be held to its six-month promise.

- **The contract is illegal.** A contract is unenforceable if its object or its consideration is illegal—for example, a contract that enables prostitution, violates tax laws, or requires the destruction of records. Contracts that may indirectly aid illegal purposes will sometimes be enforced—for example, an agreement to supply gambling machines, even though they may be illegal in some states—may be enforced. Sometimes, a court will sever the illegal aspect from the agreement, leaving the rest of the contract enforceable.

Related terms: breach, material; mitigation of damages; remedies; void (voidable).

definitions

Most contracts include a list of defined terms, to clarify how the parties are using those terms in the agreements. Sometimes, these definitions are provided alphabetically in a list or an index at the beginning of the agreement. In other cases, the defined terms are integrated (that is, they are explained within the agreement, usually when they first appear).

Defined terms: Sample language

> Employee shall treat with secrecy all technology, know-how, and other data or documents that provide a business advantage over competitors (the "Confidential Information").

D

Here are some strategies to follow when defining terms in your contracts:

- **Use industry terms.** Use industry definitions if the term is commonly defined within an industry or by regulations, statutes, or a government agency (such as the IRS).
- **Define nouns; not verbs.** Definitions are typically reserved for nouns.
- **Don't use the defined term to define the term.** To avoid confusion, don't use the defined term within the definition.
- **Capitalize and use quotes.** Defined terms are commonly capitalized (and placed in quotes when first used). For example, "'Direct Competitor' means any business entity engaged in providing legal services or products directly to consumers."
- **Avoid limiting definitions.** It's usually wise to provide complete definitions ("'Confidential Information' means …") rather than to state that a term "includes" or "does not include" something else.
- **Avoid definitions within definitions.** Keep each definition discrete. For example, don't state, "'Work product' means all materials produced as a result of employment whether during regular 'Working Hours' (defined as Monday through Friday) or during overtime."

demand letter

See breach, (notice of).

depreciation

Depreciation occurs when you spread the cost or value of an asset over time, taking into account factors such as the amount of use, rate of deterioration, and obsolescence (a major issue with technology). Although the term is commonly associated with taxes—taxpayers are permitted to deduct the cost of certain business expenses over a period of years—it is broadly used in contracts and business dealings when assessing the diminishing value of business assets over time. For example, a company that is purchasing the equipment of another, will structure the price to account for the equipment's depreciation.

disclaimers

Disclaimers are a way of distancing yourself from contractual or other legal obligations. For example, maybe you're watching an ad for a new drug and it promises to cure dandruff, hair loss, bad breath, and stained teeth, and it just sounds fantastic—until it ends with a statement saying, "your results may vary" or warning that the manufacturer won't be responsible if, say, your hair turns blue or your organs fail. Statements like these, in which a seller or manufacturer explicitly disavows responsibility for certain results, are disclaimers. Like other types of exculpatory provisions—such as indemnity clauses or limitations on liability provisions—they're used to minimize risks when the results of certain behavior are uncertain. For example, the parties may put a disclaimer in their contract giving up the right to seek consequential damages, because those damages can be difficult to predict and neither party wants to be on the hook later.

Some obligations cannot be disclaimed, because law and public policy don't allow people to avoid certain obligations. For example, a provision disclaiming a certain kind of warranty may be unenforceable. For that reason, you may need a lawyer's advice to determine which obligations may be disclaimed and which may not.

A disclaimer may also be required by contract. For example, a party that manufactures a product may require resellers to use a certain disclaimer on the product. As with all disclaimers, statements like these may not be enforceable if they violate the law or public policy.

EXAMPLE: A financial accounting firm licenses its website content to a tax preparation website. As a condition of the license, wherever the information is posted, the tax website must include the following disclaimer:

> We are providing financial information, not financial advice. If you need financial advice, you should seek guidance from an accounting professional.

Related term: exculpatory clause.

discount

Everybody loves a bargain, and everyone loves a discount—a reduction in price. Discounts are used to encourage purchasing, get rid of excess inventory, and/or improve cash flow. For example, a vendor contract may provide discounts for buyers who pay promptly.

In securities sales, a discount refers to the difference between the purchase price and the issue price (or par value) of the security. In loan agreements, a discount usually refers to a reduction of some of the interest. The term "discounting" also refers to a process by which a debtor pays a fee in exchange for the right to delay or defer future payments.

drop-dead date

Don't let the name scare you. If deadlines are important to you, a drop-dead date can help. It's the last date by which something must happen, such as delivery, payment, or completed construction.

Missing the drop-dead date leads to certain consequences that are spelled out in the contract, such as cancelling the deal, taking property, or entering a judgment. The drop-dead date is often used in connection with a "time is of the essence" provision.

Related term: time is of the essence.

due diligence

Due diligence refers to the process of examining whether something—commonly a company's financial condition—meets a certain standard or whether it exhibits deficiencies. Due diligence is often required in audits or investigations conducted prior to purchasing an asset or signing a contract. The most common business and contract situation in which due diligence is associated is when a company merges or is acquired by another. (In this case, the "diligence" is due to the company's shareholders.) The company making the purchase will investigate the financial soundness of the acquisition; or alternatively, the company being purchased may request a due diligence report on the acquiring business.

Sarbanes-Oxley and due diligence. Until 2002, the diligence required for mergers and acquisitions was directed primarily at the company's financial soundness and often was accomplished with a generic audit that was rubber stamped by the company's officers and board. However, with the passage of the Sarbanes-Oxley Act in 2002, additional layers of review and diligence were required to prevent the repeat of accounting scandals, most notably the Enron debacle. Among other things, the due diligence required under the act, includes:

- CEOs and CFOs of public companies must make themselves aware of important organization details, must certify their financials, and must implement internal disclosure policies and practices.
- Public accounting firms must meet quality control and ethical standards.

D

- Companies must avoid certain types of securities fraud, tampering with documents, or conspiracy—an area that can spread diligence responsibilities to third parties such as lawyers. Violation may trigger criminal penalties.

Related term: comfort letter.

duress

Duress occurs when a party's consent to a contract is physically or mentally coerced.

A little history. Back in the 1800s, a court might enforce a contract even if it was made under the threat of a physical beating or having one's house burned down. The twisted legal thinking behind this rule was that the two incidents were separate: The victim had other legal remedies for the beating or property destruction, so the contract could still be enforced independent of the coercion. Nowadays, courts don't see things the same way. They will not enforce an agreement if one party signed it "under duress"—that is, only because the party was coerced by threats or force. The rationale is that the party under duress lacks the legal free will to refuse to sign. Therefore, the agreement was not voluntary and the contract that results must be voided.

Economic duress. Threats of physical force are rarely used as a means of inducing a contract. Instead, economic duress has emerged as a bigger issue. Economic duress (also known as "business compulsion") occurs when, for example, a supplier of goods jacks up the price on a customer who is in desperate need of goods, or one party threatens to breach an existing contract unless the other party agrees to some further demand. In these cases, the mere threat by one party to breach the contract by itself is not enough. The threatened party must also show it had no other source for the goods or services in the contract and, therefore, that suing for damages over the breach would not solve the problem.

EXAMPLE: In 1965, the Loral Corporation entered into a $6 million agreement to supply the Navy with radar equipment. Loral solicited bids from suppliers for various parts and entered into a subcontract with Austin for 23 of the 40 parts necessary for the job. In 1966, Loral entered into a second Navy contract for more radar equipment and again solicited bids. Austin was low bidder on some but not all of the parts. However, this time, Austin announced that if it wasn't awarded a subcontract for *all* of the parts, the company would stop supplying parts under the first subcontract. Loral would be punished financially under its Navy contract if it was late or failed to make delivery. The company desperately sought another supplier but could not find one that was able to provide the parts under the shortened timetable. Loral reluctantly agreed to Austin's terms. Once the Navy contract was fulfilled, Loral sued Austin to recover the difference between the original contract price and the higher price it was forced to pay because of the coercion. The New York Court of Appeals ruled that Austin's actions amounted to economic duress, and that it was liable for the extra costs.

Related terms: undue influence; void (voidable).

earn out

An earn out is a way to calculate prices that is used by the purchasers of a business, or sometimes by stockholders, in which a payment or a portion of a payment is contingent on future earnings. For example, the purchase price for a company might be structured so that 75% is paid in cash and the remaining 25% is tied to future earnings (this part is the earn out).

Related terms: acquisition agreement (sale of business); assignments (of contract); due diligence; merger; successors and assigns.

easement

An easement is a nonpossessory interest in real estate—that is, it is the right to use real property, without owning it—for example, the right to drive across a portion of property to get to other property. Most easements are "affirmative" in that they allow someone to do something. Some are "negative," in that they prohibit things from happening (no cutting down the cherry trees). Most easements are also "appurtenant," in that they involve two different pieces of property and deal with some connection between them—for example, a boundary wall (a "party wall") or access from one home to the coastline. Usually, easements are associated with the sale of real estate, either because the easement travels from owner to owner, or because a dispute has arisen as to whether the easement exists and was fully disclosed.

Related terms: appurtenance; mortgage; real estate contract; title insurance.

E

EBITDA

EBITDA is an acronym for "earnings before interest, taxes, depreciation and amortization." The resulting figure is a way to measure the actual cash flow of a business, without factoring in the effects of accounting and financing strategies. For example, if a business owns significant assets that it must depreciate, its actual cash on hand (measured using EBITDA) could be significantly higher than the income that shows up on its balance sheet (from which the depreciation is subtracted).

Related terms: amortization; depreciation; interest rates (usury).

effective date

The effective date is the date that an agreement is in force, or put another way, it's the date that the contract term commences. The signature date and the effective date may be different as is often indicated by an "as of" statement at the beginning of an agreement—"This agreement is effective as of June 10, 2011 ('the Effective Date')."

Related terms: as of; recitals; signatures.

ejusdem generis

This rule of contract construction—Latin for "of the same class" or "of the same kind"—is intended as an aid for interpreting lists of items. When all the items in a list are from the same class of things, any general reference that follows the list will refer back to that same class.

> EXAMPLE: A contract specifies that the programs to be developed will operate on "BlackBerrys, iPhones, Androids, iPads and other similar computing devices." Because BlackBerrys, Androids, iPads and iPhones are all considered mobile handheld computing devices, the term "similar

computing devices" would be interpreted to mean only other mobile devices, not laptops or desk-based computing devices.

Related term: rules of interpretation (rules of construction).

electronic agreements

An electronic contract is an agreement created and "signed" in electronic form; no paper or other hard copies are used. For example, you draft a contract on your computer and email it to a business associate, and the business associate, then emails it back with an electronic signature indicating acceptance. Electronic contracts and electronic signatures are just as legal and enforceable as traditional paper contracts signed in ink.

The E-Sign Act and state laws. The validity of electronic agreements is secured by federal law. Germaphobes rejoiced back in 2000—no more unsanitary agreements to touch; no need to reach for that virus-laden pen—when the Electronic Signatures in Global and International Commerce Act (the E-Sign Act), was enacted and removed the uncertainty that previously plagued the enforceability of e-contracts. Almost all states have adopted the Uniform Electronic Transactions Act (UETA), which establishes the legal validity of electronic signatures and contracts in a way similar to the federal law. If a state has adopted the UETA or a similar law, the federal electronic signature law won't override the state law. But if a state has adopted a law that is significantly different than the federal law, the federal law will trump it. This ensures that electronic contracts and electronic signatures will be valid in all states, regardless of where the parties live or where the contract is executed

Click to Agree. An e-contract can also be in the form of a "Click to Agree" or "clickwrap" contract commonly used with downloaded software. The user must click an "I Agree" button on a page containing the terms of the software license before the transaction can be completed and the user can actually access the product.

E

Electronic signatures. Because a traditional ink signature isn't possible on an electronic contract, people indicate their electronic signatures (or "e-signatures") in several different ways, including typing the signer's name into the signature area, pasting in a scanned version of the signer's signature, clicking an "I Accept" button, or using cryptographic "scrambling" technology to ensure that the e-signature really belongs to the person who was supposed to sign the contract.

Opting out of electronic contracts. While the federal e-signature law makes paper unnecessary in many situations, it also gives consumers and businesses the right to continue to use paper if they want. The law provides a way for consumers who prefer paper to opt out of using electronic contracts. Prior to obtaining a consumer's consent for electronic contracts, a business must provide a notice indicating whether paper contracts are available and informing consumers that if they give their consent to use electronic documents, they can later change their mind and request a paper agreement instead. The notice must also explain any fees or penalties that apply if the consumer insists on paper agreements for the transaction. And the notice must indicate whether the consumer's consent applies only to the particular transaction at hand, or to a larger category of transactions between the business and the consumer—in other words, whether the business has to get consent to use e-contracts/signatures for each transaction.

A business must also provide a statement outlining the hardware and software requirements to read and save the business's electronic documents. If the hardware or software requirements change, the business must notify consumers of the change and give consumers the option to revoke their consent to using electronic documents (without paying a penalty). Although the law doesn't force consumers to accept electronic documents from businesses, it poses a potential disadvantage for low-tech citizens by allowing businesses to collect additional fees from those who opt for paper.

Contracts that must be on paper. To protect consumers from potential abuses, electronic versions of the following documents are invalid and unenforceable:

- wills, codicils, and testamentary trusts
- documents relating to adoption, divorce, and other family law matters
- court orders, notices, and other court documents, such as pleadings or motions
- notices of cancellation or termination of utility services
- notices of default, repossession, foreclosure, or eviction
- notices of cancellation or termination of health or life insurance benefits
- product recall notices affecting health or safety, and
- documents required by law to accompany the transportation of hazardous materials.

These documents must be provided in traditional paper and ink format.

Related term: e-signature.

employment agreements

Employment agreements are contracts by which employees are hired. Most employment agreements are oral ("You're hired!" "Great, I'll see you on Monday!"). Usually, they create what's known as an at-will employment relationship. At-will means that the employee can quit at any time or can be fired at any time, for any reason that is not illegal. An employer might also ask employees to sign an offer letter, handbook acknowledgment, or other document agreeing to at-will employment. The purpose of these is to affirm the employer's right to fire at will, just in case the employee later argues that the employer needed good cause for termination.

Disadvantages of written employment agreements. Most employees don't have written employment contracts because such agreements often limit an employer's flexibility. For example, a written contract might provide that an employee will receive particular salary increases, be responsible for certain areas of operation, or be fired only for certain reasons during the contract's term. An employer can't simply end a two-year contract after six months, unless the employee commits an act that is specified in the contract as cause for termination. Similarly, if the contract promises the employee health benefits, the employer can't later stop paying for these benefits as a way to save money. The only way to change the terms of the contract is to renegotiate them, which can be difficult if the purpose of the discussion is to take away rights to which the employee is contractually entitled.

Another disadvantage of using written employment contracts is that they bring with them a special obligation to deal fairly with the employee (the "covenant of good faith and fair dealing"). If you treat the employee in a way that seems unfair to a judge or jury, you may be legally responsible not only for violating the contract, but also for breaching your duty to act in good faith.

Advantages of using written employment contracts. There are good reasons to use a written employment agreement as well, primarily when dealing with highly trained employees and executives. These include:

- **The employer wants control over the employee's ability to leave the business.** For example, if finding or training a replacement will be very costly or time-consuming for a company, an employer might want a written contract. It can lock the employee into a specific term (for example, two years), or it can require the employee to give enough notice to allow the employer to find and train a suitable replacement (for example, 90 days' notice). Although an employer can't force someone to stay with a company, an employee is likely to comply with the agreement's terms if the contract imposes a penalty for failing to do so.

- **The employee will be learning confidential and sensitive information about the business.** An employer can insert confidentiality clauses that prevent the employee from disclosing the information or using it for personal gain. Similarly, a contract that contains a noncompetition provision can protect the employer by preventing an employee from competing against the employer after leaving the company (but only in states that enforce noncompetes; some states prohibit them).

- **The employer wants to entice a highly skilled individual to work for the company.** By promising the individual job security and beneficial terms in an employment contract, the employer can "sweeten the deal."

- **An employment contract provides an employer with greater control over the employee.** For example, if the contract specifies standards for the employee's performance and grounds for termination, the employer may have an easier time terminating an employee who doesn't live up to those standards.

What goes in an employment contract? In addition to clearly describing what the employee is going to do (the job) and what the employer will do in return (salary, benefits, and so on), the employment contract can also address a number of other issues, including:

- **Duration of the job.** How long will the employee work? One year, two years, or indefinitely?

- **Employee's responsibilities.** Specific goals may be set or supervisory obligations established.

- **Benefits.** Will the employee receive health insurance, vacation leave, disability leave, and so on?

- **Grounds for termination.** For example, can the employee be terminated for failing to achieve sales goals?

- **Noncompetition.** If state law permits, the employer may want to prevent the employee from competing once the employee leaves the business.

- **Confidentiality.** Although state law requires employees to maintain secrets, the employer may spell out restrictions and add remedies in the event of a trade secret theft.
- **Ownership of the employee's work product.** The employer may want to be assured that work-related patents, copyrights, and other innovation-related rights are owned by the company, not the employee.
- **Dispute resolution.** A company may want to limit the ways that company disputes are resolved by, for example, requiring arbitration.

Related terms: confidentiality agreement; covenant not to compete; golden parachute; retention agreement (stay-on bonus).

end-user license agreement (EULA)

See clickwrap agreement.

engagement letter

An engagement letter is an agreement that defines the relationship between a business and a professional entity, usually an accountant. It's commonly used when hiring an accountant for assistance with an audit and sets forth the work to be done, the deadlines, disclaimers (usually based on standard accounting practices), and the purpose and use of the materials generated.

Related terms: comfort letter.

entity

An entity is any legally recognized organization or business form, typically a corporation, limited liability company, or partnership.

Related terms: corporation; limited liability company (LLC); partnership (general); partnership (limited); sole proprietor.

equitable estoppel

See estoppel.

equitable remedies

See remedies.

equity

Equity has a few meanings under contract law:

- **Ownership interest.** Equity is the current value of money or property invested and retained in a business or property (sometimes referred to as "owner's equity"). If you own real estate, for example, your equity is your ownership share: the value of the property less what you still owe on it. Selling equity is a common method of raising money for a business—for example, an outsider can purchase an ownership interest (shares) in your corporation. In order to accept equity investments, you must have an appropriate business entity, which usually means a limited liability company or corporation.
- **Business value.** Equity is a financial term used to describe the value of a business after deducting its liabilities from its assets.
- **Legal fairness.** Equity is the term for legal remedies that don't involve the payment of money—for example, requiring a seller to actually deliver an automobile rather than just pay financial damages. Equitable remedies—for example, requiring someone to do or not do something (an injunction)—can be ordered only by a judge, not a jury.

Related term: remedies.

escrow

An escrow account is like a safe deposit box. One or both parties place something (money, title, a sales item) into the account, which

E

is controlled by a third-party (known as the escrow agent). Only under certain conditions are the account's contents released.

Escrow and sales agreements. Typically, the items in escrow are released once payment is made or certain activities take place (or in real estate sales, what's known as "the release of contingencies," such as a house passing an inspection or a mortgage being funded). Although escrow is most commonly associated with the sale of real estate, it's also often used in auctions and online sales and to hold money, stock, or documents transferring ownership of inventions. In real estate transactions, both money and property title are placed in escrow and then disbursed when all conditions are met. In online transactions, the buyer's money is often held in escrow while the buyer inspects the goods.

Placing secrets into escrow. Sometimes, proprietary information is placed into an escrow account and released only if there is a failure or a breakdown of some sort.

> **EXAMPLE:** Medley Sauce Company agrees to supply its famous hot sauce exclusively to one food distributor. The distributor wants an assurance that if Medley can't supply the sauce, the distributor can have another company prepare it. Medley agrees to put the secret recipe into an escrow account. The escrow will release the secret recipe to the distributor only if Medley's can't or won't supply the hot sauce for more than two weeks.

The rules regarding the release of escrow items are established in an escrow agreement that is signed by three parties—the two parties to the deal and the escrow agent. Although escrow companies specialize in creating escrow accounts, anyone can serve as an escrow agent, including lawyers and banks.

Beware of escrow fraud. Fake escrow companies are often created by scam artists who prey on online shoppers, particularly on eBay and Craigslist. Red flags should go off when the escrow payments must be made via person-to-person methods, such as Western Union or MoneyGram. When in doubt, seek verification.

Related terms: mortgage; real estate contract.

e-signature

An e-signature is a digital method for confirming your acceptance of a contract. Put another way, it's a way to prove that by mouse-clicking "I ACCEPT," the other side agreed to the deal.

Validity of e-signatures. Federal law (the Electronic Signatures in Global and International Commerce Act or E-Sign Act) and state laws (the Uniform Electronic Transactions Act or UETA) have made e-signatures valid. Not surprisingly, there are many methods of preserving the digital trail that leads to "Yes."

In sales agreements, for example, the most common method is to use the "I Agree" button as the gateway to the next step in a purchase process. Unless you check the box accepting the terms, you cannot move to the next screen and actually make your purchase. In nonpurchase agreements, simply typing out your name and acknowledging that it is your e-signature will usually suffice. Some companies also require slashes before and after the name (for example, "/RichardStim/"). Although any documented form of assent should qualify as an e-signature these days, some parties prefer to use "digital signatures," which provide secure cryptographic methods of ensuring that the right person assented to the agreement.

Cryptographic and XML signatures. Cryptography is the science of securing information. It is most commonly associated with systems that scramble information and then unscramble it. Security experts currently favor the cryptographic signature method known as Public Key Infrastructure (PKI) as the most secure and reliable method of signing contracts online.

PKI uses an algorithm to encrypt online documents so that they will be accessible only to authorized parties. The parties have "keys" that allow them to read and sign a document, and which prohibits anyone else from accessing and signing it. Since the passage of the e-signature law in 2000, the use of PKI technology has become more widely accepted. Many online services offer PKI-encrypted digital signature systems that function much like PINs for bank cards.

In addition, the organization that sets Web standards for the Internet, the World Wide Web Consortium (W3C), developed XML-compliant guidelines for digital signatures. The results of their working group are discussed at the W3C website, www.w3.org/Signature.

estoppel

Estoppel occurs when someone does or says something that another party relies on in changing his or her position. In that case, a court will prevent the first person from later denying, retracting, or withdrawing the actions or words or claiming that they should have no legal effect. It is called an estoppel because, as stated by the 17th century English legal scholar, Edward Coke, "a man's own act or acceptance stoppeth or closeth up his mouth to allege or plead the truth."

Estoppel as a defense. Estoppel is often used as an affirmative defense—a defense in a lawsuit that doesn't contest the main claim but instead asserts mitigating facts The key elements when asserting the estoppel defense are that (1) one party made a representation, (2) the other party reasonably relied upon it, and (3) that reliance resulted in an injury.

EXAMPLE: A mortgage company began foreclosure proceedings after the owner's payments were late on a property. The owner contacted an officer of the mortgage company, who made an oral promise to delay the foreclosure and give the property owner time to make a "forced sale" on the property. The mortgage company then proceeded with the foreclosure despite its officer's statements. In the foreclosure lawsuit, the mortgage company asserted that the oral promise was not binding because the mortgage agreement could be modified only in writing (based on the state's statute of frauds.) The New York Court of Appeals disagreed and permitted the property owner to use the defense of estoppel, stating "no one shall be permitted to found any claim upon his own inequity or take advantage of his own wrong. The Statute of Frauds was not intended to offer an asylum of escape from that fundamental principle of justice."

Promissory or equitable estoppel. Courts and lawyers refer to estoppel as both "equitable estoppel" and "promissory estoppel." Historically, promissory estoppel was used to refer to a promise or statement made before the contract was formed, while equitable estoppel was often used to describe statements made *after* contract formation. In practical terms, the term "estoppel" is sufficient for all of these situations.

Estoppel to enforce promises. Estoppel isn't only a defense; it can also be used offensively, to enforce a promise or a gift. The enforcement is limited to the damage caused by the other person's reliance on the promise.

EXAMPLE: Your aunt promises to give you her car and her comic book collection. You really need a new car, and you tell you aunt that you are going to sell your old clunker in reliance on her promise. After you sell your car, she reneges on her gift. Her promise to give you the car could be enforced under an estoppel theory because you relied on it in selling your car. The comics are another story, however: You didn't do anything in reliance on this promise, so you can't use estoppel to enforce it.

evaluation agreement

If you want to make sure that the person or company you hire to evaluate your idea doesn't steal it, you should use either an evaluation agreement or an option agreement. A basic evaluation agreement states that certain material is being submitted to a company for evaluation, and that the company will pay the creator if it decides to use the idea. An evaluation agreement leaves the creator free to submit the idea to others, while an option agreement usually establishes exclusivity, meaning the creator may not show the idea to others during the option period.

Evaluation agreements require confidentiality. In a sense, an evaluation agreement is a souped-up confidentiality agreement. And it poses the same challenge when you are trying to convince a company to sign one: The company may already be considering a similar idea in-house, and signing the agreement may limit that development. There are ways to work around this—for example, by recognizing existing development—but if you are concerned about a loss of rights or don't know whether you can trust the company, it's best to consult a lawyer before making the modifications. Below is a sample evaluation agreement.

Completing the Evaluation Agreement. Insert the names of the parties. If any of the parties are corporations or partnerships, indicate the correct business form—for example, "Musto Motors, a California general partnership."

- **The Submission.** Insert a phrase describing the idea. On a separate sheet write a description of the idea, label it Attachment A, and attach it to the agreement.

- **Review and Evaluation.** This section prohibits the company evaluating the submission from using it without entering into an agreement for payment. In other words, the company has two choices: Enter into an agreement or don't use the idea. In some idea submission agreements and in many option agreements, an additional agreement is attached, which the parties will sign if the company wants to use the idea. Sometimes, only the basic business terms are attached. For example, you might attach a sheet that explains the percentage of profits or the per-unit payment due if the idea is used.

- **Nonexclusivity.** This establishes that the arrangement is not exclusive and that you are free to show the idea to others. If the evaluating party wants the exclusive right to consider the idea, it may enter into an option agreement as described above.

Evaluation Agreement

Evaluation Agreement

_____ ("Disclosing Party")

and _____ ("Evaluating Party")

agree as follows:

1. The Submission. Disclosing Party wishes to have Evaluating Party examine and evaluate a submission tentatively known as "_____" and more specifically described in Attachment A to this Agreement (the "Submission") with an eye toward assisting in the exploitation of any products, services, or other commercial exploitation derived from materials contained in the Submission.

2. Review and Evaluation. Evaluating Party wishes to review the Submission and consider whether, in its opinion, the Submission can be marketed to the parties' mutual benefit. The materials furnished by Disclosing Party shall be used by Evaluating Party solely to review or evaluate the Submission. After evaluating the Submission, Evaluating Party will either offer to enter into an agreement with Disclosing Party for exploitation of the idea or return the Submission to Disclosing Party and agree not to market or participate in the marketing or exploitation of any product or service described in or derived from the Submission.

3. Nonexclusivity. Disclosing Party retains the right to submit the Submission to others while it is being evaluated by Evaluating Party.

4. Confidentiality. The materials submitted by Disclosing Party describing the Submission constitute valuable confidential information of Disclosing Party. The loss or outside disclosure of these materials or the information contained within them will harm Disclosing Party economically. Evaluating Party agrees to hold the Submission confidential and will not disclose it to any person other than its evaluators and other members of its staff who have reason to view the Submission.

Evaluation Agreement

Evaluating Party shall exercise a high degree of care to safeguard these materials and the information they contain from access or disclosure to all unauthorized persons. All applicable rights to the Submission remain vested in Disclosing Party. The foregoing provisions apply with equal force to any additional or supplemental submissions and other materials submitted or to be submitted by Disclosing Party to Evaluating Party with respect to the same subject matter of the Submission.

5. Joint Venture. Nothing contained in this Agreement is deemed to constitute either party a partner, joint venturer, or an employee of the other party for any purpose.

6. Severability. If a court finds any provision of this Agreement invalid or unenforceable as applied to any circumstance, the remainder of this Agreement will be interpreted so as best to effect the intent of the parties.

7. Integration. This Agreement expresses the complete understanding of the parties with respect to the subject matter and supersedes all prior proposals, agreements, representations, and understandings. This Agreement may not be amended except in a writing signed by both parties.

8. Waiver. The failure to exercise any right provided in this Agreement does not constitute a waiver of prior or subsequent rights.

This Agreement and each party's obligations are binding on the representatives, assigns, and successors of each party. Each party has signed this Agreement through its authorized representative.

Disclosing Party	Evaluating Party
By: _____	By: _____
Printed Name: _____	Printed Name: _____
Title_____	Title:_____
Date: _____	Date: _____

- **Confidentiality.** This paragraph establishes that you own the idea and any additional submissions and that they must be maintained in confidence.
- **Miscellaneous.** For explanations of the Joint Venture, Severability, Integration and Waiver provisions, see the relevant entries in this book.

Related terms: confidentiality agreement; license agreement.

exclusive dealings

See antitrust.

exculpatory clause

Exculpatory clauses (such as indemnifications, disclaimers, and waivers), relieve one or both parties from liability under certain circumstances. For example, the owner of a parking lot may issue a parking stub agreement that disclaims any liability if the car is damaged in the lot. An exculpatory clause will not be enforced by a court if it is grossly unfair ("unconscionable") or otherwise violates public policy. This is more likely to occur when the clause is a contract of adhesion—a one-sided agreement that the other party wasn't able to negotiate. In certain cases—for example when a landlord seeks to be relieved of any liability for negligence—the states are divided as to whether such clauses should be enforced.

Related terms: contract of adhesion (adhesion contracts); disclaimers; indemnity (hold harmless provision); waiver.

executed contract

An executed contract is one that has been performed by both parties.

E

execution

Execution of a contract refers to the parties actually doing what they promised in the contract. (To "execute" means to carry out or perform an obligation.) This term is often misused to refer to the signing of an agreement, but it actually means the completion of each party's contractual obligations.

executory contract

An executory contract has not been fully performed—that is, either one or both parties still have obligations to fulfill under the agreement.

exemplary damages

See damages, compensatory.

exhibit

See addendum.

face amount

The face amount (also known as the "sum insured") is an insurance term referring to the amount listed on the face or first page of an insurance policy. It commonly refers to the amount that will be paid if certain conditions are met—for example, the death of the insured or the maturity of the policy.

Related term: insurance contract (insurance policy).

failure to perform

Just as it sounds, this refers to one party's failure to meet a material obligation of a contract by a certain time. The failure must be of such importance that it amounts to a material breach—for example, the failure to renovate and repair an apartment complex so that it meets applicable building codes. The term is commonly used in construction contracts.

Related terms: anticipatory breach (anticipatory repudiation); breach (material).

fax signatures

Still using a fax machine? Good news! Faxed contract signatures are presumed to be valid. To make sure, it is wise to include a "counterparts" provision in your agreement. Note, in the absence of a signature, one court determined that the fact that the fax machine had been programmed to print each page with the name of the party did not satisfy the requirement that the agreement be signed.

Related terms: counterparts; e-signature; signatures

Federal Acquisition Reform Act (FARA)

The Federal Acquisition Reform Act (FARA) and the Federal Acquisition Regulations (FAR, found in Title 48 of the United States Code of Federal Regulations) set guidelines, safeguards, fees, whistleblower protections, and administrative rules for federal contracts.

Related term: acquisition agreement (FAR).

fee shifting

Fee shifting is another way of saying that someone else will pay your attorneys' fees (or vice versa). Usually it refers to a contract provision in which the prevailing party in a contract dispute is awarded reasonable attorneys' fees, rather than each party paying its own lawyer.

Related terms: attorneys' fees; boilerplate.

fictitious business name

If you're a sole proprietor, a fictitious business name is any name that doesn't include your last name (or in some states, your full legal name) or seems to suggest that other people are involved in your business (such as John Brown & Associates). In the case of other business entities, a fictitious business name is any name that doesn't precisely match a corporate, partnership, or limited liability company name.

If you do business under a fictitious name (often called a "DBA," for "doing business as"), you probably have to register that name with your state or county government, by filing a registration certificate (along with a fee) and running a statement in a local newspaper. The state wants you to register your name so it can track you down if your business does something wrong, such as ripping off consumers, breaching contracts, or skipping out on loans or bills. There are also some practical reasons to register your name. For example, some banks won't let you open a business bank account under your fictitious name unless you show them a registration certificate. And you may not be able to enforce a contract you signed using your business name unless you can show that you registered it properly.

Related terms: signatures; sole proprietor.

fiduciary (duty, relationship)

Fiduciary, derived from the Latin words *fides* (faith) and *fiducia* (trust or confidence), refers to a person whose relationship with another creates a special obligation of trust, confidence, or responsibility (a "fiduciary duty"). Certain advisors are automatically classified as fiduciaries to those they serve; the list includes legal guardians, executors, trustees, lawyers, partners, title companies, stockbrokers, directors, confidential financial advisors, doctors, and real estate brokers. But regardless of the title or profession, a person who is handling someone else's affairs may be categorized as a fiduciary, especially if that person has superior knowledge and training.

> **EXAMPLE:** Anthony Marshall, the son of socialite Brooke Astor, served as her legal guardian during her waning years (she suffered from dementia). As her legal guardian, he had a fiduciary duty to put her interests above his when advising her and handling her affairs. Instead, he embezzled a few hundred million dollars from the estate and, with help from an attorney, forced his mother to change her will for their benefit. Marshall and the attorney were convicted of fraud and embezzlement in 2009.

Higher standard. Fiduciaries must exercise the highest degree of care required under the law and must fully disclose all material facts that affect their decisions. A fiduciary should not profit from the relationship unless the details are disclosed to the other person, who must consent. For example, it would be a breach of fiduciary duty for a lawyer to represent both parties in a contract negotiation, unless the lawyer told both parties and both consented to the arrangement. Similarly, a stockbroker (who earns commissions on client stock purchases) must tell clients that he benefits when they invest in a company.

Contracts and fiduciaries. A person in a fiduciary position, such as a lawyer, trustee, or executor, may make recommendations or statements regarding contracts to those whose interests they are obligated to protect. A fiduciary may even be a party to such agreements. Because it is difficult to waive fiduciary obligations, a fiduciary who is participating in a business deal must make complete written disclosures of all information relevant to the situation. Breaches of fiduciary duty may lead to costly lawsuits that take the dispute out of the realm of contract law and into the personal injury area, where punitive damages (damages intended to punish the party at fault) and damages for pain and suffering may be available.

Related terms: agent; beneficiary; power of attorney.

financing statement

If you're making a secured loan (one that gives you the right to take the property securing the loan—the collateral—if the borrower doesn't pay), you may want to file a financing statement. Once filed, the statement officially puts any interested parties on notice that you (the lender) have established a security interest in the property. That prevents someone from later arguing that they didn't know you had dibs on the property (for example, if you're battling with a debtor in bankruptcy court). The financing statement (often referred to as a UCC Financing Statement, a UCC statement, or a UCC-1 or UCC-3) is filed in the state where the person who owes the money (the debtor) is located. If a company is the debtor, the statement is filed in the state where the company is registered. Each state's UCC statute designates the office where these statements must be filed, often the registry of deeds and, in some states, the UCC office.

Related term: secured transaction.

First page of the California UCC Financing Statement

UCC FINANCING STATEMENT
FOLLOW INSTRUCTIONS (front and back) CAREFULLY

A. NAME & PHONE OF CONTACT AT FILER [optional]

B. SEND ACKNOWLEDGEMENT TO: (Name and Address)

THE ABOVE SPACE IS FOR FILING OFFICE USE ONLY

1. DEBTOR'S EXACT FULL LEGAL NAME – insert only one debtor name (1a or 1b) – do not abbreviate or combine names

1a. ORGANIZATION'S NAME			
OR 1b. INDIVIDUAL'S LAST NAME	FIRST NAME	MIDDLE NAME	SUFFIX
1c. MAILING ADDRESS	CITY	STATE	POSTAL CODE	COUNTRY

| ADD'L INFO RE ORGANIZATION DEBTOR | 1e. TYPE OF ORGANIZATION | 1f. JURISDICTION OF ORGANIZATION | 1g. ORGANIZATIONAL ID#, if any | ☐ NONE |

2. ADDITIONAL DEBTOR'S EXACT FULL LEGAL NAME – insert only one debtor name (2a or 2b) – do not abbreviate or combine names

2a. ORGANIZATION'S NAME			
OR 2b. INDIVIDUAL'S LAST NAME	FIRST NAME	MIDDLE NAME	SUFFIX
2c. MAILING ADDRESS	CITY	STATE	POSTAL CODE	COUNTRY

| ADD'L INFO RE ORGANIZATION DEBTOR | 2e. TYPE OF ORGANIZATION | 2f. JURISDICTION OF ORGANIZATION | 2g. ORGANIZATIONAL ID#, if any | ☐ NONE |

3. SECURED PARTY'S NAME (or NAME of TOTAL ASSIGNEE of ASSIGNOR S/P) – insert only one secured party name (3a or 3b)

3a. ORGANIZATION'S NAME			
OR 3b. INDIVIDUAL'S LAST NAME	FIRST NAME	MIDDLE NAME	SUFFIX
3c. MAILING ADDRESS	CITY	STATE	POSTAL CODE	COUNTRY

4. This FINANCING STATEMENT covers the following collateral:

5. ALTERNATIVE DESIGNATION [if applicable]: ☐ LESSEE/LESSOR ☐ CONSIGNEE/CONSIGNOR ☐ BAILEE/BAILOR ☐ SELLER/BUYER ☐ AG. LIEN ☐ NON-UCC FILING

6. ☐ This FINANCING STATEMENT is to be filed [for record] (or recorded) in the REAL ESTATE RECORDS.   Attach Addendum   [if applicable] | 7. Check to REQUEST SEARCH REPORT(S) on Debtor(s) [ADDITIONAL FEE]   [optional] ☐ All Debtors ☐ Debtor 1 ☐ Debtor 2

8. OPTIONAL FILER REFERENCE DATA

FILING OFFICE COPY – NATIONAL UCC FINANCING STATEMENT (FORM UCC1) – CALIFORNIA (REV. 01/01/08)

F

forbearance

Forbearance occurs when a lender postpones foreclosing on a debt to give the borrower time to make up overdue payments. It's best to put forbearance arrangements in writing. However, an oral forbearance agreement may be enforceable through estoppel.

Related terms: estoppel; promissory note.

force majeure

To guarantee that you aren't obligated or found in breach of contract after a disaster strikes, most contracts include a force majeure provision (sometimes known as an "act of God" clause) that excuses or delays performance in the event of unforeseen natural disasters. For example, if you have a manufacturing agreement with a company in Kansas and a tornado delays operation of the manufacturing plant for three months, the manufacturing agreement would be suspended for three months. In other words, performance is often excused if it's rendered impractical by a supervening event over which you have no control.

Not for matters under the parties' control. Beware of a force majeure that is used for business contingencies, such as union disputes, technical failures, or supply shortages. The provision is not intended for matters that either party can control.

Force majeure: Sample language

In the event of an act of God, such as fire, riot, act of public enemy, war, or similar cause not within the control of the parties, the party affected by such action has the right to suspend the term of this Agreement. The party may suspend the term only for the duration of any such contingency. Neither party shall suspend its obligation to make payments. At the conclusion of the contingency, the Agreement will be reinstated.

Related terms: act of God; boilerplate.

foreclosure

Foreclosure occurs when you fall behind on your property payments and your lender uses state procedures to sell the property. In some states, the lender has to file a lawsuit to foreclose (judicial foreclosure). In others, the lender can foreclose without going to court (nonjudicial foreclosure). In a judicial foreclosure, there are various notice requirements and, ultimately, a lawsuit and judicial ruling permitting the sale of the property. In a nonjudicial foreclosure, things go faster because no court has to get involved.

Related terms: mortgage; real estate contract.

franchise agreement

Under a franchise arrangement, the franchisee (the person obtaining rights) is permitted (or "licensed") to sell certain products or services and use certain trademarks and other information that belong to the franchisor. In return for these rights, the franchisee pays an ongoing royalty as well as fees for training and other services and, sometimes, a marketing fee to boot. In addition, the franchisee commonly pays a one-time fee upfront (this is sometimes called a disclosure fee, because it unlocks the information that makes the franchise valuable). At the center of the exchange is a document known as a Franchise Disclosure Document (sometimes hundreds of pages long) that usually includes the contract and the rules for the franchise arrangement.

A little history. Credit for the modern franchise arrangement is attributed to Ray Kroc, the mastermind behind the McDonald's franchise. He didn't invent the fast-food restaurant, but he was the first to realize that the efficient and consistent hamburger preparation (pioneered by the McDonald brothers), combined with excellent customer service and aggressive marketing, could be the key to a new industry. The linchpin for Kroc's success, however, was to borrow the franchising idea popularized by Howard Johnson and then to expand it further by acquiring real estate to be leased to the franchisees.

F

Advantages. The advantages of a franchise arrangement are that once the initial investment is made (often in the hundreds of thousands of dollars), the franchisee has instant name recognition and consistent products. This can be a tremendous advantage in competitive industries, such as fast food, car care, hair care, insurance, tax preparation, and commercial cleaning.

Disadvantages. A franchise agreement is brokered with a large company that has superior bargaining power, typically using a form agreement that allows for little modification. That's one reason why, when reviewing franchise agreements, you should keep in mind these potential disadvantages:

- **Exclusivity within territory.** Nearly every franchisor reserves the right to operate anywhere it wants, so an investment in a smoothie franchise may prove unprofitable if another one springs up across the street.

- **Dispute resolution.** Most franchise agreements establish strict rules about how disputes will be resolved and where you must sue. In one case, a Michigan couple that had acquired a Burger King franchise were forced to travel to Florida. Franchise agreements may also place limits on how much you can recover if you win a lawsuit. In addition, these agreements sometimes require franchisees to waive certain legal rights—for example, the right to a jury trial.

- **Royalty payments.** Most franchise agreements require that franchisees make royalty payments to the franchisor each month based on a percentage of sales. These payments (and additional fees) can, if disproportionate to potential revenues, swiftly eat into the franchisee's net profits.

- **Supply pricing.** Does the agreement allow the franchisor to designate the franchisee's supplier of goods and services? A franchisor may claim that this is to maintain quality control, but often franchisors receive payments from the vendors. This may result in the franchisee having to pay higher prices on supplies.

- **Restrictions on post-term competition.** Is there a noncompete clause built into the franchise agreement? By purchasing a franchise, the franchisee may be unwittingly limiting business opportunities for years after the contract expires.
- **Advertising fees.** Many franchisees are obligated to make regular contributions to the franchisor's advertising fund. But franchisors maintain broad discretion over how to administer that fund. In a case against a muffler shop franchise, for example, it was discovered that the company (the franchisor) was using the advertising fund for costs wholly separate from advertising, yet the court ruled in the franchisor's favor, saying that it had no fiduciary duty to its franchisees.
- **Unfair termination.** Even the slightest impropriety, such as being late on a royalty payment or violating the franchise's standard operating procedure, can be sufficient cause for the franchisor to terminate the agreement. While most franchisors are not this strict, the contract sword still hangs over the franchisee's head.

Related terms: license agreement; trademark (servicemark).

fraud (misrepresentation)

Fraud, also known as misrepresentation, is a false statement upon which another party justifiably relies, resulting in damage. In other words, it's a lie that causes damage because someone else had a good reason to believe it—and acted accordingly. Fraud need not be an affirmative statement of false facts; it can also be concealment of the truth.

> **EXAMPLE:** Mr. King and his real estate agent did not disclose to the buyer of a California home that a woman and four children had been murdered in the home a decade earlier. The buyer learned about the incident after the sale. The court agreed with the buyer that the murders were a material fact that affected the

market value of the home, and that concealing that fact could constitute fraud.

For folks like Bernie Madoff, Charles Ponzi (inventor of the Ponzi scheme), and Kenneth Lay, there's something appealing about big bucks deception, especially when all you need to pull it off is some legal-looking paperwork. But as Sophocles said, "Things gained through unjust fraud are never secure." Scam artists and fraudsters are subject to a variety of penalties and remedies, ranging from contract rescission to punitive damages to jail time.

The elements of fraud. To win a fraud case, the injured party must typically prove all of the following elements:

- The defendant made a false and material statement (or in some cases, deliberately concealed a material fact).
- The statement was made intentionally.
- The injured party relied on the statement and was deceived by it.
- The injured party suffered harm because of the deception.

EXAMPLE: In 1963, 18-year-old Peter Roberts was working as a sales clerk at Sears Roebuck when he invented and patented a quick-release ratchet wrench. His boss suggested that they show the wrench to company executives. The executives liked it and offered Roberts $10,000 for an assignment of the patent, but they didn't tell him that they had successfully test-marketed the wrench and planned to convert about 75% of Sears wrenches to Roberts' design. Ten years and 26 million wrenches later, Roberts sued Sears for fraud, claiming the company intentionally downplayed the sales potential for his invention and should have disclosed the true facts. He won his case and was awarded $1 million.

Reliance. In order to prove fraud, the injured person must show that it was reasonable to rely on the false statement, which was material to the ultimate decision. For example, it would be reasonable to rely on someone's promise to sell you a ticket to Paris, but not a ticket to Mars. However, the law cuts victims a lot of slack here. (As one 19th-century judge stated, "no rogue should enjoy his ill-gotten plunder for the simple reason that his victim is by chance a fool.") Even if a reasonable person might doubt the statements or investigate the situation further, "[r]easonable care does not mean that a person must check out all statements made to induce the transaction."

F

> **EXAMPLE:** Mr. Fisher, a test pilot at Boeing, sought a reliable retirement investment. He settled on a franchise called Mr. Harold's Toupee Establishment. The owner of the franchise assured Fisher that Mr. Harold's had thirty years of experience and made the "highest quality" hairpieces "custom to order" in the United States. He also assured Fisher that he could earn $25,000 in annual profit. All of this turned out to be untrue. Customers complained about the low quality of the hair pieces, which were in fact imported from outside the country, were not made to order, and were "junk" according to another maker of hair pieces who inspected the products. Fisher earned only $3,000 in his first year before closing up shop and suing for fraud. Mr. Harold's responded that there was no fraud because (1) Fisher had an obligation to investigate the financial claims and the quality of the wigs before buying a franchise, and (2) much of what Fisher was told didn't play a material role in his decision to invest. The Kansas Supreme Court disagreed. It was difficult for Fisher to investigate the quality of the wigs since the nearest wig supplier was another Mr. Harold's. The court also indicated that false predictions of profits amount to fraud when they are gross misstatements of fact, and when one of the parties has superior knowledge about the subject matter of the agreement (as Mr. Harold's did here).

Types of fraud. Some misrepresentations may be innocent (the party was unaware that it was a lie and had no reason to know otherwise), negligent (the party should have known it was lie but was careless), or intentional (the party knew it was a lie and made the statement with the purpose of misleading the other party). In addition, some misrepresentations may be material to the agreement ("the car has a brand new engine"), and some may not be material ("the car has brand new windshield wiper blades"). Similarly, there is a distinction between nondisclosure (when a party has no legal obligation to mention something) and fraudulent concealment (when a party acts to hide the truth or to prevent the other party from getting at the truth). Some states permit someone to sue over any fraudulent contract statements; other states allow a fraud lawsuit only if the misrepresentation is material to the agreement.

Puffing and opinions. While material misrepresentations are forbidden, a certain amount of hyperbole is an essential lubricant to the wheels of capitalism. The law recognizes this, especially in the area of sales and promotions. For that reason, it is not a misrepresentation to state "This is the hottest car in the world" or "This is the most beautiful house on the street." However, it would be a misrepresentation for a used car salesman to say, "This car is worth $25,000" when the *Bluebook* value is only $2,000. Generally, if the statement is capable of being measured or the puffery is related to specific attributes, the statement may be subject to false advertising claims. In other words, the more the puffery sounds like factual claims, the more likely it is actionable.

> **EXAMPLE:** Pennzoil advertised that its motor oil "outperforms any leading motor oil against viscosity breakdown" and provides "longer engine life and better engine protection." A court determined that these statements were measurable, went beyond puffery, and were "literally false."

The remedies. Fraud is different from other contract claims because the victim has a few choices about how to handle the deception. Typically, someone who is duped into signing a contract (sometimes referred to as "fraud in the inducement") has these remedy options:

- **Innocent or negligent misrepresentation.** When the misrepresentation is innocent or negligent, the defrauded party can rescind (void) the contract and return the parties to where they were before the agreement was made. Usually, this means the defrauded party gets his or her money back and gives back the product that was the subject of the misrepresentations.

- **Intentional misrepresentation.** If the fraudulent statement is intentional—that is, the person knew it was a lie—the defrauded party can either: (1) rescind the contract and return the parties to their precontract state; or (2) enforce the contract (or "affirm" it) and seek damages. The damages, depending on the state, may be the "benefit of the bargain" (the value of the property as represented minus its actual value) or out-of-pocket damages (the amount paid for the property minus its actual value).

F

Because a claim of fraud can be brought as a tort (not a contract claim), it is possible for the injured party to seek special damages to punish the bad behavior ("punitive damages"), as well as damages for pain, suffering, and other emotional distress caused by the fraud.

The crime of fraud. Many federal and state statutes make fraud a crime. These statutes are typically tied to specific activities, including:

- **Securities fraud.** This usually occurs when consumers are induced to buy (or pay too much for) shares of a company's stock because important information about the company is concealed.

- **Insider trading.** This happens when someone with special knowledge (unknown to the public) about a business' activities buys stock in that company.

- **Credit card fraud.** The most common example of this occurs when a person runs up thousands of dollars in credit card charges, knowing that it will be impossible to pay them back.

- **Bankruptcy fraud.** Like credit card fraud, this happens when someone runs up huge debts with the intention of declaring bankruptcy to avoid repayment.

- **Telemarketing fraud.** A typical telemarketing scam might include soliciting for a fake charity.
- **Embezzlement.** This occurs when an employee deceives an employer by siphoning away company accounts.
- **Money laundering.** Money laundering is the financing of legitimate activities with money obtained illegally.
- **Home repair fraud.** A typical example occurs when a consumer makes an advance payment after being duped into signing a scam home repair contract. ("We were driving around the neighborhood and thought your roof needed repair.")

Related terms: defenses (breach of contract); estoppel; fraud in the inducement; fraudulent conveyance; negligence; remedies; tort; unjust enrichment.

fraud in the inducement

Fraud in the inducement is basically another name for fraud or misrepresentation, although it is intended to apply to a specific situation—the use of trickery or falsehoods to entice people to enter into agreements that they would never have signed if they knew the facts. Such behavior sometimes occurs in consumer loan arrangements (for example, when a lender tells a customer that an abnormally high interest rate is standard in the industry).

Related terms: defenses (breach of contract); estoppel; fraud (misrepresentation); fraudulent conveyance; negligence; remedies; tort; unjust enrichment.

fraudulent conveyance

This term, commonly used in connection with bankruptcy proceedings, refers to the transfer (or "conveyance") of real property to someone else for the purpose of preventing creditors from getting hold of it. In other words, it's the old "give it to the brother-in-law to hide it from the bank" scheme.

A fraudulent conveyance can be the basis of a lawsuit when an insolvent property owner schemes to keep assets away from a creditor by giving them to someone friendly to his cause. Most states have adopted some version of the Uniform Fraudulent Transfer Act, which allows a creditor to go after property a debtor transferred to another person without receiving reasonably equivalent value in return. Under these laws, the creditors of the business can void the transfer or get a judgment against the new owner of the assets and seize them to pay the debts.

frustration

See avoidance (and frustration).

further assurances

A further assurances provision is basically a "do the right thing" provision. It requires the parties to take whatever actions are necessary to complete the deal. Of course, you might presume that the parties would take these actions anyway, but this provision is intended to obligate everybody to act in good faith, just in case. The provision originated in real estate contracts, in which buyers wanted assurances from sellers that they would guarantee marketable title. The use gradually spread until the provision became standard boilerplate.

Some legal experts question whether these provisions have any effect. A majority of states imply a standard of good faith and fair dealing into all contracts, and most courts presume that the parties will not obstruct each other's ability to complete a transaction. Nevertheless, this type of provision may give the parties some extra comfort, particularly if there are any lingering doubts as to future cooperation and assistance. It can be helpful in situations where transferring real, personal, or intellectual property requires perfecting the title or some government filing and is also wise when the contract requires obtaining government permits or approvals.

Further assurances: Sample language

Each party shall use all commercially reasonable efforts to take, or cause to be taken, all necessary actions required to complete the obligations contemplated by this Agreement.

F

Related terms: best efforts; guarantee; knowledge (to the best of).

GAAP

This is an acronym for "generally accepted accounting principles," conventions and rules that establish the professional standards for business accounting.

Getting to Yes

This classic book by Roger Fisher and William Ury (Houghton Mifflin) teaches how to negotiate a contract. The authors emphasize that to reach agreement (to get to "yes"), the negotiating parties must:

- separate the people from the issues (that is, remove emotion from the equation)
- look beyond the negotiating parties to see who or what is the real interest or influence affecting each party
- generate options to create a problem-solving environment, and
- neutralize conflict by sticking to objective and easy-to-justify principles of fairness.

Related terms: mediation; negotiation.

golden parachute

A golden parachute refers to an agreement by which a departing executive receives a payment (for example, severance pay, bonuses, or stock options). A golden parachute arrangement can be part of an executive's original employment contract or part of a severance package when the executive leaves. Often, the golden parachute is an element of a retention agreement, an arrangement in which a company contracts to retain key employees after a sale or merger. Some golden parachutes, however, do not require a retention arrangement and may simply be triggered by a termination or a change in company ownership, regardless of whether the executive stays or departs.

> **EXAMPLE:** When Mike Bellotti announced that he was quitting his job as University of Oregon basketball coach to provide commentary at ESPN, many people were surprised to learn that Bellotti would receive $2.3 million from the University. Curiously, there was no prior written agreement in place providing for the payment. Although the university termed the procedure a "buyout," it was the same as a golden parachute—an agreement to step aside quietly when the University terminated his oral contract.

Related term: retention agreement (stay-on-bonus).

good faith and fair dealing

Every party to a contract must act in good faith. This requirement, known as the "implied covenant of good faith and fair dealing," is presumed to be a part of every contract.

The precise definition of good faith and fair dealing may vary from state to state and from contract to contract, but it refers generally to the duty to act honestly and equitably toward the other parties to an agreement. In contracts for the sale of goods, for example, the Uniform Commercial Code defines the good-faith duty to mean "honesty in fact and the observance of reasonable commercial standards of fair dealing."

When one party does not act in good faith, the contract can be considered breached under the laws of most states. In some states, breaching the covenant of good faith and fair dealing may also constitute a tort—a personal injury that gives rise to a legal claim. The good-faith obligation applies only once a contract is in place; it does not apply to precontractual discussions. It applies to attempts to resolve contract disputes, as well.

When good faith and fair dealing is at issue. In order to breach the implied covenant of good faith, the breaching party must exhibit some fairly egregious behavior. That behavior is measured by an objective, reasonable person's standard. Some examples of acts that courts have found to breach the covenant are:

- An insurance company deliberately and unreasonably denied claim requests.
- An employer fired employees specifically to prevent them from being eligible for sales commissions.
- A property owner, seeking to get out of a deal, denied access to the party responsible for constructing a home, thus preventing that party from getting financing.
- A real estate agent took a secret payment from the other party in order to get his client to sign a sales contract.
- A distributor signed an exclusive distribution arrangement with a manufacturer and then "sat" on the product in order to enable a competitor to gain market share.
- A landlord signed a lease for commercial property and then permits the previous tenant to stay over during the new tenant's term.
- The owner of a business sold it and agreeds not to compete, and then loan money to a relative to create a competing business.

Remedies. In the event that a party claims a breach of the implied covenant of good faith and fair dealing, the remedies are usually the same as for breach of contract. That is, the wronged party can seek compensation for damages that might reasonably be foreseen by the parties (excluding punitive damages). If breach of the covenant is treated as a tort (personal injury claim) under state law, then compensatory and punitive damages are also available.

Related terms: fraud (misrepresentation); negligence; remedies; tort.

governing law

See choice of law (governing law).

grace period

A grace period—despite its spiritual ring—is just another term for a cure period, the time between when something (usually a payment) is contractually due and when the party who is owed the money or obligation can take action to enforce it (that is, before the debtor is penalized). For example, if you are late making an insurance payment, the insurance company will continue to insure you during the grace period; typically, you have at least two or three weeks between the date your payment was due and the date the company will cut off your coverage. Grace periods are common in credit arrangements, mortgages, and insurance contracts.

Related terms: boilerplate; cure (cure period); remedies.

grant

A grant is a transfer of rights or property from one party to another. It may involve tangible property (a grant deed for the transfer of real estate, for example) or intangible property (such as a grant clause transferring the right to reproduce digital content). The grant is documented in the grant provision of an agreement. An example of a grant clause for intangible property is shown below.

Grant of rights for website posting: Sample language

Grant of Rights. Publisher grants to Website Company a non-exclusive, worldwide license to use, reproduce, distribute, display, and transmit the Publisher Content set forth in Exhibit A in electronic form via the Internet and third-party networks (including, without limitation, telephone and wireless networks). Such use will be solely: (a) in connection with the presentation of the Publisher Content within the Website Company Sites; or (b) to permit individual users of the Website Company Sites to download and print the Publisher Content.

A grant can also refer to a provision in a loan or security agreement in which a security interest in property (the collateral) is granted to a creditor.

Related terms: license agreement; real estate contract.

gross

Gross, as used in "gross income" or "gross sales," refers to the total amount received prior to making any deductions (such as for taxes). It is often used in conjunction with "net," which refers to the gross minus deductions.

Related terms: gross sales; net.

gross negligence

Negligence is the legal term for actionable carelessness. If someone has a duty to act with care but fails to do so and you are hurt as a result, you may sue for negligence. For example, if a driver rolls through a stop sign and hits you in the crosswalk, you would have a personal injury claim for negligence.

Gross negligence involves much worse behavior. Rather than just carelessness, gross negligence shows a reckless disregard for the rights or safety of others. From a lay persons perspective, the distinction is often that typical negligence is perceived as an "accident"— for example, an old-fashioned rear-ender in traffic—while gross negligence is perceived as being almost willful—for example, a collision caused by someone who is driving while intoxicated or racing. A finding of gross negligence triggers larger court awards, often including punitive damages.

Gross negligence has three common applications in contract law:

- **Insurance contracts.** Many policies provide coverage for negligent acts; after all, one purpose of insurance is to protect you from risks caused by your own carelessness. However, most policies don't cover acts that are grossly negligent.

G

- **Risk allocation.** Clauses in contracts that deal with allocating risk—for example, indemnities, insurance, or warranties—may define the risks according to negligence or gross negligence. For example, one party may seek indemnity only if the other party is grossly negligent
- **Lawsuits related to contracts.** Because negligence is a tort (a personal injury claim), the available damages in these cases go beyond what's available in a straight breach of contract case. For example, if you hire a construction crew who robs your home, and you later learn that the contractor hired convicted felons without screening them, you would have a contract claim for the work that didn't get done—and possibly a tort claim for gross negligence, in which you could seek not only damages for your stolen property, but also compensation for your emotional distress and punitive damages to punish the contractor's reckless behavior.

Related terms: negligence; remedies; tort.

gross sales

Gross sales refers to the total money received from sales during a specific period. It is distinguished from "net sales," which are gross sales minus deductions (deductible expenses permitted under a contract).

Related terms: gross; net.

guarantee

Guarantee has several meanings under contract law:

- **Promise to pay.** It is an alternate spelling for "guaranty," a promise to assume someone else's financial obligations.
- **Pay or play.** In movie contracts, a guarantee is a promise that a performer will receive some payment if the picture is canceled or is made without the performer (an arrangement also known as "pay or play").

- **Warranty.** Guarantee is sometimes used as a synonym for a "warranty," a promise or an assurance by one party as to the quality, specification, conditions, or accuracy of some activity or goods.

Related term: representations and warranties.

guaranteed minimum annual royalty (GMAR)

A guaranteed minimum annual royalty (GMAR) payment is a yearly advance against anticipated royalties. A GMAR is used in licensing and manufacturing agreements when a party who owns a valuable innovation, trademark, or creative work (the "licensor") wants to be assured of receiving at least a certain amount of money each year (paid by the "licensee"). Typically, the licensee must pay the GMAR each year, regardless of whether the product has earned back the previous year's payment.

> **EXAMPLE:** Bunkee Toys licenses the right to make Bob's patented water gun. The contract requires Bunkee to pay Bob $10,000 each year as an advance against Bob's anticipated royalties. Bunkee paid the $10,000 in 2010, and despite the fact that Bob's toy actually earned only $9,000 in royalties that year, Bunkee still has to come up with another $10,000 for Bob in 2011.

On the other hand, if the earned royalties exceed the GMAR, the company must always pay the difference. For example, if Bob earned royalties of $11,000 in one year, Bunkee must pay Bob the extra $1,000 at the end of the year. Below is an example of a GMAR provision.

G

Guaranteed Minimum Annual Royalty Payment: Sample language

Guaranteed Minimum Annual Royalty Payment. In addition to any other advances or fees, Licensee shall pay a guaranteed minimum annual royalty (the "GMAR") as follows: $_____ . Licensee shall pay the GMAR to Licensor annually on _____ . The GMAR is an advance against royalties for the twelve-month period commencing upon payment. Royalty payments based on Net Sales made during any year of this Agreement will be credited against the GMAR due for the year in which such Net Sales were made. In the event that annual royalties exceed the GMAR, Licensee shall pay the difference to Licensor. Any annual royalty payments in excess of the GMAR will not be carried forward from previous years or applied against the GMAR.

Related terms: license agreement; royalty.

guaranty/guarantor

A guaranty (also spelled "guarantee" and "guarantie") is a promise by one person or entity (the "guarantor") to pay the debt or assume the financial obligations of another. A guaranty is one type of contract that must be in writing to be valid. (This requirement, imposed by the statute of frauds, is intended to make sure that the contract is authentic and the parties knew what they were getting into.)

Historically, a guaranty was considered to be different from a surety, a contract in which one person agreed to be jointly liable for the debt of another. Because both arrangements have the same result—somebody else is on the hook for the debt—those distinctions have largely disappeared; most courts now consider a guaranty and a surety as synonyms.

Related terms: cosigner; promissory note; secured transaction; statute of frauds.

handshake agreement

Also known as a gentlemen's agreement, a handshake agreement is another way of referring to an oral agreement. The idea is that gentlemen are true to their word, so no documents are required to ensure that the parties live up to their obligations. (Gentlemen or no, certain contracts must be in writing to be enforced, per the statute of frauds.)

Related term: oral contracts.

handwritten changes

Parties sometimes edit contracts by hand, either before or after the contract is signed. In general, the same rules apply regardless of when the changes are made: The changes are valid only if both parties agree to them.

Changes before execution. If a handwritten change to an unsigned contract is considered "material"—in other words, it affects the other party's decision to accept or reject the deal—then the change will be considered a counteroffer, not a modification.

The resulting contract will be enforced only if the party who made the change can show that the other party knew of the change and accepted it. Even if the change is *not* material, it can still wreak havoc if one party later claims not to have known about it. A court may sever the changed portion or, in rare cases, invalidate the whole agreement. The solution to this problem? Either rewrite the entire contract to include the changes or have all of the parties initial the changed portion, to show that they read it.

Changes after execution. Handwritten changes to an existing contract are generally ill-advised. Many written contracts describe how and when modifications can be made, and handwritten changes typically aren't permitted. This means that, even if both parties intended to abide by a change when it was made, a court may not enforce the change later. A better solution is to either prepare a separate amendment as required by the contract or restate and simply create and sign a new version of the contract.

Related terms: accord and satisfaction; amendment; oral contracts.

hold harmless

See indemnity (hold harmless provision).

illegal contract

A contract is illegal if it violates the law or public policy. (Public policy refers to the moral and ethical principles upon which the legal system is created.) Courts will not enforce an illegal contract.

> **EXAMPLE:** In the 1890s, two British thieves, Everet and Williams, entered into a contract to divide their spoils. When Williams failed to honor the agreement, Everet sued. The British courts refused to enforce the agreement because it violated the law and public policy.

The rationale for not enforcing illegal contracts is to deter their creation.

> **EXAMPLE:** Two contractors who were both bidding for a public job entered into a secret agreement under which they would share the profits if either of them won (an illegal practice because it fraudulently restrains trade). One company won the bid but later refused to share the profits. The other contractor sued. The Supreme Court refused to enforce the contract, stating, "To refuse to grant either party to an illegal contract judicial aid for the enforcement of his alleged rights under it tends strongly towards reducing the number of such transactions to a minimum."

Two bases for illegality. A contract may be illegal if (1) the consideration is illegal (for example, one party promises to pay with stolen merchandise); or (2) the subject or purpose of the contract is illegal (for example, the parties agree to provide gambling equipment or facilities in a state where gambling is illegal).

Sometimes, either the consideration or the purpose of the contract is illegal, but not both. For example, the parties may have a perfectly legitimate construction contract (a legal purpose), except that the contractor will be paid in cocaine (an illegal form of consideration). Or, the parties may be making an illicit drug deal (an illegal purpose), with the purchaser using his earnings from a day job to pay for the drugs (legal consideration). Sometimes, both the consideration and the underlying contract are illegal, the classic example being an extortion contract (extortion is a crime, and the consideration is a promise *not* to hurt someone who pays up, also illegal).

Direct versus indirect aid. A contract is not illegal if it assists only *indirectly* in the commission of a crime that is not considered "serious."

> EXAMPLE: Graham, the owner of an illegal exotic animal business, contracts to purchase 200 pounds of pet food from PetStar. After the food is delivered, Graham is arrested for illegally selling an ocelot. PetStar sues Graham for the money he owes for the food under the contract. Graham tries to get out of paying by claiming that the contract is void because it has an illegal object—to provide supplies for an illegal enterprise. But, because selling exotic animals is not considered to be a serious crime and because it is not illegal to sell pet food, a court would likely enforce the agreement, even though it provided indirect assistance to Graham in his illegal enterprise.

Some exceptions. As a general rule, an illegal contract is presumed to be void and unenforceable. However there are some exceptions:

- **Severable provisions.** If the illegal aspect of the contract is severable (and that portion doesn't go to the "heart" of the agreement), the remainder of the contract may be enforced. For example, if a payment clause in a construction contract contains an illegal penalty provision, that penalty provision may be severed and the rest of the agreement enforced.

- **Divisible/separable consideration.** In a variation on the severable provision exception described above, legal portions of an agreement may be enforced if they are supported by "separable consideration." For example, a man made an oral agreement to sell his wheat for $5,000, his tractor for $3,000, and his marijuana for $25,000. That last part is probably unenforceable. However, a court could sever the illegal drug sale from the agreement and enforce the other two purchases (the wheat and the tractor).

- **Locus poenitentiae.** (Latin for "place of repentance.") Even if a contract is illegal (and, therefore, void), one party may recover damages if that party "repents" and disavows the contract and its illegal purpose before any illegal act takes place. For example, if Faith makes a down payment on a tasty ocelot from Graham's exotic animal palace, but then changes her mind (repents) and asks for her money back before the animal is delivered, she is entitled to get her money back. A court will enforce this exception under a quasi-contract theory: The court isn't enforcing the illegal contract itself, but is instead enforcing the repenting party's right to get out of it.

- **Not in pari delicto.** (Latin for "equal fault.") Under this theory, the party who bears a smaller share of the blame for an illegal contract may be entitled to compensation. It works as follows: If Party A has provided some benefit to Party B (for example, by paying money or delivering goods), and Party A is not as blameworthy as Party B in regard to the illegal act (not in pari delicto), then a court may allow Party A to recover its consideration under a quasi-contract theory. This rule doesn't apply if the illegal aspect of the contract violates public morals; in that case, everyone is considered blameworthy and nobody can rely on this exception.

EXAMPLE: Wickstead contracts with Ray to sell him stock in Wickstead, Inc. Ray pays $20,000 for the stock. The contract is illegal because it violates blue-sky laws (laws that regulate the sale of securities). However, Ray is less blameworthy (not in pari dilecto) than Wickstead, who owns the company and knows the laws that regulate securities sales. Violations of blue-sky laws are not considered to be against public morals (for example, as compared to a crime that causes injury to a person). Therefore, a court is likely to require Wickstead to give Ray back his $20,000 as a quasi-contract remedy.

Timing counts. How courts treat an illegal arrangement also sometimes depends on timing. If the law changes after a contract was made (turning what was a legal contract into an illegal one), the contract is treated as "impossible" and performance is excused. If an offer was made and the law changed prior to acceptance, the offer is considered terminated.

Related terms: fraud (misrepresentation); impossibility (of performance); public policy.

implied contract

A contract is implied if it is neither written nor stated explicitly, but is instead created by law or circumstances. An implied contract can be either "implied in fact" or "implied in law."

Implied in fact. An implied-in-fact contract is made when the conduct and actions of the parties demonstrate an intent to create a contract, even though there is no express documentation or agreement.

EXAMPLE: For the past ten years, Don has brought his vintage Chevy into Paul's Garage for a tune-up on his birthday, January 10th. He usually drops it off after hours and picks it up the following evening. On January 10, 2010, Don drops off his

Chevy at Paul's Garage without saying anything. An implied contract for a tune-up is created by the conduct of the parties.

Implied in law. An implied-in-law contract (also known as a quasi-contract) is not really a contract but simply an obligation that the court will enforce to achieve fairness (or, alternatively, to prevent one party from being "unjustly enriched").

EXAMPLE: Emily is new to town, so she's not sure what to do when her Toyota breaks down one night. She pushes it to Paul's Garage, which is nearby, and leaves it there, hoping to have it towed home the next day. She leaves a sign, "Needs fixing. I'll come by tomorrow." The next day, Paul assumes that a customer has dropped the car off for repair and fixes it. When Emily returns, she happily realizes that Paul has fixed her car and drives off without paying him. Even though no contract was created—because there was no offer or acceptance—a court will, out of fairness, require Emily to pay the reasonable value of Paul's services.

Related terms: statute of frauds; unjust enrichment; void (voidable).

implied covenant of best efforts

See best efforts.

implied covenant of good faith and fair dealing

See good faith and fair dealing.

impossibility (of performance)

When unforeseeable events make it impossible to perform an existing contract, a court may step in and excuse performance. This principle, referred to as "the doctrine of supervening impossibility," was established by a British court in the 1863 case, *Taylor v. Caldwell.*

EXAMPLE: Caldwell and Bishop owned a concert hall. They contracted to rent it to Taylor and Lewis, who planned to use it for four massive events (which would include a forty-piece military band, fireworks, a ballet, aquatic and circus events, and shooting exhibitions). A week before the first event, the concert hall burned down. Taylor and Lewis sued Caldwell and Bishop, claiming they had to either provide the venue or pay damages. A British court ruled that the contract was premised on the fact that the concert hall existed. Because the hall was destroyed by the fire (and through no fault of either party), the court found that it was impossible to fulfill the terms of the contract, and all parties were excused from their obligations.

Destruction of contract subject matter. The principle of impossibility is usually triggered by the destruction (or similar utter unavailability) of the contract's subject matter. However, the fact that something (for example, a wheat harvest, a tour bus, or a telephone system) has been destroyed does not necessarily guarantee that a court will excuse performance. When considering whether performance is impossible, courts examine (1) the event causing the destruction (whether it was unexpected or within either party's control), (2) whether the destruction actually makes performance impossible (or whether performance could be completed in another reasonable way), and (3) whether one of the parties was better prepared to assume the risk of the event. For example, did the contract provide or imply alternate courses of performance or include insurance for such events?

Other bases for impossibility. Other events besides destruction may make performance impossible. These include:

- **Apprehension of danger.** If dangerous conditions develop that may cause one or both parties to fear for their safety, the parties may be excused from performance. For example, an agreement to cater an event may be impossible if a bomb threat has been called in at the event.

- **Death or illness.** If death or serious illness prevents one party from personally performing, a court will relieve the parties from their obligations. This is subject to some exceptions. The obligation must require personal performance—for example, a theatrical performance, a commissioned artwork, or a lecture—and the parties must treat it as nondelegable (that is, neither party would accept some third party stepping in at the last minute to perform the services).
- **Change in law.** If, after the parties enter into the contract, laws or regulations change so as to make performance illegal, the contract may be excused for impossibility. For example, a company that contracts to export cryptography software to Dubai would be excused from performing if a regulation were subsequently passed prohibiting the export of such programs to Dubai.
- **Failure of delivery method.** If it is impossible to deliver goods or to make payments as provided in the agreement, performance may be excused (for example, if the port to which you were supposed to deliver the goods has been closed). Before finding impossibility, a court will look to see whether a commercially reasonable substitute for delivery or payment is available.

Impossibility provisions. In order to create some predictability in the face of unpredictable events, parties to a contract may include provisions that anticipate impossibility, such as:

- **Force majeure (or "acts of God") provisions.** These usually excuse or postpone performance if a natural disaster hits.
- **Strike clauses.** Striking employees may make it impossible to perform a contract. However, a court is less likely to excuse performance if the striking employees work for one of the parties (versus working for third parties). For that reason, contracts sometimes include "strike clauses" establishing what will happen in the event of a strike.
- **Changed site condition.** In construction contracts, it's common to include a "changed site condition" or "differing site

conditions" provision. These provisions anticipate the possibility that the conditions at a site may change from what is expected (for example, buried logs may be discovered, making it more difficult to pour a foundation) and establish what will happen if they do. Usually, this requires some kind of equitable (fair) adjustment. For example, the parties might agree that a higher price may be changed if unforeseen conditions make the job more difficult. The purpose of these clauses has been to shift (or share) the risk of adverse subsurface or latent physical conditions from the contractor, who normally bears these risks under a fixed-price contract.

Related terms: act of God; force majeure; impracticability (of performance).

impracticability (of performance)

Impracticability of performance is a close cousin to impossibility (in many states, they are considered synonymous). Impracticability occurs when it is possible but financially impractical to perform the contract due to unforeseen changes.

Courts are often reluctant to allow parties to avoid performing contractual obligations because of impracticability. The thinking is that the parties negotiated the arrangement and should be bound by its financial terms. However, case law originating in California has supported the doctrine of impracticability. These cases indicate that where the cost of performance is considerably more than anticipated in the contract and the increase is due to unforeseen factors, performance will be excused. For example, impracticability may apply if the ability to supply goods is made more costly due to wartime shortages, embargos, or similar events. Also, the Uniform Commercial Code, a set of rules for contracts for goods, establishes that performance may be excused when the "failure of presupposed conditions" creates an impracticability. Keep in mind that courts will not apply the doctrine of impracticability simply because the price for goods shoots up (or falls down) as a result of natural market fluctuations.

Related terms: act of God; force majeure; impossibility (of performance).

incidental damages

See damages, incidental.

including without limitation

This phrase (or its variation, "included but not limited to") is intended as a method of indicating that a list of things in a contract is not exhaustive—that is, simply listing a few of the items in a category doesn't preclude other things from falling within that category, as well.

> **EXAMPLE:** A contract provides that, "The software will operate on mobile handheld computing devices, including without limitation BlackBerrys, Palms, iPhones, Androids, and iPads." The examples of devices in the contract is illustrative—to demonstrate what mobile handheld devices are—and does not limit the contract to just those devices.

Related terms: antecedent, rule of the last (also last antecedent rule, last antecedent doctrine); interpretive provisions; mistake; plain meaning rule; rules of interpretation (rules of construction).

incorporation by reference

Incorporation by reference is a legal drafting mechanism that enables the parties to include language from one document within another. It's commonly used in contracts when referring to other contracts, exhibits, attachments, or addendums. For example, two companies enter into a confidentiality agreement to discuss a merger. A few weeks later, they decide to go ahead with the merger. They want to retain the confidentiality provisions from the first contract, so they include language in the merger contract stating "the Confidentiality Agreement entered into on June 1, 2010 and its obligations are incorporated by reference into this Agreement."

Related term: addendum

indemnity (hold harmless provision)

Indemnity is a powerful shield that requires one party to defend the other against certain legal claims. Indemnity is used because parties to contracts often want to limit their own contractual risks or shift some of those risks to the other party. For example, someone hiring a contractor does not want to be responsible if the contractor's employee injures a third party while on the job. One of the most popular tools for limiting third-party liability is an indemnity provision. Practically speaking, this means providing a legal defense (paying for a lawyer) and paying any damages awarded.

> **EXAMPLE:** Katy hires Flambo, a website creation company, to build her corporate website. The contract states that if a third party sues Katy over copyright or trademark claims arising from Flambo's construction of the site, Flambo will defend the lawsuit and pay any damages. Unbeknownst to Katy, Flambo steals its website content from CNN. CNN learns of the theft and sues Katy for copyright infringement. Flambo must defend the lawsuit and pay any damages awarded to CNN for the theft.

Of course, the obligation to indemnify is effective only if the indemnifying party is able to pay. If the indemnifying party is insolvent, the indemnity provision is worthless.

Indemnity provisions are also sometimes referred to as "hold harmless" provisions because the language for an indemnity provision often states "company A shall hold company B harmless from any losses …."

Controlling indemnity. If you must indemnify the other party, consider these strategies:

- **Beware of broad indemnity provisions.** Avoid indemnity provisions that are unusually broad. For example, stay away from a provision that indemnifies the other party for any breach of the agreement. Try to rein in an indemnity clause so that it applies to specific injuries to third parties only, and to situations that you can control. That way, you can avoid having to pay out on an indemnity provision by avoiding the conduct that triggers the provision.

- **Require prompt written notice of the third-party claim.** It would be unfair if the other party ignored a claim or settled it secretly without your knowledge and then came after you for payment.

- **Attempt to limit it to a lawsuit or even a final decision by a court.** If you are indemnifying another party, try to limit your obligation to situations where a lawsuit is filed. That prevents you from having to pay simply because somebody is threatening to sue or complaining about something. A more protective standard would require you to pay only if you lost the legal battle with the third party.

- **Attempt to cap the indemnity.** This is perhaps the most difficult modification to get the other party to agree to because it limits your liability to a specific amount—for example, you never must pay more to indemnify than you earned under the agreement.

Other factors that may matter to the parties are whether the party being indemnified can participate in the defense with counsel of its own choosing and at its own expense; and whether the matter can be settled solely by one party or requires consent of both.

Indemnity provisions are often one-sided—that is, one party provides the indemnity and the other stands to receive it. In some cases, the parties seek mutual indemnity, where each indemnifies for its own obligations. Below is a mutual indemnity provision incorporating many of the elements discussed above.

Mutual indemnity: Sample language

> **Indemnity.** Each party shall indemnify the other and hold the other harmless from any damages and liabilities (including reasonable attorneys' fees and costs), arising from any breach of each party's respective warranties as defined in this Agreement provided (a) such claim arises solely out of a breach of the warranties, (b) the party providing indemnification (the indemnitor) gives the other party (the indemnitee) prompt written notice of any such claim; (c) such indemnity is applicable only in the event of a final decision by a court of competent jurisdiction from which no right to appeal exists; and (d) that the maximum amount due from indemnitor to indemnitee will not exceed the amounts paid to indemnitor under this Agreement from the date that indemnitor notifies indemnitee of the existence of such a claim.

Related terms: boilerplate; exculpatory clause; representations and warranties.

indenture

This archaic term applies to a contract that binds an individual either to repay a debt or to perform services. The United States was established with considerable help from indentured servants who were bound to work for several years in return for their passage to North America.

Related term: specific performance.

independent contractor

An independent contractor (IC) is a person who typically provides specialized services on a per-project basis for a number of businesses. Jesus Christ was an independent contractor (a carpenter) and so was Michelangelo (a commissioned painter). ICs include plumbers, architects, and bookkeepers, as well as piano tuners, tree trimmers, and dog trainers.

ICs are typically hired to perform services that require a certain level of skill, experience, and sometimes licensing. You can hire an IC on an ongoing basis—for example, to maintain your website periodically or to do your accounting each year. ICs also work by the job—for example, to remodel a home office or help a business launch a product line.

Independent contractor versus employee. Someone who works for you is either an IC or an employee. The distinction is important. An employee is not running his or her own business but is working for yours, following the rules you set and meeting the standards you require, often at your workplace. You can exercise a lot more control over an employee, from setting work hours to imposing a dress code to dictating exactly how the employee does every aspect of the job. Although you can hire an employee for a short-term project (such as helping you with a seasonal mailing crunch or gift-wrapping items during a holiday rush), it's more common to hire employees on an open-ended basis, until the work runs out or the employee quits or doesn't meet your expectations.

Some companies misclassify workers as ICs when they are really employees. There are some incentives to hiring ICs: The employer doesn't have to pay or withhold payroll taxes, provide benefits, pay unemployment, provide workers' compensation insurance, or follow worker protections laws (on everything from minimum wage to prohibitions on discrimination) for ICs, as it does for employees. But misclassifying employees can be costly, and there are plenty of ways you can get caught if you misclassify a worker. For example, if someone you hired as an IC applies for unemployment, your state's unemployment insurance agency might decide that the worker was really an employee—and is entitled to unemployment compensation. Something similar might happen with the Internal Revenue Service, or your state's workers' compensation board or tax agency.

Independent contractor agreements. Independent contractor agreements are used for a wide range of services—for example, child care, home repair, commissioned artwork, housekeeping, consulting, training, or a host of other tasks. Despite the differences, most IC agreements share (in addition to standard boilerplate provisions) the following common elements:

- **Description of services.** The agreement should describe in as much detail as possible what the contractor is expected to do. You must word the description carefully to show only the results you expect the IC to achieve; if you explain how to achieve the results, you might be creating an employment relationship. For example, you can state that a room should be painted with one coat of primer and two coats of paint. But you should not state that the painter must wear a white uniform and gloves, remove paint by hand scraping, take lunch at a particular time, and so on.

- **Payment.** This provision explains how the contractor will be compensated, usually by fixed fee (sometimes in installments) or by a unit of time.

- **Expenses.** The expense provision usually includes an itemization of the expected expenses and the method of payment or reimbursing the IC.

- **Tools, equipment, and office space.** The contract should explain who should supply the tools and equipment for the job (usually the contractor) and where the work will be performed.

- **Permits and licenses.** This provision explains which party is responsible for obtaining the proper permissions and licenses needed to perform the tasks.

- **Ownership of work product.** In some types of IC agreements, the ownership of the product can be a key issue. For example, when hiring a wedding photographer, the copyright for the wedding photos is owned by the photographer unless the IC agreement contains a provision transferring ownership (either an assignment or a "work for hire" provision).

- **Taxes and insurance.** This clause typically establishes that all tax obligations and insurance will be paid for by the IC.
- **Indemnity.** Some IC agreements require the IC to pay for any third-party claims brought against the client as result of the IC's work.
- **Workers' compensation insurance.** Many IC agreements require the IC to carry workers' compensation insurance for both the IC and any employees of the IC.
- **Term and termination.** In this section, the parties set out the length of the agreement and how it can be terminated. Often, either party has the right to terminate, or alternatively, either party may terminate with cause (that is, a material violation of the agreement).
- **Independent contractor status.** In this provision, the parties mutually declare that the contractor is an independent contractor, not an employee. A typical provision follows.

Independent contractor status provision: Sample language

> **Independent Contractor.** Contractor is an independent contractor, and neither Contractor nor Contractor's employees or contract personnel are Client's employees. In its capacity as an independent contractor, Contractor agrees that Contractor has the right to perform services for others during the term of this Agreement. Contractor also has the sole right to control and direct the means, manner, and method by which the services required by this Agreement will be performed as well as the right to hire assistants as subcontractors or to use employees to provide the services required by this Agreement. Contractor understands that neither Contractor nor Contractor's employees or contract personnel are eligible to participate in any employee pension, health, vacation pay, sick pay, or other fringe benefit plan of Client.

Simply making a statement like this will not prevent the IRS or some other government agent from claiming that the parties are really in an employee-employer relationship. In other words, actions speak louder than words. The statement helps, but what will seal the deal is how you and the worker act and interact.

To guard against IRS misclassification disasters, some IC agreements include the following language:

Waiver of rights: Sample language

If Contractor is subsequently classified by the IRS as a common law employee, Contractor expressly waives any rights to any benefits to which contractor was, or might have become, entitled.

CAUTION

Language like this may not be enforced. As with any waiver of legal rights, a court will devote special scrutiny to this type of statement and may even sever it from an agreement if it is considered unduly oppressive.

Related terms: construction agreement; service agreement; works made for hire.

injunction (injunctive relief)

If one party has breached an agreement or been found liable for some other form of injury or damage, a court may issue an injunction: a court order requiring the losing party in the lawsuit to either take or refrain from taking some action. Sometimes, an injunction is issued while a lawsuit is pending, to maintain the status quo while the court hears the evidence and decides what to do.

EXAMPLE: On May 3, 2010 certain versions of Microsoft Office disappeared from sales channels. The software giant was on the receiving end of an injunction ordering it to stop selling the product after that date because it contained certain processes that infringed a patent. The injunction accompanied a $200 million verdict against Microsoft.

A party that violates an injunction will be considered to be in contempt of court and subject to sanctions. This makes the injunction a highly sought remedy in certain types of contract litigation, for example, a dispute in which a confidentiality agreement was breached.

> **EXAMPLE:** Mr. Huffines invented a new type of garbage compressor. He confided his trade secret designs to the Hyde Corporation, which manufactured it for more than a year under a license agreement and then terminated the contract. However, Hyde continued to manufacture the device after canceling the contract. Huffines sued and won his lawsuit against Hyde Corporation. As part of its judgment, the court issued an injunction prohibiting the Hyde Corporation from any further use of Huffines' trade secrets.

Three types of injunctions. Injunctions come in three forms:

- **Temporary injunctions or temporary restraining orders** (TROs). These are issued in the earliest stages of litigation and generally last only for a week or two, giving the court time to decide whether to grant a preliminary injunction. They are restricted to situations in which the person seeking the injunction is on the brink of suffering some irreparable injury and needs to stop some action immediately while the case is decided. For example, a temporary injunction might be issued to prevent a neighbor from beginning work on an addition that would block another neighbor's view or to prevent a competitor from releasing a new product that allegedly appropriates another company's trade secret.
- **Preliminary injunctions.** Courts issue preliminary injunctions prior to the start of trial if there is a strong showing that one party is likely to prevail at the trial and that party will suffer greater economic harm than the other if the injunction is not granted. Preliminary injunctions can last as long as it takes to get to trial, sometimes even years.

- **Permanent injunctions.** These are, as billed, permanent prohibitions against taking or refusing to take a particular action. They are issued as part of the final judgment in a case.

Bonds. Before issuing a temporary or preliminary injunction, the court may require the party seeking the injunction to post a bond to compensate the other party for any harm caused by the injunction in the event that the party seeking the injunction does not prevail in the end.

Injunctive relief provisions. Getting an injunction can be expensive and time-consuming. In order to avoid some of that legal work, some agreements include a provision like the one below. Such provisions are basically an admission by the parties that the harm caused by a breach would be irreparable and, therefore, that an injunction should be granted in case of breach. This provision enhances a party's ability to obtain an injunction by eliminating one argument the other party could make. Ultimately, however, it's up to the judge whether to order an injunction; your agreement can't force the judge to do so.

Injunctive relief: Sample language

> **Injunctive Relief.** The parties understand and acknowledge that any breach of this Agreement may cause the nonbreaching party irreparable harm, the amount of which may be difficult to ascertain. Therefore, the parties agree that the nonbreaching party may apply to a court of competent jurisdiction for an order restraining and enjoining the following activities: _____, and for such other relief as the nonbreaching party shall deem appropriate. Such right of the nonbreaching party is to be in addition to the remedies otherwise available at law or in equity.

Related terms: remedies; specific performance.

installment contract (divisible/severable contracts)

Installment contracts are distinguished by the fact that they are performed in connection with a series of periodic or incremental payments, deliveries, or other actions. The contract usually sets forth the specific dates or events that trigger these sequential actions. Typical examples would be a lease, mortgage, or vendor contract. Under the Uniform Commercial Code (a set of laws adopted in some form by all states), an installment contract is defined as an agreement that authorizes or requires the delivery of goods in separate lots that will each be separately accepted—for example, a contract to supply coffee supplies or toner cartridges weekly to an office.

Divisible or severable. Installment contracts are sometimes referred to as severable or divisible contracts. This status affects what happens when one party breaches the agreement. If a divisible contract is breached, then the breaching party can still recover for each portion of the contract that has been performed minus any damages caused by the breach.

> **EXAMPLE:** Rocky signs a one-year contract to work for Lisa as a personal assistant at $300 a week. After four weeks, Rocky quits. Even though Rocky breached the agreement by quitting, he is still owed the four weeks of pay, minus any damages that Lisa may have against Rocky for the breach.

Most installment contracts are divisible. However, there may be cases where an installment contract is not considered divisible. The test is whether the parties would have been willing (had they considered it) to accept the partial or installment payments or whether the installments are simply for the convenience of spreading out payment as the work progresses. Under this analysis, an employment agreement is usually considered to be divisible, while a construction agreement with incremental payments may not be considered divisible because the parties' overriding goal is to complete the construction.

Related terms: construction agreement; severability (savings clause); Uniform Commercial Code.

insurance contract (insurance policy)

An insurance contract (or insurance policy) is a risk allocation agreement in which an insurance company (the insurer) agrees to pay the holder of the policy (the insured) upon the occurrence of a specific event. These contracts are unique in that the insured only "wins" (receives the payout) if an unfortunate event occurs. Or, as satirist Ambrose Bierce defined insurance: "an ingenious modern game of chance in which the player is permitted to enjoy the comfortable conviction that he is beating the man who keeps the table." Policies are commonly issued for insuring against property damage, ill health and disability, the need for long-term care, death, automobile accidents, malpractice, business interruption, and claims of personal liability.

Common elements. Modern insurance contracts are constructed by establishing coverage for broad categories of claims—for example, fire, natural disasters, death—and then narrowing those categories down with a series of exclusions and conditions. The cover page (or "declarations page") is customized to indicate the important details of the policy and the remainder is typically an assembly of form documents. Because of the unequal bargaining power between the insurance company and the insured and because most policies are nonnegotiable form agreements, insurance policies are traditionally considered contracts of adhesion.

The following terms are common to most insurance contracts:

- **Claim.** A claim is your notification to an insurance company that you believe a payment is due to you under the terms of the policy.
- **Commission.** This is a fee or percentage of the premium you pay to an insurance broker or agent.
- **Conditions.** These are the duties and events that must occur to justify the coverage.

- **Declarations.** The declarations page serves as a cover sheet and is a summary of all the basic information in the policy, such as the name of the insured, the addresses, the risks covered, and policy period.
- **Deductible.** The deductible is the amount of out-of-pocket expenses that you must pay before the insurance payment begins. For example, if your deductible for business equipment loss is $1,000 per year and you suffer $1,000 in damages in one year, there will be no payment under the policy.
- **Endorsement.** An endorsement is paperwork that is added to your policy and that reflects any changes or clarifications in the policy.
- **Exclusions.** Exclusions are things your insurance policy will not cover.
- **Policy.** The policy is the written document or contract between you and the insurance company.
- **Premium.** The premium is the periodic payment you pay to the insurance company for the benefits provided under the policy.
- **Rider.** A rider is a special provision attached to a policy that either expands or restricts the policy.
- **Underwriter.** This is the person or company that evaluates your business and determines what insurance you may qualify for.

Regulation. Insurance companies and insurance contracts are primarily regulated under state laws (most states have an administrative agency to oversee insurance companies doing business within the state). The primary issues that arise in insurance company disputes is that the insurer unjustifiably or unfairly denies a claim, the insurer delays paying a claim, or the insurer places an unfair burden of proving a claim on the insured. Claims against insurers typically involve allegations of bad faith (insurance companies are held to a higher standard of care than most commercial enterprises), breach of contract, or violation of state insurance statutes. In some states, claims may be brought as a lawsuit or via a complaint to a state administrative agency.

Related terms: bilateral contract (versus unilateral contract); contract of adhesion (adhesion contracts).

intangible property (intangible assets)

Intangible property is any property that you cannot hold in your hand. In other words, it is abstract rather than material and is usually represented by a document—for example, a stock certificate or a patent. Intangible property relates to contracts in three important ways:

- **Transfer and sale of intangibles.** Contracts for the sale or license of intangibles are an essential element of international commerce. From patent licenses to franchise agreements, these contracts document the grant or transfer of ownership and also provide evidence of the market value for these assets.
- **Intangible property as business assets.** It is reported that if all of the physical assets of the Coca Cola Company were destroyed, the company could still sell its prime intangible asset—the Coca-Cola trademark—for billions of dollars. (And imagine what it could charge for its number one trade secret: the recipe for Coke.) The value of intangible property is an important part of valuing a business, and intangibles often figure prominently when a business is sold. Intangible assets include a wide range of nonphysical assets from customer goodwill (the reputation and relationship with customers a business has built over time) to trade secrets (confidential information not known to competitors).
- **Contracts *as* intangible property.** As explained above, the value of a purchased business includes the value of its intangible assets, which, in turn, includes the value of contracts to which the business is a party. For example, a retention agreement that requires employees to continue to work for the company after a sale may have value as an intangible asset, as might a favorable business lease or vendor contract.

Related terms: intellectual property; license agreement.

integration

In the process of negotiating and drafting a contract, the parties may make many oral or written statements. Some of these statements make it into the final agreement; others don't. An integration clause (sometimes called an "entire understanding" provision) states that the contract you are signing is the last word on the contract's terms; neither you nor the other party can rely on statements made in the past or earlier drafts of the agreement. Without an integration clause, either party could try to claim rights based on promises made before the deal was signed.

An integration provision also applies to statements made after the contract is signed. Those promises or statements will be binding only if they are made and agreed to formally (that is, by a signed written amendment to the agreement).

Integration provision: Sample language

Integration. This Agreement expresses the complete understanding of the parties and supersedes all prior representations, agreements, and understandings, whether written or oral. This Agreement may not be altered except by a written document signed by both parties.

Related terms: amendment; boilerplate; statute of frauds.

intellectual property

Intellectual property refers to any legally protected product of the human mind. Whether you're currently holding a printed version of this book, reading it as an eBook, or reading it as a Web page, it qualifies as intellectual property (IP). The types of IP protected by law are:

- **Copyrights.** Copyrights are granted for original creative expressions produced by authors, composers, artists, designers, programmers, and similar creative types. Copyright protection lasts a long time, often more than 100 years. A written agreement—either a work made for hire, an assignment, or a license (see below)—is necessary to transfer copyright. Some copyright transfer agreements are unique to the type of work being transferred and include details specific to the industry. For example, a music publishing agreement may differ dramatically from a book publishing agreement or a software development agreement.

- **Patents.** There are three types of patents: utility, design, and plant. Utility patents (the most common type) are granted to the inventor of a new, nonobvious invention. Utility patents are awarded for new processes, machines, manufactures, or compositions of matter, or new uses of any of the above. The utility patent owner has the exclusive right to make, use, and sell the invention for a limited term—usually 17 to 18 years. A design patent (for a new but nonfunctional design) is awarded to nonfunctional, ornamental, or aesthetic design elements of an invention or product and lasts 14 years after the date the patent issues. A plant patent is a granted for asexually or sexually reproducible plants (such as flowers) and expires 20 years from the date the patent was filed.

- **Trademarks.** A trademark is any distinctive name, design, logo, slogan, or other signifier used to identify and distinguish products and services. A written agreement—usually either an assignment or a license—is needed in several trademark transactions: to pay someone to create a trademark; to license an existing trademark to someone else to use; to sell a trademark; or to enter into cobranding agreements whereby two trademarks are used together.

- **Trade secrets.** A trade secret is any confidential information that gives a business a competitive advantage and is not known by competitors. Like any other form of intellectual property, trade secrets can be transferred by assignment or license. Trade secrets are often protected by the use of nondisclosure agreements.

Contracts and IP. Inventors make money off their IP by granting others the right to use and exploit the property. These grants generally take the form of contracts. These transfer agreements spell out many things besides the "grant" of rights; they also include promises, assurances, obligations, and responsibilities—for example, they may indicate which party will take a trespasser to court.

Types of IP contracts. There are two basic kinds of contracts transferring IP rights:

- **Assignment.** An assignment is a contract (or a provision within a contract) in which intellectual property is permanently transferred. Sometimes, in return for the assignment, the party selling the property might get either a lump sum or a continuing payment known as a royalty. In some cases, an assignment may provide for the return of the intellectual property under certain conditions—for example, if the new owner fails to exploit (that is, try to earn revenue from) the innovation. When this occurs, the rights revert (go back) to the original owner. Some assignments—for example, for patents or registered trademarks—must be recorded with the U.S. Patent and Trademark office (USPTO).

- **License.** A license is a contract by which the owner of intellectual property gives someone permission to use or exploit intellectual property rights for a limited time or in a limited way. In a sense, a license is the owner's promise not to sue over someone else's use of the owner's intellectual property. A license may be simple—the right to duplicate a photo on a website—or it may be more complex—the right to incorporate one patented device within another to create a new product. A license may be exclusive or nonexclusive and may be restricted by territory, time, media, purpose, or virtually any other factor desired by the parties. Exclusive licenses must almost always be in writing to be valid. It's often wise to record exclusive licenses with the appropriate government agency (except in the case of trade secrets, which won't remain secret for long after they're put in the public record).

Who owns IP. Issues over IP ownership sometimes arise when an employee creates an invention. Regardless of whether there is a written contract addressing the issue, an employer usually owns the rights to any innovation, creative work, or trade secret if it was created within the scope of employment. The term "scope of employment" (sometimes referred to as "course of employment") refers to whether the work is within the range of activities expected from the employee. As one court stated, the question is whether the employee was hired and paid to do the type of work that resulted in the IP. When referring to patentable inventions, the principle is usually phrased as whether the employee was "employed to invent." If so, the IP belongs to the employer.

Related terms: intangible property (intangible assets); license agreement; trademarks (service mark); works made for hire.

interest rates (usury)

Interest is a fee charged for borrowing money; it is the profit earned by the money lender. The rate at which it is paid is usually expressed as a percentage of the sum due.

Usury and contracts. Interest rates have been a subject of controversy ever since Jesus chased the money changers from the temple. Today, interest rates are capped by state usury laws ("usury" refers to illegally high interest rates) as well as laws regulating specific consumer transactions. If a loan agreement includes an interest rate that exceeds the amount permitted by state laws, it will not be enforced. These state laws affect contractual relationships in two ways: they limit the interest rates that can be charged as penalties, and they limit the interest rates that can be applied when loaning money.

> **EXAMPLE:** In California, the interest rate maximum for consumer loans is 10%. MyCalifornia Bank lends money to Josh at 10.5%. Josh refuses to pay his loan, claiming that the interest rate is illegal. A California court will invalidate the loan agreement.

But what about credit cards? Did you ever wonder why all credit card companies seem to be based in South Dakota or Delaware? That's because these two states don't limit consumer interest rates, which means resident credit card issuers can charge interest of 20% or more. In 1978, the Supreme Court ruled that national banks can charge customers throughout the country any interest rate allowed by the institution's home state. Hence, a California bank that operates its credit card division in South Dakota will not be subject to California's usury laws.

Related term: promissory note

interference with contractual relations (interference with prospective economic/business advantage)

These are two legal theories that may enable you to recover for your injuries in the event someone goes behind your back to undermine your contractual relationship with someone else. The general concept underlying both theories is the same: Somebody has stepped in between you and another party and unfairly cost you some money by screwing up the relationship. If you already have a contract with the other party, you can sue for interference with contractual relations. If you don't (or don't yet) have a contract, you can sue for interference with prospective economic advantage. In either case, you will be pursuing a personal injury (tort) claim, for which your damages could include not just your actual out-of-pocket losses as a result of the failed business relationship, but also compensation for your emotional distress and punitive damages.

> EXAMPLE: Bobby is a reality TV star and her ex-boyfriend gives an interview packed with half-truths about her. (No, she didn't ride in the buff on his Harley; she wore a skin-colored bathing suit.) The network learns of the story and cancels Bobby's reality show contract. Bobby can't sue the ex-boyfriend for breach of contract because she doesn't have a contract with him. Yet,

she still suffered a contractual injury. So, she sues her ex for interference with contractual relations.

Interference with contractual relations. In most states, when you sue someone who meddles in your contractual relationship, you must prove all of the following: (1) There was a valid contract between the you and a third party; (2) the defendant (the person that meddled in your affairs) knew about the contract; (3) the defendant acted intentionally to induce a breach or disruption of the contractual relationship; (4) the contractual relationship was, in fact, breached or disrupted; and (5) you suffered harm as a result.

> EXAMPLE: Mr. and Mrs. Shamblin owned some lots in a real estate development. The couple entered into contracts to sell two units to Mr. and Mrs. DeLage. After entering into these sales contracts, the Shamblins retained real estate agents (Mr. and Mrs. Berge) to sell their remaining units. Unbeknownst to the Shamblins, their real estate agents tried to convince the DeLages to cancel their sales contract with the Shamblins and enter into a sales agreement with one of the other owners of lots in the development for a lower price. The DeLages eventually did just that. The Shamblins successfully sued their real estate agents for tortious interference with their contractual relations with the DeLages.

To prevail on this type of claim, you don't have to show that the other party to the contract cancelled or backed out of the deal; it is enough to show that the contractual relationship has been damaged severely. As one court pointed out, you don't have to prove an injury to the contract itself, but to the contractual relationship.

Also, the person you are suing (the defendant) may not be a party to the agreement. You may have a different contractual relationship with the defendant, but the defendant cannot be a party to the contract for which you are claiming interference.

EXAMPLE: MumboJumbo, a video game maker had entered into an agreement with PopCap to make and sell games in North America. MumboJumbo was awarded $4.6 million when it was shown—via a series of internal emails—that PopCap deliberately interfered with a contract between MumboJumbo and one of its key retailers. Even though MumboJumbo and PopCap had their own contractual relationship, that wasn't the source of the lawsuit. PopCap interfered with a different contract, to which it was not a party.

Interference with a prospective economic advantage. To prove interference with prospective economic advantage, you don't have to prove that you had a contract with a third party. Instead, you must show only that you had some type of business relationship that you reasonably expected would benefit you financially. Courts permit a wider range of meddling when there is no contract to protect, so it can be harder to win this type of claim. Still, the tort of interference with prospective economic advantage protects the same basic interest—the stable economic relationship between the two original parties.

EXAMPLE: A real estate agent had oral agreements with two couples to arrange an exchange of their respective properties. A bank representative convinced the two couples they could cut the agent out of the deal and save the fee. When the agent sued the bank for interfering with his prospective economic advantage, the bank argued that the oral agreements between the agent and the couples were invalid (such contracts must be in writing to be enforced). Because there was no valid contract, the bank contended that it was free to upstage the deal. A California court disagreed and noted that the tort of interference with a prospective economic advantage did not require a contract, merely an advantageous business relationship.

Related terms: good faith and fair dealing; negligence; remedies; tort.

interpretive provisions

In addition to the basic terms of a deal, many contracts also contain interpretive provisions, which explain how the parties intend for the contract to be read and enforced. Interpretive provisions can be used to "opt out" of the usual rules that courts apply when interpreting contracts; they are also occasionally used to limit or shift the risks of contracting.

> **EXAMPLE:** Bradley Manufacturing enters into a supply agreement with Mischa. Bradley requires Mischa to sign its standard agreement, which contains many provisions favoring Bradley. Bradley also includes an interpretive provision stating that the parties mutually drafted the agreement. The usual rule courts apply is that ambiguities in a contract are construed against the party that drafted it. Bradley's interpretive provision ensures that it won't be subject to this rule.

Types of interpretive provisions. Interpretive provisions may deal with a range of issues including … well, including the word "including."

> **EXAMPLE:** An interpretive clause may state: Whenever the term 'including' is used in this Agreement, it means 'including' without limiting any preceding word or description. That enables the drafter of the agreement to not have to always state "including, but not limited to …" when providing a list of items.

Other interpretive provisions include (but are not limited to):

- **Headings.** A provision may state, "The headings of this Agreement and of individual paragraphs are for ease of reference only and not to be taken into account for the purpose of its construction or interpretation."
- **He/she.** To avoid sexist overtones, a contract may include a statement that any references to a specific gender are applicable for either gender.

- **Mutual drafting.** As noted above, a provision may be included stating that the agreement was mutually drafted. Because statements like these are often blatantly untrue (as in the Bradley Manufacturing example, above), lawyers have come up with a different approach to achieve the same outcome. They instead use language like, "This agreement has been drafted by our counsel as a convenience to the parties only and will not, by reason of such action, be construed against the party represented by the drafting counsel."
- **Definition of terms.** Some practitioners routinely include a definition of terms in all contracts. These definitions can be used to define common language used in the agreement or can be used to define esoteric references or industry jargon. For example, a software development contract may include a definition of "mobile apps."

Related terms: mistake; plain meaning rule; rules of interpretation (rules of interpretation).

invoice

An invoice is a bill, often itemized, that the seller of products or goods sends to the buyer. By itself, an invoice rarely serves as a contract because it is prepared by one party and doesn't indicate or prove that the other party accepted or agreed to it. In other words, the unless the recipient acknowledges its terms (by signing it, for example) it will not bind.

> EXAMPLE: A wheat merchant claimed that another man converted (stole) his wheat. The accused man claimed there was a contract for the wheat and pointed to some invoices. The U.S. Supreme Court disagreed: "An invoice is not a bill of sale, nor is it evidence of a sale. It is a mere detailed statement of the nature, quantity, and cost or price of the things invoiced … standing alone, it is never regarded as evidence of title."

Related terms: bill of sale.

ipso facto clause

Latin for "by the fact itself," an ipso facto clause is a contract provision stating that the contract may be terminated if one party declares bankruptcy. (The "facto" in this situation is the bankruptcy: The fact alone that one party declares bankruptcy is supposedly enough to end the contract.)

Here's an example from the termination section of a license agreement:

Ipso facto clause: Sample language

> **Termination in the event of bankruptcy or insolvency.** This Agreement may be terminated with immediate effect at any time by notice in writing if either party shall (i) apply for or consent to the appointment of, or the taking of possession by, a receiver, custodian, trustee, or liquidator of itself or any of its property or assets, (ii) become generally unable to pay its debts as they mature, (iii) make a general assignment for the benefit of creditors, (iv) be adjudicated bankrupt or insolvent, (v) file a voluntary petition in bankruptcy or a petition or answer seeking reorganization or an arrangement with creditors or take advantage of any bankruptcy, reorganization, insolvency, readjustment of debt, dissolution, or liquidation statute, or an answer admitting the material allegations of a petition filed against it in any proceeding under any such law.

Are these clauses enforceable? With rare exceptions, ipso facto provisions are unenforceable—that is, you will not be able to terminate the agreement if the other party goes bankrupt. Once the other party files for bankruptcy, all of its property and debts—including your contract—are under the control of a federal bankruptcy court trustee. Only the trustee can determine your rights and obligations under the agreement. The bankruptcy court can keep your contract rights tied up for months or even years while the trustee attempts to sort out the financial mess. Your agreement could even be assigned to another company in order to pay off creditors. These rules are derived from Section 365(e)(1) of the Bankruptcy Code which states that ipso facto clauses are unenforceable in bankruptcy with certain exceptions. Although these termination provisions are often included in agreements, they are almost always invalid and should be avoided.

Related term: severability (savings clause).

issuer

An issuer is any individual or entity that provides or allots something, typically, a corporation that issues shares of stock or a financial institution that issues credit cards.

J

joint and several liability

Joint and several liability allows someone to pursue one of several parties for the full amount of a debt or judgment.

> **EXAMPLE:** Melvin signed a contract with the Joe & Bob Partnership. After Joe and Bob breached the contract, Melvin sued for damages and was awarded $10,000. Under state law, Joe and Bob share joint and several liability. Melvin knows that Bob is broke and Joe is wealthy, so he goes after Joe for the full amount. If Job wants Bob to pay his fair share, he will have to sue Bob himself.

Distinguished from its components. Joint and several liability is distinguished from its component elements as follows:

- **Joint liability** refers to the mutual liability of each party for the other's debts. For example, in some instances, a parent may be jointly liable for a grown child's debts and vice versa.
- **Several liability** refers to instances where the parties are each responsible for their own debts. For example, in some cases, a wife may be responsible only for her own debts, not her husband's debts.

In a joint and several liability arrangement, the creditor has the best of both worlds and may seek compensation for the full amount of a debt or injury from any or all of the responsible parties. The liable parties must sort out their reimbursements among themselves.

The 1% rule. The principal of joint and several liability explains why a person who may bear only the smallest fraction of legal responsibility for an accident may end up having to pay the full financial judgment and then seek reimbursement from the more culpable parties. Under law, general partners are almost always jointly and severally liable for each others' debts. This is one reason companies create corporations or LLCs: Individual owners are typically not liable for debts and liabilities of these business structures (although the business itself is). Joint and several liability is commonly created by contract. For example, a loan agreement may establish that cosigners are "jointly and severally liable" for the debt.

Related terms: buyer in due course; cosigner; partnership (general); promissory note.

joint venture

J

A joint venture is an association or enterprise created between two or more people or businesses with a specific business goal, usually for a fixed time period (after which it is dissolved). Joint ventures (or JVs) are symbiotic, strategic, or mutually beneficial contractual alliances, usually combining complementary strengths in a specific market or industry.

> **EXAMPLE:** Anyone with a sweet tooth was probably happy to learn of the frozen dessert joint venture created between Nestle and Haagen-Dazs. As the press release for the JV announced, "Both partners offer complementary product lines in two distinct segments of the ice cream category—Haagen-Dazs with its presence in superpremium pints, and Nestle with its unique novelty line."

What a JV is not. A joint venture describes a strategic contractual relationship. It is not:

- **A merger.** A merger is a fusion of two companies, usually involving a transfer of stock ownership. In a JV, the parties typically retain their company identities and do not transfer corporate stock.

- **An acquisition.** An acquisition is a form of merger in which one company obtains ownership of another. A JV does not result in a transfer of ownership.
- **A statutory business entity.** A JV, by itself, is not a corporation, an LLC, or a partnership. In other words, forming a JV does not create statutory benefits like limited liability. However, the JV agreement can also establish a business entity. For example, the JV agreement may state that the parties shall form a corporation, a limited liability enterprise, a partnership, or some other legal structure to accomplish the goal.

The JV agreement. The key elements of a joint venture agreement are:

- **A statement of purpose.** This explains why the joint venture is being formed and sets out the common goals and interests of the parties.
- **Financial (or other) contributions.** Each party contributes something to the venture; this provision states each contribution.
- **Agents' and parties' authorization.** A JV agreement typically authorizes certain people (either the parties or their appointed agents) to take certain actions. For example, only certain people may have the power to make payments or sign contracts in the name of the JV.
- **Revenue.** The agreement establishes what happens to revenue earned by the JV and how it is distributed to the parties (the proportional shares).
- **Expenses.** This details how the JV's expenses will be paid and how it may cap expenses under certain conditions.
- **Liabilities.** This sets out each party's (and the agent's) liability for activities resulting from or instigated by the JV.
- **Term.** Most JVs are built around a specific task—for example, to construct a building or establish a distribution channel—and often are discontinued once the action is complete. In other cases, the JV expires after a fixed term. In some

cases, the JV continues until the parties mutually agree to terminate it.

- **Further assurances.** A JV agreement should include a provision that the parties will act in good faith by devoting sufficient resources to the project and complying with obligations.

I am not a joint venturer. Because many parties don't want their arrangement to be mistaken for a joint venture (usually for liability reasons), a statement announcing that an arrangement does not create a joint venture is included in many business contracts, usually in what's called a "No Joint Venture" provision.

No joint venture: Sample language

> **No Joint Venture.** Nothing contained in this Agreement places the parties in the relationship of agent, employee, franchisee, officer, partners, or joint venturers. Neither party may create or assume any obligation on behalf of the other.

Related terms: boilerplate; partnership (general)

judgment creditor

When a judge awards a financial victory to one side in a contract dispute, that's not the end of the matter. The winner—the judgment creditor—may have to chase the loser (the judgment debtor) in order to enforce the court's judgment and actually get some money. Judgment creditors can use court-ordered methods, such as attaching income or wages or getting a writ of execution (in which a sheriff seizes real or personal property).

jurisdiction (subject matter; personal)

Jurisdiction refers to the location of the court where you may file a lawsuit. You may file only in a court has the power to hear the type of dispute (known as "subject matter jurisdiction") and the power to issue a decision that will bind the parties (known as "personal jurisdiction"). If you file a case in the wrong court, the other party may get it moved to another court (perhaps one that's less convenient or favorable to you) or even get the case dismissed altogether.

Subject matter jurisdiction. You have two basic choices when considering which courts have subject matter jurisdiction: federal court or state court. In most cases, state court is the right choice. Federal courts have subject matter jurisdiction in only two kinds of cases:

- **Cases that arise under a federal law (called "federal question" cases).** For example, if you are suing for patent infringement, breach of a federal government contract, or violation of federal antitrust laws, you may sue in federal court.

- **Diversity of citizenship cases.** Federal district courts also have subject matter jurisdiction if you are suing a citizen of a different state (or a foreign national), and you are asking for at least $75,000 in money damages. (The minimum dollar amount may be responsible for the old saying, "Don't make a federal case out of it.") If a federal court has jurisdiction based on diversity of citizenship, the subject matter of the case doesn't matter. Federal courts have diversity jurisdiction only if there is "complete diversity" between plaintiffs and defendants; in other words all of the plaintiffs (if you are suing with someone else) must be citizens of a different state than all of the defendants. For diversity jurisdiction purposes, people are generally citizens of the states in which they maintain principal residences, and they can be citizens of only one state at a time. A corporation can be a citizen of two states, however: the state in which it is incorporated and the state in which it maintains its principal place of business.

EXAMPLE: Bluegrass Corp., a corporation with headquarters in Kentucky, sues a company incorporated in Washington for $300,000 for breach of contract. Bluegrass could file the complaint in a federal court in either Kentucky (its state of residence) or Washington (where the defendant resides). However, if Bluegrass was suing a number of defendants, and even one of them was a resident of Kentucky, it could not sue in federal court at all. Because one defendant and the plaintiff are both residents of the same state, there isn't complete diversity and the federal court has no jurisdiction.

State court subject matter jurisdiction. The odds are overwhelming that a state court will have subject matter jurisdiction in almost any lawsuit you want to bring. State courts almost always have the power to hear cases involving events that took place in that state, defendants who reside in that state, or defendants who are served with a summons and complaint (the initial court documents) in that state. Unless your case involves one of the few types of cases over which federal courts have exclusive jurisdiction, the state court in the state where you live will probably have jurisdiction to hear your contract dispute, as long as it has personal jurisdiction over the other party (as explained below).

Personal jurisdiction. The nearly universal rule is that the courts in a state have personal jurisdiction over all people or businesses that are citizens of or do business in that state.

> **EXAMPLE:** You have a contract dispute with a resident of Chicago. You sue in an Illinois state court for breach of contract. It doesn't matter where you live or where the events leading up to the lawsuit took place, because an Illinois state court has personal jurisdiction over all citizens of Illinois.

Other ways to get personal jurisdiction. Personal jurisdiction rules can be a bit stickier when you file a lawsuit in a state other than the one where the defendant is a citizen or does business. You can't just sue someone in your home state if the defendant doesn't live in your state, has never been in your state, and doesn't do business in your state.

EXAMPLE: Debbie is a Texas citizen vacationing in Florida. While in Florida, Debbie buys what she is told are two brand new "fully loaded" computer systems at Kevin's Computer Shop. Debbie later learns that the computers are loaded with reused parts and won't perform the tasks that Kevin claimed. Debbie cannot sue Kevin in her home state of Texas. Texas has no personal jurisdiction over Kevin because Kevin is not a citizen of Texas nor does he do business there.

To protect a defendant from being sued in a "hostile" and possibly distant location, personal jurisdiction rules require that the facts make it fair for a court to exercise power over a noncitizen. Here are standard situations in which courts have personal jurisdiction over noncitizens:

- **Defendant served while in the state.** The defendant enters the state where you filed suit after the case is filed, even if only for a short visit, and you serve the defendant with the court papers (normally a summons and complaint). (As in the children's game of "You're It," you have to find and "tag" the defendant with the papers while the defendant is in the state.)

- **The parties are subject to a jurisdiction provision.** Some contracts contain a jurisdiction provision (also known as a "forum-selection" provision), in which the parties waive personal jurisdiction rights and consent to personal jurisdiction in a specific state or county.

- **Defendant has some contacts within the state.** The defendant (individual or business) has engaged in at least a small but significant amount of activity that constitutes minimum contacts in the state where you've filed the lawsuit (and the case involves that activity). The minimum contacts requirement generally means that a defendant must have enough of a connection to the state where a case has been filed for a judge to conclude that it's fair for the state to exercise power over the defendant. A judge would probably conclude that minimum contacts exist in the following situations:

- A business with its headquarters in another state maintains a branch office, store, or warehouse in the state where the suit is filed.
- A business with its headquarters in another state sends mail order catalogs into the state where the suit is filed.
- An individual who is a citizen of another state solicits business by making phone calls to customers or publishing advertisements in the state where the suit is filed.
- An Internet service provider that is a citizen of another state does business with paid subscribers or takes online orders from customers in the state where the case is filed.

Related terms: boilerplate; jurisdiction provision (forum selection provision).

jurisdiction provision (forum selection provision)

Jurisdiction provisions—sometimes called forum-selection clauses—require the parties to consent in advance to the jurisdiction of a specific court and give up the right to complain about jurisdiction in other locations where they might otherwise be entitled to file. In other words, if either party files a lawsuit arising out of or relating to the contract, it must be filed in the agreed-upon court.

Pack your bags. Forum selection provisions are often overlooked during negotiations—relegated to the "fine print" category—and their full impact is usually not felt until months or years later.

EXAMPLE: A couple opened a Burger King franchise in Michigan. Their franchise agreement with Burger King included a forum selection clause in which they consented to jurisdiction in Florida. Later, when problems arose, the couple argued that they were not aware of the meaning of this provision and shouldn't have to travel to Florida. The courts upheld the jurisdiction clause and the couple was forced to fight Burger King in the Sunshine State.

Not always enforceable. Two states, Idaho and Montana, refuse to honor these provisions. In other states, courts enforce these provisions only if the parties have some contact with the state beyond the contract provision—for example, they must do business with the state's citizens.

Not the same as choice of law. Jurisdiction provisions are sometimes confused with choice of law (also known as "governing law") provisions. Although the two provisions are often combined in the same contract clause, each provision establishes a separate requirement. A jurisdiction provision sets out where a case can be filed (personal jurisdiction). A "governing law" provision sets out which state's laws will be used to make a decision in a dispute.

Below is an example of a typical jurisdiction provision.

Jurisdiction: Sample language

> **Jurisdiction.** Each party (a) consents to the exclusive jurisdiction and venue of the federal and state courts located in [*insert county and state in which parties agree to litigate*] in any action arising out of or relating to this agreement; (b) waives any objection it might have to jurisdiction or venue of such forums or that the forum is inconvenient; and (c) agrees not to bring any such action in any other jurisdiction or venue to which either party might be entitled by domicile or otherwise.

Related terms: boilerplate: jurisdiction (subject matter; personal).

jury trial, waiver of

If the idea of 12 strangers watching you for eight hours a day bothers you, then consider adding a jury waiver provision to your contract. If your contract dispute goes to court, a jury waiver provision will prevent either party from requesting a jury trial. Instead, the matter will be heard by a judge (in what is known as a "bench trial").

Not always enforceable. In two states, California and Georgia, these predispute jury waivers will not be enforced. In addition, a jury waiver may not be enforced when used within certain types of agreements. For example, Maryland, Massachusetts, and New York will not enforce jury waiver provisions in residential leases. In addition, these provisions generally will not be enforced unless the parties waive the right "knowingly and voluntarily."

Why waive the right to a jury? Jury waivers are usually sought by companies that perceive jurors as likely to be biased against them or because of the potential savings in money (less spent on attorneys' fees) and time (bench trials are much faster). Or, they may be included out of a concern that a jury would not grasp the technical nature of the dispute.

Below is an example of typical jury waiver language.

Jury waiver: Sample language

Jury Waiver. Each party, to the extent permitted by law, expressly and voluntarily, waives any right to a trial by jury in any dispute arising under or related to this Agreement. An original counterpart or a copy of this Agreement may be filed with any court as written evidence of the consent of each party to the waiver of its right to trial by jury.

Related term: boilerplate.

K

The letter K is sometimes used as shorthand by lawyers and law students to refer to a contract.

key person insurance

Once known as key man insurance (or "keyman"), this is a life insurance policy on the indispensable person(s) in a business. The policy is paid for by the business, and proceeds are payable to the business, in case of the key person's death. This type of policy protects against the devastation a business can suffer if a crucial person—generally a partner or founder—dies; it provides money to keep paying the bills while you figure out what to do. And when you're trying to borrow or raise significant amounts of money, lenders or investors may require you to get key person coverage on one or two crucial players in your business.

For a partnership or other business that relies heavily on the efforts of more than one person, key person insurance can be a lifesaver. For example, if one partner is an introverted type who invents and engineers products, while the other partner raises capital, sells products, and generally represents the business to the public, both partners are essential to the company's success. If either dies, the other could use the proceeds of a key person policy to stay afloat while searching for another partner or coming up with some new business strategies.

If you run your business alone and have no employees, however, you can skip the key person coverage. The sad fact is that if you die, your business is very likely going down with you. To protect your family against the risk of losing your income, buy a personal life insurance policy instead.

Related term: insurance contract (insurance policy).

knowledge, to the best of

To avoid overpromising something in a contract, you can qualify your assurance by stating that you are making the representation "to the best of my knowledge."

Why it's sometimes necessary. Because contracts are packed with promises and assurances, sometimes it's not possible to say that you absolutely can or cannot guarantee something. For example, if you are an inventor, a party that's licensing your invention may want you to promise that your soon-to-be-patented device does not infringe any other patent. You've thoroughly researched existing inventions in your field and haven't found any infringements, but what if there's an invention out there that you didn't uncover? That's when it's useful to trot out the phrase, "to the best of my knowledge."

This shifts the standard from an absolute standard (no infringements) to a qualified standard (no infringements that I know about). You could still be held liable for breach of contract based on infringements. However, it won't be enough to show that there is a similar device out there; instead, the other party will have to base its claims against you on the meaning of "knowledge." Courts interpret this as what a person in that position should have reason to know, based on a diligent search.

Related term: exculpatory clause.

lease

A lease is a rental agreement. Nowadays just about anything can be leased. For example, Cinderella could—credit willing—bypass her fairy godmother and lease a Dolce & Gabbana gown, an Hermès Birkin handbag, and a horse-drawn carriage (or even a stretch limo) to deliver her to the ball. Using a lease, one person (the lessee) pays for the exclusive right to possess and use the property of another (the lessor) for a stated period of time. Leased property commonly includes apartments, homes, commercial property, vehicles, boats, office equipment, appliances, and tools.

Key elements of a lease. The key provisions in a lease are:

- **Property description.** The property must be described specifically enough for the parties (or a court, if it comes to that) to clearly identify what was leased.
- **Term.** This provision establishes the length of the use. Although leases can be oral or written, a lease that lasts for more than one year should be in writing to comply with the Statute of Frauds.
- **Payment.** This provision describes the amount and frequency of the rental payments (and how they will be delivered).
- **Restrictions on use.** Typically, leases also identify what the lessee cannot do with the property (for example, a residential lease may prohibit pets or subletting).

Lease regulation. State and federal laws regulate consumer leasing. These laws seek to curb abuses that result from the unequal bargaining power of the parties to a lease (the property owner typically has much more clout than the renter). For example, the federal Consumer Leasing Act, which applies to leases of longer than four months for cars, furniture, appliances, and similar personal items, requires the property owner to provide a written statement detailing the amount of any advance payment and/or security deposit, when payments are due, and any external fees that will be charged.

Federal and state laws also provide a three-day cooling-off period, during which consumers have a right to cancel many types of consumer leases without penalty. Laws and regulations also set strict requirements for vehicle and residential leases.

Related terms: lease (commercial property); lease, residential (rental agreement); lease, vehicle.

lease, commercial property

A commercial lease is an agreement to rent real estate to someone who will use it for commercial purposes. Like a residential lease, a commercial lease grants the right to possess property for a limited time and purpose. However, commercial leases are distinguishable from residential leases as follows:

- **Length.** Commercial leases usually last five or more years, much longer than the typical residential lease.
- **Negotiated terms.** Commercial leases are more likely to be negotiable than residential leases, which landlords often present as "take it or leave it" arrangements.
- **No consumer protections.** Commercial tenants don't have the consumer protections—for example, strict laws regarding the return of security deposits or detailed requirements for evictions—that residential tenants have.
- **More expensive to breach.** Commercial leases are usually harder and more expensive to break than residential leases.

Factors for a commercial tenant to consider. If you're looking to rent space for your business, make sure to consider these issues when you're sizing up a potential property:

- **Local restrictions.** A commercial tenant needs to be sure that the space can be used as planned under local land-use (zoning) rules. You can find these rules at your local planning department or, if your town has one, your local business development office; many cities post their zoning ordinances online.

- **Modifications.** Commercial tenants are often concerned about modifications—for example, will you need to add cubicles, raise a loading dock, or rewire for better communications? If so, are the space and the landlord amenable to these changes?

- **Restrooms and parking.** Make sure there are enough restrooms to meet the needs of your employees and customers. Also, find out how difficult it is to park on the street nearby. Some commercial rentals come with guaranteed off-street parking.

- **Heat, ventilation, and air conditioning.** If you're a fresh air junkie, find out if the windows open in any commercial space you're looking at (it's not an option in many newer buildings). Also, find out who controls and pays for heat and air conditioning—and when it's generally on. If any of your employees will be working odd hours, you'll want to make sure that you have access to heat and air.

- **Soundproofing.** For businesses that make noise, soundproofing between walls and floors should be a priority.

- **Storage.** Will your business require storage for inventory, files, or materials? If so, find out whether space is available.

- **Other tenants.** If you're renting space in a commercial building, find out who the other tenants are. You probably don't want to share space with a competitor; an especially loud or controversial business might also be a minus.

- **Security.** Does the building offer security? This may be an issue depending on location, hours, and type of business.

Negotiating the lease. Here are some issues and terms that often come up in the negotiation of a commercial lease:

- **Gross versus net lease.** In a gross lease, the tenant pays a basic rent, usually based on square footage. The landlord pays for all property expenses, such as utilities, taxes, and maintenance. In a net lease, the tenant pays a fixed rental charge plus a portion of the building's property taxes, insurance, and maintenance costs.

- **Security deposit.** Many commercial landlords require tenants to pay one or two months' rent up front as a security deposit. The landlord will dip into this deposit if the tenant fails to pay the rent or other sums required by the lease, such as insurance or maintenance costs.

- **Alterations.** Unless the tenant is fortunate enough to find space that was previously owned by an identical business, the tenant will need to modify the space to fit its needs and tastes. These modifications are known as improvements or "build-outs." In some markets, the landlord typically pays for them; in others, the tenant pays.

- **Property tax increases.** Under a net lease, the tenant may have to pay a pro rata portion of increases in the building's property taxes—for example, if the tenant rents one-fifth of the total space in the building, the tenant may be obligated to pay one-fifth of any increase.

- **Common area maintenance costs.** In a net lease, the tenant pays for common area maintenance (CAM)—a percentage of the costs of maintaining the lobbies, hallways, garages, and elevators. Sometimes the tenant also pays to maintain the heating, ventilation, and air conditioning system (referred to as "HVAC").

- **Insurance.** A net lease tenant usually contributes to the cost of insurance for the building. This gets tricky if another tenant— for example, a bail bond business—causes the building's insurance costs to go up. In addition, the lease will likely require the tenant to carry a renter's commercial liability policy.

- **Rent fluctuations.** An important consideration is whether the rent can change during the lease term—and if so, by how much. Many gross leases include an "escalation clause" that sets a fixed monthly rate with periodic increases. The increases may be a flat percentage or amount, such as 3% a year or $.10 per square foot per year. Or, the increase may be variable and tied to increases in a national indicator, often the Consumer

Price Index (CPI). In this case, if the tenant is paying $5,000 a month and the CPI jumps 5% in one year, the monthly rent will jump to $5,250. In some markets, tenants have more clout and can negotiate a cap on the increases.

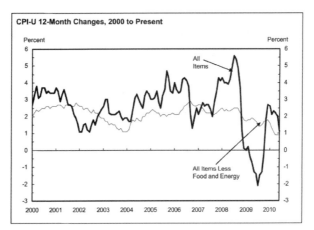

Provided by the Bureau of Labor Statistics

- **Personal liability for rent.** The tenant will be personally liable for any amounts due if the tenant is a sole proprietor or a general partner. If the tenant is a corporation or limited liability company (LLC), the landlord can reach only the assets of the business. In that case, the tenant's personal assets are not at risk unless the tenant signs a personal guarantee: a promise that the tenant will pay any debts arising from a breach of the lease. In certain real estate markets, the landlord may waive the guarantee, limit it to the first year or two of the lease, or ask for a larger security deposit instead. Tenants who are uncomfortable with a personal guarantee usually try to keep the lease short, perhaps limited to a one-year term.
- **Length of obligations.** If things go south and the tenant can't pay rent, the tenant may be sued for the remaining value of the lease. For that reason, some start-ups, uncertain of their future, prefer leases of a year or less or even a month-to-month

tenancy. Of course, if the business really takes off, the tenant may be forced to renegotiate—or even relocate—quickly.

- **If rent is not paid.** Most leases give the tenant 30 days to "cure" a first failure to pay rent, which means that the tenant has 30 days to pay before the landlord can terminate the lease and begin eviction proceedings. The landlord also may take some "self-help" measures, such as deducting the money from the security deposit (which the tenant will then have to replenish). Although the landlord is legally entitled to all of the rent through the end of the lease term, most states require the landlord must take reasonable steps to find a new tenant and credit the new rent money against the original tenant's debt (this is called the landlord's duty to mitigate damages).

- **What if the tenant can't stay?** A tenant who needs to vacate can either try to sublet the property (see "Subleasing," below) or offer to buy out the lease. With a buyout, the tenant negotiates a lump sum payment—usually an amount that's considerably less than the remaining rent on the lease. That will end fears of a lawsuit (and large judgment) against the tenant and help the landlord cover vacancy costs when looking for a new tenant.

- **Resolving disputes.** Some commercial leases require arbitration, mediation, or payment of attorneys' fees in the event of a dispute. Arbitration and mediation are ways to iron out problems without going to court. An attorneys' fee provision awards attorneys' fees and court costs to the winner of any dispute, which can get expensive in a hurry.

- **Can the landlord move the tenant from space to space?** Believe it or not, some commercial leases give the landlord the right to substitute other space—in the building or elsewhere—for the space described in the lease.

- **Special lease restrictions.** Some landlords prohibit tenants from doing certain things—for example, using kilns or cooking food. Of course, the tenant will want to make sure that it can run its business while abiding by these restrictions.

- **Subleasing.** Sometimes, the ideal space for a business is one that someone else is renting. Someone who rents from a tenant is called a subtenant. The subtenant must abide by the terms of the landlord's deal with the original tenant. The subtenant should obtain a copy of the prime lease (the one between the landlord and tenant) and check for issues like whether the landlord's consent is needed for subletting, whether the landlord must consent to improvements, which charges will pass through the prime lease to the subtenant, and whether the subtenant be responsible for common area maintenance, taxes, and insurance.

lease, residential (rental agreement)

A residential lease is a contract permitting someone to occupy and possess another's property as a residence. Typically, the renter (the tenant) pays the owner (the landlord) on a monthly basis.

Lease versus rental agreement. A residential lease and a residential rental agreement are similar in most ways. Both types of contracts give a tenant the right to use and possess residential property in exchange for monthly rent payments. However, the residential property industry recognizes these distinctions between leases and rental agreements:

- **Length of the tenancy.** A rental agreement typically lasts only from one month to the next (week-to-week agreements are also possible). The rental agreement automatically renews unless it is terminated by either the landlord or tenant, by giving the proper amount of written notice (typically, 30 days). A residential lease almost always covers a longer, fixed term, such as one year.
- **Fixed versus variable rental rates.** With a lease, the landlord can't raise the rent or change other terms of the tenancy until the lease runs out (unless such changes are explicitly allowed by the contract or the tenant agrees to them in writing).

- **Ability to terminate.** A landlord can't terminate the tenancy before the lease expires unless the tenant fails to pay the rent or violates another significant term of the lease or the law. With a month-to-month rental agreement, the landlord can terminate with proper notice.

In most instances, if the tenant continues to live on the property after a lease expires and no new lease is signed, the arrangement becomes a month-to-month tenancy.

Key terms in residential lease and rental agreements. Here are some of the most important items that arise in the negotiation of a residential lease or rental agreement:

- **Naming all tenants.** Each adult who lives in the rental unit, including both members of a married or unmarried couple, is typically named as a tenant and must sign the lease or rental agreement. This makes each tenant legally responsible for all obligations in the lease, including the full amount of the rent and the proper use of the property. This also means that the landlord can legally seek the entire rent from any one of the tenants if the others skip out or can't pay; and if one tenant violates an important term of the tenancy, the landlord can terminate the entire tenancy for all tenants on the lease or rental agreement.

- **Limits on occupancy.** The lease/rental agreement will likely specify that the rental unit is the residence of only the tenants who have signed the lease and their minor children. This guarantees the landlord's right to determine who lives in the property—ideally, people whom the landlord has screened and approved—and to limit the number of occupants. The landlord may evict a tenant who allows a friend or relative to move in, or sublets the unit, without permission.

- **Term of the tenancy.** Rental agreements usually run from month to month unless terminated by the landlord or tenant. Leases, on the other hand, typically last a year or more. The landlord generally determines which type of contract will be used.

- **Rent.** The agreement should specify the amount of rent, when it is due (typically, the first of the month), and how it must be paid, such as by mail to an office address. To avoid confusion and head off disputes, the rent provision should spell out acceptable payment methods (such as personal check only), whether late fees will be due if the rent is not paid on time, the amount of the fee, whether there's any grace period, and any charges that apply if a rent check bounces.

- **Deposits and fees.** The use and return of security deposits is a frequent source of friction between landlords and tenants. To avoid confusion and legal hassles, the agreement should be clear on: the dollar amount of the security deposit (which must comply with any state laws setting maximum amounts), how the landlord may use the deposit (for example, to repair damage caused by the tenant) and how the tenant may not use it (such as applying it to last month's rent), when and how the landlord will return the deposit and account for deductions after the tenant moves out, and any legal nonreturnable fees, such as for cleaning or pets. It's also a good idea (and legally required in a few states and cities) to include details on where the security deposit is being held and whether interest on the security deposit will be paid to the tenant.

- **Repairs and maintenance.** The landlord and tenant's responsibilities for repair and maintenance should be spelled out in the agreement, including: the tenant's responsibility to keep the rental premises clean and sanitary and to pay for any damage caused by the tenant's abuse or neglect; the tenant's obligation to tell the landlord about defective or dangerous conditions in the rental property, with specific details on the procedures for handling complaint and repair requests; and restrictions on tenant repairs and alterations, such as adding a built-in dishwasher, installing a burglar alarm system, or painting walls without permission.

- **Entry to rental property.** The lease or rental agreement should clarify when the landlord has a legal right to access the property—for example, to make repairs—and state how much advance notice the landlord will give the tenant before entering.
- **Restrictions on tenant illegal activity.** For the benefit of the landlord and the tenants, the agreement should include an explicit clause prohibiting disruptive behavior, such as excessive noise, and illegal activity, such as drug dealing.
- **Pets.** If the landlord does not allow pets, the contract should be clear on the subject. If the landlord does allow pets, the lease should identify any special restrictions, such as a limit on the size or number of pets or a requirement that the tenant will keep the yard free of all animal waste.
- **Other restrictions.** The lease or rental agreement must comply with all relevant laws, including rent control ordinances, health and safety codes, occupancy rules, and antidiscrimination laws. State laws are especially key. They often set security deposit limits, notice requirements for entering rental property, tenants' rights to sublet or bring in additional roommates, rules for changing or ending a tenancy, and specific facts the landlord must disclose (such as past flooding in the rental unit).

Any other legal restrictions, such as limits on the type of business a tenant may run from home, should also be spelled out in the agreement. Important rules and regulations covering parking and use of common areas should be specifically mentioned in the lease or rental agreement.

Example of a residential rental agreement. Below, we have provided an example of a month-to-month residential rental agreement, reproduced from *101 Law Forms for Personal Use* (Nolo). The major difference between this and a residential lease agreement is the addition of a term—a time period for the lease, after which it is renewed.

Month-to-Month Residential Rental Agreement

Month-to-Month Residential Rental Agreement

This Agreement is entered into between _____ ("Tenant") and _____ ("Landlord"). Each Tenant is jointly and severally liable for the payment of rent and performance of all other terms of this Agreement.

1. Identification of Premises. Subject to the terms and conditions in this Agreement, Landlord rents to Tenant, and Tenant rents from Landlord, for residential purposes only, the premises located at _____ _____ , ("the premises"), together with the following furnishings and appliances: _____ _____ . Rental of the premises also includes: _____ .

2. Limits on Use and Occupancy. The premises are to be used only as a private residence for Tenant(s) listed in this Agreement, and their minor children. Occupancy by guests for more than _____ _____ is prohibited without Landlord's written consent and will be considered a breach of this Agreement.

3. Term of the Tenancy. The rental will begin on _____ , ____, and continue on a month-to-month basis. Landlord may terminate the tenancy or modify the terms of this Agreement by giving the Tenant _____ days' written notice. Tenant may terminate the tenancy by giving the Landlord _____ days' written notice.

4. Payment of Rent. Tenant will pay to Landlord a monthly rent of $_____ , payable in advance on the first day of each month, except when that day falls on a weekend or legal holiday, in which case, rent is due on the next business day. Rent will be paid to _____ at _____ or at such other place as Landlord designates, in the following manner

Month-to-Month Residential Rental Agreement (continued)

unless Landlord designates otherwise: _____
_____ .

5. Late Charges. If Tenant fails to pay the rent in full before the end of the _____ day after it's due, Tenant will pay Landlord a late charge of $_____ , plus $ _____ for each additional day that the rent remains unpaid. The total late charge for any one month will not exceed $_____ . Landlord does not waive the right to insist on payment of the rent in full on the date it is due.

6. Returned Check and Other Bank Charges. If any check offered by Tenant to Landlord in payment of rent or any other amount due under this Agreement is returned for lack of sufficient funds, a "stop payment," or any other reason, Tenant will pay Landlord a returned check charge of $_____ .

7. Security Deposit. On signing this Agreement, Tenant will pay to Landlord the sum of $_____ as a security deposit. Tenant may not, without Landlord's prior written consent, apply this security deposit to the last month's rent or to any other sum due under this Agreement. Within __ _____ after Tenant has vacated the premises, returned keys, and provided Landlord with a forwarding address, Landlord will return the deposit in full or give Tenant an itemized written statement of the reasons for, and the dollar amount of, any of the security deposit retained by Landlord, along with a check for any deposit balance.

8. Utilities. Tenant will pay all utility charges, except for the following, which will be paid by Landlord: _____
_____ .

9. Assignment and Subletting. Tenant will not sublet any part of the premises or assign this Agreement without the prior written consent of Landlord.

Month-to-Month Residential Rental Agreement (continued)

10. Tenant's Maintenance Responsibilities. Tenant will: (1) keep the premises clean, sanitary, and in good condition and, upon termination of the tenancy, return the premises to Landlord in a condition identical to that which existed when Tenant took occupancy, except for ordinary wear and tear; (2) immediately notify Landlord of any defects or dangerous conditions in and about the premises of which Tenant becomes aware; and (3) reimburse Landlord, on demand by Landlord, for the cost of any repairs to the premises damaged by Tenant or Tenant's guests or business invitees through misuse or neglect. Tenant has examined the premises, including appliances, fixtures, carpets, drapes, and paint, and has found them to be in good, safe, and clean condition and repair, except as noted in the Landlord-Tenant Checklist.

11. Repairs and Alterations by Tenant. (a) Except as provided by law, or as authorized below, or by the prior written consent of Landlord, Tenant will not make any repairs or alterations to the premises, including nailing holes in the wall or painting the rental unit. (b) Tenant will not, without Landlord's prior written consent, alter, rekey, or install any locks to the premises or install or alter any burglar alarm system. Tenant will provide Landlord with a key or keys capable of unlocking all such rekeyed or new locks as well as instructions on how to disarm any altered or new burglar alarm system.

12. Violating Laws and Causing Disturbances. Tenant is entitled to quiet enjoyment of the premises. Tenant and guests or invitees will not use the premises or adjacent areas in such a way as to: (1) violate any law or ordinance, including laws prohibiting the use, possession, or sale of illegal drugs; (2) commit waste (severe property damage); or (3) create a nuisance by annoying, disturbing, inconveniencing, or interfering with the quiet enjoyment and peace and quiet of any other tenant or nearby resident.

Month-to-Month Residential Rental Agreement (continued)

13. Pets. No animal, bird, or other pet will be kept on the premises, except properly trained service animals needed by blind, deaf, or disabled persons and _____ under the following conditions:

_____

_____

_____

_____ .

14. Landlord's Right to Access. Landlord or Landlord's agents may enter the premises in the event of an emergency, to make repairs or improvements, or to show the premises to prospective buyers or tenants. Landlord may also enter the premises to conduct an annual inspection to check for safety or maintenance problems. Except in cases of emergency, Tenant's abandonment of the premises, court order, or where it is impractical to do so, Landlord shall give Tenant _____ notice before entering.

15. Extended Absences by Tenant. Tenant will notify Landlord in advance if Tenant will be away from the premises for _____ or more consecutive days. During such absence, Landlord may enter the premises at times reasonably necessary to maintain the property and inspect it for needed repairs.

16. Possession of the Premises. If, after signing this Agreement, Tenant fails to take possession of the premises, Tenant will still be responsible for paying rent and complying with all other terms of this Agreement. If Landlord is unable to deliver possession of the premises to Tenant for any reason not within Landlord's control, including, but not limited to, partial or complete destruction of the premises, Tenant will have the right to terminate this Agreement upon proper notice as required by law. In such event, Landlord's liability to Tenant will be limited to the return of all sums previously paid by Tenant to Landlord.

Month-to-Month Residential Rental Agreement (continued)

17. Tenant Rules and Regulations. ☐ Tenants acknowledge receipt of, and have read a copy of, the tenant rules and regulations, which are attached to and incorporated into this Agreement by this reference.

18. Payment of Court Costs and Attorneys' Fees in a Lawsuit. In any action or legal proceeding to enforce any part of this Agreement, the prevailing party [*choose one:* ☐ shall not ☐ shall] recover reasonable attorneys' fees and court costs.

19. Disclosures. Tenant acknowledges that Landlord has made the following disclosures regarding the premises:

☐ Disclosure of Information on Lead-Based Paint and/or Lead-Based Paint Hazards

☐ Other disclosures: _____

20. Authority to Receive Legal Papers. The Landlord, any person managing the premises, and anyone designated by the Landlord are authorized to accept service of process and receive other notices and demands, which may be delivered to:

☐ The Landlord, at the following address: _____

_____ .

☐ The manager, at the following address: _____

_____ .

☐ The following person at the following address: _____

_____ .

21. Additional Provisions. Additional provisions are as follows: _____

_____

_____

_____

_____ .

Month-to-Month Residential Rental Agreement (continued)

22. Validity of Each Part. If any portion of this Agreement is held to be invalid, its invalidity will not affect the validity or enforceability of any other provision of this Agreement.

23. Grounds for Termination of Tenancy. The failure of Tenant or Tenant's guests or invitees to comply with any term of this Agreement or the misrepresentation of any material fact on Tenant's rental application is grounds for termination of the tenancy, with appropriate notice to Tenant and procedures as required by law.

24. Entire Agreement. This document constitutes the entire Agreement between the parties, and no promises or representations, other than those contained here and those implied by law, have been made by Landlord or Tenant. Any modifications to this Agreement must be in writing and signed by Landlord and tenant.

Tenant	Landlord
Signature: _____	Signature: _____
Name: _____	Name: _____
Date: _____	Date: _____

lease, vehicle

About a quarter of all new cars are leased rather than purchased outright. In a culture that prizes spiffy new cars, it's no wonder that a massive auto-leasing industry has sprung up to provide anyone (at least anyone with a sufficiently good credit rating) to possess one.

There are some advantages to auto leasing. You get to drive a new car, typically without worrying about the warranty expiring. You may even have lower monthly payments than you would if you purchased a car on an installment payment plan.

Common provisions in car leases. In addition to the elements that appear in all leases—such as a description of the property, monthly payments, term (length of rental), and limitations on the lease—some provisions and issues are specific to vehicle leases, including:

- **Lease-to-purchase arrangements.** If the lease provides for a buy-out at the end of the term, the consumer may end up paying more than the vehicle is worth. In situations like this, it's best to calculate what it's going to cost to buy the car before signing the lease—and then decide whether the car is worth what you'll have to pay to get it.

- **Mileage fees.** Most leases require per-mile payments, which makes them disadvantageous for long-distance drivers.

- **Early termination provisions.** Some vehicle leases penalize consumers for ending them early by requiring a large payment or using a complex formula to calculate the penalty. In addition, some vehicle leases require a balloon payment if the consumer defaults.

- **Insurance requirements.** Some vehicle leases require "gap" insurance. If the vehicle is stolen or totaled, gap insurance pays the difference between what is owed under the lease and what the dealer can recover on the vehicle (assuming it's not stolen), which could amount to thousands of dollars.

- **Maintenance and repairs.** Will the consumer or the leasing company have to pay for maintenance and repairs? Does the warranty cover the entire length of the lease and all miles driven? What about "excessive wear and tear?" Most leases hold the lessee responsible for these costs.

Both the Federal Trade Commission (at www.ftc.gov) and the Federal Reserve Board (at www.federalreserve.gov) provide information to help you understand your rights when leasing a car.

leasehold

This is an archaic term describing the land or property being leased. *See* lease.

legal opinion

This term may refer to either:

- **A court's legal decision.** Some (but not all) judicial decisions include a written statement explaining what the court has decided and why. These opinions range from one or two sentences to hundreds of pages long. Most appeals court decisions include a written opinion. Some legal opinions serve as precedent (legal authority for other courts) while others do not. Some opinions are published; some are called "unpublished," which means they may not be used for any reason beyond resolving the dispute between the parties to that lawsuit. Even unpublished opinions are often publicly available via the Internet.
- **A lawyer's legal opinion.** In many cases, a company may seek a written statement from its legal counsel (sometimes called a "qualified legal opinion") providing advice about a contract or other legal matters. For example, it is common for a lawyer to provide a legal opinion as to whether a bond or stock or other security has been duly authorized and issued.

Related term: comfort letter.

legalese

Rather than use simple terms and phrases, some lawyers resort to technical, confusing jargon, commonly referred to as "legalese." Although some legal terms have very precise meanings (as explained throughout this book), legalese is often used just because of inexperience, laziness, lack of self-confidence, or even misguided desire to impress clients and justify high bills.

A little history. You may wonder how legal professionals (who actually speak the same language as mere mortals in their everyday lives) have come up with such a convoluted approach to writing. One reason, as explained by contract expert Tina L. Stark, has to do with historical battles. According to Stark, after France conquered England in 1066, the French language infiltrated British courts and English lawyers, unsure that a French word had the same meaning as the English, often included both. The results are phrases such "goods" (English) and "chattel" (French), "breaking" (English) and "entering" (French), and "right, title" (both English) and "interest" (French). This linguistic oddity has carried through for centuries and encouraged even more redundancies.

The birth of plain English. Described by one scholar as "pompous, atrocious prose spouted to undeserving clients," legalese was the unfortunate native tongue for most lawyers until the mid-1970s, when two events began to turn the tide. In 1975, attorneys for Citibank created the first reader-friendly consumer loan agreement by eliminating legal jargon, using short, clear sentence structure, adding white space, and using a less intimidating typeface. At the same time, a movement began on the West Coast by former Legal Aid attorneys seeking to give consumers access to the law. This evolved into the legal self-help industry (led by Nolo, the publisher of this book), with hallmarks that include simple explanations of the law and easy-to-understand agreements. The Citibank contracts and the popularity of self-help law gave rise to the "plain-English" legal movement, an approach to legal writing that has now been adopted as a requirement for certain consumer agreements in some states.

L

What's wrong with legalese? As long as everyone agrees on the precise meaning of a legal term, there's no harm in using it. The problem is that legalese can be vague. Even when it isn't, most people aren't exactly sure what it means. If you're drafting, negotiating, or signing a contract, you'll want to know exactly what you're agreeing to. Ambiguous language in a contract can lead to court battles down the road, if the parties didn't interpret it the same way. Leaving legalese out of your contracts makes it much more likely that you'll get the benefit of your bargain—and stay out of the courtroom.

Related terms: interpretive provisions; mistake; plain meaning rule; rules of interpretation (rules of construction).

lessor/lessee

The lessor owns the property subject to the lease. The lessee pays for the right to use and possess the property.

Related terms: lease, lease (commercial property); lease, residential (rental agreement); lease, vehicle.

letter agreement

Dear Reader: A letter agreement is simply a contract written in letter format. A letter agreement is as enforceable as any other valid contract. The only distinction is that it is drafted on letterhead, includes the typical letter formalities (date, address, and endearments), and contains a signature line for the other party. The contract terms are placed within the body of the letter. In keeping with the less formal nature of the correspondence, the drafter may replace the names of the parties with pronouns—for example, "You agree to work for me for a period of one year." It is common to include two signed versions of the letter and ask the other party to sign and return one copy.

Below is an example of a letter agreement, in this case, a release for the rights to use an interview.

Letter Agreement: Interview Release

Letter Agreement: Interview Release

Re: Interview Release

Dear _____ :

This letter, when signed, will confirm that you consent to the recording of your statements and grant to _____ ("Company") and Company's assigns, licensees, and successors the right to copy, reproduce, and use all or a portion of the statements (the "Interview") for incorporation in the following work _____ _____ (the "Work").

You permit the use of all or a portion of the Interview in the Work in all forms and media including advertising and related promotion throughout the world and in perpetuity. You grant the right to use your image and name in connection with all uses of the Interview and waive the right to inspect or approve use of your Interview as incorporated in the Work.

You release Company and Company's assigns, licensees, and successors from any claims that may arise regarding the use of the Interview including any claims of defamation, invasion of privacy, or infringement of moral rights, rights of publicity, or copyright. You acknowledge that you have no ownership rights in the Work.

Company is not obligated to utilize the rights granted in this Agreement.

You have read and understood this agreement and you are over the age of 18. This Agreement expresses the complete understanding of the parties.

You agree to the terms of this release by signing and dating, and returning this letter to me.

Very truly yours,

_____

Interview Subject's Signature: _____

Date: _____

letter of credit

A letter of credit is a written assurance provided for a company in an international transaction that payment on the deal is guaranteed by a bank. In other words, the check really *is* in the mail.

How a letter of credit is created. Here are the steps necessary to create a letter of credit:

1. The buyer of goods in one country (the applicant) contacts a bank in that country (the issuing bank).
2. The applicant asks the issuing bank to provide a letter of credit to the seller of the goods (the beneficiary).
3. The beneficiary provides the letter of credit to a local bank (the advising or confirming bank).
4. Once the goods have been supplied (that is, the seller's end of the contract has been fulfilled), the beneficiary provides the documents required by the applicant to the advising bank.
5. Once it is satisfied that all conditions have been met, the advising bank contacts the issuing bank and requests payment.

A letter of credit involves two contracts. There are two agreements at work when a letter of credit is issued: the underlying sales or service agreement; and the letter of credit. Banks don't want to get involved in what happens with the sales agreement; they are obligated only to confirm the requirements of the letter of credit agreement—that is, that the required documents have been provided, typically some combination of these:

- **Commercial invoice.** A document that describes the goods and buyer/seller contact information
- **Letter of indemnity.** A document that provides certain guarantees and assurances regarding the goods or shipping documents
- **Bill of lading.** A document issued by a commercial carrier that evidences receipt of the goods.
- **Warranty of title.** A written assurance by the seller that the seller has clear title to the merchandise.

Irrevocable and negotiable letters. Most letters of credit are irrevocable, which means that the arrangement cannot be terminated without the agreement of the issuing bank, the confirming bank, and the beneficiary. Even if the letter of credit is revocable, it cannot be revoked once the beneficiary provides the necessary documentation. Letters of credit are also usually negotiable, which means that the beneficiary can designate anyone to receive the payment. To be considered negotiable, the letter of credit should include an unconditional promise to "pay on demand." That guarantees that upon requesting demand for payment (and providing a warranty that all conditions of the agreement have been met), the bank will pay up to the holder of the letter.

Related terms: bill of sale; guaranty/guarantor; indemnity (hold harmless provision); invoice.

letter of intent

After agreeing to the essential terms of a business deal, the parties may prepare and sign a letter of intent (also known as a "memorandum of understanding" or "term sheet"). The letter of intent sets forth the agreed-upon terms and establishes a date when the parties plan to enter into a formal agreement. A letter of intent usually does not create a binding contract. Even if the parties sign it, either party can still reject the deal for any reasonable basis. For example, the parties may sign a letter of intent but then reject the final contract because one party has a good-faith disagreement about a warranty or an indemnity provision.

Binding or nonbinding? Depending on how it is drafted, a letter of intent may bind the parties, and disputes occasionally arise regarding this issue. To avoid this result, most letters of intent specifically state they are not binding agreements. So why bother preparing and signing one, if it can't be enforced? Most companies use a letter of intent because it serves as a guide for a final agreement, establishes that both parties will work in good faith to consummate the deal, and provides some comfort level to the parties as they progress through the contract negotiation. Note that even though a letter of intent rarely creates a binding agreement regarding its subject mater, it may contain some elements that become binding—for example, a confidentiality provision.

Good faith is required. A letter of intent, like an agreement in principle, usually requires the parties to act in good faith in pursuing their contracting goals. This means that the parties must deal fairly and reasonably with each other—not blow the other party off for arbitrary reasons. Courts in most states will enforce this good-faith requirement even if they do not enforce the actual terms of the letter of intent.

Introductory language for a letter of intent. Typically, the parties don't want to be bound by a letter of intent. To make sure the letter isn't binding, it should include language to that effect. Below is a sample that accomplishes this goal.

Letter of Intent: Sample introductory language

Dear _____ :

This letter reflects our discussions regarding the terms and conditions of the proposed agreement for _____ , more specifically described below. Please review this letter of intent, and if it accurately reflects our discussions, return a copy with your signature. We will then proceed to a written draft of the agreement. Thanks for your cooperation.

Letter of Intent. This document is a Letter of Intent only. It is not intended to be, and will not constitute in any way, a binding legal agreement.

Related term: agreement in principle

license agreement

A license is like a lease for intangible property. In a license agreement, the owner (the "licensor") of intellectual property—usually a copyrighted item, trade secret, creative work, trademark, patented invention, or other proprietary material—lets someone else (the "licensee") use, sell, or otherwise commercially exploit the property for a period of time. In return, the licensor receives money—either a one-time payment or a continuing payment based on a percentage of sales (known as a royalty). A license differs from a sale of rights (sometimes called an "assignment") because the licensor always retains ultimate ownership of the licensed material. In other words, the licensee isn't paying to purchase the property outright, but to use it for a limited period of time.

Licensing of rights. The licensor may make this kind of agreement only if the licensor controls the right to make and sell the work, a right typically granted by intellectual property laws governing copyright, trademark, trade secrets, and patents. In other words, without a license, the licensee could be sued for using the protected work. If the work is not protected, no license is necessary; anyone can make and sell the property without fear of legal repercussions.

Common license agreement provisions. Here are the provisions often found in a license agreement:

- **The licensed work.** This section identifies what is being licensed. Often, the licensed item is described in greater detail in an exhibit attached to the agreement.

- **The licensed product or licensed use.** This section describes the manner in which the licensee will use the licensed work (that is, the resulting work that will be sold, distributed, or otherwise exploited by the licensee).

- **Grant.** The grant of rights officially permits the licensee to use the work, describes the legal rights being licensed, and states whether the rights are exclusive or nonexclusive. If the rights are exclusive, only the licensee may use and sell the property;

otherwise, the licensor is free to license the same property to others.

- **Sublicensing.** A sublicense allows the licensee to turn around and license its rights to another company. For example, a licensee may want to grant rights to other companies in the United States or in foreign countries, where the licensee is not prepared to play an active role itself. This provision describes whether sublicensing is permitted and under what conditions.
- **Reservation of rights.** Under contract law, if you do not grant a specific right, you have retained (also known as "reserved") that right. Because this is how the law works, you don't really have to include it in your agreement. Just to be on the safe side, however, most licensors prefer to include a statement that all rights not granted are reserved.
- **Territory.** You can geographically limit where the licensee can exercise rights, by defining a "territory" in your agreement.
- **Term.** By including a term provision in your agreement, you can limit how long the license lasts.
- **Payment.** Under a license agreement, the licensor is typically paid a lump sum, periodic payments, or an ongoing royalty based on a percentage of the income from sales of the licensed work.
- **Audit.** This clause gives the licensor the right to audit the licensee's records to detect and quantify any shortfalls in payment.
- **Warranties/indemnities.** Warranties are contractual promises that the licensee and the licensor make to each other. For example, the licensor often warrants that he or she is the true owner of the property and has the right to license it. An indemnity provision requires one party to pay the other's legal costs in the event of a lawsuit over the licensed property. For example, the licensor may agree to indemnify the licensee if the licensee is sued by a third party who claims to be the true owner of the property.

- **Intellectual property rights; infringement.** This provision enables the parties to decide who will seek intellectual property protection for the work or licensed uses. It may also describe how infringements will be treated (for example, which party will be responsible for contacting infringers and demanding that they stop using the property).
- **Credit.** The credit provision allows the licensor to indicate how credit for the final product or use should appear.
- **Exploitation.** This provision guarantees that the licensee will use the property, not simply sit on it. Many licensors grant a license because they want to earn money from their creative work but lack the necessary facilities, contacts, and name recognition to market their ideas on their own. The exploitation provision addresses these concerns by setting a date by which the licensee must release the licensed content and sometimes requiring that a certain amount of money be spent on advertising or promotion.
- **Approval.** This provision gives the licensor the right to look at and approve prototypes of the licensed uses or products before they go into full production or display.
- **Licensor copies and right to purchase.** This provision allows the licensor to receive a certain number of free copies or items and the specifies cost at which it can purchase additional products.
- **Confidentiality.** A confidentiality clause reminds each party to preserve the other's confidential information—and allows each to sue for breach of contract if the other slips up.
- **Insurance.** If the property will be used in connection with a product that could cause damage, the licensor may want to make sure that the licensee carries product liability insurance. Product liability insurance doesn't usually cover trademark, patent, or copyright lawsuits. The licensee will need a separate business policy for protection against infringement claims.

L

- **Termination.** Even without a termination provision, either party can terminate a license agreement if the other party commits a "material breach." However, most licensors will insist on a written termination provision and will seek some or all of the rights listed in our model agreement (below), including the right to terminate only as to a specific portion of the territory if the property is not exploited there.
- **Effect of termination and sell-off.** If the licensee breaches the agreement for any of the reasons provided under "Licensor's Right to Terminate"—for example, the licensee stops paying royalties—the licensee should not be permitted to continue profiting from the deal by selling the product. This provision provides limitations on product sell-offs.

Below is an example of a merchandise license agreement.

Clickwraps and end-user agreements. In addition to the commercial licenses described above, a second type of license has been popularized by the software and Internet industries. Originally known as "shrinkwrap" licenses—so named because the buyer entered into the agreement by breaking the shrinkwrap packaging—these licenses place limitations on the buyer of software or the user of Internet services (known as "clickwrap licenses"). Now commonly referred to as end-user licenses, these agreements establish limitations on the right to use digital materials, such as software, stock photos, downloaded music and movies, and similar products.

Related terms: clickwrap agreement; guaranteed minimum annual royalty (GMAR); intangible property (intangible assets); intellectual property; royalty

Merchandise License Agreement

Merchandise License Agreement

This License Agreement (the "Agreement") is made between _____ _____ (referred to as "Licensor") and _____ (referred to as "Licensee").

The parties agree as follows:

1. The Work. The Work refers to the work described in Exhibit A. Licensor is the owner of all rights to the Work and Licensee shall not claim any right to use the Work except under the terms of this Agreement.

2. Licensed Products. Licensed Products are defined as Licensee's products incorporating the Work specifically described in Exhibit A (the "Licensed Products").

3. Grant of Rights. Licensor grants to Licensee ☐ an exclusive license or ☐ a nonexclusive license to reproduce and distribute the Work in or on the Licensed Products. Licensor grants to Licensee the right to modify the Work to incorporate it in or on the Licensed Products provided that Licensee agrees to assign to Licensor its rights, if any, in any derivative works resulting from Licensee's modification of the Work. Licensee agrees to execute any documents required to evidence this assignment of copyright and to waive any moral rights and rights of attribution provided in 17 U.S.C. § 106A of the Copyright Act.

4. Sublicense. Consent required. Licensee may sublicense the rights granted pursuant to this agreement provided: Licensee obtains Licensor's prior written consent to such sublicense; and Licensor receives such revenue or royalty payment as provided in the Payment section below. Any sublicense granted in violation of this provision is void.

5. Reservation of Rights. Licensor reserves all rights other than those being conveyed or granted in this Agreement.

L

Merchandise License Agreement (continued)

6. Territory. The rights granted to Licensee are limited to _____
_____ (the "Territory").

7. Term. The "Effective Date" of this Agreement is defined as the date when the agreement commences and is established by the latest signature date. This Agreement commences upon the Effective Date and extends for a period of _____ years (the "Initial Term"). Following the Initial Term, Licensee may renew this agreement under the same terms and conditions for [*number of periods*] consecutive [*number of years in rental period*] year periods (the "Renewal Terms"), provided that Licensee provides written notice of its intention to renew this agreement within thirty (30) days before the expiration of the current term. In no event does the Term extend beyond the period of United States copyright protection for the Work.

8. Payments. All royalties ("Royalties") provided for under this Agreement accrue when the respective Licensed Products are sold, shipped, distributed, billed, or paid for, whichever occurs first.

9. Net Sales. Net Sales are defined as Licensee's gross sales (the gross invoice amount billed to customers) less quantity discounts or rebates and returns actually credited. A quantity discount or rebate is a discount made at the time of shipment. No deductions will be made for cash or other discounts, commissions, manufacturing costs, uncollectible accounts, or for fees or expenses of any kind that the Licensee may incur in connection with the Royalty payments.

10. Advance Against Royalties. As a nonrefundable advance against royalties (the "Advance"), Licensee agrees to pay to Licensor upon execution of this Agreement the sum of $ _____ .

11. Licensed Product Royalty. Licensee agrees to pay a Royalty of _____% of all Net Sales revenue of the Licensed Products ("Licensed Product Royalty").

Merchandise License Agreement (continued)

12. Payments and Statements to Licensor. Within thirty (30) days after the end of each calendar quarter (the "Royalty Period"), an accurate statement of Net Sales of Licensed Products, along with any royalty payments or sublicensing revenues due to Licensor, will be provided to Licensor, regardless of whether any Licensed Products were sold during the Royalty Period. All payments are to be paid in United States currency drawn on a United States bank. The acceptance by Licensor of any of the statements furnished or royalties paid does not preclude Licensor questioning the correctness at any time of any payments or statements.

13. Audit. Licensee shall keep accurate books of account and records covering all transactions relating to the license granted in this Agreement, and Licensor or its duly authorized representatives shall have the right upon five days' prior written notice, and during normal business hours, to inspect and audit Licensee's records relating to the Work licensed under this Agreement. Licensor shall bear the cost of such inspection and audit, unless the results indicate an underpayment greater than $ _____ for any six-month (6-month) period. In that case, Licensee shall promptly reimburse Licensor for all costs of the audit along with the amount due with interest on such sums. Interest accrues from the date the payment was originally due and the interest rate will be 1.5% per month, or the maximum rate permitted by law, whichever is less. All books of account and records are to be made available in the United States and kept available for at least two years after the termination of this Agreement.

14. Late Payment. Time is of the essence with respect to all payments to be made by Licensee under this Agreement. If Licensee is late in any payment provided for in this Agreement, Licensee shall pay interest on the payment from the date due until paid at a rate of 1.5% per month, or the maximum rate permitted by law, whichever is less.

Merchandise License Agreement (continued)

15. Licensor Warranties. Licensor warrants that it has the power and authority to enter into this Agreement and has no knowledge as to any third-party claims regarding the proprietary rights in the Work that would interfere with the rights granted under this Agreement.

16. Indemnification by Licensor. Licensor shall indemnify Licensee and hold Licensee harmless from any damages and liabilities (including reasonable attorneys' fees and costs) arising from any breach of Licensor's warranties as defined in Licensor's Warranties, above.

17. Licensee Warranties. Licensee warrants that it will use its best commercial efforts to market the Licensed Products and that sale and marketing of the Licensed Products will conform with all applicable laws and regulations, including but not limited to all intellectual property laws.

18. Indemnification by Licensee. Licensee shall indemnify Licensor and hold Licensor harmless from any damages and liabilities (including reasonable attorneys' fees and costs):

   a. arising from any breach of Licensee's warranties and representation as defined in the Licensee Warranties, above;

   b. arising out of any alleged defects or failures to perform of the Licensed Products or any product liability claims or use of the Licensed Products; and

   c. any claims arising out of advertising, distribution, or marketing of the Licensed Products.

19. Intellectual Property Registration. Licensor may, but is not obligated to, seek in its own name and at its own expense, appropriate copyright registrations for the Work. Licensor makes no warranty with respect to the validity of any copyright that may be granted. Licensor grants to Licensee the right to apply for registration of the Work or Licensed Products provided that such registrations are applied for in the name of Licensor and

Merchandise License Agreement (continued)

licensed to Licensee during the Term and according to the conditions of this Agreement. Licensee shall have the right to deduct its reasonable out-of-pocket expenses for the preparation and filing of any such registrations from future royalties due to Licensor under this Agreement. Licensee shall obtain Licensor's prior written consent before incurring expenses for any foreign copyright applications.

20. Compliance With Intellectual Property Laws. The license granted in this Agreement is conditioned on Licensee's compliance with the provisions of the intellectual property laws of the United States and any foreign country in the Territory. All copies of the Licensed Product as well as all promotional material must bear appropriate proprietary notices.

21. Licensor Credits. Licensee shall identify Licensor as the owner of rights to the Work and Licensee shall include the following notice on all copies of the Licensed Products: "_____ . All rights reserved." Licensee may, with Licensor's consent, use Licensor's name, image, or trademark in advertising or promotional materials associated with the sale of the Licensed Products.

22. Infringement Against Third Parties. In the event that either party learns of imitations or infringements of the Work or Licensed Products, that party shall notify the other in writing of the infringements or imitations. Licensor shall have the right to commence lawsuits against third persons arising from infringement of the Work or Licensed Products. In the event that Licensor does not commence a lawsuit against an alleged infringer within sixty days of notification by Licensee, Licensee may commence a lawsuit against the third party. Before filing suit, Licensee shall obtain the written consent of Licensor to do so, and such consent will not be unreasonably withheld. Licensor will cooperate fully and in good faith with Licensee for the purpose of securing and preserving Licensee's rights to the Work. Any recovery (including, but not limited to,

Merchandise License Agreement (continued)

a judgment, settlement, or licensing agreement included as resolution of an infringement dispute) will be divided equally between the parties after deduction and payment of reasonable attorneys' fees to the party bringing the lawsuit.

23. Exploitation Date. Licensee agrees to manufacture, distribute, and sell the Licensed Products in commercially reasonable quantities during the term of this Agreement and to commence such manufacture, distribution, and sale by _____ . This is a material provision of this Agreement.

24. Advertising Budget. Licensee agrees to spend at least _____ % of estimated annual gross sales for promotional efforts and advertising of the Licensed Products.

25. Approval of Samples and Quality Control. Licensee shall submit a reasonable number of preproduction designs, prototypes, and camera-ready artwork prior to production as well as preproduction samples of the Licensed Product to Licensor to assure that the product meets Licensor's quality standards. In the event that Licensor fails to object in writing within ten (10) business days after the date of receipt of any such materials, such materials will be deemed to be acceptable. At least once during each calendar year, Licensee shall submit two (2) production samples of each Licensed Product for review. Licensee shall pay all costs for delivery of these approval materials. The quality standards applied by Licensor shall be no more rigorous than the quality standards applied by Licensor to similar products.

26. Licensor Copies and Right to Purchase. Licensee shall provide Licensor with _____ copies of each Licensed Product. Licensor has the right to purchase from Licensee, at Licensee's manufacturing cost, at least _____ copies of any Licensed Product, and such payments will be deducted from royalties due to Licensor.

Merchandise License Agreement (continued)

27. Confidentiality. The parties acknowledge that each may have access to confidential information that relates to each other's business (the "Information"). The parties agree to protect the confidentiality of the Information and maintain it with the strictest confidence, and no party shall disclose such information to third parties without the prior written consent of the other.

28. Insurance. Licensee shall, throughout the Term, obtain and maintain, at its own expense, standard product liability insurance coverage, naming Licensor as an additional named insured. Such policy must provide protection against any claims, demands, and causes of action arising out of any alleged defects or failure to perform of the Licensed Products or any use of the Licensed Products. The amount of coverage will be a minimum of $ _____ , with no deductible amount for each single occurrence for bodily injury or property damage. The policy will provide for notice to the Licensor from the insurer by Registered or Certified Mail in the event of any modification or termination of insurance. The provisions of this section will survive termination for three years.

29. Licensor's Right to Terminate. Licensor shall have the right to terminate this Agreement for the following reasons: (a) Failure to Make Timely Payment. Licensee fails to pay Royalties when due or fails to accurately report Net Sales, as defined in the Payment Section of this Agreement, and such failure is not cured within thirty (30) days after written notice from the Licensor. (b) Failure to Introduce Product. Licensee fails to introduce the product to market by the date set in the Exploitation section of this Agreement or to offer the Licensed Products in commercially reasonable quantities during any subsequent year. (c) Failure to Maintain Insurance. Licensee fails to maintain or obtain product liability insurance as required by the provisions of this Agreement.

Merchandise License Agreement (continued)

30. Effect of Termination. Upon termination of this Agreement ("Termination"), all Royalty obligations as established in the Payments Section will immediately become due. After the Termination of this license, all rights granted to Licensee under this Agreement terminate and revert to Licensor, and Licensee will refrain from further manufacturing, copying, marketing, distribution, or use of any Licensed Product or other product that incorporates the Work. Within thirty (30) days after Termination, Licensee shall deliver to Licensor a statement indicating the number and description of the Licensed Products that it had on hand or is in the process of manufacturing as of the Termination date.

31. Sell-Off Period. Licensee may dispose of the Licensed Products covered by this Agreement for a period of 90 days after Termination or expiration except that Licensee shall have no such right in the event this agreement is terminated according to the Licensor's Right to Terminate, above. At the end of the post-Termination sale period, Licensee shall furnish a royalty payment and statement as required under the Payment Section. Upon Termination, Licensee shall deliver to Licensor all original artwork and camera-ready reproductions used in the manufacture of the Licensed Products. Licensor shall bear the costs of shipping for the artwork and reproductions.

32. Attorneys' Fees and Expenses. The prevailing party shall have the right to collect from the other party its reasonable costs and necessary disbursements and attorneys' fees incurred in enforcing this Agreement.

33. Governing Law. This Agreement is governed in accordance with the laws of the State of _____ .

34. Jurisdiction. The parties consent to the exclusive jurisdiction and venue of the federal and state courts located in _____ in any action arising out of or relating to this Agreement. The parties waive

Merchandise License Agreement (continued)

any other venue to which either party might be entitled by domicile or otherwise.

35. Waiver. The failure to exercise any right provided in this Agreement is not a waiver of prior or subsequent rights.

36. Invalidity. If any provision of this Agreement is invalid under applicable statute or rule of law, it is to be considered omitted, and the remaining provisions of this Agreement are in no way affected.

37. Entire Understanding. This Agreement expresses the complete understanding of the parties and supersedes all prior representations, agreements, and understandings, whether written or oral. This Agreement may not be altered except by a written document signed by both parties.

38. Attachments and Exhibits. The parties agree and acknowledge that all attachments, exhibits, and schedules referred to in this Agreement are incorporated in this Agreement by reference.

39. No Special Damages. Licensor shall not be liable to Licensee for any incidental, consequential, punitive, or special damages.

40. Notices. Any notice or communication required or permitted to be given under this Agreement will be sufficiently given when received by certified mail or sent by facsimile transmission or overnight courier.

41. No Joint Venture. Nothing contained in this Agreement is to be construed to place one of the parties in the relationship of agent, employee, franchisee, officer, partner, or joint venturer to the other party. Neither party may create or assume any obligation on behalf of the other.

42. Assignability. Licensee may not assign or transfer its rights or obligations pursuant to this Agreement without the prior written consent of Licensor. Any assignment or transfer in violation of this section is void.

Merchandise License Agreement (continued)

Each party has signed this Agreement through its authorized representative. The parties, having read this Agreement, indicate their consent to the terms and conditions by their signature below.

Licensor

Licensee

Signature: _____

Signature: _____

Name: _____

Name: _____

Date: _____

Date: _____

L

licensee/licensor

The licensee is the person or entity that pays for licensing rights. The licensor is the owner of intangible property who grants licensing rights.

Related terms: clickwrap agreement; guaranteed minimum annual royalty (GMAR); intangible property (intangible assets); intellectual property; license agreement; royalty.

lien

You can get a lien on someone else's property when that person owes you money. A lien gives the person who holds it (the lien holder) the right to require the property owner (the debtor) to pay a debt before selling or giving away the property. A lien may even give the lien holder the right to force a sale of the property in order to get repaid. In other words, a lien is a little bit like when you were younger and you claimed "dibs" on something, except you get to claim dibs on something that belongs to somebody else, like their home, car, or other property.

> **EXAMPLE:** Tom has a lien on Jerry's home. Jerry puts his home up for sale. The title company discovers the lien and tells Jerry that it cannot grant clear title (which is necessary for Jerry to sell his home) until Tom is paid and removes the lien.

There are two types of liens. Consensual liens are voluntarily entered into by the property owner, who agrees that a lien will be granted if the debt is not paid. Nonconsensual liens are not voluntary: They are the result of a court order or legal right. For example, a court might order that a lien be placed on a debtor's property, or a contractor who isn't paid for repair work might file a "mechanic's lien" on the customer's home.

Consensual liens. A lien may be part of a loan agreement. For example, someone might borrow money and provide property as a guarantee (collateral or security) against the debt. A common example is a mortgage, in which the lender is granted a lien on the property that's the subject of the mortgage. If the debtor defaults, the bank has the right to foreclose on the property to get its money back.

Nonconsensual liens. If a lien is nonconsensual, the debtor doesn't have to agree to allow the property lien. For example, the federal government may obtain a lien against property for failure to pay income taxes (a tax lien) or the winner of a lawsuit may obtain a lien after the loser fails to pay a judgment (a judgment lien).

Related terms: judgment creditor; mechanic's lien; promissory note; remedies.

limited liability company (LLC)

The limited liability company (LLC) is a form of business entity that combines some of the best feature of corporations (limiting the owners' personal liability) and sole proprietorships and partnerships (the owners file the same tax documents as sole proprietorships and partnerships). An LLC can be formed by one or more people. LLCs have largely replaced corporations as the favorite choice among small business owners.

Because an LLC is considered to be a legal entity separate from its owners, the company, not the owners (or directors and employees), is liable for debts and contractual obligations. That is, the owners of an LLC, as well as the directors and employees, are not personally liable for the business liabilities. However, as with corporations, owners are liable for debts that are personally guaranteed, tax debts, and claims resulting from owners' negligence.

Taxation. An LLC is taxed like a partnership or, for a one-owner LLC, as a sole proprietorship. LLC income, loss, credits, and deductions are reported on the individual income tax returns of the LLC owners. The LLC itself does not pay income tax (although it may have to pay annual state fees). If you switch from sole proprietor or general partnership to an LLC, there won't be any changes in how you do your income tax reporting. That's because, like sole proprietorships and partnerships, most LLCs are pass-through entities. Pass-through taxation means that you report the money you earned from your business on your individual tax return and pay tax at individual income tax rates.

Creation. To start an LLC, you must file articles of organization with the state business filing office. You and the other owners should also prepare an operating agreement to spell out how the LLC will be owned, how profits and losses will be divided, how departing or deceased members will be bought out, and other essential ownership issues. Most start-up business owners prefer LLCs because reporting and paying individual income taxes is easier than the corporate alternative.

Related terms: corporation; partnership (general); personal liability; sole proprietor.

limited partnership

A limited partnership is a type of business entity that enables certain partners to avoid ("limit") personal liability for the partnership's activities. Limited partnerships consist of one or more general partners and one or more limited partners. The general partners manage the business, fund its operations, or perform services and share in the profits. Limited partners do not participate in business management; they only invest money. In return for giving up any say in how the business is run, their liability is limited to the amount of their investment, and they are not personally liable for business debts.

Suitable for specific projects. Limited partnerships have been used for businesses that were created for a specific project—for example, to produce a movie or construct a housing development. Using this business structure, an entrepreneur can obtain investment income from a number of limited partners, who do not have to worry about being personally liable. A major disadvantage of using this type of arrangement is that the entity must abide by certain legal formalities, such as filing with the state government, and must also have a written partnership agreement if required by state law. Other disadvantages are that limited partners cannot have any input in business decisions, so they have little control over how their money is spent. Also, general partners can be personally liable for all business debts. With the rise in popularity of limited liability companies (LLCs), limited partnerships have been used less frequently.

Related terms: corporation; limited liability company (LLC); partnership (general); personal liability; sole proprietor.

line of credit

There's nothing more comforting for a business than to know that a bank has extended a line of credit—an agreement to provide the business with a loan (or series of loans) up to a specific cap or limit. The business doesn't have to tap this source, but the money is there if needed.

A line of credit is granted for a period of time, often to conform to a company's fiscal year or to meet the requirements of shareholders. Lines of credit can be structured in many ways—for example, there can be varying interest rates, tiered loan levels, or limitations based on company revenues—but the basic principle remains that if the company needs a cash infusion, the money is available.

Related terms: promissory note; revolving loan.

liquidated damages

Liquidated damages are the parties' estimate, made when they sign the contract, of the damages that would be caused by a breach. If the contract is later breached, the breaching party must pay the agreed-upon amount of liquidated damages, unless that amount is so much higher than the actual damages that it serves as a penalty rather than an estimate.

> **EXAMPLE:** Bob's Diner contracts to buy milk from Tom's Dairy. Tom realizes he must purchase 10 additional cows in order to meet the demands of the new contract. He's worried

that Bob's Diner may breach or cancel the agreement before the cows are paid off. So, Tom includes a provision in the milk supply agreement requiring Bob to pay Tom $5,000 (which is half the cost of the cows) plus any lost profits if Bob breaches the agreement during the first year. By attempting to estimate damages beforehand, Tom has created a liquidated damages provision.

Damages versus penalties. Liquidated damages provisions have some advantages: They avoid uncertainty when assessing damages, and they discourage litigation because the parties don't have to wait for a court to determine their liability. But liquidated damages provisions are not always enforceable, even if they are negotiated and agreed to by the parties. Sometimes, a party with superior bargaining power insists on a liquidated damages provision that demands too much. Also, courts are often skeptical of allowing contracting parties to determine their own remedies; judges believe that they should perform this task themselves.

What's enforceable? In order to be valid, a liquidated damages clause must meet these criteria:

- **Difficult to estimate.** Courts are more likely to enforce a provision if the injury is difficult to estimate when the contract is created. Some injuries—for example, the loss of profit from a sale—are easy to predict. Other injuries—for example, harm caused by the theft of trade secrets—are much harder to estimate.

- **Reasonable assessment/not a penalty.** Courts are less likely to enforce a provision if it penalizes or punishes the breaching party. In other words, if the predicted damages are grossly disproportionate to the actual injury, it becomes a penalty or punishment. For example, a provision in a rental agreement that required double rent payments for holdover tenants was found to serve primarily to penalize the tenant, not to accurately reflect the landlord's damages. As one legal scholar stated, "If the damages provided for in the contract are grossly disproportionate to the actual harm sustained, the courts usually conclude that the parties' original expectations were unreasonable." When making a reasonableness analysis, courts consider what would have been reasonable at the time of contracting, not at the time of breach (with the exception of sales of goods contracts under the Uniform Commercial Code, as explained below).

Liquidated damages and the U.C.C. Article 2 § 2-718(1) of the Uniform Commercial Code (which applies to all transactions or sales of goods) varies slightly from the rules discussed, above. When considering the validity of a liquidated damages provision, the reasonableness of the damage estimate can be measured in light of the anticipated harm (at the time of contracting) or the actual harm (at the time of the breach).

Statutory requirements. Most states have laws regulating liquidated damages. For example, California Civil Code § 1671 states that a "provision in a contract liquidating the damages for the breach of the contract is valid unless the party seeking to invalidate the provision establishes that the provision was unreasonable under the circumstances existing at the time the contract was made." Sometimes, statutes are more specific and regulate specific industries or transactions. For example, Connecticut law regulates consumer contracts as follows:

"**Enforceability of liquidated damages provision in consumer contracts.** (a) No provision in a written contract for the purchase or lease of goods or services primarily for personal, family or household purposes that provides for the payment of liquidated damages in the event of a breach of the contract shall be enforceable unless (1) the contract contains a statement in boldface type at least twelve points in size immediately following such liquidated damages provision stating "I ACKNOWLEDGE THAT THIS CONTRACT CONTAINS A LIQUIDATED DAMAGES PROVISION", and (2) the person against whom such provision is to be enforced signs such person's name or writes such person's initials next to such statement. Nothing in this section shall validate a clause that is a penalty clause or is otherwise invalid under the law of this state."

Predicting how a court will act. How do you know whether a court will invalidate a liquidated provision? Unfortunately, despite all of the explanations about penalties and reasonableness, above, it's not always easy to predict how a court will rule. Here are some things to keep in mind:

- **The sophistication of the parties.** Some courts take a more laissez faire approach and permit a wider range of "reasonableness" than others, particularly when the parties negotiated the contract are fairly sophisticated. For example, courts are less likely to invalidate a liquidated damages provision in an agreement between two attorneys than in an agreement made by nonattorneys.

- **Consumer contracts, preprinted agreements, and bargaining disparity.** In certain cases, particularly consumer contracts such as car rental agreements or gym memberships, courts are more likely to invalidate if there is great disparity between the relative bargaining power and sophistication of the parties. As a general rule, liquidated damages provisions in preprinted contracts (and provisions that use the term "penalty") are usually subject to higher scrutiny. For example, the following provision, from a health club contract, is likely to be found unenforceable by many courts (state laws may differ, see below) because it acts a penalty by requiring a customer to pay the entire year's fees regardless of when the breach occurs or the reasons for the breach.

Liquidated Damages: Sample language which is unlikely to be enforced

Liquidated Damages. If you repudiate this contract, breach any provision, or don't make a payment within five days of your due date, we can require you to pay the entire balance of what you still owe under the annual contract.

Hedging their bets. The party drafting the contract may attempt to circumvent the liquidated damages issues by including special language explaining that the parties recognize the difficulties in estimating damages and have mutually agreed that the provision is reasonable. On the other hand, in 2006, a California court upheld a liquidated damages provision in a standardized preprinted form agreement for broadband Internet services as follows:

Liquidated Damages: Sample language which is enforceable

Liquidated Damages. Charges for late payment and nonpayment are liquidated damages intended to be a reasonable advance estimate of our costs resulting from late payments or nonpayments by our customers, which costs will not be readily ascertainable, and will be difficult to predict or calculate, at the time that such administrative late fee(s) and related charges are set because it would be difficult to know in advance: (a) whether you will pay for the Service on a timely basis, (b) if you do pay late, when you will actually pay, if ever, and (c) what costs we will incur because of your late payment or non payment ....

The court was also persuaded by the fact that the fees and charges were posted at the company's website and mailed to subscribers before any late fees were charged (and by the fact that late fees did not exceed $4.75).

Keep in mind, however, that adding language such as "costs will not be readily ascertainable and will be difficult to predict" will not automatically make your liquidated damages provision enforceable. In other words, just because you say it's not a penalty doesn't mean that a court will agree. However, it does show that the issue was discussed and reviewed by the parties.

Related terms: breach, material; damages, compensatory; damages, consequential; void (voidable).

living together contract

Living together agreements (also known as "nonmarital agreements") were first popularized in the late 1970s following the California Supreme Court's ruling in *Marvin v. Marvin* that established four contract principles:

- Unmarried couples may make written contracts.
- Unmarried couples may make oral contracts.
- If a couple hasn't made a written or an oral contract, the court may examine the couple's actions to decide whether an "implied" contract exists.
- If a judge can't find an implied contract, the judge may presume that "the parties intend to deal fairly with each other" and find one partner indebted to the other by invoking well-established legal doctrines of equity and fairness.

Although *Marvin* applies only in California, other states have applied similar principles to couples that are living together. These days, almost all states enforce contracts between unmarried partners (although some states will enforce only written contracts).

Who needs one? Unmarried partners in a long-term, serious partnership who are concerned about the legal consequences of dealing with money and property and who are planning to mix assets or share expenses should use a living together agreement.

The issues. A living together agreement should address the following issues:

- **Property and finances.** A living together agreement should cover all of the partners' property, including the property each brought to the relationship and the property either or both accumulate during it.
- **Expenses.** The agreement should cover how expenses will be handled during the relationship. For example, how will the partners divide the day-to-day costs for food, utilities, laundry, housing, and the like, especially if expenses increase or decrease? Some common solutions are: (1) Each partner pays his or her own way—that is, whatever costs they incur, (2) the

partners split 50-50, or (3) each contributes in proportion to income.

- **Separation or death.** It's wise to cover what will happen if the partners split up or if one dies. It may simply say that if the partners separate, each will have the right to take immediate possession of separate property and that all jointly owned property will be divided equally. If there is property that is owned together, but not in equal shares, the agreement should specify a method for dividing it. As for death, without properly prepared documents, members of an unmarried couple have no right to inherit property from one another. The living together agreement can specify how the partners want to provide for each other; it will serve as strong evidence of a couple's intentions. Be aware, however, that writing out a plan in the living together agreement is not enough. Each partner should also use a will, living trust, or other estate planning documents to ensure that the plan is carried out.

- **Dispute resolution.** It's wise to include a method for resolving disagreements that might later arise out of the agreement. Many living together agreements include a provision requiring mediation, followed by arbitration if necessary.

What happens if you get married? A living together contract will be enforceable after marriage only if it was created shortly before your marriage, at a time when you both planned to marry. To be enforceable, prenuptial (or premarital) contracts must be made in contemplation of marriage.

Related terms: marriage contract; prenuptial agreement.

loan agreement

See promissory note.

mailbox rule

The mailbox rule—popularized before overnight deliveries, fax, and email—provides that if one person sends an offer by mail (that is, the U.S. Postal Service), a contract is created once the other party places an acceptance into the mail (that is, drops it in the mailbox).

Related term: offer and acceptance.

make whole

Make whole has two meanings in contract law:

- **To compensate for a breach.** To make someone whole means to fully compensate someone for an injury. For contract purposes, this refers to fully compensating the victim of a breach. For example, if an employee was fired without good cause in breach of a two-year employment contract, that person is entitled to be made whole by being reinstated for the full term of the contract and paid for any lost wages, benefits, or other monetary harm caused by the firing.
- **Paying off a loan before it is due.** Loan agreements often include a make-whole provision (also known as a make-whole "call") that includes a method or formula for compensating the lender if the loan is paid off prior to the date of maturity (the date when the final installment payment is due).

Related terms: acceleration clause; damages (compensatory) clause.

marriage contract

The marriage relationship is a contract. By participating in a state-sanctioned marriage, the happy couple makes mutual promises and agrees to divisions of property and to certain rights and obligations regarding the offspring of the union. However, contracts to marry—where one party promises to marry another—are not enforced by courts. (If the reasons for this are not obvious to you, please review the history of women's emancipation.)

Marriage-related contracts. Although contracts *for* marriage are not enforced, contracts about the marriage (or its aftermath)—such as premarital (or prenuptial) agreements—are legally enforceable. Unmarried couples living together can also enter into agreements establishing obligations and property rights sometimes known as partnership, nonmarital, or "living together" agreements.

Related terms: living together contract; prenuptial agreement.

material adverse change (MAC)

A material adverse change (or MAC) refers to an important change in conditions, always for the worse. For example, a contract may state that "barring any MAC, the merger shall occur on June 1." Although fairly vague, the term is generally considered to refer to something that a reasonable company in a similar situation would consider a significant commercial change. To avoid misinterpretation, some companies specify the financial standards for determining whether a MAC has occurred.

material adverse effect

See material provision.

material breach

See breach, material.

material provision

A material provision is any clause or element of a contract that is essential for the contract to be enforceable. For example, in a sale of goods contract, the material provisions would include the description of the goods, the price, and the date of shipment or delivery.

The status of a contract provision—that is, whether or not it is material to the contract—often affects whether failing to comply with that provision amounts to a material or partial breach of the contract. Rather than rely on a judge's discretion or interpretation of the law, the parties can include a provision in the contract that a breach of certain provisions will be considered material. For example, a clause may state that certain provisions—payments, maintenance of insurance, or sales goals—will be considered material, and failing to fulfill these conditions will be a material breach. In more complex agreements, the term "material adverse effect" is used to accomplish basically the same result. For example, in a merger agreement, certain activities may be said to have a material adverse effect on the merger, such that their occurrence would result in the failure of the merger (or breach of the merger agreement).

Related terms: breach, material.

materials lien

See mechanic's lien.

maturity (maturity date)

Maturity (sometimes known as "maturity date") refers to the date on which an obligation must be repaid, or alternatively it may refer to the date of the final payment in a series of installment payments.

mechanic's lien

A mechanic's lien—which, by the way, has nothing to do with the people who work on your car—is a legal claim against property. It can be filed by anyone who provides materials or labor on a construction project and doesn't get paid. A mechanic's lien (sometimes also called a "materials" or "materialmen's" lien) is not a contract: It's a legal remedy for someone who has been the victim of a breached construction or supply contract. What's unique about mechanic's liens is that they operate as if the property itself (not the property owner) is responsible for the debt. The suppliers or workers who are owed money can force a property sale at auction if something isn't worked out.

How is a mechanic's lien created? Typically, a mechanic's lien is created as follows:

1. A property owner hires a contractor for a construction or improvement project.

2. The contractor hires subcontractors and contracts with suppliers for materials.

3. The suppliers and subcontractors (sometimes referred to as "contributors") work for the contractor; they do not contract directly with the property owner. These contributors give the property owner notice that describes the goods or services they are contributing to the project.

4. The notice is (typically) delivered to the property owner within 20 to 30 days of when the goods and services are first contributed. These so-called "20-day notices" are not liens; they are informational notices that enable the property owner to check in with contributors at the end of the construction process to make sure they've been paid.

5. If a contributor isn't paid, the contributor files a document called a "claim of mechanic's lien" at the county recorder's office for the county where the real estate is located.

6. The contributor then has a period of time—typically between two to six months—in which to either work out the payment problem or file an action against the owner to enforce the lien, which may ultimately lead to the property being sold at auction. If the enforcement action isn't filed by the statutory deadline, the lien becomes invalid.

The reality. Mechanic's lien enforcement lawsuits are seldom filed within the mandatory period, which should mean that the lien has no further effect. Even so, an old lien on property can negatively impact the owner's ability to sell because many title insurance companies will refuse to clear title unless the lien is removed, either by a release from the lien claimant or by court order. In most states, getting a court order is simple and straightforward when it is clear that the mechanic's lien claimant failed to meet the enforcement deadline.

The rationale. A property owner who has been subjected to a mechanic's lien may have to pay twice for the same materials or work: once to the main contractor; and a second time to the supplier or subcontractor who was never paid by the main contractor. State laws are typically more concerned about protecting those who provide labor or materials than about the perceived unfairness of making the owner pay twice for the same work. The owner, after all, can sue the contractor (or subcontractor or supplier) to recover the funds. The subcontractor or supplier, either because of its financial position or lack of contractual relationship, may not have the same opportunity.

Avoiding mechanic's liens. A property owner can head off issues regarding mechanic's liens in two ways:

- **Make sure that everyone gets paid.** Rather than relying on the general contractor, a property owner can pay off the subcontractors and materials suppliers directly. The owner can write a number of checks, each jointly made out to the general contractor and to a particular subcontractor or material provider. The check may be cashed only if the ultimate beneficiary endorses it, which will help ensure payment and eliminate the risk of a mechanic's lien. This is a common procedure, especially near the end of a project.
- **Get waivers.** Another approach is for the property owner to ask the contractor for lien waivers from everyone the contractor is responsible for paying. (A provision requiring waivers is shown below.) In California and many other states, a contractor must provide a waiver for all work for which the contractor has been paid (in the absence of a performance or similar bond), before accepting any further payment from the owner for additional

work. In some states, contractors and subcontractor may not "waive" their mechanic's lien rights until payment is actually made, but other states permit such waivers.

Drafting a lien waiver provision. The contract clause below is designed to provide some protection for property owners. First, the contractor warrants (promises) that no liens will be recorded. In other words, the contractor promises timely payment to suppliers and subcontractors. But what if the contractor breaks the promise? The second part of this clause states that the property owner won't make a final payment until receiving written notice from each supplier and subcontractor that they've been satisfactorily paid. In construction law lingo, the last payment is contingent on the contractor giving you the following things in writing:

- lien waivers or releases, in which subcontractors and suppliers promise that they will not record a lien on your property, or
- acknowledgments of full payment, in which subcontractors and suppliers state that they have been paid by the contractor and so have no grounds for filing a lien against you.

Lien waivers requirement: Sample language

Contractor represents and warrants that there will be no liens for labor or materials or appliances against the work covered by this Agreement, and agrees to protect and hold Owner free and harmless from and against any and all liens and claims for labor, materials, services, or appliances furnished or used in connection with the work.

To protect Owner against liens being filed by Contractor, sub-contractors, and materials providers, Contractor agrees that final payment to Contractor under this Agreement shall be withheld by Owner until Contractor presents Owner with lien waivers, lien releases, or acknowledgment of full payment from each subcontractor and materials supplier.

Related terms: construction agreement; lien.

mediation

In mediation (a form of alternative dispute resolution), a neutral third person helps the parties talk through their dispute and try to come up with a mutually acceptable compromise. (Or as the lawyer Abraham Lincoln advised, "Discourage litigations. Persuade your neighbors to compromise whenever you can.")

The mediator's role. Some mediators suggest possible outcomes, but a mediator normally has no authority to render a decision. It's up to the parties themselves—with the mediator's help—to come up with a resolution that's acceptable to everyone

Advantages. The advantages of mediation over litigation are that:

- Legal precedents or the whim of a judge do not dictate the resolution; you and the other party decide how to handle a dispute.
- If your contract dispute has undiscovered or undisclosed issues, mediation—unlike a structured court battle—gives you the opportunity and the flexibility to deal with them, too.
- Because mediation doesn't force disputants to undergo the fear and sometimes paranoia of the courtroom—where a judge or jury can stun either party with a big loss—people who choose mediation tend to be more relaxed and open to compromise.

The mediation process. While mediation is not as formal as going to court, the process is more structured than many people imagine. A typical mediation involves distinct stages:

- **Mediator's opening statement.** After the disputants are seated at a table, the mediator introduces everyone, explains the goals and rules of the mediation, and encourages each side to work cooperatively toward a settlement.
- **Parties' opening statements.** Each party is invited to describe what the dispute is about, its effects, and some general ideas about resolving it. While one person is speaking, the other is not allowed to interrupt.
- **Joint discussion.** The mediator may try to get the parties talking directly about what was said in the opening statements. This is the time to determine which issues need to be addressed.

- **Private caucuses.** The private caucus is a chance for each party to meet privately with the mediator (usually in a nearby room) to discuss the strengths and weaknesses of each position and new ideas for settlement. The mediator may caucus with each side just once or many times, as needed. These meetings are considered the guts of mediation.
- **Joint negotiation.** After caucuses, the mediator may bring the parties back together to negotiate directly.
- **Closing.** This is the end of the mediation. If an agreement has been reached, the mediator may put its main provisions in writing as the parties listen. The mediator may ask each side to sign the written summary of the agreement or suggest they take it to lawyers for review. If the parties want, they can write up and sign a legally binding contract. If no agreement was reached, the mediator will review whatever progress has been made and advise everyone of their options, such as meeting again later, going to arbitration, or going to court.

Finding a good mediator. Organizations like JAMS/ENDISPUTE, the American Arbitration Association, and Judicate offer mediation services nationwide, while a number of regional groups do a similar job. Mediators also often advertise in lawyer directories. (Nolo, the publisher of this book, operates a nationwide lawyer directory at www.nolo.com.)

Do you need a lawyer? Generally, you don't need a lawyer in mediation because the parties are trying to work together to solve their problem—not trying to convince a judge or an arbitrator of their points of view. In addition, mediation rules are few and straightforward, so you don't need to make objections or argue about the law. However, you may want to consult with a lawyer before the mediation to discuss the legal consequences of possible settlement terms. You may also want to make a lawyer's approval a condition of any agreement you reach.

How does mediation end? The vast majority of mediations result in settlements. If a mediation is successful, the parties will leave with a signed agreement or, at the very least, a signed memorandum outlining what the parties agreed to. The parties have the choice of making the agreement enforceable in court or not—many people want to be able to ask a judge to enforce the settlement in the future if the other party doesn't live up to the agreement. If the parties don't reach a resolution in mediation, nothing has been lost (except the opportunity to privately resolve the matter). The parties can still take legal action if that's what they feel is needed.

Related terms: alternative dispute resolution (ADR); arbitration; boilerplate.

meeting of the minds

A meeting of the minds is considered an essential element of contract formation; the term is considered synonymous with "mutual assent," "mutual agreement," and "offer and acceptance." Although these synonymous uses are fine, there is a subtle distinction between "meeting of the minds" and "mutual assent." A meeting of the minds means that the parties both intended to agree to the same thing; in other words, that the parties actually understood each other.

The subjective versus the objective standards. A meeting of the minds is a subjective standard that emphasizes the intentions of the parties, as they perceive them.

> **EXAMPLE:** Bob's Orchard offers to sell Tom all of his apples for $5,000. Bob delivers the apples and Tom says, "No, I thought you were offering all your Apple computers." If Tom actually believed he was buying computers—a much different objective than what Bob had in mind—then there was no meeting of the minds.

However, under modern contract law, Tom would have to pay for the apples. For the last century, courts have moved to an objective standard of mutual assent. Courts look at the acts and words of the parties, not at the thoughts in their heads. Using that standard, it would be clear, for example, that Bob is in the business of selling fruit and not computers, and that the words used to create the contract objectively indicate that fact. As Judge Learned Hand stated:

> *A contract has, strictly speaking, nothing to do with the personal, or individual, intent of the parties. A contract is an obligation attached by mere force of law to certain acts of the parties, usually words, which ordinarily accompany and represent a known intent.*

In other words, although the term, "meeting of the minds" is still used to demonstrate one of the elements of contract formation, it's true meaning (a subjective standard) is no longer the basis for demonstrating mutual assent.

Related terms: mutual assent; offer and acceptance.

memorandum of understanding

See letter of intent.

merger

Mergers are accomplished when one company (the "surviving company") acquires another company (the "merged-out" or "target" company). Often, this is facilitated by an exchange of stock; the target company shareholders sell back their stock in exchange for shares in the surviving company.

Mergers and acquisitions. Technically, acquisitions are distinguishable from mergers as follows: In an acquisition, the merged-out company is absorbed (or "swallowed") by the surviving company; in a merger, the two companies coexist as one new entity. However, in reality, there is often little distinction between a merger and an acquisition.

> **EXAMPLE:** NationsBank purchased Bank of America in 1998 for $64.8 billion. The arrangement was strictly an acquisition. However, it was publicly referred to as a merger and, although

NationsBank called the shots, it also changed the name of its company to Bank of America. In this sense, it appeared to the public as if Bank of America had made the acquisition, which was not the case.

Mergers and consolidations. A "consolidation" is a type of merger that occurs when two relatively equal entities fuse to form a unique new entity. In a consolidation, the stock of both companies is often retired and new stock is issued for the new entity. As with acquisitions, characterizing transactions as either a merger or consolidation may prove elusive.

EXAMPLE: In 2000, America Online (AOL), riding an Internet high, purchased Time Warner for $164 billion. The new company, AOL Time Warner, appeared to be a fusion or consolidation combining new and old media thinking. In its earliest days, AOL Time Warner was dominated by AOL, and the new company's chairman was the former head of AOL. By 2002, after the Internet bubble burst, losses of $99 billion were attributable to AOL. The new entity dropped AOL from its name, reverting back to Time Warner, and removed the former-head of AOL as chairman. In 2009, AOL was spun off as a separate company.

Basic provisions. Merger and acquisition agreements are complex agreements—don't try drafting one of these at home. The three key elements of these agreements are descriptions of:

- **The merger process.** The nitty gritty details of the merger—for example, how and when shares will be exchanged or retired and how payments will be made and funded—is explained in a series of "merger" provisions. Typically, these activities are accomplished with the assistance of an "exchange agent," a third party who facilitates the transfers. Merger activities are timed around a closing date, at which time, certain requirements must be met.

- **Surviving and merged-out corporations.** Depending on how the agreement is structured, some procedures are described that enable the surviving company to operate and also how the merged-out corporation will be shut down.
- **Representations and warranties.** Compared to typical contracts, the representations and warranties in a merger agreement take up a disproportionate amount of space and cover a wide range of elements. These provisions are especially important because they are used to verify the previous research or "due diligence" that led to the decision to merge. These reps and warranties may cover capitalization, compliance, financial conditions, subsidiaries, authorizations, existing contracts, taxes, employees, labor issues, insurance, intellectual property, assets, and customers.

Related terms: acquisition agreement (sale of business); private placement.

merger provision

See integration.

minimum contacts

Minimum contacts is a standard used to determine whether a particular court has the right to bind the parties by its decision (referred to as "personal jurisdiction"). As a general rule, a court can exercise personal jurisdiction over the defendant (the party being sued) if the defendant has at least "minimum contacts" in the state—that is, the defendant has engaged in at least a small but significant enough amount of activity in the state to conclude that it's fair for the state to exercise power over the defendant. What constitutes sufficient minimum contacts often arises in contract disputes when the parties to the contract are from different states.

The problems with obtaining personal jurisdiction. As a general rule, courts in a state have personal jurisdiction over all people and businesses that are citizens of or do business in that state. So if you contract with someone from Iowa, you can always sue that person in Iowa. Similarly, you can always obtain personal jurisdiction if the parties voluntarily consent to personal jurisdiction, for example, by including a jurisdiction provision in an agreement. But there are many situations in which a state cannot claim personal jurisdiction over both parties to a contract, especially if one of the parties is not a resident or does not do business there.

Minimum contacts. To determine whether it has personal jurisdiction over a nonresident, a court examines whether that party has some contact within the state. If the nonresident has engaged in at least a small but significant amount of activity, that constitutes "minimum contacts" in the state—and the court has jurisdiction. Some examples of activity courts have found to add up to minimum contacts include:

- A business with its headquarters in another state maintains a branch office, store, or warehouse in the state where the suit is filed.
- A business with its headquarters in another state sends mail order catalogs into the state where the suit is filed.
- An individual who is a citizen of another state solicits business by making phone calls to customers or publishing advertisements in the state where the suit is filed.
- An Internet service provider that is a citizen of another state does business with paid subscribers or takes online orders from customers in the state where the case is filed.

A "minimum contacts" claim is stronger when the claim relates to the purpose of the "contacts." Assume that you want to sue a nonresident business, Abel Co., in your state, and you believe the court has jurisdiction because Abel maintains a bicycle warehouse in your state. If your claim relates to a bicycle that you picked up at the warehouse, a judge is likely to conclude that it's fair to exercise personal jurisdiction over Abel Co. and allow your suit to proceed. But if your claim against Abel Co. grows out of a totally separate problem that has nothing to do with bicycles, the judge may conclude that Abel Co. does not have enough "minimum contacts" and dismiss your case at Abel Co.'s request.

Minimum contacts and the Internet. The rules for minimum contacts sometimes become fuzzier when applied to companies that have a strong Web presence.

> **EXAMPLE 1:** A Pennsylvania court was able to obtain personal jurisdiction over a California Internet service provider that had 3,000 Pennsylvania subscribers. The act of processing the Pennsylvania applications and assigning passwords was sufficient to demonstrate the minimum contacts needed for personal jurisdiction.

> **EXAMPLE 2:** A Texas court gained personal jurisdiction over an out-of-state online gambling enterprise because the gambling operation entered into contracts with Texas residents to play online gambling games, sent emails to Texas residents, and sent winnings to Texas residents.

Legal scholars are of the opinion that it is unfair to make every website owner subject to personal jurisdiction in every state simply because the site is viewable there. Similarly, sites that merely post information without making sales, called "passive sites," are unlikely to incur personal jurisdiction except in the state where their owner resides or does other business.

> **EXAMPLE:** A Minnesota website did not sell its nutrition products directly over the Web, but instead directed consumers to email the company's distributors. When a Texas company sued in Texas for patent infringement, the court found that the site was passive and, so, didn't create sufficient contacts to Texas to give the court personal jurisdiction over the defendant.

However, sites over which credit card sales or other active business is conducted, called "interactive sites," are more likely to satisfy the minimum contacts requirement.

EXAMPLE: A California man running a website called "nfltoday. com" earned revenue from his website through advertising, specifically through the sale of sports betting ads. The site was generating substantial income through interstate commerce and was disrupting marketing efforts by the National Football League in New York. When the NFL sued for trademark infringement (both parties were using the trademark "NFL" for football-related services), a court determined that the site was not passive and had sufficient contacts with New York to allow the New York court to exercise jurisdiction.

Avoiding personal jurisdiction. If you enter into significant contracts with out-of-state companies, try to avoid contract provisions that require you to waive personal jurisdiction in your state or require that you submit yourself to jurisdiction in a distant state.

Related terms: jurisdiction (subject matter; personal); jurisdiction provision (forum selection provision).

minors

See capacity (to contract).

misrepresentation

See fraud (misrepresentation).

mistake

Contract mistakes come in various sizes and forms. In some cases, the parties can resolve the mistakes in an equitable manner either by voiding the contracts or reforming (rewriting) them. In other cases, the resolution can be more contentious. The remedy for the mistake depends on the type of error. Here are some common types of contract mistakes:

- **Unilateral mistake (when one party makes a mechanical mistake).** "Never interrupt your enemy when he is making a mistake," Napoleon Bonaparte told his officers. Although that approach may work on the battlefield, it will not necessarily work in the world of contracts. A unilateral mistake is a mistake made by one of the parties and refers to a mechanical error (like a typo as to the price) that has to do with the contract terms or subject matter. (It doesn't refer to a business or judgment error, such as making a bad deal—for example, you mistakenly thought the price of potatoes would go up.) If one party makes a mistake and the other is aware (or should have been aware) that a mistake was made (known as a "palpable" mistake), then no contract can be created. On the other hand, if the party didn't know and shouldn't have known of the other party's mistake—for example, a bid was low but not extraordinarily low—then in most states, the contract will be enforced, mistake and all.

- **Mutual mistake (both parties are mistaken about the same material fact).** The parties have mutually assented to something but they both made an incorrect assumption about some material element of the contract. For example, if Tom sells his all-terrain vehicle to Bobby but both men are unaware that (1) the vehicle was stolen that morning, or (2) the state legislature banned sales of all-terrain vehicles, then a mutual mistake was made and either party can void the agreement. A mutual mistake might also be made if the parties misidentify something or someone. For example, Bob contracts with a pet store to buy a cat named Pickles, but the store has two cats named Pickles and each party to the sale was referring to a different cat.

- **Mistake based on ambiguity.** Some mistakes are based on ambiguity, a situation in which an essential element of a contract might have different interpretations. For example, a commercial lease agreement might have one clause stating that the tenant shall maintain the entire premises and another clause stating that the landlord shall maintain the lobby. This contextual ambiguity is obviously a mistake, but who is supposed to maintain the lobby? In this situation, courts try to determine which interpretation of the contract is more reasonable and assess the obligation accordingly. For example, if industry practices indicate that landlords commonly maintain the lobby *and* the landlord supplied the contract, the landlord would likely have to maintain the lobby.

- **Typos and mistranscription.** What happens when the secretary typing up the agreement leaves off a few zeroes and neither party notices? An unhappy party can have the error corrected by "reforming" (rewriting) the contract properly. However, if there is a dispute over the issue, the unhappy party has the burden to demonstrate that the written agreement didn't properly comprise the original oral agreement.

Related term: void (voidable).

mitigation of damages

When one party breaks a contract, the other party is entitled to compensation for the breach, with one big caveat. The party that didn't breach must have done whatever is reasonably possible to limit the damages.

> **EXAMPLE:** Ed signs a one-year residential lease to rent an apartment from Theo. After two months, Ed breaks the lease and vacates the apartment. Theo cannot simply let the apartment sit vacant, allow the remaining ten months to roll by, and then ask Ed for ten months of unpaid rent. Theo must make a reasonable effort to mitigate damages by renting the apartment to someone else. If Theo does rent to someone else, the damages Ed has to pay are reduced accordingly.

The principle of mitigating damages (also known as the "doctrine of avoidable consequences") requires the victim of a contract breach to take reasonable steps to reduce the damages, injury, or cost and to prevent them from getting worse.

Reasonableness. A key factor in determining the obligation to mitigate is the "reasonableness" of the mitigating opportunity. A party seeking compensation for a breach cannot recover if damages could be avoided by "reasonable effort, without undue risk, expense, or humiliation." In the case of employment contracts, for example, for an employee who was wrongfully terminated, a "reasonable effort" does not mean that person is obliged to seek or accept any job that may be available. Only work in the same field and of the same quality need be accepted.

EXAMPLE: The actress Shirley MacLaine signed a contract with a movie studio to appear in a musical film, *Bloomer Girl*. The movie studio canceled the production and offered similar pay to MacLaine if she would appear in the film drama, *Big Country, Big Man*. Aside from the difference in genre (musical versus drama), *Big Country* would be filmed in Australia, not California, where MacLaine lived, and MacLaine did not have final approval as to screenplay and director. MacLaine sued the studio and the studio defended by claiming that MacLaine had a duty to accept the *Big Country* part in order to mitigate her damages. The California Supreme Court disagreed and held that the *Big Country* offer was substantially different from—and inferior to—the original contract.

Related terms: damages, consequential; remedies

morals clause

A morals clause, usually found in contracts with public figures, prohibits bad personal behavior. Originally popularized by film studios, morals clauses were used to keep actors in line and prevent their public image from being tainted by improper sexual activity, drinking, or drug use. If they misbehaved, they could be fired without breaching the contract.

Nowadays, these clauses are most often used in television and advertising contracts with celebrity athletes or actors. Occasionally, a morals clause may appear in the news—for example, in 2005, model Kate Moss was dropped from her Chanel contract because of drug use—but these clauses are usually not the subject of litigation because celebrities often prefer not to further publicize their questionable personal behavior. A typical clause might look something like this:

Morals clause: Sample language

> **Morals Clause.** Model agrees to conduct herself according to public conventions and morals and agrees that she will not do or commit any act or thing that will tend to degrade her or that will tend to insult or offend the community or prejudice the company and its products in general.

M

Use of a morals clause in a typical employment contract is generally not recommended. Some states prohibit discrimination on the basis of arrest or criminal conviction, and the federal government prohibits discrimination based on disabilities, which some morals clause litigants have argued (mostly unsuccessfully) includes alcoholism.

mortgage

A mortgage is a loan agreement to purchase real estate. The lender advances the money, charges interest on the repayment, and acquires a lien on the property. If the borrower fails to make payments, the home can be sold (or "foreclosed") to pay back the lender.

Key mortgage terms. Some of the key terms a mortgage may include are:

- **Fixed-rate mortgage.** With this type of mortgage, the interest rate and the amount you pay each month remain the same over the entire mortgage term, which is traditionally 15 or 30 years.
- **Adjustable-rate mortgage (ARM).** With an ARM, the interest rate fluctuates according to interest rates in the economy. Initial interest rates are typically offered for a set period (sometimes as short as one month). This discounted interest rate is lower than the going rate for fixed-rate mortgages. When the initial discount period ends, the interest rate adjusts according to current market rates. The amount of the adjustment is tied to a market-sensitive number called the "index." A "margin" is the factor or percentage a lender adds to the index to arrive at the interest rate you pay over the market rate. Though your interest rate can increase if the index does, there usually is a maximum limit, called the "life-of-the-loan cap" (usually, five or six percentage points above the initial rate). A periodic cap limits the amount your interest rate can go up or down at each adjustment period, such as going up 2% annually, with your payments increasing accordingly.
- **Negative amortization.** Sometimes called "deferred interest" or "interest advances," negative amortization happens when you have a payment cap that limits only the amount your monthly payment can go up (not the total you owe, which is not capped). If your interest rate increases and your monthly payment doesn't cover the interest owed that month, the extra money is simply added onto the mortgage total you owe, often with the result that you'll owe larger payments in the future or a large balloon payment at the end of the mortgage.
- **PMI and impound account.** Lenders may require private mortgage insurance (PMI) if you're making a down payment of less than 20%. PMI insures the lender if you don't pay the mortgage. Some lenders require you to set up an impound account

M

when you close the house purchase, where you deposit up to a year's payments of PMI. In addition, you make monthly payments into the impound account for property taxes and homeowner's insurance, which, in turn, are paid by the lender or company that services the loan. To avoid PMI, you can take out a second mortgage to cover the difference between the amount of money you have for your down payment and the 80% first mortgage.

- **Assumable loan.** A loan that a creditworthy buyer can take over (assume) from a seller. Most fixed-rate loans are not assumable.

- **Prepayment penalty.** This is a charge for paying off your mortgage early.

- **Rate lock-in.** This is a lender's guarantee to make a loan at a particular interest rate, even if the market changes. The lock-in is usually for a specific time period, such as three to six weeks.

- **Debt-to-income ratio.** Also called lender qualification, this refers to the ratio of your monthly mortgage payments (including insurance and property taxes) plus long-term debts, to your income.

- **Monthly carrying costs.** This is the sum of your monthly payments for your mortgage principal and interest, homeowner's insurance, and property taxes.

- **Points and loan costs.** These are fees associated with getting a mortgage, which usually add up to 2% to 5% of the cost of the mortgage. Points make up the largest part of lender fees, with one point equaling 1% of the loan principal. Not all loans have points, but often, loans charging points have a lower interest rate. If you will own a house for many years, paying relatively high points to get a lower fixed rate of interest is usually a good idea—the cost of points is more than paid for by the reduction in interest payments over the life of the loan. But the reverse is also true—if you will move in three to five years or fewer, try to pay as few points as possible, even if you pay a little more interest, because it takes several years for the monthly interest savings to offset the initial high cost of points.

Which is better—a fixed- or adjustable-rate mortgage? Because interest rates and mortgage options change often, the choice of a fixed-rate (where the interest rate stays the same over the life of the loan) or an adjustable-rate (where the interest rate fluctuates based on market indicators) mortgage should depend on:

- the interest rates and mortgage options available when buying a house
- the buyer's view of the future (generally, high inflation will mean ARM rates will go up and lower inflation means that they will fall)
- the buyer's personal financial and investment goals, and
- the buyer's willingness to take a risk.

As a general rule, when mortgage rates are low, a fixed-rate mortgage is the best bet for many buyers. Even if rates could go a little lower in the short run, an ARM's teaser rate would adjust up soon, and you wouldn't gain much if you planned to stay in the house for more than a few years (the broker can tell you your break-even point). In the long run, ARMs are likely to go up, meaning many buyers will be best off locking in a favorable fixed rate now and not taking the risk of much higher rates later. Keep in mind that lenders don't just lend money to purchase homes; they also lend money to refinance homes. For example, if a buyer takes out a fixed-rate loan now, and several years from now interest rates have dropped, refinancing may be an option.

Does it make sense to pay more points for a lower interest rate? Paying points in order to lower a mortgage interest rate can be difficult because the buyer must come up with a few more thousand dollars by the closing. However, over time the savings in interest payments can be worth it.

EXAMPLE: Because one point is 1% of the loan principal; if Ed were borrowing $250,000 at two points, he'd pay $5,000 up front. There is normally a direct relationship between the number of points lenders charge and the interest rates they quote for the same type of mortgage, such as a fixed rate. The more points Ed pays, the lower Ed's rate of interest, and vice versa.

Before deciding whether it's worth paying points, factor in how long you plan to own your house. The longer you live there (or pay on the mortgage), the better off you'll be paying more points up front in return for a lower interest rate. On the other hand, if you think you'll sell or refinance your house within two or three years, it's a better idea to get a loan with as few points as possible. You can check a site such as www.homes.com to quickly compare combinations of interest rates and points.

Related terms: interest rates (usury); mortgage; promissory note; real estate contract; title insurance.

mortgage satisfaction

A document, issued by a lender, that is recorded in a county government office and indicates that the buyer of a home has paid off a mortgage.

Related term: mortgage.

most favored nation

This term (also better referred to as a "most favored customer" provision or "antidiscrimination" clause) refers to a provision in which one party promises to treat the other party as well as it treats its most favored customers. It typically provides that if the party setting the prices gives a better price to another customer, that price will also apply to the contract. In other words, it establishes an obligation to provide an equal or comparable rate.

EXAMPLE: Qwickdraw.com licenses articles for reproduction to RockVClub.com, a rock-climbing website, at $50 an article. There is a most favored nations provision in the license agreement. Qwickdraw enters into a similar license with another company at $45 an article. Qwickdraw must now lower its rate to RockVClub.com to match the $45 price.

Most favored nations provisions are often used in sales, service, health care, and licensing agreements. Below, is an example.

Most favored nations provision in a sales agreement: Sample language

Most Favored Nations. In the event at any time, during the life of this agreement, Vendor shall sell the same materials or service, under similar quantity and delivery conditions, to any customer at prices below those stated in this Agreement, Vendor will immediately extend such lower prices to Company.

Most favored nations clauses have also appeared in settlement agreements for large personal injury case settlements. If the defendant settles for more money with another party in the future, it will have to make up the difference to the plaintiff.

Antitrust and related concerns. In some cases, a most favored nations provision may violate antitrust laws (statutes that prohibit price fixing and other types of monopolistic behavior by large companies). Because they guarantee the other party the benefit of the same price offered to someone else, they have a tendency to fix prices, which could limit the ability of smaller companies to compete. Maryland, Indiana, and Colorado are among the states that have banned the use of these provisions in health care agreements (in which a doctor agrees to provide the lowest comparable reimbursement rate to an insurer).

Related terms: antitrust; boilerplate.

mutatis mutandis

In contract drafting, this Latin phrase refers to the fact that a clause or obligation is transferred from one agreement to another and that any minor changes in language required to make the transfer will be made. (Simplified from the Latin, this means "considering the necessary changes that must be made.") For example, if the parties want to transfer the warranties (with minor changes for the names of the parties) from an old license agreement to a new one, the new agreement might state that "the parties warrant to each other, as if contained in this agreement, mutatis mutandis, the warranties made in the License Agreement of 2009." As a general practice, it is better to avoid use of this term and to include the actual language in the new agreement. Or, alternatively, if the material is to be incorporated without any changes, to use the phrase, "incorporated by reference."

Related term: incorporation by reference.

mutual, mutuality

When an obligation is mutual, it is reciprocal or shared.

mutual assent

Mutual assent refers to the shared desire of the parties to enter into an agreement. Mutual assent is considered to be an essential element of contract formation. Whether the parties have mutually assented is judged objectively, based on their words and actions. The actions comprising an offer and acceptance commonly demonstrate mutual assent.

Related terms: acceptance; meeting of the minds; offer and acceptance.

mutual mistake

See mistake.

negative covenant

See covenant.

negligence

Under the law, all of us have an obligation to act with ordinary and reasonable care in any given situation. Negligence occurs when someone fails to act with reasonable care and, as a result, someone else is injured. For example, Tim may not have intended to cause an accident by blowing through a red light, but his careless behavior was the primary cause of Sarita's resulting injuries. Tim is negligent.

Shifting negligence liability with contracts. Contracts are sometimes used to shift one party's liability for negligent behavior. For example, in a contract for a storage locker, the storage company may disclaim any damage to the property even if it is the result of the company's negligence. Whether a court will enforce such a provision is not always clear. In some situations—employment contracts, contracts with public utilities, and contracts with common carriers (businesses that transport people or goods)—such clauses will never be enforced. In other situations—for example, a residential landlord who disclaims negligent acts—courts are split as to whether to honor the provisions. As a general rule, an exculpatory clause will not be enforced by a court if it is grossly unfair ("unconscionable") or otherwise violates public policy. This is more likely to occur if the bargaining positions of the parties are grossly unequal, if the clause only applies against one party, if there is a public interest in regulating the activity that's the subject of the contract, and if the agreement is a contract of adhesion—a one-sided agreement that the other party wasn't able to negotiate.

Related terms: exculpatory clause; gross negligence, personal liability; tort.

negotiable instrument

A negotiable instrument is an unconditional commitment to pay money. Common examples are checks and promissory notes. Negotiable instruments can be traded (bought and sold) and treated like money. They are governed by Article 3 of the Uniform Commercial Code

Related term: banker's acceptance.

negotiation

Contract negotiation is the process of give and take the parties go through to reach an agreement. Or as they often say in business, "You don't get what you deserve; you get what you negotiate."

Risks and revenues. In a typical contract negotiation, each party compromises on some issues in order to get what it really wants. Although there are always lots of details to work out, most contract negotiations boil down to two essential factors—risks and revenues.

> EXAMPLE: A landlord in a residential lease negotiation wants to obtain a profitable rental income (revenue) while also guaranteeing the right to swiftly remove the tenant and protect the property if something goes wrong (risks). Sam, a landlord, is aware that his risks may be lower if he rents to Camille, a qualified tenant with strong recommendations and who stayed at her previous rental for fourteen years. Sam considers Camille's offer to sign a one-year lease for a lower rental price. Sam knows that a bad tenant can cost him many months of lost revenue (not to mention lost time and legal fees). He agrees to Camille's lower offer because the lower risk she presents is worth accepting lower revenue.

Business and legal negotiations. Often, contract negotiations have two distinct stages: negotiation of the basic business terms followed by negotiation of the legal terms.

> EXAMPLE: Sam agrees to rent his residential property to Camille. At a walk-through at the rental home, Camille negotiates for a one-year lease at $1,500 a month. She agrees to pay the first and last months' rent up front, along with a security deposit. She will move into the house in one month. Sam and Camille shake hands and Sam promises to send along a "standard" lease agreement.
>
> A week later, Camille obtains the written lease. It includes all of the basic terms she and Sam negotiated at the house, but it also includes several objectionable provisions, including an attorneys' fee provision and a requirement that she obtain insurance. She calls Sam and the two of them negotiate these issues. Eventually, Sam agrees to take out the attorneys' fee provision, and Camille agrees to get renter's insurance. Sam revises the lease and Camille signs it.

At what point do the parties have an enforceable contract? Is it when they agree on the business terms or when the legal terms are finalized? Under contract law, there is no contract until all of the material elements of the deal have been negotiated and agreed upon. So, a legal dispute over whether and when a contract exists will boil down to whether any of the outstanding legal issues are material elements of the deal. For example, let's say that Sam refuses to budge on any of the terms of his standard lease, but Camille has already given notice at her current apartment because she believed her handshake with Sam created a contract. Whether she has a legal right to force Sam to go through with the agreement or pay her damages depends on whether the attorneys' fees and insurance provisions are material elements of the deal.

If the parties have agreed to the business terms of the deal and want to proceed before hammering out the legal details, they can use an escrow account or condition the release of funds on the execution of a written agreement. This avoids the problem of having to chase after money you laid out if the deal never materializes. If the negotiations fall apart, everyone gets back what they put in and moves on.

Lawyers and negotiation. Have you ever experienced this situation? Your company believes it has reached an agreement with another company on the business terms of a deal. Both sides bring in their lawyers to hammer out the details—and as soon as the lawyers get involved, everything goes down the tubes.

That could be because lawyers have three potentially conflicting factors at work when negotiating. They want to:

- protect their clients by minimizing risks and maximizing revenue
- act professionally, so they won't be vulnerable to malpractice claims or disappoint clients (who can always find another lawyer), and
- earn money. This last factor creates the perverse incentive: The more time it takes to hammer out a deal, the more money the attorney makes. In other words, it is profitable if either or both sides drag out the negotiation.

Although most attorneys focus primarily on the first and second factors, some attorneys are happy to let negotiations drag on as the meter runs. To some extent, the client can control this stage of negotiation by learning which issues are still in play, prioritizing the risks that matter, and instructing the attorney accordingly.

Negotiating style. As you are probably aware from watching TV shows such as *The Apprentice,* there are a variety of negotiating styles. The two most common styles are adversarial ("I will dominate you") or collaborative ("Together, we will prosper"). The various negotiating styles are, of course, employed by real people, who bring their temperaments, emotions, and personalities to the table along with their lists of terms. One negotiator might use a raised voice and threaten to storm out of the room, while another might argue in a cool, dispassionate tone.

The modern approach to contract negotiation was pioneered at Harvard University by Roger Fisher and William Ury, authors of the classic, *Getting to Yes*. These authors say that a collaborative negotiation without big emotional displays is most likely to achieve the optimum results. Anger and similar emotions tend to cloud judgment, create competition, avoid mutually beneficial outcomes, and sometimes result in a retaliatory approach to issues.

Bargaining position: the "take it or leave it" situation. One key to the outcome of contract negotiation is the relative bargaining positions of the parties. A party with vastly superior bargaining power—for example, a landlord operating during a housing shortage or an employer hiring during a recession—doesn't have to negotiate. Instead, these heavy hitters often present a contract and tell the weaker party to "take it or leave it." In cases of contracts of adhesion—form contracts that can't be negotiated—this can sometimes backfire, because the less-advantaged party may later argue that a provision is unfair or unconscionable.

If you are in the superior bargaining position, it is not always in your best interest to dictate all of the terms. As J. Paul Getty's father once told him, "You must never try to make *all* the money that's in a deal. Let the other fellow make some money too, because if you have a reputation for always making all the money, you won't have many deals."

Negotiating tactics. There have been plenty of books written about negotiating tactics. Many tips are slightly silly. For example, some suggest providing lots of caffeinated drinks and food with MSG (but don't drink or eat any yourself), then wait for your negotiation partners to give away the store in a drug-induced daze.

Others are devious and have the potential to backfire—for example, pretending to have another suitor in the wings, or insisting on negotiating items you don't really care about, so you can pretend

N

to "give in" on those and get all of the things you really want. Below we have summarized some of the more common and popular tactics. Some of these may seem like commonsense, even obvious strategies; that's because they are:

- **Break it into parts.** Some negotiations disintegrate because the parties take an "all or nothing" approach, in which the other parties must agree to all of their terms in order to move forward. A good way past this type of roadblock is to break the negotiations into sections ("compartmentalize") and reach an agreement on each part separately. This makes it feel as if you are reaching a series of solutions—and making progress—rather than battling one big war.

- **I'm only asking for what's fair.** This approach emphasizes that one party's requests are simply in line with industry standards or current market prices. This strategy relieves you of the obligation to justify your terms or spend time negotiating for them. If you emphasize that you are asking only for standard deal terms, the burden shifts to the other party to convince you that you should make an exception in this case (and to make that exception worth your while by offering concessions elsewhere).

- **The *Getting to Yes* approach.** The authors emphasize that to reach agreement (to get to "yes"), the negotiating parties must: separate the people from the issues (that is, remove the emotion from the equation), look beyond the negotiating parties to see who or what is the real interest or influence affecting each party, generate options to create a problem-solving environment, and neutralize conflict by sticking to objective and easy-to-justify principles of fairness.

- **Take control.** Controlling the location, timing, topics, and pace of negotiation (sometimes called "controlling the agenda") may create an advantage. For example, lawyers often believe that the attorney who drafts the agreement is in the contractual driver's seat. Similarly, by controlling the negotiations, you get to decide which topics are discussed and in what order. Sometimes, parties use a passive approach to take control—for example, by seeming to act as the moderator for the negotiations or by offering to "summarize" where things stand (in a letter or brief statement at the start of a negotiating session). No matter how the reins are seized, the party that frames the issues generally has more control over how those issues are eventually resolved.

- **Prioritize, prioritize, prioritize.** As indicated above, contract negotiations typically focus on revenue and risks. But clearly, some revenues and risks are more important than others. When you negotiate, you need to know what your top priorities are—usually the business or money-making opportunity offered by the deal—and how your other priorities rank below that. This will help you keep your eyes on the prize and avoid getting bogged down in issues that are not as important to you.

- **Always make sure the other side leaves negotiations feeling they've made a good deal.** Known as the "offer-concession" strategy, this means the offers you make should always leave you enough wiggle room to make acceptable concessions to the other side. Or as one businessman once put it, "The most important trip you may take in life is meeting people halfway." This also means you shouldn't start negotiations by revealing your absolute bottom line. If you instead leave yourself room to negotiate, you'll make the other party feel that they've won something—and you may be surprised to find that the other party is willing to give more than you would have been willing to accept.

- **Question rather than demand.** If the other party is taking a hard line on certain issues, ask why. Questions open up discussion; arguments often close it down.

- **Find points of agreement and end on a positive note.** This upbeat approach requires that you find opportunities to say, "You're

N

right about that," or "I agree." However small these points of agreement, they help set a collaborative tone. At the same time, if negotiations are spread over a series of meetings, always attempt to end each one positively. This too, goes a long way to establishing a more conducive, collaborative tone that is more likely to end in an agreement.

- **Do your research.** The party with more information usually has more leverage. For example, if you know that the people who put an offer on your house have already sold their own house and must move quickly, that gives you more leverage—and some extra bargaining chips. You may be able to insist on a higher price, particularly if you're willing to allow them to close the deal fast. Sometimes, even personal information about the parties may affect your ability to create a more collaborative atmosphere ("Hey, I'm racing in that triathlon, too").

- **Dealing with burnouts and ultimatums.** If the other party resorts to threats ("Agree to these terms or there's no deal") or wages a war of attrition by dragging out the negotiations, you'll have to decide what the underlying deal is really worth to you. If the ultimate prize is so valuable that you're willing to accept the other party's ultimatum or put up with endless haggling, that's fine. Similarly, if the other party has all the power (for example, it's the only known buyer for your product), then you may have to grin and bear it for a while. If not, however, the best strategy is often to walk away from negotiations that have bogged down like this. If the contract with you is really important, the other party may reevaluate its tactics and return to the table. If not, you can move on to more productive negotiations with someone else.

- **Use facts not feelings.** Successful negotiators separate business from personal, facts from feelings. They avoid letting an unpleasant personality or style drag down the negotiations. They also avoid making the negotiations seem personal by using language such as "I believe" or "I think," focusing instead on statements of fact ("If we pay this price, both parties to the venture will be at risk").

Related term: mediation.

net

Net refers to the difference between income and expenses. Generally, net is synonymous with profits—for example, "Microsoft netted $200 million this quarter."

Related terms: gross; gross sales; license agreement; net sales; royalty.

net 30 (or net 60 or net 90)

These are billing terms often used on invoices to indicate when payment for goods or services is due. The number refers to how many days the other party has to pay. For example, net 30 means that payment is due within 30 days of receipt of the goods or services.

Related term: invoice.

N

net sales

Net sales are the gross (or total) sales minus any deductible expenses permitted under a contract. Because contractual payments are often based on net sales, how they are calculated may be the subject of considerable discussion when negotiating a contract. The party that will have to make the payments may try to include more deductions (and chip away at the net sales), while the other side will want fewer deductions and higher net sales. Here's a definition of net sales from a license agreement.

Net sales: Sample language

> **Net Sales.** Net Sales are defined as Company's gross sales (the gross invoice amount billed to customers) less quantity discounts or rebates and returns actually credited. A quantity discount or rebate is a discount made at the time of shipment. No deductions will be made for cash or other discounts, commissions, manufacturing costs, uncollectible accounts, or for fees or expenses of any kind.

Related terms: gross; gross sales; license agreement; net; royalty.

nonbinding

The goal of contract law is to create enforceable arrangements—that is, arrangements that the parties must adhere to or risk exposing themselves to liability for breaching a contract. An enforceable agreement is said to be "binding" on the parties, in that it requires them to act in certain ways or face the consequences. A nonbinding arrangement is one that is not enforceable and for which no there are no mandatory obligations. For example, the recommendations of a mediator are usually nonbinding, as is a letter of intent.

Related terms: agreement in principle; letter of intent; mediation.

noncompete agreement

See covenant not to compete.

nondisclosure agreement

See confidentiality agreement.

nonrecourse

A nonrecourse loan is one that gives a lender no options beyond seizing the collateral. The lender can only go after the property securing the debt; the lender can't go after the personal assets of the debtor. If the property is worth less than the debtor owes, the lender has no recourse.

Mortgages are nonrecourse loans. Some states have laws (known as "antideficiency statutes") that have the same effect: They prevent a lender from seeking the difference between the value of the home and what is owed. These laws typically only apply to principal (or "first") mortgages and not second or third mortgages. Also, they generally protect only a debtor who is using the property as a primary residence.

Related terms: creditor; debt security; interest rates (usury); promissory note.

nonsolicitation agreement

A nonsolicitation agreement restricts a former employee's ability steal your customers or your employees. Typically, a company adds a nonsolicitation provision (also known as a "diversion" provision) to a nondisclosure or noncompete agreement, which prohibits an ex-employee from working for a competitor. Although some states limit noncompete agreements or won't enforce them at all, these states usually enforce a nonsolicitation provision, as long as it doesn't:

- unfairly restrict an employee's ability to earn a living, or
- unfairly limit a competitor's ability to hire workers or solicit customers through legitimate means.

For example, an employee's agreement not to solicit a former employer's clients will probably not be enforced if the pool of potential clients is only one or two companies. But if the customer pool is large enough to support reasonable competition, a court is more likely to enforce the nonsolicitation provision. Similarly, a nonsolicitation provision can't restrict a customer's right to take its business elsewhere, as long as that business isn't taken unfairly by the former employee (for example, by undercutting your company's prices or offering your company's customers a special discount or other promotion to switch to the new company).

Nonsolicitation Provision: Sample language

While Employee is employed by Company, and for a period of _____ thereafter, Employee shall not:

a. employ, attempt to employ, or solicit for employment by any other person or entity any Company employees;

b. encourage any consultant, independent contractor, or any other person or entity to end its relationship or stop doing business with Company or help any person or entity do so or attempt to do so;

c. solicit or attempt to solicit or obtain business or trade from any of Company's current or prospective customers or clients or help any person or entity do so or attempt to do so; or

d. obtain or attempt to obtain any Confidential Information for any purpose whatsoever except as required by Company to enable Employee's performance of duties.

N

Related terms: covenant not to compete; noncompete agreement; trade secret.

notary

A notary (also called a "notary public") authenticates signatures on contracts, affidavits, deeds, and conveyances. Parties to a contract sometimes require that the signatures be witnessed by a notary in order to provide an extra level of authentication. Usually this is accomplished by using a signature form (see below) that is printed or stamped on the document. Notaries are not permitted to offer legal advice.

Qualifications. Most states require notaries to pass a written test (usually composed of questions about the notary process and related rules), pay a fee, take an oath, and acquire insurance (bonding) if required by the state.

A Typical Notarial Signature Form

Certificate of Acknowledgment of Notary Public

State of _____)

) ss

County of _____)

On _____ , before me,

_____ , a notary public in and for

said state, personally appeared _____ ,

who proved to me on the basis of satisfactory evidence to be the person whose name is subscribed to the within instrument and acknowledged to me that he or she executed the same in his or her authorized capacity and that by his or her signature on the instrument, the person, or the entity upon behalf of which the person acted, executed the instrument.

I certify under PENALTY OF PERJURY under the laws of the State of _____ _____ that the foregoing paragraph is true and correct.

WITNESS my hand and official seal.

_____

Notary Public for the State of _____

My commission expires _____

[NOTARY SEAL]

notice

In contract law, notice refers to the process of telling the other party something or giving the other party certain information as required by the contract—for example, providing notice of insurance coverage, notice of receipt of goods, notice of termination, or notice of a force majeure event (a disaster affecting the contract). Notice provisions usually include:

- **Written notice.** Typically, notice must be given in writing. Some notice provisions require that a particular person give notice. For example, the company may be contractually obligated to give the other party's CFO notice of an audit of records relating to the contract.
- **Method of delivery.** The provision usually spells out how notice must be given—for example, by overnight delivery or certified mail.
- **Effectiveness of delivery.** The provision should also explain when delivery of notice is effective (in other words, the date when notice will be considered given). For example, a facsimile notice may be effective when the sender obtains a transmission report acknowledging delivery.
- **Name and address of recipients.** The parties usually designate the name of the person who should receive notices on behalf of the company and the address where such notice must be sent.

Notice: Sample language

> **Notices.** All notices, requests and other communications called for by this Agreement are deemed to have been given immediately if made in writing by facsimile or electronic mail (confirmed by concurrent written notice sent First Class U.S. mail, postage prepaid), if to _____ at _____ , Attn: _____ and e-mail to: _____@_____.com and if to _____ at _____ , Attn: _____ and e-mail to: _____@_____.com or to such other addresses as either party shall specify to the other. Notice by any other means is deemed made when actually received by the party to which notice is provided.

Related terms: boilerplate; breach, notice of.

novation

Novation is the act of either (1) substituting new parties to a contract, or (2) substituting new obligations for existing obligations. A novation is similar to an assignment, in that someone else is assuming a contractual duty. However, a novation creates an entirely new contract, to which both parties must agree. An assignment requires only that the assigning party provide notice of the assignment to the other party; no new contract is created, and the other party's consent is not required.

Some examples of novation might include:

- **Sales or supply contract.** Sam has to supply 10,000 ears of corn to Ben, and Ben has to supply 10,000 ears of corn to Rami's Restaurant. If everyone consents, the parties could novate the existing contracts and create a new contract in which Sam supplies 10,000 ears of corn directly to Rami's Restaurant, eliminating the middleman.
- **Substitution of new party.** Haley licenses the right to use the Hard Rock Café trademark. She no longer wishes to continue the license, but Benji does—and he has agreed to assume all the obligations of the contract. With the Hard Rock Café's consent, Haley prepares a novation agreement ending her license and creating a new one for Benji, on the same terms.
- **Sale or merger of business.** Lipincott Developments agrees to provide Internet services for Wanda's Warehouse. In their contract, Wanda insists on a novation provision stating that if Lipincott sells or merges its business to another company, the new company will enter into a new agreement with Wanda to assume Lipincott's obligations and liabilities.

Related term: assignment (of contract).

N

obligee/obligor

The obligee is the person (usually referred to as a "creditor" in a financial transaction) entitled to the benefit of a contractual obligation. In other words, the obligee is the person to whom the obligation is owed. The obligor (the "debtor" in financial agreements) is the person who must perform the obligation.

Related terms: debt; interest rates (usury); mortgage; promissory note.

offer and acceptance

When you click the "Place Your Order" button at Amazon.com, tell the cab driver where you want to go, or hand a $20 bill to the cashier at the movies, you are accepting an offer to enter into a contract. All of these actions—despite the lack of fanfare—communicate the mutual assent that is essential to form a contract. Both an offer and an acceptance communicate an unconditional willingness to be bound—and without them, there's no deal.

Offers. Here are a few things to keep in mind about offers:

- **Not forever.** Offers do not stay open indefinitely. As a general rule, the person making the offer can withdraw it at any time before the other party accepts. Unless a time limit is provided in the offer, it will be assumed to be open for a "reasonable" period of time, which may depend on the industry or trade.
- **Objective standards.** Offers are judged objectively. When reviewing the situation, a court will be more interested in how a reasonable person would consider the offer than in the actual intent of the person who made the offer.

- **Must contain essential elements.** An offer should include the essential elements of the contract. It should define with some specificity the subject of the transaction, when it will happen, the price for the transaction, and any conditions that must occur for the contract to go forward. This might sound like a lot of information, but most of us convey these details in our everyday transactions. For example, you might tell your neighbor's kid, "I'll give you $20 a day to walk the dog while I'm out of town next Monday and Tuesday." Or, your mechanic may tell you, "I can replace the tires for $800, but it won't be finished until tomorrow." In either case, if the neighbor's kid or you say "okay," you have a deal.

Is an advertisement an offer? With some exceptions, an advertisement is not considered an offer; it's officially considered as "an invitation to bargain" (or more formally, it is known as an "invitation to treat"). The person making the advertisement is not obligated to sell to every customer who responds to the ad (although some consumer laws may mandate sales under certain circumstances).

Some forms of advertising—for example, an advertisement for bounty hunters to bring in a bail-skipper—may be accepted by the performance of the bounty hunter. These arrangements—where acceptance can be established by performance rather than an agreement—are referred to as unilateral contracts.

There is no acceptance if ... Occasionally, one party disputes whether the other accepted an offer. In general, acceptance has not occurred if:

- One party's response to an offer doesn't communicate a readiness to be bound ("Sounds good, let me think about it").
- The response has strings attached ("I'm willing to do it if you'll pay me ten thousand dollars more").
- The offer is based on lies ("You said you had title to the car.")

Also, if the person making the offer indicates how the other party must accept it—"Call me with your response before Saturday"—then, the other party must accept under those conditions to create a contract. In this example, accepting on Sunday will not create a contract.

Conditional acceptance, the mirror image rule, and counteroffers. As a general rule, an acceptance must be on the same terms as the offer (known as the "mirror image rule"). When one party responds to an offer with additional conditions or qualifications, the response is generally considered to be a counteroffer, not an acceptance. A counteroffer isn't an acceptance because it materially changes the terms of the proposed contract. Legally, a counteroffer is considered a rejection of the original offer and the proposal of a new offer in its place.

> **EXAMPLE:** A customer asks a carpenter to build a cabinet for $1,000 and the carpenter replies, "Okay, if you also pay for my supplies." The carpenter has made a counteroffer. The customer must accept the counteroffer in order for an agreement to be formed.

However, under the Uniform Commercial Code—legal rules governing the sale of goods—the rules are sometimes more liberal. Under these rules, a qualified acceptance might create a binding contract, despite adding new conditions, unless the modifications cause surprise or hardship as in "I accept your offer to sell your car, but you'll have to arrange to deliver it to California, instead of New York."

Acceptance by actions. Acceptance isn't always communicated by words; sometimes actions suffice. For example, if a buyer places an order to buy goods at a certain price, and the seller responds by shipping the goods, the seller's actions signal acceptance of the offer. However, silence by itself—that is, if one party doesn't say or do anything—rarely constitutes acceptance. That principle is derived from a 19th-century English contract case in which a man offered to buy a horse and stated that unless he heard otherwise from the seller, "I consider the horse mine." The British court ruled that his assumption didn't create a contract; the other party's acceptance had to be clearly expressed. Acceptance of goods that weren't ordered may also create a binding contract except when a consumer receives unsolicited merchandise. For example, in California, the receipt of unsolicited merchandise is an unconditional gift, which the recipient need not return or pay for.

Open offers and options. Parties that want some time to consider an offer—for example, for a home purchase—can enter into an option agreement. In an option agreement, one party pays for the exclusive right to accept an offer during a fixed period. This gives the potential buyer an opportunity to consider the deal without having to worry that someone else will snap it up—or that the terms of the deal will change—in the meantime.

Related terms: meeting of the minds; mutual assent; Uniform Commercial Code.

oral contracts

Oral agreements (also known as "handshake deals" or "gentlemen's agreements") can be made in an instant, don't require any legal assistance (or billable hours), and are usually just as enforceable as written contracts. Best of all, they are based on trust, a principle that's often buried in the verbose, voluminous world of written contracts. Unfortunately, that's also where the big disadvantage comes in: What if one party remembers the deal differently (or pretends to)? What if someone shows up falsely claiming to have made an oral contract with you? Or what if you and the other person were never on the same page to begin with—but you didn't realize it because you didn't have to go through the process of negotiating and hammering out a written contract? To guard against these problems, legal rules require certain contracts to be in writing to be enforceable.

The statute of frauds: Preventing fraudulent use of oral contracts. For most of human history, contracts were oral. But lawmakers quickly realized that this time-honored tradition left honest men (the only gender with the legal power to enter into a contract at the time) open to false charges by liars who claimed to have an oral agreement to buy land or a horse, usually on the cheap. So, in 1677, Britain's Parliament created "An Act for the Prevention of Frauds and Perjuries," commonly known as the "Statute of Frauds." The law proclaimed that six types of contracts could be enforced only if they were in writing. These included:

- **Executor-administrator provisions.** The executor of a will could not make an oral promise to pay a debt of the estate.
- **Suretyship provisions.** A contract in which someone guarantees another party's debt or other obligation had to be in writing.
- **Promises to marry.** Contracts promising to marry had to be written, not oral.
- **Land contracts.** Contracts to sell land had to be in writing.
- **Contracts lasting more than one year.** Contracts that could not be performed within one year had to be written.
- **Contracts to sell goods.** In a separate section, the law required certain contracts for the sale of goods to be in writing.

Almost three centuries later (in 1954), Britain repealed most of its statute of frauds, retaining only the land and suretyship provisions. Why the change of heart? According to one member of the committee reforming the law, the statute caused more fraud than it prevented because it allowed people to get out of handshake deals when no writing existed.

U.S. adoption of the statute of frauds. Despite Britain's repeal, most American states have adopted and continue to enforce some version of the statute of frauds. The types of contracts that must be in writing vary from state to state.

Below is California's statute. Like the laws of many states, it focuses on three issues: real property (leasing and real estate sales contracts); loans; and contracts that can't be performed within a certain time period (one year, or the lifetime of one of the contracting parties). These categories appear in many statutes of frauds because they deal with important transactions that are especially likely to engender misunderstandings or create fertile breeding grounds for deception.

California's Statute of Frauds (Cal. Civ. Code Sec. 1624(a))

(a) The following contracts are invalid, unless they, or some note or memorandum thereof, are in writing and subscribed by the party to be charged or by the party's agent:

(1) An agreement that by its terms is not to be performed within a year from the making thereof.

(2) A special promise to answer for the debt, default, or miscarriage of another, except in the cases provided for in Section 2794.

(3) An agreement for the leasing for a longer period than one year, or for the sale of real property, or of an interest therein; such an agreement, if made by an agent of the party sought to be charged, is invalid, unless the authority of the agent is in writing, subscribed by the party sought to be charged.

(4) An agreement authorizing or employing an agent, broker, or any other person to purchase or sell real estate, or to lease real estate for a longer period than one year, or to procure, introduce, or find a purchaser or seller of real estate or a lessee or lessor of real estate where the lease is for a longer period than one year, for compensation or a commission.

(5) An agreement that by its terms is not to be performed during the lifetime of the promisor.

(6) An agreement by a purchaser of real property to pay an indebtedness secured by a mortgage or deed of trust upon the property purchased, unless assumption of the indebtedness by the purchaser is specifically provided for in the conveyance of the property.

(7) A contract, promise, undertaking, or commitment to loan money or to grant or extend credit, in an amount greater than one hundred thousand dollars ($100,000), not primarily for personal, family, or household purposes, made by a person engaged in the business of lending or arranging for the lending of money or extending credit.

For purposes of this section, a contract, promise, undertaking or commitment to loan money secured solely by residential property consisting of one to four dwelling units will be deemed to be for personal, family, or household purposes.

If one of these contracts is not reduced to writing, it can't be enforced. However, the parties remain free to make and honor these oral agreements. The purpose of the statute is to protect a party that wants out of a claimed oral contract (or wants to escape liability for breaching such a contract).

In addition, California, like most states has adopted a version of the Uniform Commercial Code (UCC) that requires that certain contracts for the sale of goods must be in writing. The UCC section states: "A contract for the sale of goods for the price of $5,000 or more is not enforceable by way of action or defense unless there is some record sufficient to indicate that a contract for sale has been made between the parties and signed by the party against which enforcement is sought or by the party's authorized agent or broker."

Oral contracts that cannot be performed within one year. A contract that, by its terms, cannot be performed within one year—for example, an agreement to supply paper to an office for five years—must be in writing. But an open-ended agreement—for example, an agreement for "permanent" employment without any term or time limits—need not be in writing. And, a contract that could be performed within a year, even if that would be unlikely, need not be in writing.

EXAMPLE 1: In a California case, an oral employment agreement tied an employee's payments to the employer's annual receipts Although the agreement implied a length of more than one year, the agreement *could* be terminated at any time. Because the agreement could be terminated within one year, a court ruled that the agreement was valid and did not violate the state of frauds.

EXAMPLE 2: In a New York case, the actress Patty Duke made an oral agreement, in December 2004, to perform in a play about Golda Meir from September 2005 to May 2006. She was terminated before the show began. When she tried to enforce the contract, the theater company argued that the agreement was invalid because it would have taken more than a year (from when the contract was entered into) to complete it, and was therefore one of the types of contracts that must be in writing to be enforced. A court disagreed, noting that the contract could have been performed within one year if the theater company exercised its option to terminate the show early, for example, in November 2005.

In the same manner, a month-to-month oral agreement for rental property is enforceable. Even though such contracts often last more than a year, it is possible for the agreement to be performed within a year—for example, if the tenant moves out or the landlord evicts within that time. Also, an oral contract that is to be performed when someone dies is considered to be enforceable in most states because death can occur at any time (and, therefore, it can occur within one year).

Oral contracts for the sale of land. The statute of frauds seeks to prevent fraudulent transfers of land. Nowadays, it's rare that anyone would consider a real estate sale final without a written agreement. The issue usually arises in one of these contexts:

- **Oral agreements to engage an agent or broker.** In some states, like California, the statute of frauds requires that real estate agent agreements must be in writing; most states don't impose this requirement.

- **Oral agreements to transfer timber and crops.** The term "land" is interpreted to mean all tangible property that isn't personal— that is, all property other than goods. Under this definition, the sale of crops or timber (considered goods) would not be considered a sale of land. The rule is not so clear when it comes to minerals, however. Most courts have held that when the landowner is doing the mining, this is a sale of goods; but when the buyer is doing the mining, it's a sale of land that must be in writing.

- **Oral modifications to written land sales agreements.** If you have a written real estate contract, an oral change to that contract may be enforceable. It depends on whether the underlying written agreement permits oral modifications and whether the oral modification has been acted upon. For example, if the parties orally agreed to change the price, the buying party paid that amount, and the selling party accepted it, then the oral modification is more likely to be enforced.

Oral contracts for the sale of goods. A written agreement is required for the sale of goods valued at either more than $500 (under older laws) or more than $5,000 (under state laws that are more current). "Goods" refers to things that are tangible; intellectual property doesn't count. Historically, oral agreements for the sale of goods are treated differently than all other types of oral agreements under the statute of frauds. For example, the U.C.C. rules are more liberal as to what satisfies the statute of frauds; all that is needed is "some record sufficient to indicate that a contract for sale has been made." The law is also satisfied if the receiver of the goods confirms receipt and knows the contents of the delivery.

What does it mean to be "in writing"? To satisfy the statute of frauds, there must be some document that memorializes the agreement and includes the essential contract terms. It must include the subject matter of the agreement, identify the parties, and demonstrate the parties' assents (usually by signature or some other acknowledgment). As noted above, a party enforcing a contract for the sale of goods need only demonstrate a sufficient record of the transaction; a detailed receipt might be enough.

Partial performance. An oral contract that is supposed to be in writing per the statute of frauds will not be enforced even if there is partial performance—that is, if either or both parties have fulfilled some of their contractual obligations. However, a court may step in and provide some other remedy, such as restitution. For example, if an oral contract is made to deliver water over two years and delivery has begun and was accepted, a court will likely take the necessary steps to make sure that the supplier is compensated for the goods that have already been delivered.

Related terms: parol evidence rule; quasi contract; restitution; statute of frauds; void (voidable).

par (par value)

Par (sometimes referred to as par value) refers to the face value of a security. For example, in the case of a debt security such as a United States Treasury Bond, the par value is the amount, printed on the bond, that will be repaid when the bond matures. For shares of stock, the par value printed on the certificate is the minimum price the issuing company agreed to accept for the stock when it was initially offered; in this context, the par value is a promise to investors that the stock won't be sold for less than that price. Typically, it's a fraction of the actual (or market) value of the security.

parol evidence rule

The parol evidence rule prevents one party to a written contract from introducing evidence in court that contradicts, changes, or adds to the terms of the contract. In other words, if the parties have a complete written contract, that's the final word on the subject. (Although parol evidence refers literally to oral statements, the term is now used to refer to any extrinsic evidence—that is, evidence outside of the contract itself—whether in written or oral form.)

The parol evidence rule often comes up when one party wants to introduce evidence about previous negotiations or discussions to show that the parties really intended something different from, or something in addition to, what the final contract says. Here's how it works. Let's say you sign a contract to purchase property. The seller sends you a letter assuring you that he will remove a dilapidated barn on the premises before you take possession of the property. That agreement doesn't make it into the 20-page standard real estate sales agreement your realtors draw up. When the seller doesn't remove the barn, you sue and attempt to present the letter as evidence of the seller's agreement. The court refuses to look at the letter because it constitutes parol evidence. Your written sales agreement is the final word on the sale and it doesn't mention the barn. Case closed.

Unintegrated, integrated—and partially integrated. Whether and how the parol evidence rule operates depends on whether the parties intended for the written contract to encompass the entire agreement between them. Legally, this is referred to as an "integrated" contract, one in which all aspects of the agreement are integrated into the final written document. A court that is considering whether to admit parol evidence can find that a written contract is integrated, unintegrated, or partially integrated.

- **Integrated.** If the parties to a contract intend their agreement to be the complete and final expression of their deal, then it is considered integrated. In that case, the parol evidence applies. With a few exceptions (discussed below), no contradictory or supplementary evidence of discussions or documents can be introduced. The parties' intent in this regard is determined by a range of factors, including the language and degree of specificity in the agreement. If the contract includes an explicit integration clause (see below), that's very strong evidence that they wanted the contract to be the final word on the subject.

- **Unintegrated.** If the parties didn't intend the agreement to be the final expression of their agreement, it is considered unintegrated. In this situation, evidence of prior discussions and other documents can be introduced to contradict the contract.

- **Partially integrated.** An agreement is partially integrated if it is intended as the final statement on what the agreement covers, but it is not a complete and exclusive statement of the parties' whole deal. For example, the parties might sign one contract that contemplates a second additional and complementary agreement. If an agreement is partially integrated, precontract discussions can be introduced to supplement—that is, to understand what's missing—but not to contradict the agreement.

Integration/merger clauses. To avoid surprises and make sure the parol evidence rule applies, lawyers routinely include a clause stating that the contract is intended to be the final agreement of the parties. This type of clause is referred to as "integration," a "merger," or an "entire agreement" clause. These provisions typically state that the agreement "expresses the complete understanding of the parties with respect to the subject matter and supersedes all prior proposals, agreements, representations and understandings."

Courts will generally go along with these provisions and keep parol evidence out. However, courts are free to question whether the provision is valid and occasionally may disregard one if, for example, it is found in a one-sided contract of adhesion or a contract that is otherwise unconscionable. Many courts view integration provisions as creating a presumption of integration, which can be rebutted under certain circumstances. Even if the integration provision is valid and the court honors it, one of the exceptions to the parol evidence rule may apply.

Exceptions to the parol evidence rule. Even if an agreement is integrated or partially integrated, a court may still consider parol evidence if one of these exceptions applies:

- **Interpretation.** Courts have carved out various exceptions to permit the use of extrinsic evidence (materials not included with the agreement) in order to interpret an agreement. If the agreement is clear and complete, no outside evidence will be allowed. If, however, a key contract term is ambiguous (for example, it has one meaning in plain English and a different usage in the trade or industry), a mistake was made when writing/transcribing the agreement, or the parties are not properly identified, a party may be allowed to present extrinsic evidence to show what the parties intended. In some cases, parol evidence may be allowed to fill a "gap" in the terms of the agreement, if the party can show that the agreement is not complete or does not address that issue.

- **Fraud.** Extrinsic evidence may always be introduced to prove that one party lied, acted unconscionably, created duress, or did something else that would make the contract or its provisions invalid or illegal.

- **Lack of consideration.** Extrinsic evidence is admissible to show that the consideration stated in the contract was not actually paid. For example, if a contract states that "For consideration of $100 ..." and no money ever changed hands, the party who got ripped off could present evidence to that effect. This type of evidence isn't seeking to contradict or add to the contract's terms, but to show that the contract, as written, has not been honored.

- **Subsequent modifications of existing agreements.** The parol evidence rule bars written or oral statements only if they were made prior to the written agreement or oral statements made at the time the contract was signed. It does not apply to statements made after the contract was created. However, if the contract itself prohibits oral modifications—for example, it includes a statement such as, "This Agreement may not be altered except by a written document signed by both parties"— then that will typically prevent the parties from introducing evidence of later oral modifications. We say "typically" because historically, a requirement that changes be made in writing was viewed with suspicion by the courts and often disregarded. (Or as Justice Cardozo once stated, "The clause which forbids a change, may be changed like any other.")

Related terms: fraud (misrepresentation); integration; oral contracts; quasi contract; statute of frauds; void (voidable).

participation agreement

Every contract is a participation agreement, in that the parties participate in performing their contractual obligations. But the term has a more specific meaning when applied to these types of agreements:

- **Debt financing arrangements.** The term "participation agreement" is most often used to describe a contract in which one party assumes someone else's obligations and rights under a debt financing arrangement. It works like this: You are a party to a debt financing contract, such as a bank loan. You transfer your rights to a second party (the "participant"). The participant must now fulfill your obligations and responsibilities under the contract, although—unlike an assignment or a novation—the participant has no direct contractual relationship with the third party.

- **Multibank loan agreement.** In banking, a participation agreement (also known as a "participation loan") is an agreement in which several banks all contribute to (or participate in) a loan to a single customer.

- **Agreement to create a well.** The Internal Revenue Service defines a participation agreement as "an agreement between two or more parties to share in the cost and production of a well."

- **Profit participation agreements.** Another type of participation agreement is a profit participation (or sharing) arrangement, in which one of the parties receives (or participates in) the profits from an enterprise. The arrangement was popularized by movie contracts in which an actor or a director takes no—or only a very small salary—in exchange for a piece of the gross or net profits from a motion picture.

- **Leveraged leases.** On some occasions, the term participation agreement refers to an agreement between lenders, owners, lessors, and other participants in a leveraged lease, a complex arrangement in which the lessors and lenders participate in the financing of a project.

P

- **Activity participation.** The term participation agreement is often loosely used to refer to agreements that contemplate one party's participation in a certain activity, which is usually the subject of the contract. These may range from participation in a charity event to participation in the construction of a building.

parties

Parties are the people or entities that have mutually agreed to the contract and are bound by its terms and conditions. In the case of written agreements, the parties are typically identified as the people or entities that signed the agreement. Although the parties were once referred to as "party of the first part," "party of the second part," and so on, few attorneys still use this archaic terminology.

When in court .... In court cases, parties are the people or entities who are suing (called the "plaintiffs") or being sued (the "defendants").

partnership (general)

A partnership is a business arrangement in which two or more people operate a business together and share its profits and losses. A partnership is the starting point for many famous companies, mostly because it's so easy to get off the ground. The arrangement is informal, doesn't require any government registration, and can be terminated fairly easily. However, once a business takes off— that is, it's making money and attracting customers—the partners usually become concerned about personal liability. A partnership does nothing to limit the liability of individual partners for business debts, lawsuits against the business, and so on. *Any* partner can be personally liable for all of the partnership debts. This concern over liability usually leads successful partners to convert their partnership to a limited liability structure, such as a limited liability company (LLC) or corporation.

EXAMPLE: In 1976, when Steve Wozniak and Steve Jobs brought their first Apple 1 computer to the Homebrew Computer Club in Palo Alto, California, few people took them—or their computer—seriously. Once the two partners started taking orders, however, their low-cost ($666.66) microcomputer system slowly began to sell. Nine months later, Jobs and Wozniak filed incorporation documents, converting their partnership to a corporation.

Most partnerships are general partnerships, which means simply that all partners have the same rights and responsibilities for running the business. When you begin a business with another person, you have automatically created a general partnership. A general partnership is different from a limited partnership, a business structure in which one or more of the partners is only an investor and plays no role in managing the business. In a limited partnership, the limited partners enjoy limited liability. They are liable for business debts only up to the amount they have invested in the business; their personal assets are not at risk. Even in a limited partnership, however, the general partners—the people who actually run the business—are liable for all of the business's debts and lawsuits, just like all of the members of a general partnership.

A general partnership isn't a separate entity for tax and liability purposes. There is no legal distinction between the owners and the business. That means the owners don't have to jump through any special hoops to create a partnership, but it also means that they don't get any special treatment when it comes to taxes and other liabilities.

Taxation. A general partnership is a pass-through tax entity. The profits (and losses) pass through the business entity to the partners, who pay taxes on any profits on their individual returns at their individual tax rates. Even though a partnership does not pay its own taxes, it must file an "informational" tax return, IRS Schedule K-1 (Form 1065). In addition, the partnership must give each partner a copy of this form showing the proportionate share of profits or losses that each partner must report on an individual 1040 tax return. A partner pays taxes on his or her entire share of profits, even if the partnership chooses to reinvest the profits in the business rather than distributing them to the partners.

Liability. Each partner is personally liable for business debts and legal claims against the business. (The partnership can get liability insurance to cover most claims.) What's more, a creditor of the partnership can go after any general partner for the entire debt, regardless of that partner's ownership interest. Any partner may bind the entire partnership (in other words, the other partners) to a contract or business deal.

Formalities. A partnership does not have to pay any government formation fees or register as a general partnership. In addition, it's not strictly necessary to create a written partnership agreement among the partners.

However, drafting a partnership agreement is a very good idea, because it allows the partners to make their own decisions about how they will manage the business, pay its expenses, divide its profits, admit new partners, handle a partner's departure, and all of the other issues that might come up over the lifetime of the business. Without a partnership agreement, state laws will determine all of these issues for the partnership, no matter who you and your partners want to handle things. These state law provisions usually say that profits and losses of the business should be divided equally among the partners (or according to the partner's capital contributions, in some states), and they impose a long list of other rules. Creating a written partnership agreement allows the partners to make rules that conform to their own individual needs and the needs of their business.

A typical partnership agreement should cover issues such as how profits and losses will be divided, partnership draws (payments in lieu of salary), and the procedure for selling a partnership interest back to the partnership or to an outsider. Below is a sample agreement, along with an explanation of the major provisions.

Partnership Agreement

Partnership Agreement

Partners. _____

(the Partners), agree to the following terms and conditions.

Partnership Name. The Partners will do business as a partnership under the name of _____ .

Partnership Duration. The partnership [_Choose one:_ ☐ began ☐ will begin] on _____ . It will continue

[_Choose one_]

   ☐ indefinitely until it is ended by the terms of this agreement.

   ☐ until _____ , unless ended sooner by the terms of this agreement.

Partnership Office. The main office of the partnership will be at _____ _____ . The mailing address will be:

[_Choose one_]

   ☐ the above address.

   ☐ the following address: _____

Partnership Purpose. The primary purpose of the partnership is _____ _____ .

Capital Contributions. The Partners will contribute the following capital to the partnership on or before _____ .

A. Cash Contributions

Partner's Name	Amount
	$
	$

Partnership Agreement (continued)

B. Noncash Contributions

Partner's Name	Description of Property	Value
_____	_____	$ _____
_____	_____	$ _____
_____	_____	$ _____

Capital Accounts. The partnership will maintain a capital account for each Partner. The account will consist of the Partner's capital contribution plus the Partner's share of profits and less the Partner's share of losses and distributions to the Partner. A Partner may not remove capital from his or her account without the written consent of all Partners.

Profits and Losses. The net profits and losses of the partnership will be credited to or charged against the Partners' capital accounts

[*Choose one*]

☐ in the same proportions as their capital contributions.

☐ as follows: _____ .

The partnership will only make distributions to the Partners if all the Partners agree.

Salaries. No Partner will receive a salary for services to the partnership.

Interest. No interest will be paid on a Partner's capital account.

Management. Each Partner will have an equal say in managing the partnership.

[*Choose one*]

☐ All significant partnership decisions will require the agreement of all the partners.

Partnership Agreement (continued)

☐ Routine partnership decisions will require the agreement of a majority of the partners. The following partnership actions will require the agreement of all the Partners:

☐ borrowing or lending money

☐ signing a lease

☐ signing a contract to buy or sell real estate

☐ signing a security agreement or mortgage

☐ selling partnership assets except for goods sold in the regular course of business

☐ other: _____ .

Partnership Funds. Partnership funds will be kept in an account at

_____ , unless all

Partners agree to another financial institution. Partnership checks:

☐ may be signed by any Partner.

☐ must be signed by all the Partners.

☐ must be signed by _____ Partners.

Agreement to End Partnership. The Partners may unanimously agree to end the partnership.

Partner's Withdrawal

☐ The partnership will end if a Partner withdraws by giving written notice of such withdrawal to each of the other partners.

☐ Upon the withdrawal of a Partner, the other Partners will, within 30 days, decide either to end the partnership or buy out the withdrawing Partner's interest and continue the partnership. A decision to buy out the withdrawing Partner's interest and continue the partnership requires the unanimous consent of the remaining Partners.

P

Partnership Agreement (continued)

Partner's Death

☐ The partnership will end if a Partner dies.

☐ Upon the death of a partner, the other Partners will, within 30 days, decide either to end the partnership or buy out the deceased Partner's interest and continue the partnership. A decision to buy out the withdrawing Partner's interest and continue the partnership requires the unanimous consent of the remaining Partners.

Buy-Out. If the remaining Partners decide to buy the interest of a withdrawing or deceased Partner the remaining Partners, within _____ days after that Partner's withdrawal or death, will pay the withdrawing Partner or the deceased Partner's estate:

☐ The amount in the capital account of the withdrawing or deceased Partner as of the date of withdrawal or death.

☐ The fair market value of the interest of the withdrawing or deceased partner as determined by the partnership's accountant.

☐ Other: _____ .

General Provisions

Entire Agreement. This is the entire agreement between the parties. It replaces and supersedes any and all oral agreements between the parties, as well as any prior writings. Modifications and amendments to this Agreement, including any exhibit or appendix hereto, are enforceable only if they are in writing and are signed by authorized representatives of both parties.

Successors and Assignees. This agreement binds and benefits the heirs, successors, and assignees of the parties.

Notices. Any notice or communication required or permitted to be given under this Agreement is sufficiently given when received by certified mail, or sent by facsimile transmission or overnight courier.

Partnership Agreement (continued)

Governing Law. This Agreement will be governed by the laws of the State of _____ .

Waiver. If one party waives any term or provision of this agreement at any time, that waiver will only be effective for the specific instance and specific purpose for which the waiver was given. If either party fails to exercise or delays exercising any of its rights or remedies under this agreement, that party retains the right to enforce that term or provision at a later time.

Severability. If a court finds any provision of this Agreement invalid or unenforceable, the remainder of this Agreement will be interpreted so as best to carry out the parties' intent.

Attachments and Exhibits. The parties agree and acknowledge that all attachments, exhibits, and schedules referred to in this Agreement are incorporated in this Agreement by reference.

No Agency. Nothing contained herein will be construed as creating any agency, partnership, joint venture, or other form of joint enterprise between the parties.

Attorneys' Fees and Expenses. The prevailing party shall have the right to collect from the other parties its reasonable costs and necessary disbursements and attorneys' fees incurred in enforcing this Agreement.

Jurisdiction. The parties consent to the exclusive jurisdiction and venue of the federal and state courts located in____[county]_____ ____[state]_____ , in any action arising out of or relating to this Agreement. The parties waive any other venue to which any party might be entitled by domicile or otherwise.

Arbitration. The parties shall settle any controversy or claim arising out of or relating to this Agreement by arbitration in ____[county]_____ ____[state]_____ , in accordance with the rules of American

Partnership Agreement (continued)

Arbitration Association and judgment upon the award rendered by the arbitrator(s) may be entered in any court having jurisdiction. The prevailing party shall have the right to collect from the other parties its reasonable costs and attorneys' fees incurred in enforcing this agreement.

Date signed: _____

By: _____

Printed Name: _____

Address: _____

By: _____

Printed Name: _____

Address: _____

P

Completing the Partnership Agreement. Your partnership agreement should address these issues:

- **Partnership Name.** If you're going to use a business name for your partnership that's different than the names of the partners—for example, Miraculous Windchimes, instead of Furry, Brown, and Wind chimes—you should include the partnership's formal name in your agreement. Before you choose a name, make sure no other business is already using it.

- **Partnership Duration.** A partnership may be created for a specific period and have a fixed duration (for example, five years) or it may exist indefinitely until termination. You should specify the duration of the partnership in your agreement.

- **Partnership Purpose.** It's helpful to state the partnership's mission or purpose in the agreement, if for no other reason than to make sure you and your partners agree on your common goals.

- **Capital Contributions.** The dates and amounts of each partner's contributions to the partnership should be tracked in the agreement, as well as the status of the contribution (that is, whether the partner chipped in cash or property.

- **Capital Accounts.** A capital account is a bookkeeping technique for keeping track of how much of the partnership assets each partner owns. Each capital account starts out with the amount the partner invests in the partnership. To that figure the partner adds his or her share of the profits and deducts losses. The partnership agreement should specify how capital accounts will be calculated.

- **Profits and Losses.** There are many ways to divide the profits and share the losses. Most partnerships choose to assign each partner's share of profits and losses in proportion to the capital each has invested in the partnership. Not all partnerships want to divide profits this way, however. For example, the partners might decide that one partner should receive a greater share

P

of the profits in exchange for spending more time working on the partnership business. Of course, this isn't the only way to recognize the contribution of a partner who's doing extra work. You could still allocate profits in proportion to contributions while compensating the partner who's putting in more time in some other way (by paying that partner a salary, for example).

- **Salaries.** Generally, a partner's reward for doing work for the partnership is a share of the partnership profits. However, there's no legal or tax-related reason why the partners can't agree to hire one or more partners as employees who will receive a salary for their services. The partnership agreement should spell out the details of these types of arrangements.

- **Management.** Your partnership agreement should spell out how day-to-day decisions will be made. When it comes to important decisions, such as whether to take out a bank loan or where to rent space for the business, all partners should have a say in the outcome. But it can be hard to achieve unanimity on every single decision, especially in a large partnership. Most partnership agreements establish a majority vote on routine decisions (because it allows more flexibility) and require unanimity only on major business decisions. Of course, for a small partnership to succeed, the partners need to have both shared goals and confidence in one another's judgment. If those elements don't exist, pages of rules as to how decisions should be made won't help. Or, put more bluntly, if you don't trust your partners and enjoy working with them, don't bother creating a partnership in the first place.

- **Partnership Funds.** Most partnership agreements establish where the financial accounts will be held and which partners will have signing authority.

- **Ending the Partnership.** The agreement should make clear that the partnership can be ended if all the partners agree.

- **Partner Withdrawal or Death.** Unless your partnership has a written agreement stating otherwise, the law says your partnership will end if any partner decides to leave. In addition, if your partnership has no agreement to the contrary, a partner can't transfer his or her partnership interest to someone else. This means that, unless you agree in writing to a different plan, if one partner leaves, the partnership assets will be liquidated, bills will be paid, and the partners will be cashed out. As with a partner's withdrawal, a partner's death will end the partnership unless you agree in the partnership agreement to handle it differently.
- **Buy-Out.** Many partnership agreements establish a formula or method for buying out the interest of a withdrawing or deceased partner.

Related terms: corporation; limited liability company (LLC); limited partnership; personal liability; sole proprietor.

partnership (limited)

See limited partnership.

patent

Patents are a form of intangible intellectual property, the most common of which is a utility patent granted to the creator of a new, nonobvious invention. Inventions are categorized as new processes, machines, manufactures, or compositions of matter or new uses of any of the above. The utility patent owner has the exclusive right to make, use, and sell the invention for a limited term—usually 17 to 18 years. Other patents include design patents for new and nonfunctional designs and plant patents for asexually or sexually reproducible plants.

Patents and contracts. Patents are often the subject of two types of contracts:

- **Assignment.** An assignment is a contract (or a provision within a contract) in which a patent is permanently transferred.

• **License.** A license is a contract by which the owner of a patent gives someone permission to use or exploit intellectual property rights for a limited time or in a limited way.

Related terms: copyright; intangible property (intangible assets); intellectual property; license agreement; patent; trademark (service mark); works made for hire.

payment

See consideration.

payment in kind (PIK)

Payment in kind refers to compensation paid in something other than cash—for example, goods or services. In the world of securities, a payment-in-kind bond or stock (known as a "PIK") pays dividends or interest not in cash, but in the same form as the underlying security—that is, either as a bond or stock.

performance bond

A performance bond is a contract among three people: (1) The party who receives the benefit of the performance (the "obligee")—for example, a landowner who is having a home built; (2) the principal, who does the work—for example, the contractor building the home; and (3) the insurer, who insures that the job will get done. Under a performance bond agreement, the insurer guarantees that the principal will finish the job satisfactorily. If for some reason the principal can't accomplish the task, the performance bond will compensate the obligee, up to the limits of the bond, for any losses. Performance bonds are commonly used for specific projects—for example, construction of a building or producing a movie.

Related terms: construction agreement; mechanic's lien.

personal guaranty (guarantee)

A personal guaranty (sometimes spelled guarantee) is a contract in which someone (the "guarantor") pledges to personally repay or make good on a debt. A personal guaranty may be required as a condition of getting a loan for your business if you have formed a limited liability structure, such as a corporation or limited liability company (LLC). Suppliers, banks, and landlords know that corporate shareholders or LLC members don't have personal liability for the corporation or LLC's debts, so many of them won't extend credit or loan money to a small LLC or corporation—especially a new company that hasn't yet established a profitable track record—without the owner's personal guarantee.

When you sign a personal guarantee for a particular loan, lease, or contract, you promise that you will pay the debt personally if your business does not. Put another way, you agree, contractually, to give up your limited liability for that debt. If the business can't pay, the creditor may sue you to take your personal assets.

Signing a personal guaranty isn't the only way to make yourself personally liable for a debt. If you are a sole proprietor or general partner (that is, you have not formed a liability-limiting business entity), you are automatically liable for the debts of the business. Even if you have formed an LLC or a corporation, you may be personally liable for a debt if you sign the contract creating the debt personally, rather than in the name of your business.

Related terms: corporation; limited liability company (LLC); limited partnership; partnership (general); promissory note; sole proprietor.

personal liability

The personal assets of a party who is personally liable can be used to pay off a contract breach or a debt. As a general rule individual business owners (sole proprietorships), and general partners are personally liable for business debts; owners of corporations and LLCs are generally not liable for their business's obligations. However, don't assume that forming an LLC or a corporation will always shield all of your personal assets. Even if you operate as a corporation or an LLC, a creditor can still go after your personal assets if:

- **You personally guarantee a loan or lease.** Most lenders and landlords condition small business loans and leases upon the business owner's personal guarantee. The only way you could escape these debts is for the business and each owner seeking protection to file for bankruptcy.
- **You owe federal or state taxes.** If your business fails to pay income, payroll, or other taxes, the IRS or the state tax agency can try to recover the unpaid taxes personally from you or the other directors, officers, and owners of your LLC or corporation.
- **You act negligently.** If you run a business subject to potential negligence claims—for example, an establishment open to the public, or a manufacturer of consumer products—you can be personally liable for the damage. In these cases, buying insurance will usually do you more good than will forming a corporation or an LLC.
- **You fail to abide by corporate rules.** If you don't take corporate responsibilities seriously—for example, you mix corporate and personal funds and don't keep records of meetings and shareholders—a judge may strip away the asset protection feature of the corporation or LLC. It's called "piercing the veil."

Related terms: corporation; limited liability company (LLC); limited partnership; partnership (general); sole proprietor.

plain meaning rule

The plain meaning rule, which has been adopted by some states but is not followed in others, governs the interpretation of contracts (and to some extent, statutes). In a nutshell, the rule says that if the plain meaning (or "commonsense" meaning) of a contract's language taken in context is evident, that is how the language must be understood. The court should not go outside of the document and consider external evidence (such as prior negotiations) to understand what a word, phrase, or provision means. If the plain meaning is not clear, external evidence may be used to assist in the interpretation.

The modern trend disfavors the plain meaning rule and seeks to understand the intent of the parties, even if it differs from the way a term is usually used. As one comment to the Restatement of Contracts says:

> *Any determination of meaning or ambiguity should only be made in the light of the relevant evidence of the situation and relations of the parties, the subject matter of the transaction, preliminary negotiations and statements made therein, usages of trade, and the course of dealing between the parties.*

Plain meaning versus parol evidence. The parol evidence rule prevents one party to a written contract from introducing evidence in court that contradicts, changes, or adds to the terms of the contract, if the parties intended for their contract to be the final and complete version of their agreement. So, doesn't this conflict with the plain meaning rule, which says outside evidence should be admitted if it will assist the court in interpreting a term that does not have a plain meaning?

Contract experts and judges have distinguished the two rules this way: Evidence admitted under the plain meaning rule is used to interpret (and better understand) the agreement; it's not used to contradict the agreement. Also, the parol evidence rule (as applied in most states) allows courts to consider outside evidence if a term or provision of the contract is ambiguous, which is another way of saying that it doesn't have a plain meaning.

Related terms: interpretive provisions; mistake; parol evidence rule; plain meaning rule; rules of interpretation (rules of construction).

plea bargain

See criminal plea bargain.

power of attorney

A power of attorney (POA) is a document by which one person (the "principal") appoints another (called an "attorney-in-fact") to make certain legal decisions on the principal's behalf. (Attorneys-in-fact are so called because they are authorized to act for someone else; they have none of the rights or powers of a licensed lawyer.) If you grant power of attorney to your brother to manage your apartment building, for example, then your brother can sign rental and repair contracts on your behalf.

There are many duties that can be delegated under a power of attorney arrangement. At the same time, the delegation can also be very narrow (referred to as a "special" or "limited" power of attorney). For example, if you are going to be out of town when escrow closes on the house you are purchasing, you could grant power of attorney to someone only for the purpose of signing the final documents.

Tasks that can be delegated to an attorney-in-fact. Using a power of attorney, you can give someone broad power to handle many financial and legal obligations, including:

- using your assets to pay your everyday expenses and those of your family
- buying, selling, maintaining, paying taxes on, and mortgaging real estate and other property
- collecting Social Security, Medicare, or other government benefits
- investing your money in stocks, bonds, and mutual funds
- handling transactions with banks and other financial institutions
- buying and selling insurance policies and annuities for you
- filing and paying your taxes
- operating your small business
- claiming property you inherit or are otherwise entitled to
- transferring property to a trust you've already created
- hiring someone to represent you in court, and

- managing your retirement accounts.

Although oral powers of attorney will be enforced in some cases and in some states, it is generally recommended that these grants be in writing. In some states, they must be witnessed; often, they must be notarized.

Durable power of attorney. A power of attorney expires automatically if the principal becomes incapacitated (that is, unable to make decisions). To avoid the potential problems this can cause, you can create a "durable" power of attorney, which remains in effect if the principal becomes incapacitated or disabled.

For example, if you want someone to make medical decisions for you after you become incapacitated, you need to prepare a durable power of attorney for health care (sometimes known as an "advanced medical directive"). Similarly, if you want someone to manage your finances if you are incapacitated, you must prepare a durable power of attorney for finances. If you would prefer that the power of attorney not go into effect until you are unable to make your own decisions, you can create what's known as a "springing" durable power of attorney (it springs into effect when you become incapacitated).

A durable power of attorney automatically ends at the principal's death. It also ends if the principal (or a court) revokes it.

Below is an example of a limited power of attorney for real estate that allows you to give someone the authority to buy or sell a piece of real estate for you or to conduct any other business concerning real estate that you own. It is commonly used when the principal is unavailable or lives far away from the property and wants someone else to manage it in that person's absence. A power of attorney for real estate is a "conventional" power of attorney, meaning that it automatically expires if you become incapacitated or die. As explained above, if you want a document that will stay in effect even if you become incapacitated, you need a "durable" power of attorney. Not all states require witnesses and a notary, but their signatures are included in the sample agreement.

Related terms: authority to bind; fiduciary (duty, relationship).

Power of Attorney

RECORDING REQUESTED BY

AND WHEN RECORDED MAIL TO

_____

_____

Power of Attorney for Real Estate

I, _____ *[name of principal]* _____, of _____ *[city]* _____ ,

_____ *[county]* _____ , _____ *[state]* _____ , appoint

_____ *[name of attorney-in-fact]* _____, of _____ *[city]* _____ ,

_____ *[county]* _____ , _____ *[state]* _____ , to act in

my place with respect to the real property described as follows: _____

_____ .

My attorney-in-fact may act for me in any manner to deal with all or any part of any interest in the real property described in this document, under such terms, conditions, and covenants as my attorney-in-fact deems proper. My attorney-in-fact's powers include but are not limited to the power to:

1. Accept as a gift or as security for a loan, reject, demand, buy, lease, receive, or otherwise acquire ownership or possession of any estate or interest in real property.

2. Sell, exchange, convey with or without covenants, quitclaim, release, surrender, mortgage, encumber, partition or consent to the partitioning of, grant options concerning, lease, sublet, or otherwise dispose of any interest in the real property described in this document.

3. Maintain, repair, improve, insure, rent, lease, and pay or contest taxes or assessments on any estate or interest in the real property described in this document.

Power of Attorney (continued)

4. Prosecute, defend, intervene in, submit to arbitration, settle, and propose or accept a compromise with respect to any claim in favor of or against me based on or involving the real property described in this document.

However, my attorney in fact shall not have the power to: _____ _____ _____ _____ .

I further grant to my attorney-in-fact full authority to act in any manner both proper and necessary to the exercise of the foregoing powers, including _____ and I ratify every act that my attorney-in-fact may lawfully perform in exercising those powers.

This power of attorney takes effect on _____ , and shall continue until terminated in writing, or until _____, whichever comes first. In the event of my incapacity or death, this power of attorney will terminate immediately.

I agree that any third party who receives a copy of this document may act under it.

Revocation of the power of attorney is not effective as to a third party until the third party has actual knowledge of the revocation. I agree to indemnify the third party for any claims that arise against the third party because of reliance on this power of attorney.

Signed this _____ day of _____ , _____ .

State of _____ , County of _____ .

Signature: _____

Social Security number: _____

P

Power of Attorney (continued)

Witnesses

On the date written above, the principal declared to me that this instrument is his or her power of attorney for real estate, and that he or she willingly executed it as a free and voluntary act. The principal signed this instrument in my presence.

Name: _____

Address: _____

County: _____

Name: _____

Address: _____

County: _____

P

Power of Attorney (continued)

Certificate of Acknowledgment of Notary Public

State of _____)
) ss
County of _____)

On _____ , before me,

_____ , a notary public in and for

said state, personally appeared _____ ,

who proved to me on the basis of satisfactory evidence to be the person

whose name is subscribed to the within instrument and acknowledged to

me that he or she executed the same in his or her authorized capacity and

that by his or her signature on the instrument, the person, or the entity

upon behalf of which the person acted, executed the instrument.

I certify under PENALTY OF PERJURY under the laws of the State of _____

that the foregoing paragraph is true and correct.

                     WITNESS my hand and official seal.

                     _____

                     Notary Public for the State of _____

[NOTARY SEAL]   My commission expires _____

Signature of Attorney-in-fact

By accepting or acting under the appointment, the attorney-in-fact
assumes the fiduciary and other legal responsibilities of an agent.

Signature of Attorney-in-fact: _____

preamble

See recitals.

prenuptial agreement

A prenuptial agreement (also known as an "antenuptial agreement," "premarital agreement," or just a "prenup") is a written contract created by two people before they are married. A prenup typically lists all of the property each person owns (as well as any debts) and specifies what each person's property rights will be after the marriage.

Who needs a prenup? While prenups are often used to protect the assets of a wealthy fiancé, couples of more modest means are increasingly turning to them for the following reasons:

- **To pass separate property to children from prior marriages.** A marrying couple with children from prior marriages may use a prenup to spell out what will happen to their property when they die, so that they can pass on separate property to their children and still provide for each other, if necessary. Without a prenup, a surviving spouse might have the right to claim a large portion of the other spouse's property, leaving much less for the kids.

- **To clarify financial rights.** Couples with or without children, wealthy or not, may simply want to clarify their financial rights and responsibilities during marriage.

- **To avoid arguments in case of divorce.** Couples may want to avoid potential arguments if they ever divorce by specifying in advance how their property will be divided and whether or not either spouse will receive alimony. (A few states won't allow a spouse to give up the right to alimony, however; in most others, a waiver of alimony will be scrutinized heavily and won't be enforced if the spouse who is giving up alimony didn't have a lawyer.)

- **To get protection from debts.** Prenups can also be used to protect spouses from each other's debts and may address a multitude of other issues as well.

If a couple does not make a prenup. If you don't make a prenuptial agreement, your state's laws determine who owns the property that you acquire during your marriage, as well as what happens to that property at divorce or death. (Property acquired during your marriage is known as either marital or community property, depending on your state.) State law may even have a say in what happens to some of the property you owned before you were married. If you make a prenup, you can make your own decisions about how to handle these issues.

Making a valid prenup. Traditionally, courts scrutinized prenups with a suspicious eye. Historically, prenups almost always required the less wealthy spouse (often the woman) to waive legal and financial benefits. Prenups were also thought to encourage breakups.

As divorce and remarriage have become more prevalent, however, and with more equality between the sexes, courts and legislatures are increasingly willing to uphold premarital agreements. Today, every state permits them, although a prenup that is judged unfair or otherwise fails to meet state requirements will still be set aside.

Because courts still look carefully at prenups, it is important to negotiate and write up your agreement in a way that is clear, understandable, and legally sound. If you draft your own agreement, you'll want to have separate lawyers review it and at least briefly advise you about it. Otherwise, a court is much more likely to question its validity.

What can be included? A prenup can be used for the following purposes:

- to create a system to keep finances separate
- to protect each other from debts
- to provide for children from prior marriages
- to keep property in the family

- to define who gets what in the event of a divorce (some states forbid or restrict agreements about alimony)
- to clarify responsibilities during the marriage
- to establish whether to file joint or separate income tax returns or to allocate income and tax deductions on separate tax returns
- to determine who will pay the household bills—and how
- to decide whether to have joint bank accounts and, if so, how to manage them
- to reach agreements about specific purchases or projects, such as buying a house together or starting up a business, or
- to establish how to handle credit card charges.

What you can't include in a prenup. State laws differ as to what matters are considered off-limits. However, as a general rule, any agreement to do something that is illegal or against state-defined public policy will be considered unenforceable and may even jeopardize other valid aspects of the premarital agreement. For that reason, you cannot restrict child support, custody, or visitation rights. No state will honor agreements limiting or giving up future child support. A handful of states similarly limit your ability to give up your right to alimony (also called "spousal support" or "separate maintenance") if there is a divorce. Other states permit such waivers. These variations in state laws are another good reason to get the advice of a lawyer when drafting a prenup.

Related terms: living together contract; marriage contract.

prepayment

See promissory note.

prepayment penalty

See promissory note.

priority

If a person or business owes money to various people and entities, the order in which everyone gets paid is referred to as "priority." Priority becomes very important when a debtor doesn't have enough assets to pay everyone back.

Priority debts must be paid before other debts, which are moved to the back of the line and sometimes are never repaid.

As a general rule, secured creditors (those with debts secured by collateral) have priority over unsecured creditors. Other factors that may determine priority in a particular situation include bankruptcy laws (which establish that certain types of debts have priority over others), provisions regarding payment included in loan agreements (these sometimes claim priority), and public policy laws that make certain debts more important (these debts include child or spousal support, some taxes, student loans, and criminal fines or restitution).

private placement

A private placement is the sale of a company's stock to a limited number of private investors, without placing the stock for sale on a public stock exchange. When making a public offering of stock, a company usually has to abide by the complex federal laws (most of which are part of the Securities Act of 1933) requiring registration of the shares. These rules are intended to protect investors by providing enough information about the stock and the company to allow outsiders to make an educated decision about the investment.

A company that makes a private placement is exempt from these rules, as long as it meet certain requirements. For example, it can sell only to a limited number of investors, and those investors must be in a position—either because of their relationship to the company or because of their investment savvy—to make an educated decision about purchasing the stock without needing to see a prospectus and other documents that would otherwise have to be provided.

P

privity

Privity is a principle of contract law that prohibits anyone—except the parties to the contract (those who are "privy" to it)—from suing to enforce a contract. In other words, unless you signed a contract, you can't show up in court and ask a judge to enforce the provisions. That can be a problem, particularly if you are third party who benefits from the agreement but did not sign it. Luckily, there are some exceptions to the rule, which allow certain outsiders to seek enforcement of a contract

Intended third-party beneficiaries. Intended third-party beneficiaries can sue to enforce a contract even though they are not parties. Third parties who are receiving a gift or benefit (donee beneficiaries)—for example, the person named as a beneficiary of an insurance policy, trust, or annuity—can ask a court to enforce the contract. So can third parties who are assigned rights under loan agreements (called "creditor beneficiaries").

Product negligence and privity. Prior to the 20th century, companies used privity as a shield to protect themselves from the claims of consumers injured by their products. Because a consumer purchased the product from a dealer, broker, or store (and not directly from the manufacturer), the manufacturer argued that it had no direct contractual relationship (in other words, no privity) with the consumer. Therefore, the manufacturer had no obligation to compensate the consumer for any loss. By the 1920s, courts had chipped away at the concept of privity and extended a manufacturer's duty of care (a concept based in tort, not contract law) to anyone who could be foreseeably injured by a product placed into commerce.

Related term: product liability.

product liability

Product liability refers to the legal responsibility of a company that makes, sells, or distributes a product that causes an injury. Product liability claims are generally grouped into three categories:

- **Defective manufacture.** This category involves a product that have been defectively manufactured in some way, meaning that a mistake was made either at the factory or at some point between the factory and wherever the product was purchased, resulting in a faulty product.
- **Defective design.** This category of claims involves products that were defectively designed, meaning that the products are dangerous in some way even though they were correctly manufactured. These cases do not involve a single faulty product, but rather an entire line of products that are claimed to be unreasonably dangerous.
- **Failure to warn.** This category of claims involves a failure to provide adequate warnings or instructions regarding the proper use of the injury-causing product. These claims are sometimes referred to as "defective marketing" claims.

These days, product liability lawsuits are most often brought as tort (personal injury) cases, for which more significant damages are available, than as contract cases. But contract law has been an important factor in assessing whether a company should be liable to consumers for a defective product and in allowing parties to avoid or shift liability for faulty products.

A little history. Modern product liability rules evolved from contract law. When the 20th-century began, consumers who were injured by a faulty product could generally receive compensation for their injuries only if they could prove they were in a contractual relationship (or "privity," as the lawyers say) with the product manufacturer. That changed in 1916, when Benjamin Cardozo (then sitting as a judge at the New York Court of Appeals) ruled that Buick Motor Company could not avoid liability for a defective wheel simply because a Buick dealer—rather than the Buick Motor Company itself—sold the car to the consumer. With this holding, Cardozo chipped away at the concept of privity and found that the manufacturer owed a duty of care to anyone who could be foreseeably injured.

P

Approximately fifty years later, in a case involving a wood-working machine, California Supreme Court Justice Roger Traynor established a rule of strict liability for defective products that would soon be adopted by nearly all states. Traynor held that when a manufacturer puts a defective product on the market, it has liability for injuries caused by that product, regardless of whether there is a contractual relationship or proof that the company is at fault. Traynor wrote, "Even if there is no negligence, however, public policy demands that responsibility be fixed wherever it will most effectively reduce the hazards to life and health inherent in defective products that reach the market." With these words, Justice Traynor officially ended the defense of contractual privity against product liability claims.

Using contracts to shift liability. As the courts decided that no contractual relationship was necessary to sue for product liability, the creators of products realized that contracts could be used in another way: to shift the liability for defective products away from themselves and on to someone else. For example, an inventor who licenses a product to a manufacturer may, as a condition of the contract, insist that the manufacturer maintain product liability insurance and add the inventor/licensor as a named insured. This will require the insurance company to defend claims brought against the inventor as well as the manufacturer.

Similarly, the parties may seek to shift or assign liability for third party claims by including indemnity provisions, which require one party to defend the other in lawsuits brought over defects. For example, an inventor may indemnify the manufacturer against claims regarding the safety of the product's design, while the manufacturer may indemnify the inventor for claims resulting from defects in the manufacture of the product. Of course, the use of indemnification is grounded in practical realities: If a party has no money to pay an attorney, the provision is useless and the legal obligation to indemnify can't be enforced. The most prudent course of action is to have both insurance and indemnity.

EXAMPLE: George invents a leak detector, which he licenses to Plumbing Unlimited (PU). In the license agreement, George promises that the detector's design is effective and agrees to indemnify PU against any claims based on a faulty design. Unfortunately, George's design has a flaw, resulting in undetected flooding in many homes. Consumer claims are brought against PU, which demands that George indemnify and pay for the costs of the lawsuits. Unfortunately, George is broke and declares bankruptcy. Even though it negotiated an indemnity provision, PU (and its insurer) will be on the hook for the damage cause by the faulty detector.

Product warranties and disclaimers. Contracts also affect product liability through the use of product warranties and disclaimers. Warranties are assurances made about a transaction. Some warranties—known as implied warranties—are not actually spoken or written down, but are mandated by state laws. The two most well-known implied warranties are:

- **The implied warranty of merchantability.** This is a merchant's basic promise that the goods sold will do what they are supposed to do and that there is nothing significantly wrong with them.
- **The implied warranty of fitness for a particular purpose.** This warranty is a promise that the customer can rely on a merchant's advice that a product can be used for some specific purpose—for example, that a four-cup coffeemaker will, in fact, produce four cups of coffee.

Disclaimers. A disclaimer is a statement that attempts to limit responsibility. Manufacturers often try to limit their legal responsibility by disclaiming any product warranties. These implied warranties and disclaimers are not contracts between the parties— although, historically, the roots for warranties come from the contractual relationship of the buyer and seller.

P

Express warranty. An express warranty is a specific written or oral assurance about a product (for example, the packaging for a bicycle trainer warrants the parts for 90 days). Express warranties are contracts because the manufacturer, as a condition of a sale, is making a statement as to the reliability, functionality, or other quality of the merchandise. If the manufacturer doesn't keep that promise, the consumer can sue for breach of the warranty/sales contract. Further, if the seller makes an express warranty, the seller cannot disclaim any implied warranties. If the seller does not offer a written warranty, the law in most states allows the seller to disclaim implied warranties (although selling without implied warranties is not a consumer-friendly approach).

Much of what companies can and cannot do regarding express written warranties is set out in the Magnuson-Moss Act, a federal law passed in 1975. Among other things, the act ensures that warranties are available where warranted consumer products are sold (so that consumers can read them before buying); prohibits anyone who offers a written warranty from disclaiming or modifying implied warranties; and sets standards for full and limited warranties. Equally important, it modifies the remedies for a breach of warranty. Unlike a typical contract claim, the act makes a breach of warranty a violation of federal law and allows consumers to recover court costs and reasonable attorneys' fees.

Related terms: fraud (misrepresentation); gross negligence; negligence; tort.

pro rata

Pro rata refers to allocating something proportionally.

> EXAMPLE: A partnership agreement states that the annual partnership profits are to be divided on a pro rata basis amongst all of the partners. The profits in one year are $100,000 and there are five partners. Each partner receives $20,000.

profit participation

See participation agreement.

promissory estoppel

See estoppel.

promissory note

A promissory note is a loan agreement that documents the amount of a debt and the terms under which it will be repaid, including the interest rate (if any). Under a promissory note, the amount that is borrowed is referred to as the "principal," the person borrowing the money is the debtor, and the person lending the money is the creditor.

Although promissory notes are often agreements to lend a fixed sum of money—for example, a car loan or a mortgage—they can include a wide variety of other debt arrangements including credit card contracts, hedge fund loans, or so-called nonrecourse notes used in real estate transactions.

Some history. As hard as it may be to believe, until the turn of the 20th-century, most banks loaned money only to the wealthiest individuals and largest businesses. The idea of lending money to a small business or extending credit to someone who had to work for a living was virtually unheard of until banker A.P. Giannini (founder of Bank of America) introduced the concept. He began offering home loans to immigrants in 1904 and—following the 1906 earthquake—extended loans to small business owners. Based on his success, other banks soon adopted his business model, leading eventually to today's vast consumer credit and credit card industries.

Common elements of promissory notes. Promissory notes typically address the following issues:

- **Purpose of loan.** Often a promissory note describes the purpose for which the loan is intended—for example, to buy a piece of real estate—and establishes that the loan cannot be used for other purposes.

- **Secured or unsecured.** A loan can be secured (where the borrower pledges property, such as a car, as collateral to guarantee repayment) or unsecured. If the loan is unsecured and the borrower doesn't repay the loan, the lender must sue in court to get a judgment, which then makes the lender eligible to use wage garnishment or property attachments to collect on the note. The property that is used to secure the loan doesn't have to be worth the exact amount of the loan; it can be any tangible or intangible property agreed upon by the parties. If a debt is secured, the property securing the debt should be detailed in the promissory note.

- **Interest.** Most loans include interest. Interest charged on a friendly loan (money lent between people who know each other) tends to run no higher than 5% to 10%. If you loan money and want to charge a higher rate of interest, check your state law to see if the rate is legal; it may constitute the crime of usury (charging an illegally high interest rate). Of course, you may want to lend money to family or friends interest free. Be aware, however, that if the IRS learns of an interest free loan, it can magically attribute interest to the arrangement. This means that the lender will be assumed to have earned interest—and will have to report and pay tax on that interest as income—even though no interest payments actually changed hands. For most personal loans, uncharged interest can be treated as a tax-free gift to the borrower, as long as the total amount given and imputed to the borrower in a calendar year is $13,000 or less (as of 2010).

- **Maturity date.** Every loan agreement includes a date of maturity: the date on which the loan is due (or must be paid off in full).

- **Amortization.** In the 1930s, the U.S. government devised a system for paying loans that permitted a low down payment and a lengthy period of installment payments. The debtor pays the same amount every month, but more of the money goes to paying down the principal (and less of it to paying off interest) as the payment plan progresses. In order to figure out how much the monthly payments will have to be to make all of the math come out right, lenders use an amortization calculator or software program. The lender plugs in the loan amount, interest rate, and number of months the borrower will take to repay the loan. The calculator provides the monthly payment amount.

- **Prepayment; prepayment penalties.** Loan agreements usually state whether all or part of the loan can be paid off prior to the date of maturity (a process known as "prepayment"). Some contracts leave prepayment up to the discretion of the borrower or lender; some contracts prohibit prepayment, at least for a period of time (for example, no prepayment during the first two years of the loan), and some contracts require prepayment in certain circumstances. For example, prepayment of a home loan may be mandatory if the underlying property is sold. Many lenders, eager to maximize interest payments, discourage prepayment by assessing prepayment penalties: fees imposed for paying off a loan early. In some states, those fees are illegal for residential home loans. In other states, there are limits on these penalties—for example, they can be assessed only during the first two years of a home loan. If the borrower decides to prepay a portion of the loan, the lender must recalculate the monthly payments based on the new outstanding balance.

- **Repayment requirements.** Promissory notes typically include instructions as to how the payments should be made (type of delivery and location of lender) and when (for example, what date of the month). There are many ways to structure repayment of the loan. Typically, loans are repaid in monthly installments that include a mixture of interest and principal.

Sometimes, loans are repaid in a lump sum at the end of the term (the time period of the loan). Or, there might be a series of installment payments with a lump sum payment at the end (known as a balloon payment). In the case of a "demand" loan, the payment must be made when the lender demands it. There also may be cure periods for any promissory note that includes payment deadlines. For example, if payment is not received by a certain date, the borrower may have five or ten days to correct the failure.

- **Cosigners and personal guarantors.** A promissory note should identify any cosigner or guarantor (someone who will step in and pay if the borrower defaults). In the case of a business loan to an LLC or a corporation, the lender may insist that an owner of the business personally guarantee the loan—that is, promise that personal assets may be used to repay or make good on a debt. Generally, all of the people accountable for the debt are subject to "joint and several liability," which means that any of them can be held accountable for 100% of the debt.

- **Spouses.** A lender may ask the borrower's spouse to sign a loan agreement. This is likely to happen, for example, if someone is borrowing money to buy property that both spouses will use or to help finance a new business venture. A lender may not require a borrower's spouse to sign if the borrower is the only one applying for the loan, and no jointly held or community property is involved. A borrower's spouse who signs the note is legally liable for repaying the debt. Normally, if only the borrower signed the contract and didn't repay it, the other party to the agreement could get a judgment against the borrower but not against the borrower's spouse. This means that the creditor would be able to seize property that the borrower owns as sole owner, but not property that the borrower and a spouse own in both of their names or that the spouse owns solely, unless the borrower lives in a community property state such as California. But if the borrower and spouse both sign a contract and then default, the other party can sue and get a judgment against both. That judgment can be enforced by seizing the couple's joint bank account, putting a lien on jointly owned real estate, seizing property in the borrower's name alone, and seizing property in the spouse's name alone.

- **Remedies.** Many promissory notes provide remedies for late payments or a loan default (when the borrower stops making payments). Typically, the remedies include the right to accelerate the loan (to make the whole loan due if payments are missed), to proceed against any property securing the loan, or to seek attorneys' fees required for collecting the debt.

- **Witnesses; notary.** With the exception of a few states and specific types of loans, most loan agreements do not need to be witnessed or notarized. Of course, it never hurts to have the signatures witnessed and the document notarized, if there is any concern that one party will later dispute the terms of the loan agreement.

Below is a sample promissory note that must be paid back with installment payments.

Related terms: amortization; compounding (compound) interest; debt; equity; interest rates (usury); mortgage.

Promissory Note

Promissory Note

(Loan repayable in installments with interest)

Name of Borrower: _____

Name of Lender: _____

1. For value received, Borrower promises to pay to Lender the amount of
   $_____ on _[date payment is due]_ at _____ [address where
   payments are to be sent]_____ , at the rate of _____% per year from the
   date this note was signed until the date it is

   [choose one]:

   ☐ paid in full (Borrower will receive credits for prepayments, reducing
      the total amount of interest to be repaid).

   ☐ due or paid in full, whichever date occurs last (Borrower will not
      receive credits for prepayments).

2. Borrower agrees that this note will be paid in installments, which include
   principal and interest, of not less than $_____ per month, due
   on the first day of each month, until the principal and interest are paid
   in full.

3. If any installment payment due under this note is not received by Lender
   within _____ days of its due date, the entire amount of unpaid principal
   will become immediately due and payable at the option of Lender
   without prior notice to Borrower.

4. If Lender prevails in a lawsuit to collect on this note, Borrower agrees to
   pay Lender's attorneys' fees in an amount the court finds to be just and
   reasonable.

The term Borrower refers to one or more borrowers. If there is more than
one borrower, they agree to be jointly and severally liable. The term Lender

Promissory Note (continued)

refers to any person who legally holds this note, including a buyer in due course.

Borrower's signature: _____

Date: _____

Print name: _____

Location: [*city or county where signed*]_____

Address: _____

_____

proviso/provision

A proviso (or provision) refers to a contract condition: something that must happen for another contract requirement to kick in. Typically, you can spot a proviso because it includes the word "provided," as in, "John agrees to paint the truck, *provided* that Tom delivers the truck by Sunday." The problem with provisos, and the reason why they are disfavored in drafting contracts, is that they can be ambiguous. For example, in the situation described above, it's not clear whether Tom and John have reciprocal obligations or whether the delivery of the truck is a condition of its being painted. To avoid that result when drafting a contract, it is recommended that stipulated conditions use language such as "if" and "must"—for example, "If Tom delivers the truck by Sunday, John must paint it."

Related term: condition.

public policy

Contracts will not be enforced if they are against public policy—the fundamental principles of morality and fairness upon which the legal system is based. If you think that sounds vague and difficult to predict, welcome to the club. (One 19th-century English judge characterized public policy as a "very unruly horse," exclaiming, "you never know where it will carry you.")

Sources of public policy. In some cases, public policy is elaborated expressly within the law. For example, the law might state that it is against public policy to charge illegally high interest rates or to discriminate on the basis of race. In other situations, courts have defined public policy in the absence of statutory language. For example, during the early 20th century, it was against public policy to enforce agreements that involved cohabitation of an unmarried man and woman—for example, an agreement in which one partner agreed to live with and provide household services in return for a percentage of profits from a partner's book. To enforce such arrangements was thought to encourage sexual relations outside of marriage. As time went on, public policy changed, and some states started enforcing such agreements.

Another common example in which public policy affects enforcement of contracts is when unlicensed vendors render services. Although laws may require licensing and provide penalties, the statutes do not state that agreements entered into by unlicensed workers are unenforceable. Yet, courts often refuse to enforce these contracts because honoring them would violate the policy underlying the licensing laws. Similarly held to be against public policy are contracts for the sale of goods for illegal purposes (selling a gun knowing that the buyer is likely to use it for a crime), contracts that encourage gambling, or bribing someone to obtain a contract.

Related term: illegal contract.

purchase order

A purchase order (also known as a "purchase requisition") authorizes delivery of goods to one party at a price and on terms that are set forth in the order document. Some purchase orders, referred to as "open purchase orders," may be for a series of deliveries over months or years, again at the price and terms set forth. A purchase order functions as an offer until the supplier fulfills the order, when it becomes a binding contract. After fulfilling the order, the supplier typically invoices the customer (the party issuing the purchase order).

Related terms: installment contract (divisible/severable contracts); invoice.

put

A put is stock lingo for the right to sell shares at a given price and by a specific date. A call is the right to buy shares at a given price and by a specific date.

Q

quantum meruit

This term—Latin for "as much as deserved"—refers to a court-ordered payment that is made to avoid unjust enrichment (acts that result in someone getting rich unfairly). This remedy might be used if parties didn't have a valid contract, but one nonetheless provided goods or services to the other. In this situation, it would be an "unjust enrichment" to allow the second party to get the goods or services free, so a court might order that party to pay their fair market value.

Related terms: remedies; restitution; unjust enrichment;

quasi contract

A quasi contract (also referred to as an "implied-in-law" contract) is not a contract at all. It's an obligation that grows out of an unfair situation, which courts will enforce as if it were contractual. This typically comes up when goods or services are provided that benefit someone, but that beneficiary has no contractual obligation to pay for them. For example, say a lawn maintenance company mowed the wrong lawn, while the happy homeowner sat inside, aware of the mistake, and made other plans for the Saturday he planned to spend mowing it himself. There is no contract between the parties, but it would be unfair to let the homeowner enjoy the benefits of someone else's labor when he knew it was a mistake. The remedy available for these types of situations is known as restitution: making the situation right by requiring the beneficiary to pay for the goods or services.

Related terms: quantum meruit; remedies; restitution; unjust enrichment.

quitclaim deed

A quitclaim deed transfers whatever ownership interest a person has in a property. It makes no guarantees about the extent or validity of that interest. Divorcing couples commonly use quitclaim deeds, in which one spouse signs all of his or her rights in the couple's real estate over to the other. This can be especially useful if it isn't clear how much of an interest (if any) one spouse has in property that's held in the other's name. (However, a quitclaim deed doesn't relieve the person transferring ownership from the obligation to pay the mortgage on the property, if there is one.)

Quitclaim deeds are also frequently used when there is a "cloud" on title—that is, when a search reveals that a previous owner or some other person, like the heir of a previous owner, may have some claim to the property. Anyone who has an arguable or possible claim to the property can sign a quitclaim deed to transfer any rights they may have to the proper owner.

real estate contract

A real estate contract is an agreement to transfer land and any attached improvements (homes, buildings, fences, and so on). Real estate (also known as "real property") is distinguished from personal property: tangible items that aren't land or things built on land, such as cars, furniture, jewelry, clothing, appliances, and much more. In all states, a contract for the sale of real estate must be in writing or it won't be enforced.

A little history. Back in medieval days, land was transferred under the "tenurial" system, in which the feudal landowner conveyed a piece of property through a ceremony known as "livery of seisin," (delivery of an estate in land). The ceremony usually involved a physical meeting between the parties at the estate to be transferred, accompanied by an oath of transfer and a ceremonial handing over of a clump of earth or a twig (referred to as the "turf and twig" ceremony).

Real estate documents. Nowadays, the transfer of real estate still involves a meeting of the parties (the "closing"), which usually takes place at the offices of the real estate agent, the title company, or a lawyer. The parties may "meet" only on paper, each signing their stack of paperwork separately, or they may be together at the closing. Instead of handing over a ceremonial clump of land, the parties hand over a pile of documents for signature and acknowledgment. Some of these are contracts between the buyer and seller; others are between the buyer and a lender. Contractual closing documents include:

- **Promissory note.** If the buyer is borrowing money to finance the purchase, the promissory note is the loan agreement setting out the terms by which the buyer will receive the money and repay it to the lender.

- **Mortgage or deed of trust.** Again, if there is a loan, the mortgage establishes a lien on the property—the mortgage lender's right to claim the property under certain conditions. The mortgage converts the property into collateral, which the lender can take in foreclosure if the buyer fails to repay or to otherwise follow the terms of the note (known as a "default"). The lender records the mortgage with the appropriate local government office.

- **Deed or warranty deed.** A deed is the document that formally transfers ownership of real estate. It contains the names of the old and new owners and a legal description of the property, and is signed by the person transferring the property. It should accurately reflect the names of the parties and the manner in which they intend to hold the property (for example, as tenants in common, joint tenants, and so on). There are various types of deeds, the most common of which are quitclaim, grant, and warranty. A quitclaim transfers whatever interest the signer has in the property, but doesn't make any guarantees about the nature of that ownership; a grant deed implies certain promises (for example, that the title hasn't already been transferred to someone else); and a warranty deed—most commonly used in real estate contracts—transfers ownership and explicitly promises the buyer that the transferor has good title to the property, meaning it is free of liens or other claims of ownership. With a warranty deed, the transferor guarantees that he or she will compensate the buyer if the warranty turns out to be wrong. Most often, this promise is accompanied by a title insurance policy, in which the title company researches the property's history and insures that the person selling it has good title. The warranty deed may make other promises as well, to address particular problems with the transaction. It is always preferable for the buyer to obtain a warranty deed.

- **Bill of sale.** This agreement transfers personal property that's not considered part of the real property. For example, if you are purchasing a tractor, hammock, rug, or other property from the seller, you would use a bill of sale to memorialize the transaction.

Other documents. Due to government regulations, lender rules, and other requirements, most real estate sales also include plenty of supplementary documents, such as:

- **Truth-in-Lending Act (TILA) Disclosure Statement, or "Regulation Z form."** This is a document in which the lender breaks down all the payments, confirms the interest rate, the annual percentage rate ("APR"), and the total cost of the loan over its lifetime.

- **Closing statement, settlement sheet, or HUD-1 settlement statement.** This statement itemizes every payment to be made as part of the real estate sale, whether for insurance, closing costs, lien payoffs, or as part of your loan (such as points or a mortgage broker's fee).

- **Monthly payment letter.** This tells the buyer how much money will be paid in monthly loan principal and interest.

- **Affidavit of title and American Land Title Association (ALTA) statement.** In the affidavit, the seller promises that the title is clear of liens and can be transferred to the buyer. The ALTA statement is similar, but it is signed by both parties to demonstrate that they haven't done anything to cloud title to the property (such as granting an easement).

R

Following the closing, the buyer records the property deed in the appropriate public records office. In some areas, this is done electronically. In others, someone (the closing agent or a messenger) goes to the appropriate office in person. The sale hasn't truly "closed" until the deed is recorded.

Escrow. In order to ensure that the seller will receive the funds and the buyer will receive title (and to protect against the parties changing their minds), an escrow account is used. This account is a holding zone, where the money and deed are kept until the contract is final and everything can be released to the appropriate party. The deed is placed in escrow and not delivered until all the conditions of escrow have been met (including the depositing of funds). The escrow account is created by an escrow agreement. A financial institution or another escrow agent manages the transaction (in some states, real estate agents or attorneys may serve that function). Escrow agents are rarely the subject of disputes unless an agent acts illegally—for example, by embezzling funds from the escrow account.

Selling real estate "as is." An agreement to sell a home or land may include a provision stating that the buyer takes the property in its current condition (as is), without any further guarantees. The buyer must accept the property in the same condition as it reasonably appears to be at the time of sale. An "as is" provision may state that the buyer has a duty to inspect, which will further relieve the seller of certain disclosure obligations. An "as is" provision does not permit the seller to conceal defects that would not be apparent from an inspection. That type of concealment may amount to fraud.

Disputes with real estate agents. Real estate agents (or brokers) have a fiduciary relationship to their principals (whether seller or buyer), which requires them to act with loyalty, confidentiality, trust, and reasonable care. In some cases, a broker may represent both buyer and seller (known as "dual representation"). In this situation, the agent must obtain written consent from both parties and, in some states, the broker cannot collect fees from both parties. Regardless of whether representing a seller or buyer exclusively, the agent must disclose all known material facts regarding the property. This sometimes creates a dilemma when a seller deliberately lies to an agent and the agent repeats the lies to the buyer or buyer's agent.

EXAMPLE: A seller told his real estate broker that certain land included a barn. The broker repeated the statement about the barn to buyers (who planned to use the barn for their horses). It turned out that the seller had not provided an accurate representation; the barn was not fully within the property boundaries. A court held that the agent was not liable to the buyers because he didn't know, nor should he have known, that the statement was false. Absent this knowledge, the court held that the buyer's broker had no duty to investigate further on behalf of the buyers. (Note: In at least one state (California), an appellate court has held that a broker in a residential sale has an affirmative obligation to investigate all facts regarding the value of the property.)

Fraud and failure to disclose. Sellers, particularly of residential property, usually have to make a laundry list of disclosures. These often go far beyond the appearance or condition of the property and can include the existence of lawsuits threatening the property or even that the residence is a source of notoriety (for example, the site of a serial killing). If material defects are intentionally concealed or misrepresentations deliberately made, the wronged party may bypass a claim for breach of contract and sue either for the tort of fraud (a personal injury claim for which higher damages are available) or for violation of a consumer statute to protect against fraud or unfair business behavior.

> EXAMPLE: In an Illinois case, four townhouses were built with a common foundation, which an engineer later determined was sinking (eventually it sank seven to ten inches). During a preclosing walkthrough of the homes, one of the purchasers complained of cracks to the developers, who were aware of the foundation problems. The developers said that the cracks were "normal" and "a result of natural settling," and that there was a 20-year warranty on the basement and foundation (which was never produced). One developer even told a buyer "it's not like the house is going to sink or anything." The court awarded the homeowners $1.38 million as compensation, $5,000 in punitive damages, and attorneys' fees.

Easements and real estate sales. An easement is a nonpossessory interest in real estate. An easement owner has the right to use real property without owning it (for example, the right to drive or walk across a neighbor's property to get to one's own property). Most easements are "affirmative," which means that they allow someone to do something. Some are "negative," in that they prohibit things from happening (no cutting down the cherry trees).

Most easements are also "appurtenant," in that they involve two pieces of property and deal with some connection between them— for example, a boundary wall (a "party wall") or access from one home to a coast line. Usually, easements are associated with the sale of real estate either because the easement travels from owner to owner or because a dispute has arisen as to whether the easement exists and was fully disclosed.

Related terms: mortgage; statute of frauds; title insurance.

reasonable efforts

See best efforts.

recitals

Recitals (sometimes referred to as "whereas provisions") are the introductory statements in a contract that state who the parties are, place the agreement within a context, explain the purpose of the agreement, and lead the reader into the agreement. (Recitals typically end with a statement like, "Therefore, the parties agree ....") Because recitals precede the body of agreement, they are rarely considered binding elements of the contract and therefore don't create obligations or rights. However, occasionally a court has to read and interpret the recitals in order to clear up the parties' intentions.

The outdated "whereas" thing. Despite the continued use of "whereas" to introduce an agreement ("Whereas the parties desire to enter into an agreement ..."), this terminology is archaic and serves no legal purpose. Proponents of plain English contract drafting recommend leaving the whereas out.

Recitals from a Publishing Agreement

This Agreement (the "Agreement") is entered into effective June 1, 2011 (the "Effective Date") by and between KarKare, ("KarKare") with its principal place of business at 34 Bonnie Avenue, Mountain View, CA 94043 and Vehicular Traffic, a California corporation (referred to as "Vehicular Traffic"), with its principal place of business at 425 Bowles Street, Berkeley, California 94710. Vehicular Traffic is a provider of automotive content, software, and website tools, including print publications for personal and business use. KarKare is a provider of Web-enabled tools and services that assist drivers in evaluating and appreciating automobiles. In consideration for development fees specified in this Agreement, Vehicular Traffic shall develop a publication providing legal automotive information for drivers (the "Auto Law Book"). Vehicular Traffic shall distribute the Auto Law Book within its existing sales channels as well as for purposes of online display, promotion, online syndication, and download. KarKare shall acquire rights to syndicate, display, download and publish the Auto Law Book as set forth in this Agreement. The parties agree as follows:

Related terms: as of; whereas provision.

redemption

Redemption refers to either the price at which a company can repurchase (redeem) its bonds before maturity, or the repayment of a debt or security before its date of maturity.

redlining

Redlining (also called "blacklining") refers to the digital markup of a contract, usually to distinguish changes between one version of an agreement and another. Redlining is helpful when keeping track of multiple drafts of agreements as they pass back and forth amongst the parties and their lawyers. The process is now universally accomplished by word processing programs such as Microsoft Word. These programs show the sections that have been deleted ("strikeouts") and also accommodate comments.

Redlining has a different meaning when applied to consumer loan agreements: It refers to the practice of refusing to lend, or lending only at very high rates and otherwise more onerous terms, to certain people. The term originally referred to the process of drawing a red line on a map, beyond which the lender or provider of goods or services would not do business. Today, it is used to describe any practice of refusing to lend to particular groups of people, whether delineated by neighborhood or more explicitly by race or gender, for example.

Related term: reverse redlining.

refinancing

Refinancing is the process of replacing an existing debt with a new debt. For example, when you receive a credit card offer to "move" your credit card debt from one company to another, that's an invitation to refinance your debt. Refinancing is especially popular in the home loan market. Overindulgence in the practice, along with dropping home values, contributed significantly to the economic downturn of 2008 and 2009.

Related terms: compounding (compound) interest; debt; interest rates (usury); mortgage; promissory note.

reformation

Reformation is a court-imposed modification to a contract, with the purpose of making the contract reflect what the parties intended. Reformation comes into play when the parties made a deal but failed to state that deal properly. If one of the parties asks a court for reformation, a court may grant it in the following situations:

- **Transcription errors.** Reformation is available if something's gone awry in the process of transcribing the written contract, typically a typo or other typing/data entry error (or what used to be known as a "scrivener's error"). For example, the term "lessor" might appear in a contract when both parties meant to say "lessee."

- **Mutual mistake.** This occurs when both parties are operating under a misunderstanding as to terminology or the absence or presence of a condition or obligation. For example, if both parties mistakenly believed there was a provision requiring inventory to be sold off, a court may reform the agreement to put it in the contract.

- **One party's mistake; the other's fraud.** If a mistake was the result of one party's lies—that is, the liar knew and induced the mistake—a court may reform the agreement to erase the effects of the fraud. For example, if the other side deceptively removes a provision after you have read the agreement but before you sign it, a court may reform the agreement to include the provision. This is not always the outcome, as other remedies are also available for fraud.

Related terms: fraud (misrepresentation); mistake; remedies.

release (personal)

A release is an agreement by which someone waives (gives up) the right to sue over a certain activity or transaction. A personal release (also known as a "model" release) is one in which a person foregoes the right to make certain legal claims that might arise from the use of the person's likeness, such as defamation, invasion of privacy, or violation of the right of publicity. Typically, a personal release is sought when a person's name or image is being republished or broadcast.

Blanket or limited. There are two classes of personal releases:

- **Blanket releases.** A blanket (or unlimited) release permits any use of the image or name of the person signing the release and is suitable if the company or photographer needs an unlimited right to use the name or image. Stock photographers who sell their photos for unlimited purposes commonly use blanket releases.

- **Limited releases.** Celebrities and models usually sign limited releases, which specify the particular ways their images and names may be used. If the use exceeds what's permitted under the limited release, the person can sue for breach of the agreement. For example, a model who signed a release limiting use of her image for a museum brochure sued when the photo appeared on a Miami transit card.

See below for a sample unlimited personal release agreement.

release and settlement

See settlement agreement (settlement and release).

remedies

Remedies are damages or other court-ordered actions intended to resolve legal problems. If a contract is a breached, courts usually prescribe payment of damages to fix things, a return of any money paid or goods supplied, the specific performance of the contract (that is, both parties have to do the things they promised in the contract), or some combination of these remedies. The initial choice of remedy is stated by the wronged party in the court complaint. In contract law, the remedies chosen usually boil down to this choice: Do you want to undo the contract, get the benefits you should have received from the contract, or actually go through with the deal?

> **EXAMPLE:** Robert agreed to sell Andrea a painting of a long-haired dachshund for $5,000. Robert and Andrea sign a written agreement and Andrea pays Robert $5,000. After six months, Andrea still has not received the painting. She sues for breach of contract. Andrea can undo the contract by asking for the return of her $5,000 (restitution). Or she can seek the benefits she should have gotten from the contract by asking for her lost

Sample Unlimited Personal Release Agreement

Unlimited Personal Release Agreement

For consideration that I acknowledge, I irrevocably grant to _____
_____ ("Company") and
Company's assigns, licensees, and successors the right to use my image
and name in all forms and media including composite or modified
representations for all purposes, including advertising, trade, or any
commercial purpose throughout the world and in perpetuity. I waive the
right to inspect or approve versions of my image used for publication or
the written copy that may be used in connection with the images.

Release. I release Company and Company's assigns, licensees, and
successors from any claims that may arise regarding the use of my image,
including any claims of defamation, invasion of privacy, or infringement
of moral rights, rights of publicity, or copyright. Company is permitted,
although not obligated, to include my name as a credit in connection with
the image.

Company is not obligated to utilize any of the rights granted in this
Agreement.

I have read and understood this Agreement and I am over the age of 18.
This Agreement expresses the complete understanding of the parties.

Company

By: _____   By: _____

Printed Name: _____   Printed Name:_____

                                 Title:_____

Date: _____   Date: _____

R

profit: the difference between what she paid and the painting's current market value (compensatory damages), along with the return of her $5,000 plus interest. Or, instead of seeking damages or restitution, she might seek a court order requiring that Robert go through with the contract and actually hand over the painting (specific performance).

Common contract remedies are described below; each has its own detailed entry as well. Keep in mind that the application and choice of remedies can be confusing, especially if:

- each side claims that the other side breached
- the contract includes a liquidated damages clause
- the parties waived consequential damages or established some cap on liability in the contract
- there has been complete or partial performance, or
- one party claims breach while the other claims that no contract exists.

The good news is that just about every type of contract problem has been litigated, and the general rules for sorting out these disputes can be determined prior to filing a lawsuit. The not-so-good news is that as the complexity of the dispute increases, so does the need for legal assistance.

Some common court remedies are:

- **Damages.** The most common remedy for a breached contract is to give the wronged party the "benefit of the bargain." That means awarding a payment to compensate for the loss caused by the breach (known as "compensatory damages"). The court attempts to put the unhappy party in the position it would have been in if the contract had been performed. For example, if a seller breaches a contract to sell goods, compensatory damages would be the buyer's lost profit: the difference between the contract price (what the buyer would have paid under the contract) and the market price (what the buyer could have earned by reselling the goods). How damages are measured depends on whether the unhappy party is the seller or buyer, the type of goods or services that are at stake in the agreement, and whether the contract includes language that may affect the award—for example, whether there is an enforceable liquidated damages provision. In addition to compensatory damages, a court may award other types of damages, including:

- **Incidental damages.** Reasonable minor expenses incurred in dealing with a breach
- **Punitive damages.** Damages awarded to punish the wrongdoer. Punitive damages are not awarded in contract cases unless separate tort (personal injury) claims are also part of the lawsuit.

• **Restitution.** While compensatory damages attempt to put the parties where they *would have been* if the contract had been performed, restitution seeks to put the parties where they were *before* the contract was created. Put another way, the goal of restitution is to undo the contract and restore (or return) any benefits the unhappy party has conveyed. For example, if you paid $500 as an advance payment to a house painter and the painter flaked out, you could seek restitution—the return of your payment. Restitution sometimes occurs in combination with a court-ordered rescission of the contract. (Rescission officially "undoes" the contract, making it void.)

• **Specific performance.** Sometimes damages are not a suitable remedy—for example, if the goods are unique and/or the damages are difficult to prove. In those cases, a court may order one party to actually go through with the deal. Specific performance is not a popular remedy because it often requires ongoing court supervision. Also, it does not lend itself to certain contracts—for example, it would be improper to require specific performance of certain personal services contracts.

- **Injunction.** An injunction is an order by a court requiring a party to do, or to not do, something. Like specific performance, an injunction is an equitable (nonmonetary) remedy that can be ordered at the discretion of the court. Injunctions are sometimes used in conjunction with other remedies involving personal services contracts or employment. For example, if a nondisclosure agreement is breached, a court may enjoin (issue an injunction prohibiting) the breaching party from disclosing the secrets.

Noncontract remedies. Some methods of resolving contract problems are classified as contract remedies although technically they are solutions to problems in which a contract should not have been made or does not exist. These methods include:

- **Mutual rescission.** Mutual rescission occurs when both parties want to call it quits and end the contract, most often before the contract has been performed.
- **Quasi contract.** Courts may order one party to repay another or compensate for services rendered even when there isn't a contract. For example, say someone gets an estimate from a house painter. The painter mistakenly believes that the homeowner has hired him, and shows up on Monday to start painting. The homeowner is home and sees the painter start work, but says nothing all week long, hoping for a free paint job. If the homeowner refuses to pay the painter because there was no valid contract, most courts would allow the painter to sue for damages under a quasi contract theory.
- **Tort remedies.** In some cases, parties to a contract may sue for deceptive and unfair behavior, even though such behavior is not categorized as a breach of contract. These include claims of fraud, intentional interference with a contractual relationship, and in some states, breach of the implied covenant of good faith and fair dealing.

Related terms: consequential damages; exemplary damages; incidental damages; liquidated damages; mitigation of damages; remedies; specific performance; tort.

rent

See lease, residential (rental agreement).

rental agreement

See lease, residential (rental agreement).

replevin

Replevin is a special legal process to recover goods (also known as "claim and delivery"). The goal of replevin is to make someone deliver goods promptly to someone who claims ownership of the property, without having to go through a lawsuit. The process is often used by creditors seeking to obtain possession of the security or collateral for a loan—for example, a rental store seeking to recover rental furniture, or a used car dealer seeking to obtain a car for which the buyer stopped making payments.

representations and warranties

Ever wonder why contracts sometimes contain statements that start with "The Seller represents and warrants …"? This seemingly repetitious use of language has some legal significance. Here's how it works.

Representations. A representation is a statement of current fact that a party makes with the intent that the other party will rely on it.

> EXAMPLE: Gwen represents that her car had new brakes installed a week earlier. Tom justifiably relies on that representation when he buys the car from her. Gwen's statement wasn't true. Tom would have a claim for misrepresentation. However, if Tom had the car inspected before he bought it and learned that new brakes had not been installed, he would not have a claim because he no longer had a reason to rely on Gwen's representation.

Warranties. A warranty is a guarantee or promise that a statement is true. It's similar to an indemnity in that the party making the warranty must pay damages if the warranty is triggered (that is, if the statement is not true).

> EXAMPLE: Gwen warrants that her car had new brakes installed a week earlier. Tom buys the car from her. Gwen's statement wasn't true. Tom would have a claim for breach of warranty. Even if Tom had the car inspected before he bought it and learned that new brakes had not been installed, he could still have a claim against Gwen if, prior to purchasing the car, he told her that he was preserving his right to sue over the brakes.

Remedies. The remedies for misrepresentations and breach of a warranty differ. A misrepresentation can trigger a claim for fraud. If the misrepresentation was made innocently or negligently, that may result in rescinding (undoing) the agreement. If the misrepresentation was intentional, the party that was lied to could make a tort claim of fraud and seek compensatory and special damages (punitive damages). Remedies for breach of a warranty are the same as for breach of contract: The injured party is entitled to the benefit of the bargain. In Tom's case, for example, he could get a court order requiring Gwen to pay for new brakes for the car.

Related terms: condition; covenant; fraud (misrepresentation); warranties.

repudiation

See anticipatory breach.

rescission (court ordered)

As distinguished from mutual rescission, which is voluntary, a court-ordered rescission is imposed on the parties as part of the resolution of a contract lawsuit. The court grants an order that rescinds (nullifies) the contract.

Related terms: reformation; remedies; rescission (mutual); restitution.

rescission (mutual)

When the parties to a contract want to call it quits and return to their precontract position, they set aside (or "mutually rescind") their contract. Mutual rescission is like hitting the reset button: You go back to the beginning as if the contract never existed.

God save the contract. An example of mutual rescission occurred in 1976, shortly after the British record label EMI signed the punk rock band the Sex Pistols to a two-year contract. Two months after signing, the band appeared on the BBC and shocked a London audience with what was described by the press as a demonstration of "filth and fury," using language that had previously not been heard on British television. After a few additional PR disasters, the record label—reportedly under political pressure—wanted to end the arrangement. The band happily agreed to rescind the contract, once it was assured a payment of approximately $250,000.

Oral rescission. Although we recommend putting rescissions in writing, a mutual rescission can also be accomplished by an oral agreement. However, as with all oral agreements, there can be problems proving what was agreed to. For example, in one case, a boat salesman rescinded an agreement to buy ads from an outdoor advertising company, paying $50 as consideration for the rescission. Despite the oral arrangement, the outdoor advertiser later sued and won an award for the annual outdoor advertising fees. The boat salesman was forced to appeal his case all the way to the Wisconsin Supreme Court in order to get a reversal—spending significant time and money that could have been saved if the parties had simply documented the rescission in the first place.

Implied rescission. A mutual rescission can also be implied from the actions of the parties, if those actions demonstrate that both parties intend to rescind the contract. Obviously rescission by implication can create even bigger proof problems than oral rescission because it's based on assumptions and interpretations. For

R

example, a company contracted to build three injection blow-mold machines (complex devices used to create plastic containers). The company that ordered the machines never properly conveyed the specs for the machines, which made it impossible to construct them under the agreement. Because both parties failed to cooperate in the performance of the contract, mutual rescission was implied. Again, a written rescission agreement would have saved time and money.

Put it in writing. By now you get the picture. There are many advantages to putting a mutual rescission in writing. For example, a written mutual rescission agreement can provide that the other party's successors won't sue you, which protects you if the other party sells to a subsequent owner who sees the contractual dispute differently. A written rescission also makes it clear that the first contract has been terminated, which provides needed clarity if the parties execute a second contract. A written agreement may also be required by the Statute of Frauds—a law that certain contracts will be enforced only if they are in writing.

Payment? Often a mutual rescission doesn't require any money to change hands because the contract hasn't been performed. One party might pay the other as part of the rescission deal to compensate the other party for contractual duties it has already performed or to give the other party a stronger incentive to rescind, as EMI paid the Sex Pistols.

What makes a rescission legally enforceable? Rescinding a contract requires each party to release the other from any legal claims for breach of contract. To be legally enforceable, a release must satisfy two requirements:

- **The release must be voluntary.** Each side must enter into the agreement voluntarily. If one party was coerced into signing an agreement because of the other party's threats or intimidation, a court probably won't consider the rescission voluntary. In other words, it won't be enforceable.
- **The agreement must be arrived at fairly.** The parties have to be honest with each other. Judges are usually unwilling to enforce

any agreement that is the product of deceit or the result of one side taking unfair advantage of the other.

Before signing a mutual rescission. Before you agree to a mutual rescission, you should ask yourself two questions: Do both parties understand the issues that underlie the rescission? Do both parties understand what the rescission agreement accomplishes? If you answered no to either question, you may want to consult an attorney, or at least someone knowledgeable in business law who is not involved in the dispute. Keep in mind that a mutual rescission is a form of release, in which the parties give up their right to sue over the rescinded contract. If you sign a release and learn six months later that you actually suffered more monetary damage than you thought, you are out of luck unless a court declares the release unenforceable.

Never mind the Sex Pistols. By the way, the Sex Pistols eventually signed with Virgin Records and their first album included a song entitled "EMI," in which the record executives were referred to as "useless fools." (Ironically, Virgin Records was later sold to EMI. Awkward!)

Related terms: reformation; remedies; rescission (court ordered); restitution; void (voidable).

restitution

The contract's gone bad. Now imagine that you can rewind the whole deal and stop right before the handshake; all money is returned, and the parties just walk away. That's restitution, a contract remedy in which a court returns the parties to the positions they were in before the contract was made. Although many victims of a contract breach want to be compensated for their lost profits, some choose restitution instead because the damages are difficult to calculate or speculative.

What's the difference between restitution and rescission? These two terms—sometimes confused by lawyers and courts—are distinguished by timing and control. In both restitution and rescission, the parties return to where they were before a contract was made. However, rescission occurs *before* the parties have performed their contract. Rescission is usually mutual (although sometimes court ordered). Restitution occurs *after* the contract has been performed (or partially performed) and is always court ordered.

Restitution without a contract. Restitution is also used if a transaction has occurred without a valid contract, and it would be unfair to allow one party to profit from doing wrong. For example, if an arrangement is fraudulently induced—a scam artist sells fake real estate—there is no contract because there was never an honest offer to accept. However, a court may order restitution as a way for the victim to recover money lost in the deal. Restitution may also be ordered to prevent unfairness if one party provides goods or services and the other party accepts them.

When restitution isn't allowed. A court will not order restitution if the victim of the breach has fully performed his obligations and all that remains is for the breaching party to pay for the full performance. In that case, the court will award damages in the amount of the payment still owed.

Related terms: reformation; remedies; rescission (court ordered); rescission (mutual).

retention agreement (stay-on bonus)

In a merger-crazy world, what's a paranoid executive supposed to do? Get a retention agreement: a contract that requires a new owner to keep an employee on for a set period of time. Employee retention agreements (also called "stay-on agreements") are usually available only to company officers or other key employees.

A well-drafted retention agreement can benefit both the company and the employee. The employee gets an assurance of job security for a period of time, and the company gets the employee's commitment to stay on through the transition, which often adds value for prospective purchasers who want that crucial period to go smoothly.

Sample Retention Letter Agreement

Retention Letter Agreement

Date: _____

Dear _____ :

This letter serves as an offer to enter into a retention agreement (the "Agreement"). Your signature, below, indicates that you accept its terms. This Agreement is being made in order to provide sufficient incentive and encouragement for you to remain with Company following a Change in Control, as defined below. For all purposes under this agreement, "Company" shall include any successor (or parent) to Company's business and/or assets.

Change in Control. A "Change in Control" means either: (1) the acquisition of more than fifty percent of the total combined voting power represented by Company's then outstanding voting securities by a new beneficial owner; (2) a merger or consolidation of Company with any other corporation or other business entity (other than a merger or consolidation in which the same parties control more than fifty percent of Company's outstanding voting securities before and after the merger or consolidation); or (3) the sale or disposition by the Company of all or substantially all of Company's assets (unless Company remains an operating business and a going concern).

Severance Benefits. Below is a summary of the severance benefits you will receive if you are subject to Termination Upon a Change in Control of Company. To be eligible, the termination must occur during the Retention Period. The "Retention Period" refers to the period that starts upon the effective date of any agreement resulting in Change in Control of Company and ends _____ months after the effective date.

R

Sample Retention Letter Agreement (continued)

Benefit	Amount	Payment Terms
Cash severance	½ Annual base salary	Lump sum within 30 days of termination
Payment of COBRA premiums	Equivalent of two months of full monthly premiums	Lump sum within 30 days of termination

Termination Upon Change in Control. "Termination Upon Change in Control" refers to a termination by Company during the Retention Period of your employment other than:

- a termination for cause within the Retention Period or
- your resignation within the Retention Period, unless your resignation is for any of the following reasons: (a) You are no longer in an executive position in a substantive area of your competence; (b) your annual base salary or bonus has been reduced; (c) you have been denied any benefit or compensation plans or their equivalent in which you were participating immediately prior to the Change in Control; or (d) your workplace has been relocated more than 25 miles or your travel requirements have been made substantially more demanding than those existing immediately prior to the Change in Control. In the event you seek severance benefits based on resignation for any of these listed reasons, you agree to first notify the new owner and to provide the new owner 10 days to cure such basis for resignation. If the activity is not cured, the resignation is to be considered as Termination Upon Change in Control.

Receiving Severance Benefits. In order to receive the severance benefits, you are obligated to remain an employee of Company through the later of either (1) the completion of the transaction that results in Change in Control, or (2) the termination of your employment. In addition, you may elect to reduce any of the foregoing benefits to avoid the excise tax on excess payments under Section 4999 of the Internal Revenue Code. This

Sample Retention Letter Agreement (continued)

Agreement is not meant to provide any severance benefits to you under any circumstances other than those described above.

Miscellaneous. This Agreement may not be amended except in a written document signed by both parties. If a court finds any provision of this Agreement invalid or unenforceable, the remainder of this Agreement will be interpreted so as best to effect the intent of the parties. This Agreement is governed by and interpreted in accordance with the laws of the State of California. This Agreement expresses the complete understanding of the parties with respect to the subject matter and supersedes all prior representations and understandings. In the event of a dispute arising under or related to this Agreement, the prevailing party shall be entitled to attorneys' fees and costs.

By: _____

Date executed: _____

ACCEPTED AND AGREED TO

By: _____

Date executed: _____

R

How do they work? Some retention agreements may provide bonuses, a severance package, accelerated stock options, or some combination of benefits. The benefits are typically *not* paid if the employee is fired for good cause or if the employee quits other than for a "good reason." A good reason is typically some reason that involves the new owner's making life more difficult for the employee—forcing the employee to take a demotion or cut in pay, travel further to work, and so on. These reasons should be spelled out in the agreement.

Is this a golden parachute? A retention agreement is a type of golden parachute: an agreement to provide a lump sum payment to a departing executive. But it's not the only type of golden parachute. In some golden parachutes, for example, payment may be triggered by a change in ownership (sometimes referred to as "change in control"), regardless of whether the executive stays or goes.

Related terms: employment agreements; golden parachute; severance agreement.

reverse redlining

Redlining is refusing to do business with (often, to lend or extend credit to) certain groups of people. Redlining was first defined by neighborhood: Creditors would refuse to do business beyond an invisible "red line," typically in poor urban areas. Today, redlining usually refers to refusing to do business with people of a particular race or gender.

When a company engages in reverse redlining, it takes a different approach: It actively targets members of particular groups (again, usually by race or gender) for certain products. The problem is, these products typically have exorbitantly high interest rates, one-sided terms and provisions, and very few consumer protections. In other words, reverse redlining is a form of predatory lending.

Related term: redlining.

revolving loan

A revolving loan is often the loan of choice for small businesses because it is open-ended. The offer to loan up to a certain amount of money stands for a year or more, and the loan can be repaid—with the exception of certain interest and fee payments—at the discretion of the borrower. A revolving loan is typically secured by substantial property, often a business's assets. A revolving loan (also referred to as a revolving line of credit) has a cap or ceiling, and the borrower is typically free to borrow up to the cap.

In consumer contracts, the most common type of revolving loan is a credit card agreement: The consumer can charge up to the credit limit on the card and must pay it back with interest and fees.

These debts are called "revolving" because they keep rolling over from month to month. The debtor can borrow, pay the money back, and borrow again indefinitely, until either side chooses to end the deal.

Related terms: line of credit; promissory note.

royalty

A royalty is a periodic payment for the sale or license of a product or service. For example, an inventor may license his idea to a company that uses it to create a product, in exchange for an annual royalty based on sales of the product. A royalty can be calculated as a percentage of revenues minus certain deductions (called a "net royalty"), or as a gross royalty (a percentage of total sales revenue) or a per unit/per use royalty (for example, $2 per item distributed or sold). A contract may provide for royalty payments once a year, twice a year, or even four times a year. (A system of continuous royalty payments is sometimes referred to as a "running royalty.")

R

Royalty provision from license agreement: Sample language

> **Royalties.** Manufacturer agrees to pay the royalties ("Royalties"), as specified in Exhibit A, for all Net Sales of the Licensed Products ("Licensed Product Royalty"). All Royalties provided for under this Agreement accrue when the respective items are sold, shipped, distributed, billed, or paid for, whichever occurs first. Royalties will also be paid by the Manufacturer on all items, even if not billed (including, but not limited to introductory offers, samples, promotions, or distributions) to individuals or companies that are affiliated with, associated with, or subsidiaries of Manufacturer. "Net Sales" are defined as Manufacturer's gross sales (i.e., the gross invoice amount billed customers) less quantity discounts and returns actually credited. A quantity discount is a discount made at the time of shipment. Manufacturer shall not make deductions for cash or other discounts, for commissions, for uncollectible accounts, or for fees or expenses of any kind which may be incurred by the Manufacturer in connection with the Royalty payments.

Related terms: guaranteed minimum annual royalty (GMAR) intellectual property; license agreement.

rules of interpretation (rules of construction)

Rules of contract interpretation (also known as "rules of construction," because they explain how contracts should be construed) assist the court and the parties in making sense of an agreement if its meaning is in dispute. The primary rule of construction that all courts follow is that contract language should be interpreted objectively, as a "reasonable person" would understand the terms. Courts consider how a reasonable person within a similar trade, and under similar circumstances, would interpret the disputed language. This standard is the modern (post-19th-century) approach to interpretation; prior to that, courts used a more subjective standard based on the intentions of the actual parties to the agreement.

In some situations, the objective standard is mixed with other rules of construction. For example, when considering what a contract phrase, condition, or provision means, courts may look at additional external factors, such as how the language is used within the trade or industry in question. A court may also evaluate the parties' course of dealing and performance. In that case, the court examines how the parties behaved in prior contracts and arrangements and how they behaved in the course of performing a current contract. If, for example, one party has lent money to the other several times, and the other party has always made monthly payments on the loans, a court might decide that such payments are required, even if the parties' most recent contract doesn't address the issue at all. Courts may consider some of these factors more important than others; generally, the objective meaning of the contract's language is given the greatest weight.

When something is susceptible of two reasonable meanings. If, using an objective standard, a phrase or provision can be interpreted reasonably by each party in a different manner, then a court may seek out the subjective intentions of the parties. If the intent of each party is reasonable, but different, the court may void the contract.

Related terms: any/each; interpretive provisions; mistake; parol evidence rule; plain meaning rule.

savings clause

See severability (savings clause).

schedule

A schedule is a contract addendum that contains facts regarding the agreement. This material, although supplementary to the agreement, should be "incorporated by reference" to make sure it is legally binding. Schedules are often used when a company uses the same form agreement over and over but changes elements such as pricing, delivery methods, products, services, or royalties. These latter elements are provided in attached schedules.

Related term: addendum

secured transaction

A secured transaction is made in conjunction with a debt or loan agreement. The person borrowing the money agrees that the creditor can take certain property (the "collateral" or "security") if the borrower fails to pay off the loan. In an auto loan, for example, the security is usually the automobile; in a real estate sale, the security for the mortgage is the real property.

Not a loan. A security agreement is usually a separate document from the loan or promissory agreement. It's often attached to (and incorporated within) the loan. For example, when purchasing real estate, the buyer is bound by a promissory note (the home loan) and a mortgage (the security agreement). The loan agreement should include language that references the security arrangement.

Security Agreement for Borrowing Money

Security Agreement for Borrowing Money

Name of Borrower: _____

Name of Lender: _____

Grant of Security Interest. Borrower grants to Lender a continuing security interest in the following personal property: _____ _____ (the Secured Property). Borrower grants this security interest to secure performance of the promissory note dated _____ that Borrower executed in favor of Lender (the Note), which obligates Borrower to pay Lender $_____ with interest at the rate of _____% per year, on the terms stated in the Note.

Financing Statement. Until the amount due under the Note is paid in full, the Note will be further secured by a Uniform Commercial Code (UCC) Financing Statement. Borrower agrees to sign any other documents that Lender reasonably requests to protect Lender's security interest in the Secured Property.

Use and Care of Secured Property. Until the amount due under the Note is paid in full, Borrower agrees to: maintain the Secured Property in good repair; refrain from selling, transferring, or releasing the Secured Property without Lender's prior written consent; pay all taxes on the Secured Property as they become due; and allow Lender to inspect the Secured Property at any reasonable time.

Borrower's Default. If Borrower is more than _____ days late in making any payment due under the Note, or if Buyer fails to correct any violations of paragraph 3 within _____ days of receiving written notice from Lender, Borrower will be in default.

Security Agreement for Borrowing Money (continued)

Lender's Rights. If Borrower is in default, Lender may exercise the remedies contained in the UCC for the state of _____ and any other remedies legally available to Lender. Before exercising such remedies, Lender will provide at least ten days' advance notice, as provided in this agreement. Lender may, for example: remove the Secured Property from the place where it is then located; require Borrower to make the Secured Property available to Lender at a place designated by Lender that is reasonably convenient to Borrower and Lender; or sell, lease, or otherwise dispose of the Secured Property.

Notice. Any notice may be delivered to a party at the address that follows a party's signature below, or to a new address that a party designates in writing. A notice may be delivered in person, by certified mail, or by overnight courier.

Entire Agreement. This is the entire agreement between the parties. It replaces and supersedes any and all oral agreements between the parties, as well as any prior writings.

Successors and Assigns. This agreement binds and benefits the parties' heirs, successors, and assigns.

Governing Law. This agreement will be governed by and construed in accordance with the laws of the state of _____.

Modification. This agreement may be modified only in writing.

Waiver. If one party waives any term or provision of this agreement at any time, that waiver will be effective only for the specific instance and specific purpose for which the waiver was given. If either party fails to exercise or delays exercising any of its rights or remedies under this agreement, that party retains the right to enforce that term or provision at a later time.

S

Security Agreement for Borrowing Money (continued)

Severability. If any court determines that any provision of this agreement is invalid or unenforceable, any such invalidity or unenforceability will affect only that provision and will not make any other provision of this agreement invalid or unenforceable, and such provision will be modified, amended, or limited only to the extent necessary to render it valid and enforceable.

Borrower   Lender

By: _____   By: _____

Date: _____   Date: _____

S

Sample UCC Financing Statement

UCC Financing Statement

This Financing Statement is presented for filing under the Uniform Commercial Code as adopted in ___[name of your state]_____ .

....

Name of Borrower: _____

Address of Borrower: _____

_____

Name of Lender/Secured party: _____

Address of Lender/Secured party:

_____

_____

The term Borrower refers to one or more borrowers. If there is more than one borrower, they agree to be jointly and severally liable. The term Lender refers to any person who legally holds this note, including a buyer in due course.

The property listed as collateral in the security agreement is as follows [identify or describe]: _____

_____ .

This Financing Statement secures the following debt:

Promissory note dated: _____

Amount of debt: _____

Payback due date: _____

All other terms and conditions are stated in the promissory note, a copy of which is attached.

Borrower: _____

By: _____

Date: _____

S

Security agreement provision to include in promissory note: Sample language

> Borrower agrees that until the principal and interest owed under this note are paid in full, the note is secured by the following security agreement:
>
> Security agreement signed by:_____*[name of owner]*_____
>
> on:___*[date signed]*___, which gives a security interest in:___*[description of the personal property used as collateral]*_____.

Creditor precautions. There are a few precautions that lenders often take for secured transactions. First, it is crucial to accurately describe the property that will serve as collateral, to avoid fights later over what can be seized. Second, if the creditor is concerned that the borrower is slippery—for example, the borrower may be using the same security for multiple loans—the creditor may file a Uniform Commercial Code (UCC) financing statement with the appropriate state agency, typically the Secretary of State's office. This puts other creditors on notice that you have the right to take the property. Many states have a special UCC form that creditors should use.

Related terms: debt; interest rates (usury); mortgage; promissory note.

security (security interest)

See secured transaction.

sell-off provision

See termination.

service agreement

When you hire someone to do something for you, such as home repair, child care, business accounting, or tennis lessons, you are entering into a service agreement. Here are some provisions commonly found in service contracts:

- **Independent contractor or employee status.** Because there can be tax and other legal repercussions, it's important that a worker is properly classified as either an independent contractor or employee. (*See* independent contractors.)
- **Description of services.** The description of services must be accurate and satisfy both parties. If the buyer wants an opportunity to review and approve the services before paying, then an inspection and approval procedure should be included.
- **Ownership of work product.** When an employee creates something on the job, it belongs to the employer. If a contractor creates something for a hiring party, however, ownership of that work product could be at issue. In this situation, an assignment of rights should be included in the contract. If confidentiality is required, then a confidentiality provision should also be included.
- **Warranties/indemnity.** If the hiring party needs assurances— for example, that the work will be up to a certain standard or won't involve any violations of the law—or if both parties want indemnity against various legal claims, those provisions should be included in the contract.
- **Limitations on liability.** Each party may want to limit liability in the event of a dispute. Provisions to that effect may be included in the contract.
- **Termination.** Each party's right to terminate the agreement should be spelled out in the contract, including when the contract may be terminated, under what circumstances, and by whom.
- **Boilerplate.** Typical boilerplate provisions should be included as necessary.

The sample agreement below is a very basic services agreement that includes a fairly stripped-down boilerplate provision.

Related term: independent contractor.

Sample Service Agreement

Contractor Services Agreement

This Agreement is made between _____ (Company) with a principal place of business at _____ and _____ (Contractor), with a principal place of business at _____ . This Agreement will become effective on _____ (the Effective Date).

Services to Be Performed. Contractor agrees to perform the following services:

- _____

- _____

Payment. In consideration for the services to be performed by Contractor, Company agrees to pay a fee of $_____ . Contractor shall invoice Company each month during the period when services are rendered.

Expenses. Contractor shall be responsible for all expenses incurred while performing services under this Agreement.

Independent Contractor Status. Contractor is an independent contractor, not Company's employee. Contractor's employees or contract personnel are not Company's employees. Contractor and Company agree that Contractor has the right to perform services for others during the term of this Agreement, and that Contractor has the sole right to control and direct the means, manner, and method by which the services required by this Agreement will be performed. Company will not: (a) withhold FICA (Social Security and Medicare taxes) from Contractor's payments or make FICA payments on Contractor's behalf, (b) make state or federal unemployment compensation contributions on Contractor's behalf, (c) withhold state or federal income tax from Contractor's payments, or (d) obtain workers' compensation insurance on behalf of Contractor.

Sample Service Agreement (continued)

Intellectual Property Ownership. Contractor shall retain copyright in her work resulting from her services (the "Work"). However Contractor grants a nonexclusive license to Company to use, reproduce and distribute the Work created by Contractor during the term of this Agreement and afterwards.

Terminating the Agreement. Either party may terminate this Agreement at any time by giving written notice to the other party of the intent to terminate.

Limited Liability. This provision allocates the risks under this Agreement between Contractor and Company. Contractor's total liability to Company under this Agreement for damages, costs, and expenses will not exceed $_____ or the compensation received by Contractor under this Agreement, whichever is less. However, Contractor shall remain liable for bodily injury or personal property damage resulting from grossly negligent or willful actions of Contractor or Contractor's employees or agents while on Company premises to the extent such actions or omissions were not caused by Company. NEITHER PARTY TO THIS AGREEMENT SHALL BE LIABLE FOR THE OTHER'S LOST PROFITS OR SPECIAL, INCIDENTAL, OR CONSEQUENTIAL DAMAGES, WHETHER IN AN ACTION IN CONTRACT OR TORT, EVEN IF THE PARTY HAS BEEN ADVISED BY THE OTHER PARTY OF THE POSSIBILITY OF SUCH DAMAGES.

Miscellaneous. This is the entire Agreement between Contractor and Company. If any provision of this Agreement is determined to be invalid, illegal, or unenforceable, the remaining provisions will remain in full force if the essential provisions of this Agreement for Company and Contractor remain valid, binding, and enforceable. This Agreement will be governed by the laws of the state of _____. This Agreement does not create a partnership relationship. Contractor does not have authority to enter into contracts on Company's behalf.

Sample Service Agreement (continued)

Resolving Disputes. If a dispute arises under this Agreement, the parties agree to first try to resolve the dispute with the help of a mutually agreed-upon mediator in the state of _____. The parties shall share any costs and fees other than attorneys' fees associated with the mediation equally. If it proves impossible to arrive at a mutually satisfactory solution through mediation, the parties agree to submit the dispute to a mutually agreed-upon arbitrator in the state of _____ . Judgment upon the award rendered by the arbitrator may be entered in any court having jurisdiction to do so. Costs of arbitration, including attorneys' fees, will be allocated by the arbitrator.

Company

By: _____

Title: _____

Date: _____

Contractor

By: _____

Title: _____

Taxpayer ID Number: _____

Date: _____

S

setoff provision

A setoff is a method for one party to recoup losses from, or balance obligations to, another party.

> **EXAMPLE:** Kyle owes Parkay Construction $5,000 after Parkay installed a new bathroom on his houseboat. During construction, Parkay negligently damaged the houseboat's hull, causing $4,000 worth of damage. Kyle applies a "setoff" of the $4,000 (to fix the damage) against the $5,000 he owes Parkay, and pays Parkay only $1,000.

Sometimes a right of setoff is built into a contract; for example, a construction contract may permit setoffs under certain circumstances. In other cases, such as loans or other financial agreements, setoffs may be prohibited.

settlement agreement (settlement and release)

When the parties to a dispute want to end it, they must negotiate a compromise, agree on the settlement terms, and then enter into a contract. This contract (the "settlement agreement") is intended to put the dispute behind both parties for good. To accomplish that goal, each party must release the other from any legal claims. The release must satisfy two contract law requirements:

- **The settlement must be voluntary.** Each side must enter into the agreement voluntarily. If a party was coerced into signing an agreement because of the other's threats or intimidation, a court may consider it involuntary and therefore unenforceable.
- **The agreement must be arrived at fairly.** Judges are usually unwilling to enforce any agreement that is the product of deceit or the result of one side taking undue advantage of the other.

Releases are powerful documents. If you sign a release giving up your right to sue for breach of contract in exchange for $500, and learn six months later that your damages are much greater than you thought when you signed the release, you are out of luck unless a court declares the release unenforceable for one of the above reasons. Before signing a settlement and release agreement, always make sure you understand the issues that underlie the release (for example, what really happened, whose fault it was, how strong your legal claims are, and how much damage you have suffered). Also make sure you understand the effect of the settlement agreement. For example, are you giving up all possible claims against the other party or only claims you know about when you sign? If you aren't completely sure that you understand the facts and ramifications of the agreement, you may need some legal advice to help you decide whether to give up your rights.

Elements of a settlement and release. As you can imagine, settlements can be complex arrangements detailing lengthy disputes among multiple parties who have committed numerous transgressions, or they can be fairly simple (as in the sample shown below). They typically include the following provisions:

- **Description of the dispute.** A settlement usually includes a summary of the dispute. It can be as short as "The parties entered into a contract whereby Jones was supposed to perform office cleaning services for Tilden. Jones was supposed to be paid $500 per month. A dispute has arisen regarding the payments to Jones (the "Dispute")."

- **Release.** This section of the agreement legally releases the parties and their legal successors from any claims about the underlying contract or dispute. In other words, there can be no more legal wrangling over the issues you are settling after you sign the agreement.

- **Termination of the contract.** If the dispute involves a contract, the parties typically include a statement that the underlying contract is terminated.

- **No admission of liability.** This section states that neither party admits any fault or wrongdoing, that the release is being made with full knowledge of the facts (so you can't later argue you didn't understand the agreement), and that each party has

Settlement Agreement

Settlement and Release

This agreement (the "Agreement") is intended as a settlement and release effective as of the date of signature below (the "Effective Date") between:

_____ ("Party 1") and

_____ ("Party 2")

(collectively referred to as the "parties").

1. The Dispute. A dispute has arisen between the parties regarding a transaction as follows: _____

_____

(the "Dispute"). As result of the Dispute, an amount is now in dispute between the parties.

2. Release. Contingent upon fulfillment of the settlement requirements set forth in this Agreement, each party, for itself and for its heirs, successors, and assigns, voluntarily releases the other party and its heirs, successors, and assigns from any and all actions, causes of action, debts, bills, demands, damages, costs, expenses (including attorneys' fees), liabilities, or other losses known or unknown which may presently exist or later arise regarding the Dispute. This Agreement applies solely to the Dispute.

3. No Admission of Liability. This Agreement constitutes a compromise. It is not an admission of liability by either party. Each party agrees to the foregoing release with full knowledge of any and all rights it may have. Both parties acknowledge they have full authority to execute this agreement in the capacities for which they have signed below.

4. Payment. As full consideration for this Agreement, _____

_____ shall pay to _____

_____ the amount of $_____ upon execution of this Agreement.

S

Settlement Agreement (continued)

---

5. General Provisions

    a. Severability. If a court finds any provision of this Agreement invalid or unenforceable, the remainder of this Agreement will be interpreted so as best to effect the intent of the parties.

    b. Integration. This Agreement expresses the complete understanding of the parties with respect to the subject matter and supersedes all prior proposals, agreements, representations, and understandings. This Agreement may not be amended except in a writing signed by both parties.

    c. Waiver. The failure to exercise any right provided in this Agreement is not a waiver of prior or subsequent rights.

    d. Attorneys' fees and Expenses. In a dispute arising out of or related to this Agreement, the prevailing party shall have the right to collect from the other party its reasonable attorneys' fees and costs and necessary expenditures.

    e. Governing Law. This Agreement is governed in accordance with the laws of the State of _____ .

Party 1   Party 2

By: _____   By: _____

Date: _____   Date: _____

the authority to enter into this release. Authority may be at issue if you are settling a dispute with a company: You'll want to make sure that the person signing the agreement has the authority to bind the company legally.

- **Payment.** The settlement agreement explains who will be paying whom, and how much. Most settlement agreements—but not all of them—involve money changing hands. For example, one party might agree to return property, give a favorable reference, or allow the other party to keep property (such as a car) in exchange for the release.

Related terms: accord and satisfaction; remedies.

severability (savings clause)

A severability provision (or a "savings" clause), states that any invalid portion of a contract should be removed so the rest of the contract can be enforced.

Why is it necessary? Back in the way old days, if any portion of a contract was invalid, the whole agreement was likely to be considered tainted and unenforceable. Later, courts began to attempt to preserve the contract whenever possible by severing unhealthy portions of an agreement (if possible) and enforcing the rest. Eventually, lawyers began inserting boilerplate language referred to as a severability provision.

Severability provision: Sample language

Severability. If any provision of this Agreement is found to be invalid or unenforceable, the remainder of this Agreement is to be interpreted so as best to effect the intent of the parties, and to maintain the Agreement's validity and enforceability.

S

Related terms: boilerplate; remedies.

severance agreement

Severance agreements are contracts between a company and a departing employee that typically provide for a lump sum payment, continuing benefits for a period of time, and sometimes other compensation or consideration. Companies usually provide severance agreements for one of these reasons:

- **Fairness.** The company wants to treat departing employees in a humane manner that reflects the employee's contributions and the company's culture.
- **Contractual requirements.** The company may have agreed to pay certain employees severance (for example, a high-ranking executive might have an employment contract requiring severance if the employee is terminated within the contract's term). The company may have a policy of providing severance to departing employees (such as one week's pay for every year the employee has been at the company), or may simply have followed a practice of offering severance so consistently that employees have developed a reasonable expectation that they will receive severance, thus creating an implied contract.
- **Avoiding lawsuits.** The company may be concerned that the departing employee might bring legal claims against the company (for example, for wrongful termination). To head off possible problems, the company can provide a severance package in return for the employee's release of all claims.

Regardless of why a company is offering severance, it is not uncommon for companies to require a release of future claims in return for a severance package. Here are some things that employers must keep in mind when entering into severance agreements:

- **State-specific requirements.** Some states have specific requirements about what language must go into a release. And, some states dictate details, such as the typeface and font size, that must be used for the release of certain claims.
- **I gave at the office.** An employee must receive some benefit in exchange for signing the release. If an employer ordinarily

offers a severance package to employees who are not asked to sign a release, the employer will have to give something extra to employees who do sign. That should be specified in the release.

- **Be clear about the rights the employee is waiving.** The employer might state that the employee is waiving any right to sue for claims arising out of the employment relationship, including the termination of that relationship. In any case, the release must be specific enough to forestall any later claim that the employee did not know what it covered, and it must be comprehensive enough to cover every claim the employee might conceivably raise.

- **Give the employee plenty of time to decide whether to sign.** It is reasonable for an employee to take a week or two to decide whether to give up the right to sue you. The employer might even suggest that the employee consult with a lawyer to review the agreement.

- **Avoid any hint of coercion.** An employee's decision to sign a release must be voluntary, or courts will not enforce the release. An employer should not threaten or talk tough with employees to convince them to sign; that behavior risks invalidating the severance agreement.

- **Special rules apply to older workers.** If the employee is 40 years of age or older, a federal law, the Older Workers Benefits Protection Act (OWBPA), dictates what must be included in a release. Among other things, the employer must give older employees a longer period of time to review the release, allow them to revoke the agreement (in other words, to change their minds) for a limited time after they sign, and advise them in writing to consult with an attorney.

Related terms: employment agreements; golden parachute; severance agreement.

shall (versus will)

Lawyers and judges sometimes fight over the meaning of "shall" and "will," two words that are very closely scrutinized when used in contracts. Both words are examples of obligatory language because they obligate a party to do something (as opposed to words like "may" that are considered discretionary language because they allow a party to choose whether or not to do something).

"Shall" is typically interpreted to mean that a party has a duty or obligation to do something, often in the future. As a general rule (and one which is rarely followed by most contract drafters), "shall" should not be used unless it is preceded by the name or a reference to a party to the agreement—for example, "Nolo shall publish the Book"; not "The Book shall be published by Nolo."

Some contract drafters prefer "will" as an alternative to shall, although the term is not an ideal replacement. "Will" is considered appropriate when dealing with certain future events—for example declarations about future occurrences ("Once construction is complete, ten maple trees *will* be planted next to the fence.") or a warranty about future effects ("The deicer *will* be free from defects and *will* perform in accordance with specifications").

Because some commentators, particularly in other English speaking countries, believe that "shall" is also generally an inappropriate term, they have adopted the use of "is required to," instead of "shall." This usage—adopted in Australia, Britain, and Canada—has not gained much popularity in the United States. Instead, some American drafters have replaced "shall" with "must." "Must" is useful when it clearly spells out the obligation but seems heavy-handed to some. However, "must" has its place in drafting, particularly when parties intend to create an unambiguous obligation—for example, "The Tenant *must* provide notice of any alleged defect that prevents Tenant's use of the Commercial Property, no later than 24 hours after learning of the defect."

Workarounds have been proposed to the shall/will dilemma, including more use of active rather than passive voice and more precise use of verbs. However, in the absence of any clearer direction, the most prudent approach is to use "shall" instead of "will" when spelling out contractual obligations.

Related terms: interpretive provisions; rules of interpretation (rules of construction).

shrink-wrap agreement

See clickwrap agreement.

side letter

A side letter is an agreement that seeks to modify, amend, or supplement another agreement, often involving a third party, and usually made at the same time.

> **EXAMPLE:** A musician signs with a production company. The production company enters into an agreement with a record company. The record company then signs a side letter with the musician in which the musician promises to perform exclusively for the production company.

Although it is usually not an issue, a party may have trouble enforcing a side letter if the primary agreement contains an integration provision (that states it is the "entire agreement" between the parties).

signatures

Signatures refer to any handwritten (or digital) symbol that a party intends to use to indicate acceptance of a written agreement. If one party uses initials or another marking instead of a handwritten signature, it will be accepted provided it can be shown that the other party believed that the initials or marking was made with the intent to authenticate the written agreement. There is no requirement that handwritten signatures be in ink; it can be provided in pencil or

S

even typed in, again provided that the other party believed that the execution was made with the intent to authenticate the agreement.

Who signs? It is not necessary that both parties sign agreement. All that is required is that the party against whom it is to be enforced signs the agreement.

> **EXAMPLE:** Tom lends Bob $5,000 and Bob signs a promissory note. Tom does not sign the promissory note even though there is a signature line for him. Bob defaults on the loan. Tom can sue under the promissory note because Bob—the party against whom the note is to be enforced—has signed it.

It is essential that the proper parties are identified for signature—that is, that the name of each entity is spelled correctly and that in situations where one company owns another, the proper party is identified (and bound). When signing an agreement, each party must sign in relation to the business that is represented (for example, as a general partner representing the partnership). To avoid personal liability, individuals signing on behalf of corporations and LLCs should be identified in their corporate or LLC capacities, as described below. Each party must, of course, have the authority to sign. To further reinforce this, many agreements include a concluding statement such as: "To evidence the parties' agreement, each party has signed this Agreement through its authorized representative."

Preparing the signature block. The portion of an agreement reserved for signatures (sometimes referred to as the "signature block") is typically at the end of the agreement but before any addendums. It is usually preceded by a concluding statement, such as "Accepted and agreed to" or "each party has signed this Agreement through its authorized representative." Although for convenience some contract drafters prepare a separate (stand-alone) signature page, it is generally less risky—in terms of avoiding disputes—to include the signatures on the same page as other contract text. If the signatures end up on their own page, you may break the preceding page in the middle to make sure that some text precedes proper signature blocks. On the portion of the preceding page where there is white space, you can add the phrase "Intentionally left blank" or mark it with an "X."

The following rules are generally applied when determining how to draft proper signature blocks:

- **Sole proprietorship.** A sole proprietor simply signs his or her name unless operating under a fictitious business name (sometimes known as a DBA). In that case, list the name of the business above the signature line as follows:

  Flora's Haircuts

  By: _____

  Flora Cassidy *dba* Flora's Haircuts

- **Partnership.** In the case of a general or limited partnership, the only person authorized to sign an agreement is a general partner or someone who has written authority (usually in the form of a partnership resolution) from a general partner. The name of the partnership must be mentioned above the signature line, or the partnership will not be bound (only the person signing the agreement will).

  The Central City Group, a general partnership

  By: _____

  Thomas Lincoln, General Partner

- **Corporation or LLC.** In the case of a corporation or limited liability company (LLC), only a person authorized by the corporation or LLC can sign the agreement. The president or chief executive officer (CEO) usually has such power, but not every officer of a corporation has the authority to bind the corporation. (If in doubt, ask for written proof of the

S

authority. This proof is usually in the form of a corporate resolution.) The name of the corporation should be mentioned above the signature line, or the corporation may not be bound (only the person signing the agreement will).

DarkVentures, Inc.

By: _____

    Wendy Corrin, President

Speculative Ventures, LLC

By: _____

    Tom Franklin, Member

Related terms: agent; authority to bind; executed contract; execution.

sole proprietor

A sole proprietor (or "sole proprietorship") is any one-person business that is not a corporation or an LLC. In other words, if you're operating by yourself and haven't incorporated or formed an LLC, you're a sole proprietorship—the least expensive and easiest way to operate a business. A sole proprietorship is created automatically when you go into business. There is no fee to create one and no paperwork unless you are operating under a fictitious business name or DBA (doing business as), in which case, you will need to register with a local government office. One of the key distinguishing features of a sole proprietorship is that the owner is personally liable for all business debts and legal claims. From a tax perspective, a sole proprietorship is a pass-through entity. If you operate as a sole proprietor, your profits (and losses) pass through the business entity, and you pay taxes on any profits on your individual return at your individual tax rate. You report this business income on IRS Schedule

C, *Profit and Loss From Business (Sole Proprietorship)*, which you file with your 1040 individual federal tax return.

Related terms: corporation; entity; fictitious business name; limited liability company (LLC); personal liability; signatures.

specific performance

Specific performance is a contract remedy in which a court orders one party to do whatever it was supposed to do under the contract. It is usually used as a remedy when financial damages are inadequate and the subject of the contract is an especially unique piece of property—for example, a painting or an item of particular provenance (moon rocks, for example).

Specific performance won't be ordered in some circumstances; here are the rules:

- **No specific performance for personal service contracts.** Courts will never require specific performance of a service contract. For example, a court will never make a chef cook for a restaurant or force a driver to work for a bus company. Ordering someone to work for someone else smacks of involuntary servitude and may even violate the 13th Amendment to the Constitution (which abolished slavery). However, a court may order specific performance of a noncompete agreement by issuing an injunction that prevents a party from working for a competitor; preventing someone from taking a job is permissible, but requiring someone to take it is not.
- **Specific performance is usually not granted if extensive supervision is required.** Courts are reluctant to order specific performance if doing so will require a lot of monitoring and supervision. Historically, for example, courts considered construction contracts too difficult to manage (although modern courts have held that the obligations of such supervision are "exaggerated," and specific performance is merited). On the other hand, some agreements, such as a contract for insurance coverage, do not

S

require ongoing supervision, and specific performance may be ordered if other remedies are not appropriate.

- **Damages have to be inadequate.** Specific performance is rarely awarded unless damages won't adequately compensate the injured party for its losses. For example, in real estate contracts, money often cannot correct the problem because real estate is so unique. If the court can determine damages (sometimes difficult if the damages are speculative), and the award can adequately compensate the injured party's loss (that is, money can solve the problem), then specific performance probably won't be required.

- **Rules for goods.** The Uniform Commercial Code (UCC Sec. 2-716) provides a fairly liberal application of specific performance to the sale of goods ("Specific performance may be decreed where the goods are unique or in other proper circumstances"). Under this standard, courts have leeway to determine whether goods are unique, as well as payment terms, price, and "other relief as the court deems just."

Related terms: injunction (injunctive relief); remedies.

standby letter of credit

A standby letter of credit is like a guaranty; it's an assurance by a financial institution that if one party to a loan or other financial obligation fails to honor that obligation (that is, it doesn't pay the debt), the financial institution will step in and pay the loss. In other words, the financial institution is "standing by" in case of any bad news. In that way, a standby letter of credit is a hybrid contract that combines features of a surety bond or guaranty with an offer of credit. It differs from a traditional letter of credit in that a letter of credit is used as a way to facilitate a payment; it's not on standby in case of a default.

Related terms: guaranty/guarantor; surety bond.

standstill agreement

A standstill agreement is made among stockholders in order to purchase the outstanding stock from a shareholder who is attempting a hostile takeover. In other words, the hostile takeover is brought to a "standstill" once the raider is bought out.

statute of frauds

See oral contracts.

statute of limitations

Each state has a law that limits the time period for bringing various legal claims (called the statute of limitations). The time periods differ from state to state and depend on the cause of a lawsuit. Suits that are brought after the time period has expired (or after the statute has "rung") will be dismissed. In other words, if you don't file on time, you can't file at all. This issue is typically raised as a defense in a lawsuit.

When does the clock start ticking? The statutory time period usually begins once the injury is discovered (referred to the "date of harm"). Determining this date can be tricky if one party is not aware of the other party's breach. In that case, courts may create an exception and start the clock running as of the date the harm is actually discovered or, alternatively, the date when the plaintiff should have reasonably discovered the harm.

Courts take a commonsense approach to determining what's reasonable. In the case of a construction contract, for example, it is presumed that a reasonable contractor would have discovered a subcontractor's breach prior to making a final payment to the subcontractor.

S

EXAMPLE: Florida has a five-year time period to file a claim on written contracts (including performance bond agreements). A subcontractor finished its work on a school in February 2001. The contractor accepted the work and paid the subcontractor its final payment at that time. The whole school wasn't completed, however, until 2005. By 2006, the main contractor claimed that the subcontractor's work was defective and sued for breach of contract. A court dismissed the case because it was filed more than five years after February 2001, the date when the contractor accepted the work.

What state's statute applies when parties are in different states? Because each state provides different time periods for bringing various types of claims, you need to know which state's laws apply to your dispute, especially if you and the other party are from different states. First, look to the contract to see if it contains a governing law provision indicating which state's law applies. If there is no provision, the state law to be applied will be determined by a court based on various factors, such as which state's law the parties intended to govern the agreement, the location where the contract was entered into, and the location where it is to be (or was) performed.

Statute of limitations chart. The chart below lists how many years you have to bring the most common contract or contract-related legal claims. Note, like all statutes, this information may change, so review your state's law before proceeding. In addition, some states may provide different time periods for certain written contracts, most often for contracts for debts.

State Statutes of Limitations on Contract Claims

State	Written Contract	Oral Contract	Injury	Property Damage
Alabama	6	6	2	6
Alaska	3	3	2	6 (real property); 2 (personal property)
Arizona	6	3	2	2
Arkansas	5	3	3	3
California	4	2	2	3
Colorado	6	6	2	2
Connecticut	6	3	3	2
Delaware	3	3	3	2
District of Columbia	3	3	3	3
Florida	5	4	4	4
Georgia	6	4	2	4
Hawaii	6	6	2	2
Idaho	5	4	2	3
Illinois	10	5	2	5
Indiana	10	6	2	6 (real property); 2 (personal property)
Iowa	10	5	2	5
Kansas	5	3	2	2
Kentucky	15	5	1	5 (real property); 2 (personal property)
Louisiana	10	10	1	1
Maine	6	6	6	6
Maryland	3	3	3	3
Massachusetts	6	6	3	3
Michigan	6	6	3	3
Minnesota	6	6	6	6

State	Written Contract	Oral Contract	Injury	Property Damage
State Statutes of Limitations on Contract Claims (cont'd)				
Mississippi	3	3	3	3
Missouri	5	5	5	5
Montana	8	5	3	2
Nebraska	5	4	4	4
Nevada	6	4	2	3
New Hampshire	3	3	3	3
New Jersey	6	6	2	6
New Mexico	6	4	3	4
New York	6	6	3	3
North Carolina	3	3	3	3
North Dakota	6	6	6	6
Ohio	15	6	2	4
Oklahoma	5	3	2	2
Oregon	6	6	10	6
Pennsylvania	4	4	2	2
Rhode Island	10	10	3	10
South Carolina	3	3	3	3
South Dakota	6	6	3	6
Tennessee	6	6	1	3
Texas	4	4	2	2
Utah	6	4	4	3
Vermont	6	6	3	3
Virginia	5	3	2	5
Washington	6	3	3	3
West Virginia	10	5	2	2
Wisconsin	6	6	3	6
Wyoming	10	8	4	4

S

subordination agreement

A subordination agreement gives one creditor priority over another. It's often used when a home is financed a second time and the financial institution holding a second mortgage agrees to subordinate its claims to the institution holding the first mortgage. A subordination provision can also be incorporated into other agreements—for example, a subordination clause may be incorporated into corporate agreements to state that a loan to a corporation (for example, a loan from a shareholder) is subordinated to a bank's loan to the corporation.

subrogation

Subrogation refers to replacing one party with another; it is usually used when one creditor is substituted for another. A typical example might be when someone injures you and your insurance company pays your damages. Typically, your claim would be subrogated, which means that the insurance company has the right to stand in your shoes and sue the party that injured you (or at least claim a portion of the recovery from that person).

successors and assigns

Successors and assigns are people or entities that step into another party's shoes. By definition, a successor is someone who succeeds to a status or position—for example, by inheritance or by purchasing a company. An assign is someone that has acquired the position as a result of an assignment—for example, if a contract is assigned to another company. The terms, although distinguishable, almost always appear together and are considered by some to be synonymous. To guarantee that the contract will still be in effect if a successor or an assign takes over, a statement such as the one below is commonly included in agreements.

S

Successors and assigns: Sample language

Successors and assigns. This Agreement is binding upon, and will inure to the benefit of, the parties to this agreement, and their respective successors and/or assigns.

Related term: assignment (of contract).

surety

See guaranty/guarantor.

surety bond

A surety bond, like a guaranty, is a promise by one person or entity (the "surety) to pay the debt or assume the obligations of another (the "principal") if the principal cannot honor its promise to another party (the "obligee"). A bail bond is an example. The bail bond company is the surety, assuring the government (the obligee) that the accused criminal (the principal) will either show up in court or forfeit bail. Surety bonds are commonly used in the construction industry to guaranty that a contracting party will complete the work as required by the contract. In almost all states, a surety contract must be in writing to be valid. (This requirement, imposed by the statute of frauds, is intended to make sure that the contract is authentic and the parties knew what they were getting into.)

Related terms: cosigner; guaranty/guarantor; promissory note; secured transaction; standby letter of credit; statute of frauds.

surviving provisions

See termination.

term

Term refers to the time period during which a contract is in force. For example, a lease with a one-year term lasts for a year. The term is often based on one of the following criteria:

- **Performance.** The term may be tied to performance of certain tasks—for example, the contract ends once construction of a home is complete or a series of services has been performed.
- **Fixed.** The term can be for a fixed length (say, ten years).
- **Fixed with renewals.** The term can be for a fixed length (say, two years) with a series of renewals. For example, at the end of two years, the parties (or in some cases, one party) can renew the contract for one year at a time. Usually, the contract spells out the process for renewals (such as notice requirements).
- **Open-ended with right to terminate.** The term may be open-ended—that is, the contract lasts until terminated by either party or both parties. Some contracts may be terminated only for certain reasons; others may be terminated for any reason, as long as the party who wants to terminate gives the required amount of notice.

When does the term start? The term commences on the effective date, often stated in a written agreement (it may be different than the date the contract is signed). If the contract doesn't state an effective date, the contract is usually be presumed to start on the date the last party signed it.

Related terms: as of; effective date; termination.

term sheet

A term sheet is a summary of agreed-upon terms for a potential deal, sometimes attached to a commitment letter, letter of intent, or an option agreement.

Related term: letter of intent.

termination

To quote the ultimate authority—the Terminator—contract termination is the point at which the parties say "Hasta la vista, baby," and move on. Here are some of the ways a contract can terminate:

- **Both parties have fully performed.** Many contracts, particularly oral agreements, end when everybody's done what they're supposed to do. For example, you paid for the vintage Pez dispenser at eBay, and the seller has delivered it.
- **One party has committed a material breach.** If one party breaches, the other party can say, "That's it, we're done," and terminate.
- **Court-ordered termination.** Courts have the right to terminate an agreement if there was a breach or the contract was void.
- **Mutual termination.** The parties to a contract are always free to mutually terminate a contract.
- **Written contract provisions.** Contract provisions may provide a right to terminate at will or under certain circumstances (often, a set amount of notice is required).

Termination provisions. Written agreements commonly provide a system or method for terminating a contract. This section is usually titled "Termination" or "Right to Terminate," and it works in conjunction with the "Term" provision. (The "Term" provision lays out when the contract starts and ends, along with any potential renewal periods.)

Provisions can be worded so that either party (bilateral), both parties (mutual), or just one party (unilateral) may terminate an agreement. Normally, a period for cure must be included if the basis for termination is a breach of a provision, to give the breaching party some time to fix the problem.

Bilateral termination with cure: Sample language

Termination. Either party has the right to terminate this Agreement at any time if the other party breaches or fails to observe any of its obligations pursuant to this Agreement, and such breach or failure is not cured within thirty (30) days after written notice from the nonbreaching party.

Unilateral termination with cure: Sample language

Licensor's Right to Terminate. Licensor shall have the right to terminate this Agreement for the following reasons:

a. Licensee fails to pay Royalties when due or fails to accurately report Net Sales, as defined in the Payment Section of this Agreement, and such failure is not cured within 30 days after written notice from the Licensor;

b. Licensee fails to introduce the product to market by [*insert date by which Licensee must begin selling Licensed Products*] or to offer the Licensed Products in commercially reasonable quantities during any subsequent year;

c. Licensee fails to maintain confidentiality regarding Licensor's trade secrets and other Information;

d. Licensee assigns or sublicenses in violation of the Agreement; or

e. Licensee fails to maintain or obtain product liability insurance as required by the provisions of this Agreement.

Termination at will. Some agreements allow termination at will—that is, one or both parties may end a contract whenever they want, for any reason. To be valid, this "free pass" at termination must include a notice provision: a period of reasonable notification prior to termination. The contract may be terminated only after one party has given notice in the required form (typically, in writing and directed to the person named for this purpose in the contract) and the notice period (often 30 or 60 days) has passed.

A contract that includes a right to terminate at will without notice isn't valid because it's based on an illusory promise. If the other party can walk away on a moment's notice for any reason, then the contract has no substance. There's no consideration and no real obligation to do anything. In effect, a party who can terminate at will without notice is saying, "I'll do this … if I feel like it." The Uniform Commercial Code rules for the sale of goods also follow this principle and state that an agreement dispensing with reasonable notification is invalid.

Surviving provisions. Just because an agreement terminates doesn't mean that all of the obligations in the agreement terminate. For example, the parties may want to continue their obligations to maintain confidential information after the agreement ends. Or, additional payments may accrue after termination (for example, if posttermination sales are permitted). To handle situations like this, the parties often state that certain obligations will continue or survive the termination of the agreement. Typically, those provisions include confidentiality, warranties, indemnity, and payment obligations. You can indicate which provisions survive (if any) by adding a sentence at the end of the provision, such as: "This obligation shall survive any termination of this Agreement." Some agreements have a separate provision like the one below.

Survival provision: Sample language

Survival: The obligations of Sections _____ and _____ shall survive any termination of this Agreement.

It doesn't matter which method you use, but you should carefully review which sections survive termination to make sure that your interests will be fully protected—and to make sure that you don't agree to any continuing obligations that should end when an agreement terminates.

Posttermination. An agreement may also contain certain posttermination instructions—for example, requiring the return of materials or permitting posttermination sales of remaining inventory (a sell-off provision). Often, posttermination instructions like these are included in an "Effects of Termination" provision.

Posttermination (and sell-off) provision: Sample language

> **Effect of termination.** Upon termination of this Agreement, all Royalty obligations as established in the Payments Section shall immediately become due. After the termination of this license, all rights granted to Licensee under this Agreement shall revert to Licensor, and Licensee will refrain from further manufacturing, copying, marketing, distribution, or use of any Licensed Product or other product that incorporates the Property. Within 30 days after termination, Licensee shall deliver to Licensor a statement indicating the number and description of the Licensed Products that it had on hand or is in the process of manufacturing as of the termination date. Licensee may dispose of the Licensed Products covered by this Agreement for a period of three months after termination except that Licensee shall have no such right in the event this agreement is terminated according to the Licensor's Right to Terminate, above. At the end of the post termination sale period, Licensee shall furnish a royalty payment and statement as required under the Payment Section. Upon termination, Licensee shall deliver to Licensor all tooling and molds used in the manufacture of the Licensed Products. Licensor shall bear the costs of shipping for the tooling and molds.

Right to claim breach. By the way, the fact that a contract has already terminated doesn't prevent one party from later suing for breach. For example, if you licensed your invention to a company for two years, and you discover after the contract ends that the company understated its sales and owes you thousands of dollars in royalties, you may file a lawsuit even though the contract has terminated. Parties typically have three to six years (check your state's statute of limitations) after discovering the harm caused by the breach to file a lawsuit over a written contract.

Related terms: remedies; term.

third-party beneficiary

Anyone who benefits from a contract, but is not a party to that contract, is considered a third-party beneficiary. Some third parties (known as "intended beneficiaries") can sue to enforce a contract, because the parties clearly wanted them to benefit from the contract's terms. Others ("incidental beneficiaries"), can't enforce the contract; although they might benefit from the contract, that wasn't necessarily the parties' aim or one of the purposes of the contract. Whether a third party is classified as an intended or incidental beneficiary may spell the difference between getting paid or not, so it's sometimes the subject of courtroom battles.

Homer's odyssey. Back in the 1930s, Homer Le Ballister was an employee of the National Theatres Syndicate, which was being purchased by Redwood Theaters. The purchase agreement contained this clause:

> It is further understood and agreed that in the event you accept this offer and control of the said corporation is taken over by us, we will retain your Mr. Homer Le Ballister, now employed by you as manager, in some suitable position for a period of one year at a salary of not less than eighty-five dollars ($85.00) per week.

Despite the contract, Homer was fired shortly after the deal went through. Redwood Theaters claimed it didn't owe Homer anything because he wasn't a party to the agreement, which was primarily intended to benefit the two companies. In other words, they argued that Homer was an incidental, not an intended beneficiary.

The California Court of Appeals disagreed and ruled for Homer, noting that his appearance in the contract showed that the parties *intended* to expressly benefit him. "Whether or not a contract is one for the express benefit of a third person is a fact sometimes difficult to determine. The test appears to be whether an intent so to benefit the third party appears from the terms of the contract."

Two types of intended beneficiaries. Intended beneficiaries fall into two categories:

- **Someone receiving a gift or benefit.** This type of beneficiary (also known as a "donee beneficiary") is fairly common. For example, the person named as a beneficiary of a life insurance policy falls into this category. Another example would be a mother who contracts to purchase a house for her daughter to live in.

- **Someone who is owed a debt.** In this situation (involving what is known as a "creditor beneficiary"), one person contracts to lend money to another, who then repays the debt to a third party. The landmark case that established third-party beneficiary rights—*Lawrence v. Fox*—dealt with a creditor beneficiary. In 1857, Mr. Holly lent $300 to Mr. Fox. The agreement was that Mr. Fox would pay the $300 to Mr. Lawrence (the third-party beneficiary). When Fox didn't pay Lawrence, Lawrence sued. In a decision that was "well ahead of its time," the New York Court of Appeals ruled that Lawrence could sue under the agreement between Holly and Fox, even though he was not a party to it. This case became the foundation for third-party beneficiary law. (By the way, this principle of having someone else repay your debts is also sometimes referred to as "paying it forward.")

Vesting of rights. Becoming an intended beneficiary is never automatic. In other words, just because you are named in a contract doesn't give you the right to sue to enforce it. Courts require that the third-party beneficiary's rights must have "vested." This can happen in one of three ways:

- **The third party knows of, and detrimentally relies on, the rights created in the contract.** Using an example above, once the daughter, knowing that her mother is buying her a house, moves out of her previous residence in reliance on the contract, the daughter's rights have vested.
- **The third party expressly assents to the contract at the request of one of the parties.** For example, the mother and daughter tour the house with the seller, and the daughter agrees to the arrangement.
- **The third party files a lawsuit to enforce the contract.** If the seller refuses to go through with the sale, and the daughter files a lawsuit against the seller to demand specific performance, the daughter's rights have vested.

Incidental third-party beneficiaries. An incidental third-party beneficiary is someone who benefits from the contract indirectly. For example, in 1928, a warehouse owner watched his building burn to the ground because the water company allegedly provided inadequate water pressure. The warehouse owner claimed to be an intended third-party beneficiary of the contract between the water company and the city. The court disagreed, noting that it wasn't the intention of the parties to specifically assume all risks resulting from inadequate pressure. The decision limited the expansion of third-party beneficiary rights and also established an underlying policy argument: If third-party beneficiary rights "were extended too far, many potentially beneficial contracts would not be made," for fear of incurring unforeseen liability.

Labels and the law. Some companies mistakenly believe they can shift liability by improperly using the third-party beneficiary principle. For example, let's say one company is selling a truckload of lumber to a lumber distributor. The distributor may include a statement, "All customers of distributor are intended beneficiaries of this Agreement and, as such, are entitled to all rights and remedies entitled to third-party beneficiaries under law." The idea behind the clause is that unhappy customers can step in and sue the lumber supplier under the contract, rather than going after the distributor. A provision like this probably won't fly if challenged in court. It's not enough to say that someone is an intended beneficiary: That person must actually meet the criteria described above.

Related terms: additional insured; beneficiary; fiduciary (duty, relationship); quasi contract.

time is of the essence

To handle situations in which courts may not consider the timing essential—for example, for delivery of certain goods—drafters of contracts often include a statement that "time is of the essence." For example, a provision may state: "Time is of the essence with respect to all payments to be made under this Agreement." The modern view held by most courts is that a party's failure to meet the conditions of a "time is of the essence" provision amounts to a material breach. And, alternatively, most courts will not consider the timing as crucial if this language is left out. However, even with the clause, a court may give the breaching party time to cure the breach and may even disregard the provision completely if other evidence indicates that it would be unfair to enforce the provision or that the parties really didn't intend for the contract to be terminated because of a missed deadline

Why is the language needed? If the other party to a contract does not perform its obligations on time, like the White Rabbit in *Alice in Wonderland*, you may find yourself late for a very important date. Parties to a contract are sometimes surprised to learn that missing a contractual deadline does not always amount to a material breach. In many types of contracts—for example, construction, real estate sales, loans, or other nongoods contracts—courts often don't consider timing to be essential. They believe that minor deviations from a contract's schedule aren't important enough to warrant

451

damages or termination of the contract. In some circumstances, however, the parties would beg to differ. For example, the timing of a loan contract may be very important indeed, if the lender's failure to fund the loan on time means that you can't buy a house or pursue a lucrative business opportunity. For that reason, lawyers began to use "time is of the essence."

Sale of goods. In contracts for the sale of goods, courts consider delivery dates to be very important. A seller's failure to hit that date is usually considered a material breach even without a "time is of the essence" provision. That's not the case when it comes to the date for paying for the goods, however. Courts give the parties more leeway to miss these dates because a late payment can always be addressed by charging interest on the amount due.

Related terms: breach, material.

title insurance

Title insurance protects the buyer of real property from the possibility that someone else could have a lien or another claim to ownership of the property. Typically, title insurance is paid for by the buyer (except in some Western states, where sellers pay) and is approximately $1,000 or .05% of the property's purchase price. Title insurance policies usually limit the payout (the maximum you'll get if the title proves defective) to the purchase price.

What's not included? As with all insurance, a title insurance policy is sometimes defined by what's *not* covered. The common exclusions listed below can be avoided if the insured buys extra coverage ("endorsements") to insure against these items, such as:

- **Issues discovered in a preliminary investigation.** The title company will conduct a preliminary inspection of title before making a commitment to insure. Any items discovered during the preliminary inspection are excluded from coverage. For example, if the investigation reveals an easement allowing access by a utility company or existing liens on the property, those won't be covered by the policy. Title insurance covers only surprises, not known problems with the title.

- **Future events.** Anything that occurs after the policy's effective date is typically not covered. For example, if you buy a house, then your contractor puts a lien on the house when you fail to pay for a kitchen remodel, that lien isn't covered by your title insurance.

- **"Standard" exclusions.** Items such as boundary line disputes, unrecorded easements, taxes, special assessments and mechanic's liens, and mineral and water rights are generally not covered by title insurance.

Related terms: closing; deed; mortgage; real estate contract.

tort

Tort law refers to the body of law covering intentional or negligent injuries of a person or business (tort is French for "wrong"). It includes a range of injuries such as battery, assault, theft of property ("conversion"), negligence, false imprisonment ("kidnapping"), fraud, trespass, infliction of emotional distress, defamation ("libel"), invasion of privacy, product liability, strict liability, and nuisance. There are also many special business torts, such as unfair competition and intentional interference with a contractual relationship.

Torts and crimes. As you can see from the list above, many torts could also be categorized as crimes. The primary difference between torts and crimes is that in the case of a tort, the lawsuit is between private parties and the remedy is almost always money. When you are charged with a crime, you are being prosecuted by the state, not a private party, and your punishment may be a loss of freedom (confinement), although you may have to pay a fine or another financial penalty instead of, or in addition to, doing time.

Torts and contracts. Some precontract activity may give rise to a tort, such as fraud in the inducement (lying to convince another party to make a contract) or interference with a contractual relationship (coming between two parties to a contract to undermine their dealings with each other). A tort may also be committed in conjunction with a breach of contract. For example, a company's president deliberately terminates an agreement, then libels the other party in a newspaper interview.

Typically, in a contract dispute, a claim of fraud will be treated as part of the contract claim unless the injured party can demonstrate that the fraud claim is distinct from the contract claim. When the injured party can show that the claims are distinct, a court will permit one or both. (In some cases, an injured party must choose between contract and tort claims.) Parties that have a choice will typically pursue their tort claims, because the available damages are much larger. In addition to compensatory damages (which are available under either theory), a tort victim may ask for damages for pain and suffering and punitive damages that are awarded solely to punish the bad actor.

Related terms: exemplary damages; fraud (misrepresentation); gross negligence; negligence; product liability.

trade secret

A trade secret is any information that has commercial value, has been maintained in confidence by a business, and is not known by competitors. Trade secrets are protected by contracts known as confidentiality agreements or nondisclosure agreements (NDAs). A business that owns trade secrets can sue those who steal the secrets or who divulge them in violation of a legal duty—for example, after signing an NDA. Common types of trade secrets include customer lists, sensitive marketing information, unpatented inventions, software, formulas and recipes, techniques, processes, and other business information that provides a company with a business edge.

Related terms: copyright; intangible property (intangible assets); intellectual property; license agreement; patent; trademark (service mark); works made for hire

trademark (service mark)

A trademark is a distinctive word, phrase, logo, graphic symbol, or another device that is used to identify the source of a product or service and to distinguish it from competitors. Some examples of trademarks are Ford for cars and trucks, Betty Crocker for food products, and Quicken for software.

A trademark can be more than just a brand name or logo. It can include other nonfunctional but distinctive aspects of a product or service that tend to promote and distinguish it in the marketplace, such as shapes, letters, numbers, sounds, smells, or colors. Titles, character names, or other distinctive features of movies, television, and radio programs can also serve as trademarks when used to promote a product or service.

For all practical purposes, a service mark is the same as a trademark, except that trademarks promote products while service marks promote services (such as McDonald's food service, Fedex delivery service, MTV's television network service, and the Olympic Games as an international sporting event).

A trademark is often licensed for use on other products or services or is part of a larger business arrangement, such as a franchise or an acquisition (in which the trademark is considered an intangible asset). When a trademark is sold or otherwise conveyed, the owner must also convey an intangible quality referred to as the trademark's "good will." When a trademark is licensed, the owner has a legal obligation to police the use of the mark to guarantee the consistency and quality standards associated with the mark.

Related terms: copyright; intangible property (intangible assets); intellectual property; license agreement; patent; trade secret; works made for hire.

tying contracts

See antitrust.

ultra vires

Ultra vires refers to activities that are beyond the scope of legal authority. The principle was primarily applied to corporations that were acting outside the scope of their corporate charters, but, nowadays, it rarely arises—the result of changes in state and federal corporation laws.

under water

An unprofitable investment—in which a property is worth less than what was paid for it—is said to be "under water." It is used most frequently to refer to homeowners who owe more on their mortgages than their home is currently worth, a situation that often leads to foreclosure.

underwriter

An underwriter assesses the risk of taking on a new customer or account and agrees to pay if the company must assume the risk. The term is commonly associated with the insurance business, in which an underwriter decides whether it's in the company's interest to issue an insurance policy and then assumes the specific risk. In banking, the underwriter determines whether to issue a loan and guarantees the loan; in real estate, whether to issue and guarantee a mortgage; and in securities law, whether to issue and guarantee securities.

undue influence

Undue influence occurs when someone whose capacity to make decisions is diminished or weakened is subjected to psychological pressure, coercion, or unfair persuasion. In other words, excessive persuasion is used to convince someone vulnerable to such pressure.

> EXAMPLE: The pregnant wife of a man who had been shot and killed on October 30 and buried on November 1 was approached by members of her husband's family a day or two later and persuaded to deed her entire interest in her husband's estate to his children by a prior marriage. In determining that the resulting contract was a product of undue influence, the court indicated that "the only reason which we can discover for [the family's] unseemly haste is, that they thought that [the wife] would be more likely to comply with their wishes then than at some future time, after she had recovered from the shock which she had then so recently experienced."

Undue influence is usually found in situations where the parties have a special and confidential relationship of some sort (for example, lawyer-client, husband-wife, executor-beneficiary) and in which the weaker party is pressured by improper or excessive persuasion ("overpersuasion").

What is overpersuasion? As one court put it, overpersuasion is "persuasion which overcomes the will without convincing the judgment." In a well-known California case (and one of the few modern cases that doesn't involve a confidential relationship between the parties), a teacher had been arrested on charges (later dismissed) of homosexual activity. He been awake for over 40 hours and just released from police custody when school officials pressured him into resigning. In striking down the resignation, the court explained the elements that can create a pattern of overpersuasion. These included "(1) discussion of the transaction at an unusual or inappropriate time, (2) consummation of the transaction in an unusual place, (3) insistent demand that the business be finished at once, (4) extreme

U

emphasis on untoward consequences of delay, (5) the use of multiple persuaders by the dominant side against a single servient party, (6) absence of third-party advisers to the servient party, (7) statements that there is no time to consult financial advisers or attorneys. If a number of these elements are simultaneously present, the persuasion may be characterized as excessive."

Four elements of undue influence. There are many things that undue influence is not: For example, it does not involve mental illness (incapacity), misrepresentations (fraud), or threats (duress). The four elements that typically must be proved to demonstrate that a contract was the result of undue influence are:

- **Facts showing susceptibility.** There must be some proof that the weaker party was susceptible of being unfairly influenced— for example, a recent traumatic event, illness, or emotional turmoil.

- **Proof that there is opportunity to exert undue influence.** This is typically shown by the presence of a special relationship such as trustee-beneficiary, parent-child, or attorney-client.

- **Evidence of influence.** Who took the lead in the contract negotiations? Did the weaker party have access to advice from others? What did each party say and do?

- **Is there something funny about the transaction?** Does the contract have an odd odor to it—that is, does the agreement seem unnatural because the consideration is severely unbalanced and one party is giving up a lot for no apparent reason?

What's the remedy? If the wronged party does not complain—that is, the party doesn't try to end the agreement—the arrangement is presumed to be valid. If the wronged party does seek to end it, a court will void the agreement if it determines that undue influence was used. Often, undue influence is raised after the death of one of the parties. For example, the child of an aging parent might claim that a caretaker used undue influence over the parent to contract for the disposition of property or to convince the parent to change estate planning documents to benefit the caretaker.

Related terms: duress; void (voidable).

Uniform Commercial Code

Back in the early 1950s, legal scholars distilled rules about contract law (including what was then known as the Uniform Sales Act) and created a set of model laws called the Uniform Commercial Code (UCC). Uniform or model laws have no legal effect until they are adopted by state legislatures. They represent an effort by great legal minds to come up with the most sensible and common rules applied in various situations. Some uniform laws don't prove to be very popular, but this wasn't the case for the UCC: It was eventually adopted, with slight modifications, in all fifty states.

As a result of this work, sellers and buyers who operate across state lines now have consistency in the application of laws relating to certain types of contracts. (If you would like to review the UCC as applied to your state, an index of state UCC laws is available at the Cornell Law School website (www.law.cornell.edu/uniform/ucc.html).)

UCC articles. The UCC consists of eleven articles comprising ten categories of contracts:

- **Article 1: General Provisions.** This provides definitions for common contract terminology as well as certain rules used to interpret contracts that are covered by the UCC.
- **Article 2: Sales.** Article 2, regarding the sale of goods, is probably the most well-known section of the UCC and includes rules for the sale of personal (movable) property.
- **Article 2A: Leases.** This section provides rules for the leasing of personal (movable) property. It does not cover the leasing of real estate.
- **Article 3. Negotiable Instruments.** This section provides guidance on debt agreements, such as promissory notes.
- **Article 4: Bank Deposits and Collections.** This provides guidelines for banks conducting business regarding matters such as deposits and collections.

- **Article 4A: Funds Transfers.** This section offers rules on transactions transferring money between banks.
- **Article 5: Letters of Credit.** Article 5 establishes legal rules for letters of credit: written guarantees of payment made by financial institutions.
- **Article 6: Bulk Transfers.** Bulk transfer rules refer to transactions in which one party sells all (or almost all of its inventory) to one buyer, typically characterized as a liquidation or an auction.
- **Article 7: Warehouse Receipts, Bills of Lading and Other Documents of Title.** These rules pertain to agreements to warehouse or store goods.
- **Article 8: Investment Securities.** These are rules regarding the sale and ownership of stock and similar securities.
- **Article 9: Secured Transactions.** Article 9 governs agreements in which a debt or another obligation is secured by some form of collateral (property).

The UCC and its commentary. In addition to providing its model laws, the UCC also provides detailed commentary (the "Official Comments") that judges treat with deference when ruling on UCC matters. The UCC and the Official Comments are privately owned, and reproduction is prohibited under copyright law. Several sites (such as the Cornell Law School, Lexis-Nexis, and Westlaw) have licenses to reproduce the UCC. Some of these licenses include the Official Comments; some don't. Copyright law does, however, permit the reproduction of state laws that are adopted based on the UCC.

Navigating Article 2. The most important section for small business owners is Article 2, which deals with contracts for the sale of goods. Among other things, it provides guidance as to the following:

- **Definitions of goods (2-105).** Goods consist of "all things that are movable" at the time of the contract, including tangible personal property (not real estate), future goods, special or custom-ordered goods, crops, and "the unborn young of animals." It doesn't include money or commercial paper (promissory notes and so on).

- **Contracts for sales don't need to be definite (2-204).** The UCC recognizes contracts for the sale of goods as valid even if certain key terms (including price) are indefinite, as long as the parties intended to make a contract and "there is a reasonably certain basis for giving an appropriate remedy." In other words, if trade custom or other criteria can fill in the gaps, then a contract has been formed.

- **Open offers may be good for up to three months (2-205).** An offer to buy or sell goods will be held open for the time stated in the offer. If no time is stated, it will be held open for a "reasonable time," which cannot exceed three months.

- **Offers to buy goods promptly can be accepted by shipment (2-206).** An offer to buy goods for prompt shipment—for example, a purchase order requesting a current delivery—can be accepted either by a promise to ship goods or by actually shipping the goods.

- **Battle of the forms (2-207).** What happens when the buyer submits a purchase order with basic terms, and the seller submits an invoice accepting the basic terms but also includes a form agreement with different or more detailed terms? This is referred to as the "battle of the forms." Under the UCC, any additional terms in the acceptance will become part of the agreement unless: The offer limits acceptance to the terms of the offer; the terms of acceptance materially alter the terms in the offer; or a notice of objection is furnished by the buyer within a reasonable time. This section also states that when the parties conduct themselves as if they have a contract, that conduct is "sufficient to establish a contract."

- **Implied warranties (2-314 and 2-315).** All goods must be merchantable (acceptable within the trade) and fit for their intended purpose, unless such warranties are disclaimed following the procedures spelled out in the code.

- **Buyer's rights when goods don't conform (2-601).** If the goods are not as promised, the buyer can: reject all of the goods and sue for damages; accept all of the goods; or accept some, reject the rest, and sue for damages.

Amendments to Article 2. In 2003, Article 2 was amended to recognize the validity of electronic agreements, to impose the requirement that a contract must be in writing to transactions worth at least $5,000 (the former limit was $500), and to create a new category of consumer contracts, among other changes.

unilateral contracts

See bilateral contracts (versus unilateral contract).

unjust enrichment

Unjust enrichment is a catch-all phrase that encompasses any acts that result in someone getting a benefit unfairly. That may happen as a result of fraud, someone unfairly taking advantage of someone else, or acting unconscionably, or any of the many other ways one person scams another out of money.

Unjust enrichment can also happen more innocently. For example, if one party thought there was an agreement and carried out its obligations to the benefit of someone else, the other person might have to pay for those services, especially if that person knew of the mistake and did nothing to correct it.

If a contract is used as part of the unjust enrichment—for example, a scam artist signs an agreement to sell someone the Brooklyn Bridge—courts routinely void such agreements or consider them unenforceable. Courts prescribe remedies for unjust enrichment based on fairness (referred to as "equitable remedies"). These include restitution (returning the parties to where they were before the event) or an award of quantum meruit—a payment that compensates for the loss.

Related terms: defenses (breach of contract); estoppel; fraud in the inducement; implied contract; negligence; quantum meruit; remedies; statute of frauds; tort; void (voidable).

usury

See interest rates (usury).

vendor

Vendor is a generic term referring to any supplier or seller of goods or services.

verbal agreement

See oral contracts.

void (voidable)

If a contract is defined as an enforceable agreement, then it should be a misnomer to use the term "void contract" or "voidable contract." The act of voiding a contract makes it unenforceable—and therefore, no longer a contract. Nevertheless, lawyers and courts commonly use the "void" and "voidable" language, so we'll explain it here.

Void contracts. Some contracts are just plain void: They were never enforceable, and courts will treat them as if they never existed. The most famous example is a hit man's contract to murder someone. Even if the parties wrote down all of the essential terms and money changed hands, that contract obviously will never be enforced by a court (although of course, hit men probably have their own means of enforcement). Void contracts are typically those that violate the law—such as contracts to engage in wagering, money laundering, or restraint of trade, or contracts paid for in illegal consideration, such as cocaine—but they may also include contracts that lack consideration.

Voidable contracts. A contract that is voidable is a valid contract that one party can disavow and make unenforceable. A contract that is entered into under duress or as a result of mistake or undue influence is voidable by the wronged party. A minor who is a party to a contract may disavow the agreement and have it voided as well. Alternatively, in all of these situations, the party with the power to disavow such contracts can also ratify the contract and treat it as valid and enforceable.

The remedies for contracts that are voided are either to put the parties in the position they were in before the agreement (restitution) or award money for services or goods (referred to as quantum meruit). The purpose of the latter remedy is to prevent one party from being unjustly enriched.

Related terms: capacity (to contract); defenses (breach of contract); estoppel; implied contract; statute of frauds; unjust enrichment.

waiver

The term waiver has two applications in contract law:

- **Waiver of a contract provision.** Sometimes, parties want to deviate from an agreement but don't need or want to modify it. For example, one party to a nondisclosure contract might give the other party permission to disclose certain facts to certain people, even though that might technically violate the language of the contract. These deviations—in which a party waives a provision or permits something that would otherwise be prohibited—are referred to as waivers (or "consents"). Unlike an amendment, a waiver doesn't modify the agreement itself; instead, it excuses or permits specific activities that would otherwise be prohibited by the contract.

- **A waiver provision.** A waiver provision is a boilerplate clause by which the parties agree to forego or give up the right to sue for breach of a particular provision of the agreement without giving up any future claims regarding the same provision.

Waiver provision: Sample language

> **Waiver.** If one party waives any term or provision of this agreement at any time, that waiver will be effective only for the specific instance and specific purpose for which the waiver was given. If either party fails to exercise or delays exercising any of its rights or remedies under this agreement, that party retains the right to enforce that term or provision at a later time.

waiver of jury trial

See jury trial, waiver of.

warranties

Warranties are guarantees or promises that something is true. A breach of a warranty is similar to a breach of contract, for which similar remedies are available. Contracts often include statements of facts made by one party or the other, set forth under the heading, "Representations and Warranties." (See "representations and warranties" to find out why these two types of assurances are often merged in contracts.) Here, we focus on the warranties that are associated with services, goods, and consumer contracts. These warranties may be express or implied.

Express warranties. An express warranty is one that is actually stated, usually in writing. Most consumers are familiar with express product warranties that state something such as "this product is warranted against defects in materials or workmanship" for a specified time. These warranties either come directly from a seller or are included in the sales contract you sign with the seller. However, an express warranty may also be in an advertisement or on a sign in a store ("all dresses 100% silk") or in a salesperson's oral description of a product's features.

Implied warranties. An implied warranty is not spoken or written but is based on reasonable consumer expectations. Most implied warranties are imposed by state or federal laws. The two most well-known implied warranties are for "merchantability" and for "fitness."

The implied warranty of merchantability is an assurance that a new item will work if you use it for a reasonably expected purpose (for example, that a toaster will toast bread or a power drill will drill holes). This warranty applies only to the product's ability to perform its basic purpose, not to everything that could possibly go wrong with the product. For used items, the warranty of merchantability is a promise that the product will work as expected, given its age and condition.

The implied warranty of fitness applies when you buy an item with a specific (even unusual) purpose in mind. If you communicated your needs to the seller, the implied warranty of fitness assures you that the item will meet these needs. For example, if you tell a salesperson that you need a toaster that will still toast bread after you drill holes in it, because you are doing a performance art piece that involves working toasters hanging on the walls of a gallery, the implied warranty of fitness has you covered.

How long does a warranty last? An express warranty lasts for the term stated in the language of the warranty—for example, "three years after the date of purchase." The lifespan of an implied warranty depends on state law. Some states limit an implied warranty to a period of time—one or two years, for example. Others say that an implied warranty lasts only as long as any express warranty made about a product.

Can a seller avoid a warranty by selling a product "as is"? The answer depends on whether the warranty is express or implied and on the laws of the state where you live. Sellers cannot avoid express warranties by claiming the product is sold "as is." On the other hand, if there is no express warranty, sellers can sometimes avoid an implied warranty by selling the item "as is." Some states prohibit all "as is" sales. And in all states, the buyer must know that the item is sold "as is" in order for the seller to avoid an implied warranty.

Related term: representations and warranties

website development agreement

When someone hires a developer to create a website, a number of legal issues can arise. Here are the key issues that should be addressed in negotiations and in your final written contract:

- **Specifications and timelines.** It's essential for the parties to agree on the details of the website—that is, the scope and appearance—as well as the dates when work should be completed.

- **Warranties and indemnity.** It is wise for both parties to seek mutual assurances regarding their respective use of copyrights, trademarks, or any materials that may be defamatory or invade privacy.
- **Ownership of the site.** The developer should provide assurances and, if necessary, an assignment guaranteeing that ownership vests in the hiring party. The developer may retain certain rights for software or other stock elements provided.
- **Contract assignability.** To avoid the developer farming out the work to someone else, a developer contract should include a clause that prevents assignment of the agreement.
- **Objections and approvals.** The hiring party will want a simple system for approving or objecting to the developer's work (for example, an approval system that has several stages or milestones).
- **Termination.** The hiring party will want an escape hatch in case things go sour during the development process, such as a right to terminate the agreement as long as the developer is paid for work that's already completed.
- **Maintenance.** Many Web developers continue to maintain sites after completion; in other cases, a developer hands over the keys to the hiring party. Either way, the maintenance obligations, if any, should be spelled out in the contract.

whereas provision

See recitals.

wire transfer

Substitute the word "electronic" for the antiquated term "wire," and you'll get a better idea of what this term refers to—any electronic transfer of funds from one institution to another. Traditionally, wire transfers are associated with transfers from one bank account to another, but the term can also be applied to ATM or credit card payments, Western Union, or even intra-account transfers that you make at an online bank account. Wire transfers are sometimes required as the means of payment in contracts because they are considered by most businesspeople to be the most secure and efficient means of transferring funds. In the United States, wire transfers are governed by Article 4A of the Uniform Commercial Code.

Related term: Uniform Commercial Code.

workout

A system or plan, formalized with a written agreement, for resolving a debt dispute. Workouts are often negotiated in order to avoid bankruptcy. In recent years, workouts have been associated specifically with mortgage foreclosures.

works made for hire

Works made for hire refers to a contractual relationship between a hiring party and someone who will create a copyrightable work—for example, a sculpture, website, book, photograph, architecture, music, or graphic art—that gives the hiring party ownership of the work. For example, *Webster's Dictionary*, the film *Groundhog Day*, and MapQuest are all examples of works made for hire. Under copyright law, the hiring party is considered "the author" and owner of copyright in the work—even though someone else actually created it—in two situations:

- **Employment relationship.** If the person creating a work is an employee of the hiring party, and the work is created within the scope of employment, then the work is automatically considered a work made for hire. In other words, the employer owns all copyrightable work created in the course of employment by an employee. No written agreement is needed to ensure this status.

- **Independent contractor.** Here's where things get more complicated. The hiring party owns the copyright to work created by an independent contractor only if the work is commissioned, the worker signs a work made for hire agreement, and the work qualifies within one of several enumerated categories, including: a contribution to a collective work; a part of a motion picture or other audiovisual work; a supplementary work—a work prepared for publication as a supplement to a work for the purpose of introducing, concluding, illustrating, explaining, revising, commenting upon, or assisting in the use of the other work; an instructional text used in teaching—provided that it is designed for use in day-to-day teaching activity; a translation; or a test and test answer materials. Any work created by an independent contractor that does not fall within one of the above categories cannot be a work made for hire.

Employee or contractor? Because the work made for hire standards between employees and contractors differs, the first step in any analysis of copyright ownership is to determine whether the worker is an employee or independent contractor. Usually, this isn't too hard to figure out. Basically, an employee has regular tasks, receives regular paychecks, is supervised by the hiring party, doesn't run a separate business, and has payroll taxes withheld.

The catch. A common problem for many hiring parties is that they may prepare a work made for hire agreement for a contractor, but the work does not fall into one of the enumerated contract categories.

EXAMPLE: Nectar Publishing plans to publish a series of educational texts on fruit trees. The company hires Charles, an author who is not employed by Nectar, to write the books. For Nectar to own copyright as a work made for hire, Charles will have to sign a work made for hire agreement and the resulting works must fall within one of the enumerated work made for hire categories. It's possible that the works may qualify as "instructional texts," but only if they are intended to be used in day-to-day teaching activities. If the work does not fall within one of the enumerated categories, the works will *not* be works made for hire even if a work made for hire agreement has been signed. In that event, the only other method by which Nectar could acquire copyright ownership is to require Charles to assign his rights under his publishing agreement

In the alternative. Because so many works do not fit within the work made for hire enumerated categories, a clause is usually included that assigns all rights in the work to the hiring party (a "copyright assignment"). An example of this provision is included in the sample work made for hire agreement, below.

Related terms: copyright; intangible property (intangible assets); intellectual property.

Work Made for Hire Agreement

Work Made for Hire Agreement

This Work Made for Hire Agreement (the "Agreement") is made between
_____ ("Company")
and _____ ("Artist").

Services. In consideration of the payments provided in this Agreement,
Artist agrees to perform the following services: _____ .

Payment. Company agrees to pay Artist as follows: _____

_____

_____

_____ .

Works Made for Hire—Assignment of Intellectual Property Rights.
Artist agrees that, for consideration that is acknowledged, any works of
authorship commissioned pursuant to this Agreement (the "Works")
shall be considered works made for hire as that term is defined under U.S.
copyright law. To the extent that any such Work created for Company by
Artist is not a work made for hire belonging to Company, Artist hereby
assigns and transfers to Company all rights Artist has or may acquire to all
such Works. Artist agrees to sign and deliver to Company, either during
or subsequent to the term of this Agreement, such other documents as
Company considers desirable to evidence the assignment of copyright.

Artist Warranties. Artist warrants that the Work does not infringe any
intellectual property rights or violate any laws and that the work is original
to Artist.

Miscellaneous. This Agreement constitutes the entire understanding
between the parties and can only be modified by written agreement. The
laws of the State of _____ govern this Agreement. In

Work Made for Hire Agreement (continued)

the event of any dispute arising under this agreement, the prevailing party shall be entitled to its reasonable attorneys' fees.

Artist

By: _____

Printed Name: _____

Date: _____

Company

By: _____

Printed Name: _____

Title: _____

Date: _____

yellow-dog contract

An illegal employment contract (or contract provision) in which an employee agrees not to join or form a union while employed.

Related term: employment agreements.

NOLO® *Keep Up to Date*

1 Go to Nolo.com/newsletters to sign up for free newsletters and discounts on Nolo products.

- **Nolo Briefs.** Our monthly email newsletter with great deals and free information.

- **Nolo's Special Offer.** A monthly newsletter with the biggest Nolo discounts around.

- **BizBriefs.** Tips and discounts on Nolo products for business owners and managers.

- **Landlord's Quarterly.** Deals and free tips just for landlords and property managers, too.

2 Don't forget to check for updates at **Nolo.com**. Under "Products," find this book and click "Legal Updates."

Let Us Hear From You

3 Register your Nolo product and give us your feedback at Nolo.com/book-registration.

- Once you've registered, you qualify for technical support if you have any trouble with a download or CD (though most folks don't).

- We'll also drop you an email when a new edition of your book is released—and we'll send you a coupon for 15% off your next Nolo.com order!

CTRCT1

NOLO® *Online Legal Forms*

Nolo offers a large library of legal solutions and forms, created by Nolo's in-house legal staff. These reliable documents can be prepared in minutes.

Create a Document

- **Incorporation.** Incorporate your business in any state.
- **LLC Formations.** Gain asset protection and pass-through tax status in any state.
- **Wills.** Nolo has helped people make over 2 million wills. Is it time to make or revise yours?
- **Living Trust (avoid probate).** Plan now to save your family the cost, delays, and hassle of probate.
- **Trademark.** Protect the name of your business or product.
- **Provisional Patent.** Preserve your rights under patent law and claim "patent pending" status.

Download a Legal Form

Nolo.com has hundreds of top quality legal forms available for download—bills of sale, promissory notes, nondisclosure agreements, LLC operating agreements, corporate minutes, commercial lease and sublease, motor vehicle bill of sale, consignment agreements and many, many more.

Review Your Documents

Many lawyers in Nolo's consumer-friendly lawyer directory will review Nolo documents for a very reasonable fee. Check their detailed profiles at **www.nolo.com/lawyers**.

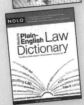

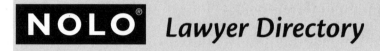